STUDIES IN ITALIAN ART AND ARCHITECTURE

15TH THROUGH 18TH CENTURIES

MEMOIRS OF THE AMERICAN ACADEMY IN ROME

Volume XXXV

STUDIES IN ITALIAN ART HISTORY

I

EDIZIONI DELL'ELEFANTE

Roma

AMERICAN ACADEMY IN ROME

Studies in Italian Art and Architecture 15th through 18th Centuries

Edited by

Henry A. Millon

THE MIT PRESS

Cambridge, Massachusetts, and London, England

Printed and bound in Italy.

Library of Congress Cataloging in Publication Data

Main entry under title:

Studies in Italian art and architecture, 15th through 18th centuries.

1. Art, Italian—Addresses, essays, lectures.
2. Art, Renaissance—Italy—Addresses, essays, lectures.

3. Art, Modern—17th-18th centuries—Italy—Addresses,
essays, lectures. I. Millon, Henry A. II. Ackerman, James S.
N6914.S78 709'.45 79-14746
ISBN 0-262-13156-0

To

Laurance and Isabel Roberts

CONTENTS

FOREWORD

FELLOWSHIPS *in Art History were initiated at the American Academy in Rome in 1947 as the Academy, under Laurance Roberts (Director 1947–1959), reactivated its facilities in Rome. The dedication of this volume is a tribute to the leadership and concern shown by the director and Mrs. Roberts in helping to include art history among the disciplines at the Academy.*

From 1947 to 1978 there have been thirty-five awards to Fellows in Art History. The first of these was Joseph Kelleher who came to study the Holy Crown of Hungary. His research was published in 1951 as Volume XIII in the Academy series Papers and Monographs.

The past few years have seen art historians in larger numbers at the Academy. The increase has been partly due to an increased interest in scholarly studies of the history of Italian art, architecture, and urbanism, and partly due to additional fellowship funds from the National Endowment for the Humanities and the Samuel H. Kress Foundation. Fellows in Art History are now located throughout the United States on faculties and curatorial staffs of university departments of art history, schools of architecture, and museums. The opportunity to use Italian archives and work with Italian art and architecture, has produced major contributions to the growth of knowledge in the field. The papers in this volume show some of the interests and directions followed in the last few years.

Publication of work done at the Academy has been a continuing concern of the Academy's Board of Trustees and its Publications Committee. Limited funds have, however, made publishing art historical articles or volumes rare occasions. Recently the Board agreed that if funds could be found the time might be appropriate for the initiation of a series of art historical publications that, while maintaining the format and numerical sequence of the other Academy series, Memoirs *(normally devoted to studies in classical history, literature, and archaeology), would be entitled " Studies in Art History." The volumes that follow may be either collections of papers or monographs. The MIT Press has graciously agreed to enter into joint publication of this first volume with the American Academy in Rome.*

Special notice should be taken of the many friends of the Academy whose encouragement and support aided the publication of this volume, particularly Bernice Davidson, Gabrielle and Paul Geier, Carol and Milton Lewine, Elisabeth MacDougall, Alfred Moir, and Phoebe and Mark Weil.

The papers in the first volume in the new series are gathered from the art historians— Residents and Fellows— at the Academy from the fall of 1973 to the summer of 1977. The papers included were gathered in the fall of 1976. Were it not for other commitments Ann Hanson, Jack Freiburg, and Amy Neff McNeary would have contributed papers as well. Anthony Clark was at the Academy when he died in November 1976. In January he was due to become Art Historian in Residence. The paper included here is the English text of his introduction to the catalogue of the Pompeo Batoni exhibition held in Lucca in 1967. Inclusion of the paper was possible with the concurrence of John Walsh and Edgar Peters Bowron, executors of the Clark Estate. There is one non—art historian among the contributors, John D'Amico, whose studies in the history of the Renaissance brought him into collaboration with Kathleen Weil-Garris. My own piece is included since I was in Rome as Director during that period.

In Rome, Lucy Gordan Rastelli ably assisted with the editing of the typescripts and printer's proofs. Katya Furse, Andrea Minutoli, and June Osterman in Cambridge received the typescripts and maintained communication with the authors as they travelled. John D'Arms, the current director of the Academy, provided valuable liaison with printer and publishers. He and Bill Lacy expedited negotiations with Roger Conover at The MIT Press. The Edizioni dell'Elefante is primarily responsible for the design of the volume. I am grateful for the encouragement received from its director, Enzo Crea, when the idea for the book was in its incipient stages.

JAMES S. ACKERMAN

I

ON EARLY RENAISSANCE COLOR THEORY AND PRACTICE *

I *Cennini and Alberti*

LEONE Battista Alberti's *De Pictura*, written in 1435, was the major treatise on painting of the early Renaissance.[1] While the first of its three books, an application of ancient and medieval optics to painting, refers in passing to the influence of atmosphere and reflected light on the appearance of colors,[2] the practical instructions to the painter on the use of pigments in the closing paragraphs of the second book (46-50) are not concerned with such local phenomena. The color transmitted by

* *Research on this paper was done largely at the American Academy in Rome in 1974/75 during my term as Resident, when I was supported by a grant from the National Endowment for the Humanities. I am grateful to both institutions for providing one of the most rewarding years of my life.*

As the basic vocabulary of color theory applied to pigments is not standardized, I explain my use of the three essential terms:

Hue *is the specific color identification, as: ultramarine blue.*

Value *is the place of a given area of pigment on a scale from light (high value) to dark (low value).*

Intensity *(also called brilliance or saturation) is the degree of vividness of a given area of pigment. The pigment in its pure form is usually at its highest intensity.*

1 Citations are from Leon Battista Alberti, *On Painting and On Sculpture: the Latin Texts of De Pictura and De Statua*, ed. and tr. by Cecil Grayson, London/New York, 1972. Grayson (" The Text of Alberti's *De Pictura* ", *Italian Studies*, XXIII, 1968, pp. 71-92) dates the text from a note in one of the manuscripts of August 26, 1435, and proposes 1436 for the Italian translation done by the author. Maria Simonelli, " On Alberti's Treatises of Art and Their Chronological Relationship," *Yearbook of Italian Studies*, 1971, pp. 75-102, persuasively argues that the Latin text is a later expansion and correction of the Italian.

2 I have discussed the first book (except for the much-studied section on painters' perspective) in a sequel to this essay, " Alberti's Light," *Studies in Late Medieval and Renaissance Painting in Honor of Millard Meiss*, New York, 1978, pp. 1-27. The two are part of an eventual book on Renaissance art and science.

rays of light from the surface of an object is assumed to be its " real " color as affected by direct light and shadow only, and cases of interference by surrounding conditions are looked on as special, with slightly negative overtones, as if they were obstacles to perceiving things rightly. Artists are not encouraged to take pleasure in or to record the kind of special environmental effects that were to be so important in later painting. The practical outcome of the advice was to encourage painters to assign a particular hue to the area within the circumscribed outline and then to modulate this by raising its value (with white) on the side toward the light and to lower it (with black) on the opposite, shadowed side. This is discussed in § 46, where Alberti expands on the " third part " of painting, " reception of light." He also suggests that

> ... you may change the color with a little white applied as sparingly as possible in the appropriate place within the outlines of the surface, and likewise add some black in the place opposite to it. With such balancing, as one might say, of black and white, a surface rising in relief becomes still more evident. Go on making similar sparing additions until you feel you have arrived at what is required.

Modeling of each object singly to achieve relief was the practice followed by Quattrocento painters, but neither Alberti nor any other writer or practitioner of the period was able to translate " light " and " shadow " into pigment equivalents in a way that fulfilled his aspirations both to realism and to effective color design.[3]

Alberti failed in this area because he did not differentiate between the behavior of light as defined scientifically or as experienced optically, and the behavior of pigment. This difference invalidates two of his fundamental principles: first that

[3] The literature on Quattrocento color and modeling is limited: I am greatly indebted to the following works, which stimulated my interest in the subject: Herbert Siebenhüner, *Über den Kolorismus in der Frührenaissance* (diss., Leipzig), Schramberg, 1935, T. Hetzer, *Tizian, Geschichte seiner Farbe*, Frankfurt a.M., 1935; John Shearman, " Leonardo's Colour and Chiaroscuro," *Zeitschrift f. Kunstgeschichte*, XXV, 1962, pp. 13-47; Samuel Cowardin, *Some Aspects of Color in Fifteenth Century Florentine Painting*, Diss., Harvard, 1962; Sir E. H. Gombrich, " Light, Form and Texture in Fifteenth Century Painting," *Journal of the Royal Society of Arts*, 112, 1964, pp. 826-49. Cf. the discussion of " the mode of relief " based on an empirical study of Quattrocento paintings by Arthur Pope, *The Painter's Modes of Expression* (*An Introduction to the Language of Drawing and Painting*, II), Cambridge, Mass., 1939, pp. 71-85, from which I have taken my color terms.

See also the valuable technical contributions of H. Ruhemann, " Technical Analysis of an Early Painting by Botticelli," *Studies in Conservation*, II, 1945, pp. 26 ff.; and M. Johnson and E. Packard, " Methods in the Identification of Binding Media in Italian Paintings of the Fifteenth and Sixteenth Centuries," *Ibid.*, XVI, 1971, pp. 145-64. Filippo Lippi alone is discussed by Ernst Strauss, *Koloritgeschichtliche Untersuchungen zur Malerei seit Giotto* (*Kunstwissenschaftliche Studien*, XLVII), Munich, 1972, pp. 60ff.

white and black are the palette equivalents of light and shadow respectively, and second, that all other colors can be produced by mixing the four primaries with white and black. The second of these perpetuated the tradition that originated in Aristotle who, however, was not concerned with pigments (see Appendix). Alberti's primaries (blue, red, green, earth color), like Aristotle's, were excessively limiting since yellow was excluded. Besides, mixing a hue with black and white normally does not alter it but merely raises or lowers its value. If white is mixed with a pure blue, the resulting pigment is a paler state of the same blue. The term " paler " is more indicative than " lighter " because in the process, the blue loses some of its intensity or impact; the majority of colors are neutralized almost as much by the addition of a bit of white as by a comparable amount of black.[4]

The modeling of all objects toward white on the light side and toward black on the dark, which results from the first proposition, is not, on the other hand, unacceptable, but it was rejected by the mass of Quattrocento painters because it was not to their taste. They, like the Impressionists, didn't mind neutralizing their colors with white, but they found that an equal application of black produced a somber and deadening effect that was particularly uncongenial to the tempera medium. Alberti recognized this preference and though he emphatically cautions (in § 47) against the excessive use of either white or black, he regards white as more dangerous, since the experienced painter will " hate work that is dark and horrid " in any case, while " we all by nature love things that are open and bright; so we must the more firmly block the way in which it is easier to go wrong."

In Alberti's procedure, the paint appears in its pure and most intense state along a band just to the light side of a line which he advises the painter to draw at the start dividing the light side of the figure from the dark.[5] This effect corresponds most closely to outdoor lighting in the full sunlight when the combined effect of glare, reflection and the adjustment of the eye to brightness lowers color perception and may make it seem that the most intense color appears roughly midway between the highest and the lowest value.

Alberti's instructions, in implying that light and dark should be kept in equilibrium,

[4] It is practical to assume that pigments are at their most intense in a pure form, though Cowardin, *op. cit.*, p. 26, points out that due to the physical constitution of ultramarine and the red lakes, the addition of a little white causes a slight rise in intensity. The effect is to increase the impression of relief in objects painted with these pigments.

[5] Book II, 47: " But if, as I explained, the painter has drawn the outlines of the surface correctly and clearly sketched the border-line between lighter and darker, the method of coloring will then be easy."

assume that objects in paintings will be illuminated by rays travelling parallel to the picture plane at 90 degrees to the centric ray coming to the eye. Thus, discounting surface variations, objects appear half in the light and half in the shadow (because cast shadows are rarely used in Quattrocento paintings, all objects are assumed to receive full direct light). Each figure is to be modeled in relief, in the nearest possible approximation of the sculptural relief of Ghiberti and Donatello (in § 46, Alberti praises " those faces which seem to stand out from pictures as if they were sculpted "); paradoxically, relief is actually more modified by " atmosphere " in the *schiacciato* panels of Donatello — which antedate the writing of *De pictura* — than in any painting done in Alberti's lifetime.

Alberti's application of ancient and medieval optics to the problems of pictorial light and color affected the way his contemporaries thought about painting more than the way they practiced it. In this respect, *De Pictura* was the opposite of Cennino Cennini's *Libro dell'arte*, written in about 1390, a manual that recorded many of the techniques practiced and taught to apprentices in late medieval workshops.[6] Alberti, though he claimed to have experimented in painting, would not have been able to give such practical advice. Anyhow it would have been contrary to his purpose to step down from the level of natural philosophy to what he would have regarded as merely " mechanical " concerns; he was trying among other things to raise the intellectual level of art and the social status of the artist.[7]

Cennini's *Libro dell'arte* may be read as a compendium of standard practices in the Florentine workshops of the later fourteenth and early fifteenth centuries; a few masters at that time might have differed with it in certain respects, but a majority would have accepted it as more or less representative of their practice. Most of its information on color relates to making and mixing pigments, but in one passage

6 Cennino d'Andrea Cennini, *The Craftsman's Handbook, The Italian " Il Libro dell'arte,"* ed. D. V. Thompson, 2 vols., New Haven, 1933 (volume of translation only, New York, 1954, 1960). The " arte " of the title should be translated " craft ", not " art." A manuscript of this kind is not likely to have been used in the workshop, since it records just the essential practices that every master would have taught to his apprentices. But this sort of recording of basic practical information for the illumination of the amateur, for posterity, or for the sheer pleasure of it became increasingly frequent in the later Middle Ages; the relaxation of guild control over trade secrets may have been a factor in this case and in comparable northern European manuals on Gothic building.

7 His description of perspective construction, however, was an instructive exception because, while it met his criteria in being the proof of a scientific theory and a paradigm of the mathematical rationalization of art, it could be read by contemporary painters as a set of instructions not yet available in the workshops for the application of a radically new technique — they could even use it without understanding the theory behind it.

where Cennini tells how color is used to model figures in fresco painting, he gives the key to his system and the basis for a comparison to Alberti's: [8]

The Way to Paint a Drapery in Fresco

> Now let us get right back to our fresco-painting. And, on the wall, if you wish to paint a drapery any color you please, you should first draw it carefully with your verdaccio; and do not have your drawing show too much, but moderately. Then, whether you want a white drapery or a red one, or yellow, or green, or whatever you want, get three little dishes. Take one of them, and put into it whatever color you choose, we will say red: take some cinabrese and a little lime white; and let this be one color, well diluted with water. Make one of the other two colors light, putting a great deal of lime white into it. Now take some of the first one, that is, the dark one; and with a rather large and fairly pointed bristle brush go over the folds of your figure in the darkest areas; and do not go past the middle of the thickness of your figure. Then take the intermediate color; lay it in from one dark strip to the next one, and work them in together, and blend your folds into the accents of the darks. Then, just using these intermediate colors, shape up the dark parts where the relief of the figure is to come, but always following out the shape of the nude. Then take the third, lightest color, and just exactly as you have shaped up and laid in the course of the folds in the dark, so you do now in the relief, adjusting the folds ably, with good draftsmanship and judgment. When you have laid in two or three times with each color, never abandoning the sequence of the colors by yielding or invading the location of one color for another, except where they come into conjunction, blend them and work them well in together. Then in another dish take still another color, lighter than the lightest of these three; and shape up the tops of the folds, and put on lights. Then take some pure white in another dish, and shape up definitively all the areas of relief. Then go over the dark parts, and around some of the outlines, with straight cinabrese; and you will have your drapery, systematically carried out. But you will learn far better by seeing it done than by reading. When you have finished your figure or scene, let it dry until the mortar and the colors have dried out well all over. And if you still have any drapery to do in secco, you will follow this method.

These instructions would be valid for most panel painting as well, but the artist particularly concerned with color effects had more flexibility on the panel: first, he could vary the thickness of his surface, letting the underlying preparation show through in the thin portions to affect the value or the tone of the surface, and second, he could more easily mix colors directly on the painting, by hatching strokes of different

[8] Cennini, *op. cit.*, ch. 71, pp. 49 f.

hues; for the most part fresco painters were constrained to mix the chosen color on the palette, or, as Cennini would suggest, in a dish.

In one respect, Cennini's practice resembled Alberti's: the problem is conceived as one of creating an illusion of relief by assuming a figure to be illuminated from one side (from at least a right angle, as indicated by the phrase " do not go past the middle of the thickness of your figure "), so that the light tones will predominate on the half toward the light and the darks on the halfs away from it. But while Alberti proposed that the darks be made by mixing the basic color of the figure with black, Cennini advises in this passage only the base (red, in his example) and white.[9] His deepest shadow is represented by the pigment at its greatest intensity — and even this has a little white in it. Transitions to more illuminated parts are made by progressive additions of white. This method, with minor variations (e. g., in panel painting, white was not widely used in the deep shadows) was followed in almost all Florentine pictures prior to the writing of *De Pictura*, and in a large number of later Quattrocento works. It produced paintings of a high value range — partly because it evolved in a period of gold-ground painting when color areas had to compete with the reflective brilliance of burnished metal — in which each figure stood out from its neighbors and from the background by virtue of its uniformity of hue. It preserved some of the character of what Hetzer called the " absolute " color of medieval painting, in which the hue remains unaltered by the position or conditions in which the object is placed. The resplendent compositions of vigorously colored figures emphasized surface patterns (the reflectivity of the high-value color patches tended to hold them to the surface), and failed to satisfy Alberti's demand for the illusion of relief in a number of other ways:

1) The least illuminated portion of the surface (the shadow) receives the most intense or saturated color, while the well-illuminated parts are progressively lessened in intensity by the addition of white. Thus the most vibrant tones occur in areas where, in the actual world in normal conditions, they appear inhibited — neutralized by the deprivation of light. As a result, the painted shadows attract the eye, and seem to advance, while the neutralized lights recede. This effect conflicts with the modeling effort, especially in the drapery of figures, where the lighter portions are always intended to advance and the darker to recede.

[9] In other notes, Cennini advised the use of black in deep shadows, notably in the instructions for modeling the Virgin's mantle in ultramarine, in fresco (ch. 83, pp. 54 f; see also chs. 78, 81, 85). I am emphasizing the passage quoted as the standard Cenninesque practice, however, because it is standard in panel painting of his time and in much of the Quattrocento.

2) Pigments of different hues in their pure, unmixed form (e. g., at their most intense) have different values: yellow and orange are bright — yellow a little more so — and blue and violet are dark. It is not just that they look respectively more bright and dark; if one tests them with a photometer they register a higher and lower reflection of light. To make a yellow of the same value as a blue, one mixes in some black or some violet, which reduces its intensity while it lowers its value; conversely, to make a blue the same value as a yellow, one adds white, again reducing intensity. Cennini and most early Renaissance Florentines did not worry about balancing values in this way; they usually used pure pigment for every shadow regardless of hue. But they did encounter many occasions on which it was necessary to represent a rose or light blue robe which, according to their system, required a great deal of white in its deepest shadows. Consequently, the difference between light and shadow in such a robe would be far less than the light-shadow difference in a neighboring figure whose robe might be deep red or blue, with the result that two adjoining figures could appear to be in different lighting conditions, or of different degrees of solidity. And because the under-and outer-garments of figures were usually of quite different hues, there could be violent value contrasts within a single figure.

3) In addition to the difference in value between one hue and another, there is also a differential of intensity due to the physical nature of the pigments. This is particularly noticeable in the unique vividness of the ultramarines made from lapis lazuli, which is much greater than that of blues made from other materials, and which attract the eye in spite of the lower value of blues in relation to other colors. The ultramarines usually overwhelm the greens, for example, which tend to be rather flaccid. Furthermore, ultramarine often held a dominant position; it was used for the sky and for the outer robe of the Virgin in altarpieces. Patrons often specified its extensive use because its preciousness, in a mercantile society, made such liberality a token of piety.[10]

10 The economic value of gold and of the constituents of pigments – particularly ultramarine, which was made from lapis lazuli, a semi-precious stone – continued to be a factor in the appreciation and commissioning of pictures during the Quattrocento, and contracts often stipulated the quality and quantity of precious materials. The phenomenon is discussed by Michael Baxandall, *Painting and Experience in Fifteenth Century Italy*, Oxford, 1972, pp. 1-27, whose observation that emphasis gradually shifted in the course of the century from the value of the materials to the value of the painters' skill is amply supported by contemporary texts. He quotes a passage from Alberti (49) advising against the use of gold to represent gold jewellery and other objects: "I would try to represent with colors rather than with gold this wealth of rays of gold... there is greater admiration and praise for the artist in the use of colors." Cowardin, *op.*

4) White objects and draperies could not be treated consistently with those done in color for the obvious reason that white can be only darkened and not lightened. The shadows of white objects were therefore down-modeled by the admixture of some low value neutral such as blue-grey or a variety of mixtures with earth colors. The neutralization of the shadows tended to make white objects look more natural than colored objects with their brilliant shadows, and in some mid-fifteenth century pictures, such as those of Piero della Francesca, white-robed figures seem to move in a more light- and atmosphere-filled ambience than their colored companions.

For all of these reasons, the work of Lorenzo Monaco, Fra Angelico, often Mantegna and Piero della Francesca, and many other early Renaissance Italians seems to be a patchwork of intense colors, each isolated from its neighbor and involved in a competition that inevitably is won by those of higher value. If this treatment of light-shadow-color had been consistently used, and carried over into landscape and domestic settings when they began to replace gold as a ground for panels, the competition and contrast would have been excessive. It would have inhibited the communication of the content of pictures and have clashed with the illusion of recession given by linear perspective.[11] But painters subdued the tones of the background, which avoided that problem of competition but caused another, by perceptually separating the people depicted from the surrounding world of nature and buildings.

Cennini recommends a second mode of modeling that was widely practiced from the later fourteenth century into the sixteenth: the color shift.[12] This involved using a low-value color such as blue to render the shadows of a red drapery, or red as the shadow of a green drapery, etc. It rarely was used to depict anything but folds of cloth, and Cennini even proposed that its purpose was to represent shot silk, the fabric woven in two colors in such a way that it appears to change from one hue to another when seen at different angles. Albrecht Dürer, writing in ca. 1512-13, suggested that color shifts were still in use, but he disapproved of them as a shading device except where shot silks were to be represented.[13] That

cit., pp. 51 ff., suggests that ultramarine was less modeled than ordinary colors to avoid diluting it and to keep it from emerging too vigorously from the plane.

11 Hetzer, *op. cit.*, pp. 26 ff. shows that Giotto broke with this tradition, using color to achieve a unity of intensity and of value between foreground and background.

12 Cennini, *op. cit.*, ch. 77 ff., pp. 53 f. Cennini's term for the shift is *colore cangiante*.

13 In his short note, "vom Farben," *Dürer: Schriftlicher Nachlass*, ed. H. Rupprich, Berlin, 1966, II, 393 f.

artists would have sought for more than a century to represent this exceptionally luxurious modern industrial product as the garb of a great variety of figures seems less likely than that they welcomed a further change to enrich the color pattern and to escape the pervasiveness of local color. Cennini's statement can be taken, however, as an engaging document in support of the economic interpretation of art, coming as it does from the foremost silk-producing town in the western world in which the silk-makers guild, the Arte della Seta, was one of the three most powerful political and social institutions, and a major patron of the arts.

Alberti wanted to change these practices by recommending the use of black for shadows in symmetry with the use of white for lighter portions. This presented in one respect an advance in verisimilitude over the prevailing method. It kept the shadows from competing in interest with the highlights by lowering their intensity, neutralizing them with black, and this made for convincing modeling. It did not, however, resolve the value contrasts in the overall composition because even though black would bring the shadows of a yellow drapery closer to those of a blue, the parts of the figures halfway between the darkest and lightest portion would be executed in pure pigment and create sharp value contrasts. But the chief obstacle was that the method threatened to destroy the decorative qualities of the Cenninesque tradition without achieving the chiaroscurò that Leonardo demanded. As white neutralized the lights, and blacks the darks, Albertian pictures would have approached the character of tinted drawings — while lacking the spontaneity of drawing — and have lost much of the expressive potential of rich color.

Dürer, in the passage just cited, appears to have held essentially to an Albertian system (though he wrote later than Leonardo) in recommending cautious modeling up and down of a basic drapery color with white and black, while warning against the danger of destroying the basic color:

> Moreover, take care, when painting anything in one color, whether it be red, blue, brown or mixed color, not to put so much light in the highlights that it departs from its own nature. For example: an uneducated person looking at your painting with a red drapery in it, says: "Look my good friend, how the drapery is such a brilliant red in one part and in the other it's white or pale colored." That is improper, and you have not done right. In such a case, you should paint a red object so that it is red all over, and the same for all colors. And the same goes for the shadows, so that it cannot be said that a brilliant red is soiled with black.[14]

[14] *Ibid.*, *loc. cit.*, An English translation of the passage is given by M. Conway, *Literary Remains of A. D.*, Cambridge, 1889, pp. 173 f. While Dürer is negative about excessive use of white and black in modeling,

Although Alberti was much concerned with the behavior of light and Cennini was not, his prescription for painted chiaroscuro was only another, slightly more mimetic, formula for modeling, equally unrelated to the unique experience of perceiving a particular object or scene at a particular time or place. Both systems could be practiced by the rule without looking at anything, just as a fictive space could be constructed in perspective without a model in actual experience. Both writers, and most Quattrocento painters, concentrated on modeling each figure in a composition separately, as a relief sculptor would have to do. As a method of painting it was therefore inescapably bound to drawing.[15] This had radical implications for the illumination of pictures: it favored a light entering the picture from left or right at a right angle to the axis of vision which would illuminate one side of the figure and put the other side in shadow. Unlike sunlight, the source is thus not localized at a specific point overhead; light, if it is consistent at all, simply blows in from the side like a gentle, steady breeze, touching all the objects alike. One figure or object does not block this effluvium from another, casting a shadow, — partly because shadows are impossible to plot unless there is a specific light source,[16] and partly because they would alter the color consistency of the individual figure, and upset the whole color system. Quattrocento figures sometimes cast shadows of an unspecific sort on the ground, but rarely on each other. Shadows often are more precisely delineated on furniture and architecture because these belong to an already-neutralized setting and the neutralizing effect of shadow does not disturb the color system, and because the flat planes simplify the problem of shadow projection. Masaccio's Pisa altarpiece of 1427 (Figs. 1 and 2) may be the first instance of both procedures: the figures in the central panel cast imprecisely defined shadows and receive light from a vague area to the left and somewhat above, and the gray throne is lit from a defineable point-source at the upper left (note especially the rosettes on the forward face).[17]

the implication of the passage is that a moderate use is expected, since he warns against shading one color with another, as yellow with blue or green.

Here, as in the Leonardo passages (cf. note 30), I understand the word usually translated as " beautiful " (*schön*, *bella*) to mean "brilliant" or "intense" (Conway, who attempted to translate into Renaissance English, used " fair ").

15 The point is emphasized by Shearman, *op. cit.*, p. 16.

16 See Thomas Kaufmann, " The Perspective of Shadows. The History of the Theory of Shadow Projection," *Journal of the Warburg and Courtauld Institutes* XXXVI, 1975, p. 25. The appearance of cast shadows in paintings purportedly illuminated by natural light (e.g., Fig. 1) is contemporaneous with the emergence of linear perspective, the reason being that the method of projection is similar. However, as Kaufmann demonstrates, a geometric system of casting shadows from a point source was not worked out until the late writings of Dürer.

17 John Shearman has proposed, partly on the basis

The rare instances in Quattrocento art of illumination by sources other than the sun were the cause of remarkable innovations in the representation of shadow and in color practice, perhaps because they forced the painter out of the mould of uniform modeling. The light that comes from a torch (as in Piero della Francesca's *Dream of Constantine* at Arezzo) or from a supernatural source within the picture, necessarily originates at a defined point and impels the artist to paint strong and inevitably dramatic chiaroscuro contrasts and low-value shadows.[18] Gentile da Fabriano, in the Nativity predella of the Strozzi Altarpiece of 1423, combined divine light emanating from the Christchild with moonlight to produce a doubled cast shadow in a notable fusion of naturalism with the supernatural. Piero again, in the predella of the Perugia altarpiece with the Stigmatization of St. Francis (Fig. 3), where the Crucifix is the source of light, completely abandoned the Cenninesque color practice he normally applied to figures to produce an astonishingly naturalistic vision of a sharp cold light descending on the figures from above, modeling them from a wholly unfamiliar angle, and throwing the surroundings into a deep neutral obscurity that appears almost nowhere else in Florentine art; this work is closer in sensibility to the naturalistic illuminations of the *Coeur de l'amour épris* (Fig. 4), a French work of the third quarter of the century,[19] than to the Florentine tradition of supernaturally lit narratives launched by Taddeo Gaddi with his starlit *Annunciation to the Shepherds* in the Baroncelli Chapel of Sta. Croce in Florence. The *Stigmatization* stands virtually alone in its time in its awareness of the interaction of light, shadow and color.

Such paintings show that the painter does not simply identify the color of each object to be represented, match it with a pigment, and apply it to his picture, as Alberti seems to imply. First, the effects of light and shadow on color perception vary with the character of the environment. The shadows of a given object seen outdoors at a distance on a sunny summer's day may appear to be a brilliant blue tinged by the color of neighboring objects, while those of the same object seen indoors and lit from a single source may appear an indescribable dark mud color. In the first instance, modeling with black would probably misrepresent the nature of the

of the distinctness of the cast shadows, a reconstruction of the altarpiece with additional figures of saints to the right and left ("Masaccio's Pisa Altar-piece: an Alternative Reconstruction," *Burlington Magazine*, CVIII, 1966, pp. 449-55).

18 A number of such cases from the early 1400s on are discussed by Millard Meiss in "Some Remarkably Early Shadows in a Rare Type of Threnos," *Festschrift Ulrich Middeldorf*, Berlin, 1968, pp. 112-18.

19 The *Coeur* manuscript is discussed by O. Paecht, "René d'Anjou et les van Eycks," *Cahiers de l'Association internationale des études françaises*, VIII, 1956, pp. 41-57.

light, and in the second, it might seem true to life. Further, the colors of pigments not only behave differently from those in nature, but are entirely dependent on the color setting in which they are used: a patch of blue paint looks to be one color when it is mixed on the palette, another when it is placed by a red, and a third when yellows are added alongside. This is one demonstration of the final point that the perceptual process itself influences our experience: Alberti wrongly believed that color is a property of the object that is conveyed to the eye; actually, the color sensation is generated in the eye from external light stimuli. It is not entirely an "objective" phenomenon.

Alberti, though he spoke of the effects of atmosphere and of reflection, was not prepared psychologically or philosophically to deal with ambiguities of this order. He would have thought it unscientific to offer different rules for different occasions. This is exactly what Leonardo decided was necessary to break out of the confines of early Renaissance color practice, and it meant for him recording innumerable observations of specific local conditions of light and color. But he was no more able than Alberti to reconcile this with his vision of science, though he was as eager to do so.

II *Color and Content*

While early Renaissance painters thought about light and color principally in terms of the problems of representing the visible world and of making internally harmonious compositions, their decisions, not always conscious, influenced a third fundamental aspect of their work, the content.

Three consequences of the prevailing and conservative color style of the Quattrocento inhibited the gravity of the message conveyed by paintings:

First, the practice of modeling (in which the pure pigment used for shadows tended to come forward because of its intensity) reduced the solidity and denseness of figures and made them what we call colloquially "light weight"; the lack of an appearance of physical gravity suggests a lack of dramatic gravity. This was a factor contributing to the rejection of the practice by Leonardo, who asked:

> *What is more important, that a figure abound in brilliance of colors or display high relief?* Only painting presents itself to its observers as if it were in relief and causes what has no substance to project from the walls. But colors honor only the masters who

> make them, for in them there is no cause for wonder except their brilliance (*bellezza*), and their brilliance is not to the credit of the painter, but of him who has generated them. A subject can be dressed in ugly colors and still astound those who contemplate it, because of the appearance of relief.[20]

Second, the need to distinguish figures in a continuum of bright, uniformly lit colors led to differentiating each one — and usually the separate garments of any single one — by hue, so that multifigured compositions often covered the entire range of the palette. Alberti approved this:

> I should like all the kinds and species of colors to appear in painting with a certain grace and amenity... if you are painting Diana leading her band, it is appropriate for this nymph to be given green clothes, the one next to her white, and the next red, and another yellow, and the rest should be dressed successively in a variety of colors, in such a way that light colors are always next to dark ones of a different kind (§ 48).[21]

Finally, the high values resulting from modeling entirely with white, and strong intensities, gave the surface a bright, candid appearance. " White ", Alberti adds in the same passage, " lends gaity (*hilaritatem*) not only when placed between gray and yellow, but almost to any color," which is one reason why he recommended caution in its use.

In the Middle Ages, when colors frequently were chosen for established symbolic inferences or for the economic value of the material, their value and intensity did not affect their message. But a new generation, seeking to give painting a psychological as well as a representational validity, and to gain dramatic impact in narrative, must have been frustrated by the cheerfulness and excitation of the traditional palette. The mood it generated was unsuited to commissions that called for the depiction of key events in the Bible and lives of the Virgin and saints, altarpieces and subjects from ancient poetry, normally of a sober nature. It was particularly incongruous in representations of the Passion of Christ, Fra Angelico's *Crucifixion*

20 Leonardo da Vinci, *Treatise on Painting*, § 123 (108); see also § 236 (110). My numbering of passages in the Treatise is explained in note 25.

21 The juxtaposition of " light " and " dark " colors is further explained in what follows in the same paragraph: " there is a kind of sympathy among colors, whereby their grace and beauty is increased when they are placed side by side. If red stands between blue and green, it somehow enhances their beauty as well as its own." Alberti, showing an unaccustomed first-hand familiarity with pictorial effects, is referring to the intensification that results from the juxtaposition of complementary colors, though the concept of complementary only began to be grasped by Leonardo (see below, p. 36).

Piero della Francesca treats the clothing of the angels in the London *Baptism* as if he were attempting to carry out Alberti's instructions.

now in San Marco in Florence (Fig. 5) being a notable example, with its festive, exhilarating color range. Alberti, in discussing the appropriate treatment of the *historia* (narrative theme) at the end of Book II and the start of Book III, chose almost exclusively dramatic events of intense emotional content and sobriety — the scene of Diana mentioned above being an exception. The discussion is dependent entirely on Roman rhetoric, particularly Ciceronian.[22] It is consequently concerned with *decorum*, or appropriateness of the style to the theme, and gives the impression that the author is on the verge of formulating a theory of genres that would have involved, *inter alia*, different color ranges for different types of theme, as Nicolas Poussin, another painter absorbed in rhetoric, attempted to do two centuries later.[23] Whether or not this was the case, Alberti's rejection of the exclusively high-value palette must have been related to an effort to find a suitable tonal range for tragic themes.

I believe that one reason why critics of the nineteenth century classed Quattrocento painters together with those of the previous century as " primitives " is that they found the products of the high-value color system emotionally naive. But even Early Renaissance commentators appear to have responded similarly. The modern popular image of Fra Angelico as a simple soul, cheerfully singing praises of the Lord does not really clash with that of Cristoforo Landino, who, describing in 1480 the Florentine painters of his century, called Angelico " vezoso (blithe) divoto et ornato molto con grandissima facilità ", while Masaccio was " optimo

22 For Alberti's roots in rhetoric, see John Spencer, " Ut Rhetorica Pictura," *Journal of the Warburg and Courtauld Institutes*, XX, 1959, pp. 26-44; Michael Baxandall, *Giotto and the Orators*, Oxford, 1971, pp. 121-39; H. Mühlmann, " Über den humanistischen Sinn einiger Kerngedanken der Kunsttheorie seit Alberti," *Zeitschrift für Kunstgeschichte*, XXXIII, 1970, pp. 127-42.

23 A theory of genres seems to me to emerge naturally from a concern for *decorum* in painting as it does in rhetoric (and in architecture, with the orders). For lack of it, Alberti seems inconsistent when he advises (§ 40) " The first thing that gives pleasure in a *historia* is a plentiful variety... I would say a picture was richly varied if it contained a properly arranged mixture of old men, youths, boys, matrons, maidens, children, domestic animals, dogs, birds, horses, sheep, buildings and provinces... provided it is appropriate to what is going on in the picture," and a moment later, " Perhaps the artist who seeks dignity above all in his *historia* ought to represent very few figures..." The two statements might be harmonious if one were taken as describing the comic genre and the other the tragic, but Alberti also says, " In a *historia* I strongly approve of the practice I see observed by the tragic and comic poets, of telling their story with as few characters as possible," which leaves the purpose of " variety " undefined. Baxandall (" Guarino, Pisanello and Manuel Chrysalorus," *Journal of the Warburg and Courtauld Institutes*, XXVIII, 1965, pp. 200 f.) offers the suggestion that Alberti is here tactfully expressing his debt to the less articulated rhetorical aesthetics of the previous generation of humanists, particularly Guarino of Verona; in that event, his next step would not have been to develop a system of genres, but to subordinate *varietas* to *dignitas*. The paradox is discussed in a still different light by Mühlmann, *op. cit.*, pp. 135 ff.

imitatore di natura, di gran rilievo universale, buono componitore, et puro sanzo ornato." [24] I'm not sure that Angelico's religious sensibility was as shallow as it has looked to later generations. He learned his craft at a time when nobody dreamed of a psychological use of color and, being of a conservative disposition, he was insufficiently inventive to create a new palette. If there has been clear leadership, Angelico and others addicted to high values might have adopted a new color system. But, in contrast to the treatment of other formal features in Quattrocento painting, every leading master struck out independently with his own experiments in color and no consensus emerged.

III *Leonardo da Vinci*

Nearly everything Leonardo wrote about painting can be found in the *Trattato della Pittura*, which his heir Francesco Melzi efficiently compiled from scattered statements in the mass of notebooks left by the artist. Leonardo had given no form to the notes, and Melzi and modern editors attempted to arrange them roughly by theme but without overcoming the lack of structure, the repetitiveness or the contradictions.[25] Any attempt to present a consistent theory based on this evidence is therefore likely to be somewhat arbitrary. Yet Leonardo's notes on color, while they constitute neither a practice manual like Cennini's, nor an element in a theoretical system like Alberti's, clarify the profound differences that distinguish his approach to color from that of his predecessors.

The notes are less concerned with the way color is used in painting than with the way it looks in nature. They are short and empirical, recording effects as perceived under different conditions, primarily in terms of light and shadow, and only secondarily in terms of hue. The method is simple — to look around without preconceptions, attending to the way in which three-dimensional effects may be translated into two-dimensional terms illusionistically. Past theory and practice

24 Landino's critique (from his Commentary on Dante's *Divine Comedy*, 1481) is discussed and analyzed in detail by Baxandall, *Painting and Experience*, pp. 114 ff. Since Baxandall has justifiably devoted almost a page to defining each of the characterizing terms, I felt that providing a translation here would distort the meaning.

25 Quotations from Leonardo's *Trattato* follow the accepted practice of English publications, giving the paragraph number first from the standard German edition of H. Ludwig (Vienna, 1882 and several later editions) and then again, in parenthesis, from the English translation of A. P. McMahon, Princeton, 1956. The latter is indispensable because it includes a facsimile of Melzi's original manuscript transcription from Leonardo's notebooks, Cod. Urb. Lat. 1270, but it greatly complicated Leonardo studies by needlessly rearranging the numeration of the paragraphs so that the double-reference system is required.

are seldom cited. It is as if Leonardo wished to begin the art again from scratch, without so much as a bow to those predecessors — chiefly northern Europeans — who had pioneered in representing in art the phenomena in nature that most interested him.

The basic difference between Leonardo's approach and that of his Italian predecessors is that while they aimed in a painting to represent objects as they knew them to be, he sought to represent the effect of things on the eye. For Leonardo, the object seen could be altered entirely in form and color by changes in the light and the surrounding atmosphere and, where it differed, in the light and atmosphere of the observer's surroundings. This distinction was of fundamental importance for Leonardo's painting, but paradoxically his actual painting is not naturalistic in the sense that the notes would suggest. Leonardo had many aims as an artist that did not get recorded on paper because they were not empirical. Conversely, many of the natural effects that he advises using for paintings occur in scenes that neither he nor other Italian Renaissance painters depicted.

Had the *Trattato* been published in Leonardo's lifetime, its chief impact would probably have been to reinforce criticism of the non-naturalistic results of Quattrocento color practice, and to urge painters to look more closely at nature. It could not have helped contemporaries to articulate an alternative color system or to integrate the empirical naturalism it champions with the theoretical ideals of Renaissance painting — classic form, proportions, and imitation in the sense of idealization.

Leonardo's description of the illusion of relief as the fundamental goal of painting echoes Alberti's, and the following passage is only one of many in the *Trattato* that suggest on first reading that his color system was no more than an expanded and more sophisticated version of the one presented in *De Pictura*:

> The primary purpose of the painter is to make a plane surface look like a body in relief detached from the plane, and he who in that art most surpasses others deserves most praise, and this particular investigation, which is the crown of the science of painting, originates in the shadows and lights or, if you wish, brightness and darkness. Therefore whoever avoids shadows avoids what is the glory of the art for noble imaginations, but gains glory with the ignorant public, who want nothing in painting but brilliance (*bellezza*) of color, altogether forgetting the brilliance and marvel of depicting a relief on what in reality is a plane surface. (T. 412 [434])[26]

26 "Brilliance" in the closing lines of the passage is a translation of "bellezza," which Leonardo does not use in the modern sense of "beauty" (as Mc Mahon translated it). As John Shearman first pointed

But there are radical differences which focus on what is meant by "shadows and lights." Alberti's concept of relief could be called *modeling*, in that he visualized raising each individual figure and object from the picture plane by working down toward black or shadow on one side and up toward white or light on the other. The composition has a consistent lighting only to the extent that the light sides of all the figures face the same way. Leonardo's concept can be called the relief of chiaroscuro, since light, rather than body, is the fundamental element and, so far as the painter is concerned, bodies and things do not exist until they are illuminated. As light falls, it reveals color, brings parts of objects forward in relief, and reflects from one object to another. Light has its own color which it casts onto objects and which mixes with the color of the objects. As light takes precedence over body, unity takes precedence over diversity, for in Alberti's system, the whole can be conceived only as a collection of modeled parts. Chiaroscuro was the cornerstone of a new, more harmonious and unified style of painting.

The painter who "avoids shadows" in the passage quoted, and is scorned by Leonardo, represents the fifteenth-century practitioner whose distaste for the dulling effects of black and for large neutralized areas led to the retention of Cenninesque shadows rendered in full or only slightly moderated intensity. Probably the "ignorant public" to which Leonardo refers in this connection encouraged many of his contemporaries to retain what he regarded as an absurd practice that flouted the evidence of everyday experience. Quattrocento painters are implicitly berated in other passages in the *Trattato*, — most memorably in the one quoted above on pp. 22-23 — and always for the reason that they prefer the excitement of colors in their full intensity to the satisfaction of representing the three-dimensionality of nature. He appears, in that statement, to regard the attraction of the picture in which all colors appear in high intensities as being comparable to that of precious stones (some colors being ground from rare minerals) and to be unworthy of an artist. He proposes to overcome the tyranny of brilliant colors by introducing the neutralization of color in a naturalistic way.

In the *Trattato*, the only form of neutralization approved is the admixture of black in shadows. In practice, however, Leonardo normally toned down the lights as well by mixing colors on the palette, sometimes with black but also with lower-

out ("Leonardo's Colour...," p. 31): "It cannot be too strongly emphasized that *bellezza di colori* does not mean 'beauty of color' in the modern sense, but the harsh brilliance of pure pigment." Elsewhere I use the term "intensity," which is inappropriate here because of Leonardo's play on the word.

value hues, and often, as in the clothing of the *Mona Lisa*, to the extent that the hue is virtually indescribable (at least, under the present screen of varnish), and changes in response to the play of light. In the *Virgin with St. Anne* (Fig. 17), the color passes beyond the stage represented by the *Trattato*; the shadows are a chromatic gray rather than black, and seem as alive and as transparent as the lights; objects no longer have a basic color but become a field for a subtle play of varied colors.

In Alberti's treatise, light is a simple phenomenon that varies only according to the nature and the direction of its source (the sun, moon, lamp-light, etc.). Leonardo's light is infinitely more complex. Not only does it have its own color according to the nature of its source, which it casts onto the objects it strikes, but it reflects from every object and takes the color from it to whatever other objects stand facing it.[27] Furthermore, the atmosphere itself is a vehicle of light as particles or " atoms " of humidity near the earth's surface catch and reflect the rays of the sun. The blueness of the sky and the blue cast given by the thickness of the atmosphere to distant objects results from our seeing the illuminated particles against a dark background — pure unhumidified air being by nature dark (an explanation based on Aristotle).[28] Thus the color of an object can be made up of its own " natural " color, the color of the source of illumination, reflections from one or more facing objects, and the atmosphere between it and the viewer.[29]

An even more significant contribution to the painter's vision was linked to Leonardo's work on the physiology of vision: the statement that the light perceived varies according to the conditions of viewing. The best illustration cited in the *Trattato* is the room that looks brightly lit when one is inside it but seems dark (and objects within it virtually colorless) when it is seen " from the piazza." [30] The reason given — correctly — is that the pupil of the eye enlarges in the reduced light of the interior and contracts in the bright light of the outdoors.

27 In *De Pictura*, Alberti discusses (§ 11) how reflected light carries the color of the object from which it is reflected, citing the case of a person walking in an open field receiving a green reflection on the face; but this is an isolated observation not integrated into his precepts for painting.

28 *Trattato* 243 (225); 226 (226); 490 (519). The theory also explains why the sky seems less blue at the horizon: in 226, Leonardo demonstrates geometrically that when we look at the horizon — along a line tangent to the earth's surface — the eye has to penetrate a greater segment of the sphere of humidified air surrounding the earth than when we look straight upwards in a line perpendicular to the earth's surface.

29 The assumption that a particular object has an intrinsic color independent of conditions of illumination and environment is Leonardo's and need not be challenged here.

30 See below, p. 34.

Because of Leonardo's concentration on chiaroscuro relief, black and white are much more important than colors in his thinking.

His black, like Alberti's, is used to represent the absence of light (black is " tenebre " in T. 213 [178]), to neutralize shadows, and discourages the general practice of shading with low value neutrals made from colors such as the mixture of complementaries:

> The shadow of bodies ought not to take on any other color than that of the body to which it is attached. Therefore, since black is not counted in the number of colors, the shadows of all the colors are taken from it. As the colors of bodies are in greater or lesser shadow, they require more or less black, provided that the color of the body is never entirely lost, except in the complete darkness contained within the boundaries of the opaque body.
>
> Therefore, painter, if you would copy nature, tinge somewhat the walls of your studio with white mixed with black, because white and black are not colors.
>
> (T. 703 [803])

There are two reasons for this rule: first, the " natural " color of the object is the only color that can appear in its shadows unless another color is reflected onto it from a facing object, (or coloration is caused by the light source or the atmosphere,) [31] second, since in this theory, shadow is the absence of light and color, there is no justification for using even neutralized color to represent it; only the non-color black is equivalent to shadow.[32]

In practice this simple precept could be carried out only in the artificial conditions of the studio, where a given object could be isolated from other objects that might reflect on it, where the effect of atmosphere could be minimized, and where, by devices like painting the studio walls as recommended in the quoted passage, even the color of natural light could be controlled.

Leonardo explained what makes reflected color objectionable in the following:

> Never will the color of the shadow of any body be a true, proper shadow, unless the object opposite, which casts the shadow, is of the same color as the body to which the shadow is given.

[31] J. P. Richter, *The Notebooks of Leonardo da Vinci*, London, 1883, 1970, § 306, from ms. G, fol. 153v: " The surface of every object partakes of the color of the (source of) illumination and of the color of the air that is interposed between the eye and that object, that is, of the color of the transparent medium..."

[32] The statement in T. 905 (980), " The shadow of verdure always takes on blue, and so does every shadow of all other objects, and it becomes more blue the farther from the eye it is and less blue the nearer it is," is not a contradiction of the precept about black shadows, but deals with the effects of the intervening atmosphere and is a special case of Leonardo's " perspective of color." T. 630 (814) also treats blue shadows and explains: " This happens because of the brightness of the air...". Cf. T. 646 (816).

> Let us suppose, for example, that I have a room whose walls are green. I say that if a blue object is seen in such a place, illuminated by the bright blueness of the air, then the illuminated side will be a very intense blue. But the shadow of such an intense blue will be ugly and not a true shadow of an intense blue because it is spoiled by green, which reverberates in it. It would be worse if the walls were tan. (T. 239 [202])[33]

Since Leonardo would have conceded that reflected and atmospheric colors of all kinds occur in the natural environment, his dicta on black shadows represent a departure from his generally naturalistic and empirical position. He accepted this inconsistency because an uncompromising naturalism would make it impossible to achieve harmonious and balanced color compositions, while consistent black shadowing could produce tonal consistency throughout a picture.

The role of white in Leonardo's theory is entirely different from its function in the Quattrocento; white is a wholly passive non-color " more receptive to any color than the surface of any other body except a mirror: "

> For that reason we shall say that because white is empty, devoid of color, when it is illuminated with the color of any luminous body it takes on the color of that luminous body. Black would not do so, for black is like a broken vessel, which is deprived of the capacity to contain anything. (T. 215 [205])

Thus, while black was made equivalent to shadow, white was not, as it had been for earlier painters, equivalent to light. That is because light in nature is colored and, when it falls on a white object, gives it a hue.[34] Leonardo cites the instance of a lady in white " in the country " whose dress will have the brightness of the sun in one part, the blue of the air in another, and the green of the fields where they were reflected.[35] Leonardo's thinking about black and white is so far from

33 Also in the Madrid Codex II, fol. 127, where green reflections on a red body are disapproved. The passage was not transcribed into the *Trattato*.

34 While emphasis on the color of light and on the independence of light from illuminated objects was new to theory, it had a history in naturalistic painting starting in the first years of the fifteenth century in some of the illuminations of the Boucicault master and the Limbourg brothers, Jan van Eyck and the majority of the major northern European masters. The progress of the latter was encouraged by the fact that white diminishes the transparency of glazes, as Leonardo noted (Richter, 277: " no white or black is transparent "), which is particularly deleterious in oil painting. Italian masters working in tempera generally avoided the problem of colored light unless they were depicting superior non-natural light, such as an apparition or an artificially lit night scene, which made these exceptions paradoxically more " naturalistic."

35 T. 785 (786).

being symmetrical that, while he advises using black non-naturalistically in order to permit the kind of tonal balance he sought in his pictures, he advises a completely naturalistic use of white, citing an example — reminding us of an Impressionist canvas — of a subject and a setting one cannot imagine his choosing for a painting. Almost every comment in the *Trattato* on the use of white is about depicting white objects.[36] I have not found any reference to the use of white to raise the value of other colors, which was the chief concern of Cennini and Alberti.

I believe, however, that Leonardo was the first writer to differentiate value from intensity, but his reticence about mixing white with other colors kept him from pursuing the issue. In a few passages, the term "chiarezza" appears to be the equivalent to our use of "value," as (T. 485 [460]).[37]

> The edge of that illuminated object will seem darkest that is seen on the lightest (*più chiaro*) ground, and similarly that will seem lightest which is seen on a dark ground. And if that edge is flush with—and seen on—a light ground of the same lightness (*chiarezza*) as itself, it will be imperceptible.[38]

The choice of the terms *chiaro*, *chiarezza* — both suggestive of light — to discuss value contrasts reminds us that in the many passages where Leonardo refers to the admixture of black to represent shadow, he never differentiates the lowering of value-*chiarezza* from the lowering of intensity-*bellezza*. This produces a dilemma

[36] I am discounting the two passages on the primary colors cited below (p. 35), in which white is associated with light, because both are paraphrases of Aristotelian and post-Aristotelian theory (see Appendix), and are not related to studio practice.

[37] Cf. T. 154 (260): "Li colori di che tu vesti le figure sieno tali che dieno gratia l'uno al altro e quando l'un colore si fa campo del altro sia tale che non paino congionti et appichati n' sieme anchora che fussino di medesima natura di colore ma sien vari di chiarezza..." If we read *natura di colore* as "hue," then the different *chiarezza* ("value") is achieved by adding or subtracting white. Another instance occurs in the passage T. 226, paraphrased in note 28 explaining that the sky seems "*più chiaro*" at the horizon than overhead: this obviously means "lighter" in the sense of higher in value, as against the greater intensity of the overhead blue, which Leonardo would call "*più bella*."

[38] This passage, besides dealing with the issue of value, is one of several that refer to optical effects on the borderlines between hues of different value, or between black and white (e.g., T. 204 (151)). The observations of this phenomenon, known today as Mach bands, are presented abstractly, without reference to practice; in fact, all of the passages cite black and white as the contrast causing the effect, though the two are almost never juxtaposed in paintings of Leonardo's time.

Recent research on Mach bands demonstrated that they are caused by the inhibition of individual receptors in the retina due to competition from neighboring receptors. See Floyd Ratliff, "Contour and Contrast," *Scientific American*, June, 1972, pp. 90-101, which discusses a number of works of art as well as recent experimental achievements. The paper is based on one of the same title in *Proceedings of the American Philosophical Society*, 115, 2, 1971, pp. 150-63.

that is the reverse of that of the Quattrocento, since achieving a tonal balance between a naturally high-value yellow and naturally low-value blue is difficult whether they are in shadow or in light. But it is not *as* difficult in the darks. In his paintings, Leonardo was able to capitalize on the fact that black minimizes such contrasts while the earlier use of white had maximized them.

The early *Madonna of the Rocks* in the Louvre (Fig. 6) is a bold realization of the new ideas; the dark setting and the directed light throw much of the picture into a shadow that helps to unify it. Although the draperies of the Virgin and angel are still conceived as having particular local colors — in fact, Leonardo's four primaries — the competition between them is reduced by the pervasiveness of shadow. In the later (London) version of the same picture, more complex chromatic means are used to draw the different colors together; the yellow drapery, for example, is modeled down with browns picked up from the landscape, and in similar ways the diverse hues are bound together coloristically rather than simply in terms of value as in the earlier picture.

In his passages relating to the effect of light and shadow on color, Leonardo was the first of the theorists to present a clearly articulated concept of color intensity (or saturation, brilliance). John Shearman first pointed this out,[39] showing that Leonardo used the term *bellezza* to convey the concept; earlier scholars, mistranslating *bellezza* as " beauty " [40] had been misleading enough to deprive it of precision but not enough to have revealed the error. The following quotation is typical (T. 242 [189]):

> Color found between the shadowed and the illuminated parts of shadowed bodies is of less *bellezza* than that which is entirely illuminated, so that the prime *bellezza* of colors is to be seen in the principal lights.

This principle is diametrically opposed to Cennini's placement of the most intense hue in the deepest shadow; and, in that it operates against using white in the highlights, it is opposed to Alberti as well. In a related passage, Leonardo openly states his opposition to the Cenninists by casting them as " the adversary " (T. 245 [193]):

> Colors placed in shadow will partake more or less of their natural intensity (*bellezza*) depending on whether they are in greater or lesser obscurity; but if the colors are

[39] See note 26 above.

[40] In T. 210 (188), the term *qualità* is used rather than *bellezza*: " The true quality of colors is known through light..." The passage was taken from Cod. Ashburnham, fol. 33, which is dated 1492. I assume that at this date Leonardo's vocabulary was not fixed.

located in luminous space, they will look the more intense the greater the splendor of the source of light.

THE ADVERSARY: The differences of color in shadow are as numerous as are the differences of color in the things shadowed.

REPLY: Colors placed in shadow will differ less and less as the shadows in which they are situated grow deeper. For this there is the testimony of those who from the squares look inside the doors of shadowed temples, where the paintings covered with different colors all appear to be enveloped in obscurity.

This concept is modified in T. 206 (190):

Different colors have their *bellezza* (greatest intensity) in different parts of themselves, and this is seen in black, which has its *bellezza* in the shadows, white in the light, and blue green and tan in half shadows, and yellow and red in the light, gold in reflections, and lake in half shadow.

The statement appears in a context that makes it ambiguous whether Leonardo is referring to colors in nature or to pigments. This is not the only ambiguity in Leonardo's system: another arises in the conflict between the two precepts 1) that a hue reaches its greatest intensity when it is most lit, and 2) that light is itself colored. In many instances the color of the light would reduce the intensity of the color of the object, as would occur in carrying out the instructions of T. 756 (869).[41] Here, in a fashion reminiscent of Cennini's mixing in little bowls, the painter is advised to use mixing spoons to measure out the relative amounts of body-color and light-color for representing the illuminated portions of a body: the amounts are determined by figuring the angle of incidence of the light source, up to a maximum of two parts light-color to one part body-color.

In practice, Leonardo tended to modify such precepts to improve the tonal harmony of pictures; the strongly illuminated yellow drape at the center of the Louvre

41 " Sia tolto un colore simile al colore del corpo che tu voi imitare, e sia tolto il colore del principale lume col quale voi aluminare esso corpo, di puoi se tu trovi che il sopra detto maggior angolo sia duplo al angolo minore, allora tu torrai una parte del colore naturale del corpo che voi imitare, e dagli due parti del lume che tu voi ch'esso riceva, et harai posto il lume duplo al lume minore di puoi per fare il lume sub duplo, togli una sola parte d'esso colore naturale del già detto corpo, e aggiongieli solo una parte del detto lume; et cosi harai fatto sopra un medesimo colore un lume il quale sara doppio l'uno à l'altro, perchè sopra una quantità d'esso colore è datto una simil quantità di lume, e l'altra quantità è datto due quantità di tale lume. E se tu voi misurare di punto esse quantità di colori habbi uno piccolo chuchiaro col quale tu possi pigliare le tue quantità eguali come posto quivi in margine [sketch of spoon]. E quando tu hai con esso tolto il tuo colore e tu lo radi colla piccola riga come far si sole alle misure delle biade quando si vende esse biade."

Madonna of the Rocks (Fig. 6) is toned down from full intensity to keep it from seeming inconsistent with its surroundings. In the *Madonna and St. Anne* (Fig. 7), the red undergarment of the Virgin, most intense in the middle tones, is paler in the yellow-white highlights.

Another innovation in Leonardo's treatment of the effect of light and shadow on color was his emphasis on the changes caused by the displacement of the observer from the immediate environment of the object to be depicted to a more (or less) illuminated environment. I have mentioned passages that cite the case of the well-illuminated room in which the objects appear to an indoor observer brightly colored while they seem to an observer standing outdoors in the sunlight dark and colorless; this is due partly to "a defect of the eye which, overcome by the excessive light of the air, contracts the size of its pupil a good deal and so loses much of its visual power." [42] The expansion and contraction of the pupil is also cited as accounting partly for the differing brilliance of the moon in day and night: these passages are the only ones I have found in which Leonardo put to use his extensive studies in the physiology of the eye in developing his painting theory. The consideration both of the observer's ambience and of its potential physiological effect represents a radically different attitude from that of the Quattrocento. In one passage Leonardo suggests the practical implications of his observation, instructing the painter never to mix colors in a light different from that of the object to be depicted; he goes on (T. 819 [872]):

> Suppose... I represent a mountain in the west, which is half shadowed and half luminous, but I wish to depict only the luminous part. I take a little piece of paper covered with that color which seems to me similar to that of the mountain, and I put it alongside the real color in such a way that there is no space between the true and the simulated, exposing it to the sun's rays, and adding different colors until each seems true, and I will continue thus with respect to every kind of shadowed and luminous colors.

The simple-minded naturalism of this proposal was not one that Leonardo followed in his painting; in fact, it wouldn't work, because as soon as other colors were

[42] See T. 202 (195); 700 (815); 628 (753), and also Ms. E, 17v and L. 41v. The manuscripts are cited in Leonardo, *Scritti scelti*, ed. A. M. Brizio, Turin, 1952, pp. 407, 453 (as noted by Carlo Pedretti, *Leonardo da Vinci On Painting: a Lost Book*. Berkeley/Los Angeles, 1964, p. 206; this volume is an indispensable source book for *Trattato* studies).

added alongside the one matched they would alter its appearance, and it would no longer look like the mountains.

Neither of the two passages in the *Trattato* that identify the primary colors (*colori semplici*) is based on studio practice. One repeats a reduced Aristotelian list (T. 254 [176]) of six: white, black, yellow, green, blue and red, the last four standing for earth, water, air and fire: T. 237 (213) adds two to that number, as Aristotle had, (though the specific colors are different): lion-colored or tan, and blackberry-colored, and discusses the making of " composite " colors from the mixture of the primaries, first one with one, then two with two, and so on.[43] In what seems to be a footnote to these lists, Leonardo adds (T. 255 [177]):

> Blue and green are not in themselves simple colors because blue is composed of light and darkness, as in the case of air; that is, it is composed of most perfect black and purest white. Green is composed of a simple and compound color... blue and yellow.

In the case of green, the apparent contradiction is due to the fact that the Aristotelian system, which did not purport to apply to pigments, conflicted with studio experience (where green results from mixing yellow and blue). The reservation about blue is more complicated. It originates in Aristotle's claim that *all* colors are made up of black and white (or darkness and light) in different proportions; I think Leonardo singled out blue because, in addition to being the color of certain objects in nature, it is the color of the sky and atmosphere as well, as discussed above,[44] and his explanation of that phenomenon involved the simple mixture of lightness and darkness.

[43] In his *Treatise on Architecture* of ca. 1460 (ed. J. Spencer, New Haven, 1965, fols. 180r ff.), Antonio Averlino, il Filarete, includes a section on drawing and painting largely borrowed from Alberti's *De Pictura*, but adjusted in specifics to observations that the author had made in the studios of painters (that he was not himself trained in painting is suggested by his open admission of ignorance with respect to the manufacture of several pigments). The treatise cannot have influenced later painting theory.

Filarete lists the same six *principali et più degni* colors as Leonardo for his basic palette (fol. 181v): white (= light), black (= shadow), red (fire), blue (air), green (grass) and yellow (gold, flowers, grass). The last two associations with nature show that Filarete had lost the thread of the tradition of aligning colors with the elements, which Leonardo sustained.

Filarete's comments on making and mixing pigments in this passage, though inexpert, are unique in the Quattrocento. Especially interesting is his apparent preference for oil as a medium (fol. 182r): " but this is another practice and another mode which is beautiful for anyone who knows how to do it. In Germany they work well in this technique, especially Master Jan of Bruges (Van Eyck) and Master Roger (Van Der Weyden)."

[44] See above, p. 28.

In spite of this conservative approach to the fundamentals, Leonardo produced a remarkable new precept of color composition. It is the first to identify complementary colors and to perceive that in juxtaposition they intensify each other (T. 258 [180]):

> Among colors of equal perfection the one which will appear to be the most excellent is that which is seen in the company of the direct opposite color (*retto contrario*). A direct opposite is a pale color with red, black with white... azure blue and golden yellow, green and red.[45]

The term *retto contrario*, implying that the colors are laid out according to a geometric figure, suggests the color wheel.[46] The advantage of juxtaposing complementary fields is that it emphasizes relief; as an alternative, Leonardo suggests (T. 190 [185]): "If you wish the proximity of one color to make another which it borders attractive, observe the rule which is seen in the rays of the sun that compose the rainbow." The image of a picture employing hues aligned according to the spectrum is curiously inconsistent with Leonardo's surviving paintings.

The notes do not show much interest in the effects of one color on another other than as a way of separating bodies: Leonardo did not investigate in his written work the way particular pigments are affected by different chromatic settings in which they may be placed.

Remarkably few of Leonardo's notes on painting deal with actual colors apart from the conditions that light, shade, atmosphere and reflection exert on colors generically. What is revealing about the corpus of color notes is the context in which they were conceived, the approach that made Leonardo the first to differentiate the workings of intensity and value and that helped him to achieve a new and radical chromatic and tonal composition. Although Leonardo was an irrepressible experimenter with pigments and media, there are not more than half a dozen notes on technical processes in the manuscripts. He overlooked even the issue that from hindsight seems to have been the most crucial in Italian painting of his generation: the differing coloristic effects and potentialities of the oil and tempera medium.

[45] Slightly different lists of favored harmonies are offered in T. 190a (183), 238 (184) and 253 (182).

[46] See also T. 258c (181): "ogni colore si conosce meglio nel suo contrario che nel suo simile..." The term *eccellentia* used in the first passage is rare: *bellezza* being more common. The reason is probably that the notes were taken from an early ms. of ca. 1492, according to Pedretti, *op. cit.*, p. 188.

IV *Conclusion*

In writing of color theory and practice from Cennini to Leonardo, I may have made it appear that there occurred a steady progress from a relatively unsophisticated level to a relatively mature level. In the early days of art history, the thesis that art advanced from the early fifteenth century to an apex in the early sixteenth century was taken for granted, and memorialized by identifying the style of Leonardo, Raphael and Michelangelo as "High Renaissance." Modern historical theory has rejected the concept of progress in art; it is now generally agreed that what matters in a work of art is its validity as an aesthetic object and as an expression of its time and place rather than the degree to which it approaches a fixed standard of perfection. But there is some ambiguity in the present subject. First, color practice is in part a theoretical and applied science, and we agree that it is proper to speak of progress in science and technology — fifteenth century artists unquestionably improved the potential range of coloristic and chiaroscuro effects in the tempera and oil media and expanded their means of achieving tonal balance. Second, early Renaissance artists did agree on a "fixed standard of perfection:" a major task of painting was held to be the representation of the three-dimensional effects of nature — and the color practice of 1500 was better able than that of 1400 to produce the desired impression of relief.

But there is also a different basis on which future generations regarded the art of the early 1500s as an advance over that of Cennini's time. The color and chiaroscuro of Leonardo and Giorgione intensified the interaction of the artist with his subject, and of the viewer with the picture in two ways — in providing means to dramatize the actors and the environment by manipulating light and dark for emotional effect, accenting one area or part of the body and suppressing another, and in developing the means of presenting the visual world perceptually rather than conceptually, as when a group of trees or a range of mountains is presented as a pattern of light and shadow rather than as a collection of autonomous objects.

These innovations deeply affected the future course of painting, since they made possible a kind and a range of emotional and sensual interplay between the viewer and the figures and objects in a picture beyond the reach even of such great dramatists as Masaccio and Giotto. And over the centuries, the artist's ability to bring us into this sort of relationship to the work of art (which was associated in the Renaissance with the art of poetry and has been called "literary" in modern criticism, but which is easier to understand as an effort to appeal to our perceptions and experiences of people and of nature) has been held to be a primary index of value in art, and constituted the fixed standard by which the Renaissance of the early sixteenth century became " High."

The fact that this is no longer the case, that twentieth-century art and taste shifted emphasis to abstract expression in form and color, has helped to restore the art of the Quattrocento in critical esteem. When we concede today that Leonardo had a better control of color and chiaroscuro than Alberti's contemporaries, we do not imply that he could therefore make better pictures, but simply that he was better able to make the kind of pictures he wished.

APPENDIX

THE ANCIENT AND MEDIEVAL TRADITION

A Renaissance artist, scientist or scholar who sought information on color could turn, in effect, to only one source: Aristotle, or to medieval or modern commentaries on or derivations from the theories expounded in his *De Sensu*, *De Anima* and *Meteorologica*. The extensive medieval literature on optics that provided the basis of much Quattrocento art theory, and particularly the study of light, vision and artificial perspective, did not, because of its theoretical-geometrical base, deal with color.

The Aristotelian system is not concerned with the behavior of pigments but with the workings of color in nature.[a] It is most fully expounded in *De Sensu* (III, 439 f.), where white and black are presented as the two poles of a color spectrum, and all other colors result from a mixture of the two in varying proportions. Simple proportions such as 3 : 4 and 2 : 3 account for most colors, but some are incommensurable. Some proportions are equivalent to musical intervals, and the concords in color — purple with crimson is cited — are like musical harmonies.

Aristotle's color is not immediately apprehended through the agency of light. Light has to combine with the atmosphere, which is the medium of communication between the color and the eye — in a vacuum there would be no color.[b] The atmosphere, consequently, cannot alter a color unless it is infused with colored matter such as smoke.

De Sensu lists " seven " (actually eight) basic colors including black and white--crimson, violet, green, blue, yellow in the sense of sunshine-color (which is to be classed with white) and gray (classed with black). *Meteorologica*, however, limits the list to the three found in the rainbow that cannot be imitated by mixing other colors (what we would call primaries): red, green and blue[c]. Yellow is said not to be actual rainbow color but results from the contrast of the red and green on either side of it in the spectrum.

The association of the primary colors (*simplices*) with the four elements seems to have originated in a text believed in the Middle Ages and Renaissance to have been by Aristotle: *De Coloribus*,[d] but the specific alignments (air and water: white; fire: yellow/sun-color;

a. Averroes, in his commentary on *De Sensu*, made a special point of the difference: while colors are infinite in nature, he said, they are finite in art; the artist (*artifex*) can only imitate the variety of nature because he is outside things, while nature is inside. Pigments are similarly finite and extrinsic (*Aristotelis... libri... cum Averroes Commentariis*, VI, Venice, 1550, fol. 192v a, § 19 ff.

b. Aristotle, *De Anima*, II, vii, 431-32.

c. *Meteorologica*, 372a ff. Leonardo owned a copy of this according to the booklist he compiled in 1504 (Cod. Madrid II, fols. 2v, 3r: " Meteura d'Aristotile ").

d. *De Coloribus*, ed. C. Prantl, Leipzig, 1881, p. 23. The first printed edition was that of Simon Portius, Paris, 1549.

earth: multicolored) were useless to painters. Alberti revived the tradition, and more practically associated air with blue, water: green, fire: red, and earth: ashen.

In sum, though the Aristotelian tradition was the only source of knowledge on the subject, it was thin, inconsistent, and, as Samuel Edgerton has emphasized in his fine review of Alberti's color sources, bedeviled by confusion over the translation of Aristotelian color vocabulary.[e]

e. "Alberti's Colour Theory: A Medieval Bottle Without Renaissance Wine," *Journal of the Warburg and Courtauld Institutes*, XXXII, 1969, pp. 109-34. One source of medieval color theory and vocabulary not discussed here is the *Liber de Sensu et Sensato*, ed. Robert Steele, Oxford, 1937, attributed by the editor to Roger Bacon. It expands on Aristotle's text by listing (Ch. XVI, pp. 74 ff.) the "grades" of each of seven basic colors, at times with vivid equivalents (*Pallidus* being the color of the juice of semi-cooked meat).

Fig. 1. Masaccio, Madonna and Child with Angels, *From Pisa Altarpiece, 1426, Florence, Uffizi Gallery.*

Fig. 2. Masaccio, Crucifix, *From Pisa Altarpiece, Naples, Capodimonte Museum.*

Fig. 3. Piero della Francesca, Stigmatization of St. Francis, *Predella from altarpiece, Perugia, Gallery 1460s?*

Fig. 4. René of Anjou(?), Livre du cuer d'amours espris, *Österreichische Nationalbibliothek, ms. 2597, fol. C, late 1450s.*

Fig. 5. Fra Angelico, Deposition from the *Cross, Florence, Museo San Marco, ca. 1443.*

Fig. 6. Leonardo da Vinci, Madonna of the Rocks, *1492, Paris, Louvre Museum.*

Fig. 7. Leonardo da Vinci, Madonna with St. Anne, *ca. 1505, Paris, Louvre Museum.*

KATHLEEN WEIL-GARRIS — JOHN F. D'AMICO

II

THE RENAISSANCE CARDINAL'S IDEAL PALACE: A CHAPTER FROM CORTESI'S *DE CARDINALATU*

In memory of Milton J. Lewine

PREFACE

WITHOUT *the American Academy in Rome, this collaborative venture would never have been thought of or attempted. A lecture by Weil-Garris reminded D'Amico of a passage in Paolo Cortesi's* De Cardinalatu, *a humanist text with which the lecturer had only the foggiest acquaintance. A look at Cortesi's chapter on the cardinal's palace, however, revealed nothing less than a letter delivered* poste restante, *directed to historians of art, but also containing messages for students of other aspects of Renaissance culture. Cortesi combines descriptions of actual Roman palaces with a careful account of the Renaissance cardinal's ideal palace, its layout, functions and painted decorations.*

De Cardinalatu *is an encyclopedic book of conduct designed for both established and aspiring prelates. Not all were born to elevated status. Ecclesiastics, like artists and humanists could embark on careers open to talent. Indeed, Cortesi wrote his treatise as part of a campaign to become a cardinal himself.* De Cardinalatu *was composed in the first decade of the sixteenth century while Julius II and his cardinals were building their opulent palaces and decorating them with works by the greatest artists of the High Renaissance. The author of the treatise, an Apostolic Protonotary, belonged to the inner circle of cardinals, papal courtiers and curial humanists. As a literary man, he was not primarily interested in the visual arts but he seemed exactly the person to provide an intimate yet oblique view of the great artistic undertakings of his time and of the patrons who set them in motion.*

D'Amico, who had been studying Cortesi from the standpoint of curial humanism had been largely unconcerned with the interest the treatise might have for art historians. Weil-Garris, on the other hand, would have been discouraged from investigating further by Cortesi's notoriously ferocious humanist Latin; a consideration which must also have contributed to the relative neglect from which this source has suffered. At first we thought it sensible for the Cortesi specialist to make an English translation of the chapter on palaces whereas the art historian was to point out matters of special interest to colleagues. As it happened, however, we each had to contribute extensively to the work of the other in order to do our own and the writing of the piece fell to Weil-Garris.

Our efforts have been aided in many ways by a number of scholars, institutions and learned friends. K. Weil-Garris's research was supported by grants from the National Endowment for the Humanities and by the John Simon Guggenheim Memorial Foundation. Our work began while she was Art Historian in Residence at the American Academy in Rome and J. D'Amico was a Fellow in Post-Classical Humanistic Studies there. It was completed while she was a visitor at the Institute for Advanced Study, Princeton. Our deepest thanks go to these beneficent institutions and, in particular, to Henry Millon and Irving Lavin for their part in making this study possible. We also enjoyed the hospitality of the Bibliotheca Hertziana and of the Princeton University Library.

Cortesi provided us with opportunities to show our ignorance of a remarkably wide range of subjects. We were foiled to some extent in this by kind and generous colleagues. C. L. Frommel, above all, lent us his matchless knowledge of Roman palaces, as did Wolfgang Lotz, Richard Krautheimer and John Shearman. Marshall Clagett helped us, with the greatest possible amiability, to deal with Cortesi's references to scientific and mechanical matters. We are indebted to James Butrica, Marjorie Woods, F. W. Locke, Rogers Scudder, Hermann Goldbrunner and Charles Davis for help with Cortesi's Latin. Peter Partner gave us the benefit of his specialized studies of papal administration. We also learned much from discussions with Richard Goldthwaite about contrasts between Florentine and Roman palace life and from Bernice Davidson and Iris Cheney about Roman cinquecento art; Charlotte Nichols, Derek Moore and Lucy Rastelli gave valuable editorial assistance. Errors of commission and omission are ours alone. We have not, indeed, aspired to a definitive account of Cortesi's ideal palace but hope to have opened the door a bit wider.

INTRODUCTION

The Genesis of De Cardinalatu

PAOLO CORTESI was born in Rome in 1471.[1] His father, Antonio, held various offices in the Roman Curia and wrote a tract against Lorenzo Valla in defense of the papacy.[2] Alessandro, Paolo's older brother, also a curialist as well as a poet and orator, was responsible for the young man's education. He took Paolo to the homes of the political and intellectual leaders of Rome and to the palaces of cardinals.[3] Among Cortesi's other teachers were Pomponio Leto, leader of the Roman humanists, and Sulpizio Verolano who edited the first Latin Vitruvius. Alessandro Cortesi died in 1490 when Paolo was only nineteen years old; but by then, his career as a humanist was already fully launched. Paolo's house became the site of an academy devoted to humanistic learning and, in particular, to literature. He occupied a number of posts at the Curia but may have been dissatisfied with his progress for, in 1503, he left Rome to take up permanent residence near San Gimignano, the town where his family had originated. There he built a villa, continued writing, and held open house for a steady stream of humanists and important personages among whom were a number of cardinals. Cortesi died at the age of thirty-nine [4] in 1510, while editing his last work, *De Cardinalatu.*

A list of Cortesi's correspondents and acquaintances shows how fully he participated in the cultural life of his time. He knew Poliziano, Marullo and Pico in Florence; Lucido Fosforo, Serafino, Pontano, Alessandro Farnese, Cardinal Adriano

1 For Cortesi's birth date see Paolo Cortesi, *De hominibus doctis dialogus,* ed. and trans. Maria Teresa Graziosi (Rome, 1973), p. viii. On Cortesi and his family see Pio Paschini, " Una famiglia di curiali nella Roma del quattrocento: I Cortesi ", *Rivista di storia della chiesa in Italia,* 11/1 (1957), pp. 1-48; Anna Gracci, " Studi su Paolo Cortesi da San Gimignano ed il suo ' De Cardinalatu ' " (Tesi di laurea, Università di Firenze, 1966-67); John F. D'Amico, " Humanism and Theology at Papal Rome, 1480-1520 " (unpublished Ph. D. Thesis, University of Rochester, 1977), ch. 2.

2 See Paschini, " I Cortesi ", p. 3 and Graziosi's introduction to *De hominibus doctis,* p. viii. On the " Antivalla " see below, text note 99.

3 On Alessandro see Paschini, " I Cortesi ", pp. 7-26 and Florio Banfi, " Alessandro Tommaso Cortese, glorificatore di Mattia Corvino Re d'Ungheria ", *Archivio storico per la Dalmazia,* 23 (1937), pp. 135-160, and more recently Ladislas Havas, " Le Panegyrique de Cortesius et les relations diplomatiques entre Matthias Corvin et la Papauté ", *Acta Classica Universitatis Scientiarum Debreciensis,* 1 (1965), pp. 57-62. Correspondence between the two brothers and Florentine friends is discussed in Fortunato Pintor, *Da lettere inedite di due fratelli umanisti (Alessandro e Paolo Cortesi), Nozze Sari = Lopez-Protto do Albaneto* (Perugia, 1907).

4 See Cortesi, *De hominibus doctis,* p. XIII.

Castellesi (a fellow Ciceronian) and the brothers Raffaele and Mario Maffei were his humanist friends in Rome. Cardinals Soderini, Piccolomini, Sanseverino, Isvalies, and Vigerio; Archbishop Cosimo Pucci of Florence; Luca de Pontremolo, Bishop of Reggio; Guidobaldo Capponi, Bishop of Cortona; Ercole d'Este, Duke of Ferrara; the Duke of Urbino, Guidobaldo da Montefeltro; Marcantonio Colonna and Piero Soderini were among the high church and secular dignitaries with whom Cortesi exchanged letters and whom he often knew personally as well.[5] Among the humanists, Ermolao Barbaro, Teodoro of Gaza, Battista Egenzio, Alessandro d'Alessandro, Bartolomeo Lampridio (a close friend of Paolo's brother) may be mentioned, as well as Michele Ferno who wrote his *Historia nova Alexandri VI* for Paolo.[6]

Cortesi was identified with the most rigorously Ciceronian wing of Roman humanism. For him and his colleagues Cicero's Latin represented the standard of perfection and the rule to which all modern writers must adhere. Cortesi first expounded this view in his early dialogue, *De hominibus doctis* (1491), which was dedicated to Lorenzo de' Medici, and he developed it further in his epistolary controversy with Poliziano.[7] Combining ideas taken from Aristotle and Horace, Cortesi maintained that the only way to raise standards in all forms of modern Latin was through the exclusive imitation of antique literary models. He saw imitation as a natural, necessary activity that does not impair the mind or render the imitator intellectually sterile. Poliziano had argued against Cortesi that imitation meant the loss of individuality but Cortesi answered that in literature the author imitates his model not like an ape but as a son imitates his father.[8] Through imitation art can be learned; elegance and variety are cultivated. In short, the limits of nature are corrected by skill and practice, by means of imitation.

5 Relevant letters are to be found in Florence, Biblioteca Nazionale Centrale, II/III/3. See below, notes 61-67.

6 See Cortesi, *De hominibus doctis*, pp. VIII-XII; also Alexander ab Alexandro, *Gentilium dierum liber sex* (Leiden, 1573), vol. II, p. 217; Michele Ferno, *Historia nova Alexandri VI ab Innocentii obitu VIII* (Rome, 1493), fol. 3 r.

7 On Ciceronianism see Remigio Sabbadini, *Storia del Ciceronianismo e di altre questioni letterarie dell'età della rinascenza* (Turin, 1885); Izora Scott, *Controversies over the Imitation of Cicero* (New York, 1910); Giorgio Santangelo, *Il Bembo critico e il principio d'imitazione* (Florence, 1950). On the *De hominibus doctis* see Graziosi, edition cited above; also Giacomo Ferraù, " Il ' De hominibus doctis ' di Paolo Cortesi ", in *Umanità e storia: scritti in onore di Adalchi Attisani*, vol. 2, (Naples, 1971), pp. 1261-1290; see also D'Amico, " Humanism and Theology ", chs. 2 and 3.

8 For the Latin see Eugenio Garin, *Prosatori latini del quattrocento* (Milan, 1958), pp. 902-911; the comparison of imitating like a son, p. 906, " Similem volo, mi Politane, non ut simiam hominis, sed ut filium parentis ".

These ideas about literature were also to be applied to the visual arts later in *De Cardinalatu*; Cortesi's attitude was typical of the classicism which dominated Roman intellectual life in the early sixteenth century and which forms a literary prelude to the passion for Vitruvian decorum which spread among the following generation of architects.[9] Cortesi put his principles of imitation into practice in his next work, the *Liber sententiarum* (1504); a theological textbook written when Cortesi had already retired to San Gimignano. In this book, Cortesi followed the rules of Ciceronian word choice to write about the basic tenets of the church, thus attempting to establish the propriety of combining classical Latin with Christian subject matter. The *Liber* emphasized the ideas of Aquinas and Scotus and pointedly omitted references to modern theologians other than Pico. Cortesi was not, however, attacking scholastic thought itself, but rather, the forms used to present it in his own day. Cortesi sought to remedy these defects of style by harmonizing scholastic, technical theology with the broader literary and cultural principles of humanist eloquence; an undertaking which brought the *Liber* and its author considerable fame.[10]

The *Liber* was intended for a new cultural leader, the Renaissance prince. The completed picture of this new cultural hero was presented in *De Cardinalatu*. The idea for the treatise developed over several years. Cortesi had initially intended to write a *De principe* but decided in favor of the *De Cardinalatu* after a conversation with Cardinal Ascanio Sforza, as we shall see below.[11] Cortesi's audience was now to be a broader one: the nobility immediately below the prince or pontiff, his major advisers and the bureaucrats. Thus, the *De Cardinalatu* reflects changes in Italian society at the turn of the century. Rome and its government took on

9 See the discussion in Paolo Portoghesi, *Rome and the Renaissance*, P. Sanders, trans., (London, 1972), ch. 1.

10 See D'Amico, "Humanism and Theology", ch. 4 and Giovanni Farris, *Eloquenza e teologia nel "Prooemium in Librum Primum Sententiarum" di Paolo Cortesi* (Savona, n.d.). An English translation of the *Prooemium* of the *Liber* can be found in Leonard A. Kennedy, ed., *Renaissance Philosophy: New Translations* (The Hague, 1973), pp. 32-37. Generally this is a good translation; however, there is one important error. Page 35 translates *De principe* as "about the fundamental truth (i.e. theology)". *De principe* refers rather to *De Cardinalatu* in its earlier form as a book on the prince.

11 For the appropriate section of Severo's letter see note 59 below and Delio Cantimori, "Questioncine sulle opere progettate da Paolo Cortesi", in *Studi di bibliografia e di storia in onore di Tommaso de Marinis*, vol. I (Verona, 1963), pp. 276-78. On Severo Varini see Augusto Cesari, *Severo Varini (Frate umanista)* (Bologna, 1884), which is essentially an expansion of Cristoforo Poggiali, *Memorie per la storia della letteratura di Piacenza*, vol. II (Piacenza, 1789), pp. 3-34. For Severo's position within the Florentine world see Sergio Bertelli, "Noterelle machiavelliane: Ancora su Lucrezio e Machiavelli", *Rivista storica italiana*, 76/3 (1964), pp. 774-792.

ever greater importance in Italian political and social life. Furthermore, the great quattrocento humanists were all dead. The center of culture as well as power had moved from Florence to Rome; from secular to predominately ecclesiastical patronage of culture. *De Cardinalatu* was designed as a response to this situation and as part of a program to put a new, humanistically educated aristocracy in place of its old counterpart. The aim of this handbook for the high ecclesiastical aristocrats was to define the cardinal in humanistic terms in order to present him as a major patron of culture.[12]

Most fifteenth century writing on cardinals is to be found in discussions on canon law and theology.[13] These themes are also important in *De Cardinalatu* but Cortesi presents the cardinal primarily as a functionary. He takes care of his own large household; he is the great bureaucrat of the Church who helps the Pope with its governance. Above all, he is an arbiter and patron of culture.

The treatise was written in a difficult, often contorted, Latin. Since Cortesi avoided the use of contemporary words, he created new meanings for ancient words when they were used to describe modern matters. A " flamen in ara litans " means for instance a priest saying Mass.

At the same time, Cortesi's language in *De Cardinalatu* is less rigidly Ciceronian in structure than are the works of his youth. Cortesi's Latin had become a critical instrument for the definition of the humanistic ideal of aristocratic life. The language of the treatise is normative. Things are " obvious " or " ought to be " or both. The cardinal is given rules by which to decide what he must do or avoid. As in the *Liber sententiarum*, Cortesi arrives at opinions on all matters by attempting to find a golden mean among contrasting points of view. The resulting position is then considered universally valid and applicable.

In his introductory letter to *De Cardinalatu* which explains the genesis of the treatise, Severo Varini Piacentino speaks of a " universum sapientiae studium et graecam illam encyclopediam ".[14] Cantimori, however, points out that *De Car-*

12 See the discussion of *De Cardinalatu* by Carlo Dionisotti, " Chierici e laici ", in *Geografia e storia della letteratura italiana* (Turin, 1967), pp. 167–185.

13 See Gigliola Soldi Rondinini, *Per la storia del cardinalato nel secolo XV*, Memorie dell'Istituto Lombardo - Accademia di Scienze e Lettere, vol. 33/1 (Milan, 1973), and Hubert Jedin, " Vorschläge und Entwürfe zur Kardinalsreform ", *Römische Quartalschrift*, 42 (1934), pp. 305–332, translated into Italian in *Chiesa della fede: chiesa della storia* (Brescia, 1972), pp. 156–192 which we cite.

14 Severo's letter, " Iam mihi persentiscere uideor non nullos criticos ei uitio uertere (id quod ego ad summam huius operis laudem pertinere arbitror) quod nimis multa in hunc librum congesserit, et minime quaque inculcauerit, quibus ego ita responsum uelim.

dinalatu cannot, itself, be identified with the four books " tetrateuchus in quo cum separatim est Medicinae, Legum et Philosophiae explicanda disputatio..." [15] mentioned by Severo. The treatise does touch on these matters but only in chapters devoted to other subjects. Either Cortesi had planned but never completed a work that followed the divisions outlined by Severo, or *De Cardinalatu* actually incorporates materials originally destined for use in an encyclopedia.

De Cardinalatu resembles humanist encyclopedias like Raffaele Maffei's *Commentaria urbana* and the various works addressed to secular princes by Pontano. All these works share essentially ethical aims: to unite all knowledge in usable form — illustrated by classical and post-classical *exempla* — in order to establish norms that could serve as guides to the conduct of life. Cortesi and his contemporaries lacked the overriding metaphysical concerns of the medieval encyclopedists but never lost sight of their own goal, derived from classical rhetoric: to move men to virtue and to regulate human action. To achieve this aim, Cortesi reviewed all the disciplines and activities of life, including the building and decoration of palaces.[16]

De Cardinalatu is divided into three books. The first provides the cardinal and, by extension, all leaders, with the rules for their early education along both humanistic and more traditional lines. The curriculum does not include the visual arts. The second book is concerned with prescriptions for the cardinal's mode of life, his house, his retainers, his official and private relationships. The third section discusses the political and ecclesiastical duties of the cardinal. It is interesting that there is no section on theology in the treatise; that subject is, however, treated exhaustively in the earlier *Liber sententiarum* which forms a prologue to *De Cardinalatu*.

Cortesi discusses the cardinal's palace in his section on the cardinal's way of

Paulo nostro propositum fuisse uniuersum sapientiae studium et Graecam illam encyclopediam in qua multum insudauerat exprimere, quae cum omnibus his qui egregie docti haberi uolunt, sit degustanda, tum uel maxime necessaria est sacrosanctis principibus quorum cognitionem nihil effugere citra ignominiam potest ".

15 See Cantimori, " Questioncine ", pp. 279-280. On the printing of *De Cardinalatu;* see Fabio Jacometti, " Il primo stampatore senese Simone di Nicolò di Nardo ", *La Diana*, 1/3 (1926), pp. 3, 11.

16 On encyclopedism see Vittorio Cian, " Contributo alla storia dell'enciclopedismo nell'età della rinascità ", in *Miscellanea di studi storici in onore di Giovanni Sforza* (Lucca, 1920), pp. 289-330, which is corrected by Carlo Dionisotti, *Gli Umanisti e il volgare fra quattro e cinquecento* (Florence, 1968), pp. 38-77 who specifically deals with Cortesi and his friend, Raffaele Maffei.

life (Bk. II, ch. ii). Unlike popes and reformers since Avignon,[17] Paolo saw no incongruity between the religious duties of the cardinal and the conspicuous display of wealth. Nonetheless, his attitudes give Cortesi an unexpected place in the history of Renaissance reform literature. He understood that it was unrealistic to expect apostolic poverty of the cardinals and proposed, instead, a rational standardization of behavior that would avoid abuse and excess. Some Roman humanists were skeptical of these views. Even Raffaele Maffei — editor of the *De Cardinalatu* — censured cardinals who spent money unnecessarily in building palaces.[18] Cortesi's attitudes were, however, shared by the majority of Roman humanists and ecclesiastics.[19] It was important to determine the ideal location of the palace and the distribution of its rooms, since these matters affected the creation of a fitting environment for a governor of the Church and a great patron. The palaces that actually existed in Rome were described from this standpoint, as *exempla*. Palaces, real or ideal, were seen as external representations of the cardinal's new cultural position.

Sources of the Chapter on Palaces

Raffaele Maffei claimed he used a thousand books to write one of his own. Cortesi, too, certainly drew on a wide literary culture when he wrote *De Cardinalatu*. Our primary interest in the chapter on the cardinal's residence has been, however, to identify the more salient characteristics of Cortesi's attitudes toward the arts and of the intellectual climate in which he flourished. We have, therefore, used the glosses as pointers to those of Cortesi's references that his contemporaries thought most important. We have, however, also noted references that Maffei and his contemporaries would have thought too obvious to warrant a gloss, but which may no longer seem so evident to modern readers.

17 See Norman Zacour, "Papal Regulation of Cardinals' Households in the Fourteenth Century", *Speculum*, 50 (1975), pp. 434-455, Jedin, *Chiesa della fede*, pp. 173-174, D'Amico "Humanism and Theology", ch. 7.

18 See Raffaele Maffei, *De institutione christiana* (Rome, 1518), bk. VIII, ch. 5, "De opibus aedificiis sumptibusque reliquis non necessariis", fols. Y 3r-4r. On Maffei see John F. D'Amico, "A Humanist Response to Martin Luther: Raffaele Maffei's *Apologeticus*", *Sixteenth Century Journal* 6/2 (1975), pp. 37-56.

19 See D. S. Chambers, "The Economic Predicament of Renaissance Cardinals", *Studies in Medieval and Renaissance History*, 3 (1966), pp. 289-313, and more recently the same historian's "The Housing Problems of Cardinal Francesco Gonzaga", *Journal of the Warburg and Courtauld Institutes*, 39 (1976), pp. 21-58.

It has, nonetheless, occasionally been difficult to trace the filiation of Cortesi's ideas. Cortesi generally follows Aristotelian ideas but often takes them from intermediate sources, such as Vitruvius or Aquinas. Cicero's short, functional description of the house in *De officiis* (I, 39) provided Cortesi with certain general requirements for the perfect house. Cicero is the model for Cortesi's language, but so is Vitruvius. Sometimes, however, Cortesi goes back to Vitruvius's own sources. Cortesi's discussion of siting and climate may draw on the often-translated *Airs, Waters, Places* by Hippocrates and not just on Vitruvian reflections of this text.[20] Plinian ideas or Plinian language also occur in Cortesi's treatise, but are not highly significant for the chapter on palaces.

Cortesi's background in Vitruvian studies was quite elaborate. His teacher, Sulpizio Verolano, was the editor of the first printed Latin Vitruvius, which was dedicated to Cardinal Raffaele Riario, and published in 1486, a year after Alberti's *De re aedificatoria.* In the 1480's through his brother, Alessandro, Paolo probably also became acquainted with Fra Giocondo, editor of the first illustrated Latin Vitruvius of 1511. In the chapter on palaces, Cortesi uses Vitruvian themes much as he had turned to the language of Cicero, that is, as a normative model to be imitated and made the basis of new invention. Alberti had complained about Vitruvius's bad Latin and, indeed, Cortesi uses Ciceronian language to correct him.[21] Cortesi, however, borrows specific words and phrases from Vitruvius. The structure of individual passages may also be derived somewhat more loosely from the antique model. He does not follow it for the sequence of subjects discussed and he often differs with Vitruvius in opinions or in the relative weight assigned to a topic.

At the same time, Cortesi also made constant use of modern sources. For matters of Roman topography, Cortesi usually turns to Flavio Biondo's *Roma instaurata* published 1471. Indeed, in Paolo's earlier *De hominibus doctis* he says that authors should be encouraged to write about historical subjects as Flavio had done, but in better Latin.[22] It may be that Cortesi thought he was taking his own advice in writing his chapter on palaces.

There are so many parallels between Alberti's *De re aedificatoria* and Cortesi's chapter on palaces, that it is virtually certain this was Cortesi's most important

20 Hippocrates, *Airs, Waters, Places,* W.H.S. Jones, trans., (Cambridge, Mass., 1939).

21 Giulio Schlosser Magnino, *La letteratura artistica,* Filippo Rossi, trans., (Florence, 1964), p. 122.

22 Cortesi, *De hominibus doctis,* pp. 44-45.

modern source. The reader is invited to consult our commentary for references to specific Albertian ideas but, as just one example, one might note here the degree to which Cortesi's account of the cardinal's palace is modeled on Alberti's chapter on the gentleman's country house. Significantly, Cortesi follows Alberti's description of the residence in terms of the functions of each space. He establishes graded zones of privacy, ranging from the fully public atrium to the most private living quarters reserved for the master (*Ten Books*, bk. V, chs. ii, iii, vii). This notion exists in Vitruvius as well, but with nothing like the emphasis and consistency given it by Alberti.[23] Cortesi, however, ransacked most other parts of the treatise as well. Our notes even suggest that Cortesi actually referred to Alberti more often than to Vitruvius himself, something one might not have expected from such a doctrinaire classicist in matters of language. We cannot demonstrate that Cortesi used any of Alberti's other works although his ideas on the utility of painting and the primacy of *historia* may reflect *De pictura* and there are a few suggestive parallels with Alberti's *Pontifex*.[24] In any event, Cortesi saw *De re aedificatoria* as it has been intended by its author: as a new Vitruvius which could be used to interpret and rationalize the antique source for the modern world. Even more important, perhaps, Alberti's example itself seems to have given Cortesi the freedom to depart boldly, not only from the revered ancient model, but also from Alberti's own text.

There were also other reasons that encouraged Cortesi to deal as freely with his modern model as with his ancient source. Indeed, Alberti's ideas had to be modified before they could be used just because he, like Cortesi, saw the palace as the outward manifestation of a social unit. For Alberti, this unit was the family with the conjugal couple at its center. Cortesi is very much aware that this model is inappropriate for the cardinal and his *familia*. Thus he is forced to invent the description of the artificial family and household of the ecclesiastical prince and of the arrangement of rooms that serves it best. Not only are women excluded from this society but so is the wide spectrum of the generations that graces Alberti's ideal family. The cardinal's residence need have no place for the children to play,

23 Richard Krautheimer, "Vitruvius and Alberti", in *Acts of the Twentieth International Congress of the History of Art* (Princeton, N.J., 1963), vol. 2, pp. 42–52 for a classic statement of Alberti's rationalization of Vitruvius and its consequences for the Renaissance.

24 Leon Battista Alberti, *On Painting and On Sculpture*, Cecil Grayson, ed. and trans., (London, 1972), Alberti's, *Pontifex* in *Leonis Baptistae Alberti Opera inedita et pauca separatim impressa*, Girolamo Mancini, ed., (Florence, 1890), pp. 71–72.

for the grandmother to take her rest or for the old men to sit in the sun as they do in Alberti's palace.[25]

The humanist tone and learning of Alberti's treatise, its intended appeal to an audience of cultivated men rather than artisans, the fact that it was written in Latin; all these things would have appealed to Cortesi. His involvement with Alberti, however, went deeper still. Paolo would have learned to admire Alberti through his friend Poliziano who had written the introduction to the first printed text of *De re aedificatoria*.[26] Cortesi had also singled out the Florentine for praise in his earlier *De hominibus doctis* and had translated into Latin a vernacular *Istorietta d'amore* believed to be by Alberti.[27] Indeed, Cortesi could see Alberti in a very specific way as his own forerunner, for Alberti, too, had been a writer of humanist treatises and a scriptor at the Curia. In the chapter on palaces, Cortesi even shares Alberti's vision of the social functions of architecture and of its mission; [28] in Richard Krautheimer's words, " ... to create dignified surroundings for the dignified actions of dignified people." [29]

In a number of instances, however, Cortesi describes his cardinal's ideal palace in far greater detail than do either Alberti or Vitruvius. Here Paolo seems to have more in common with writers of more technical vernacular treatises on architecture such as Filarete and Francesco di Giorgio. There are interesting parallels with Filarete's description of the ideal town of Sforzinda, the layout of its palaces and their embellishment. Filarete's concern with the moral dimension of painted decorations is also suggestive. For instance, Filarete's painted *storie* of antique heroes punished for wrong-doing,[30] parallel Cortesi's suggestion that the chastisement of Christian secular rulers be represented. Cortesi could have known a manuscript of Filarete's treatise but it cannot be demonstrated that the two writers share more than a common literary heritage. Cortesi's chapter also resembles Filarete more than Alberti in that the verbal descriptions of palaces seem precise enough to invite a

25 Book II of the *De Cardinalatu* is, however, concerned with the make up of the cardinal's family.

26 See Franco Borsi, *Leon Battista Alberti*, R.G. Carpanini, trans., (Oxford, 1977), p. 365.

27 Cortesi, *De hominibus doctis*, pp. 32, 93 fn. 52. Cortesi made a Latin translation of the *Historietta amorosa fra Leonora de' Bardi e Ippolito Buondelmonti*. Maria Graziosi in her introduction to *De hominibus doctis*, p. ix and note 16 accepts Alberti's authorship while Paul-Henri Michel, *La Pensée de L. B. Alberti* (Geneva, 1971, rpt), pp. 39, 307 n. 3 lists the work as apocryphal. The Latin translation was published by Anicio Bonucci, ed., *Opere volgari* (Florence, 1843-1849), vol. 3.

28 Carroll W. Westfall, " Society, Beauty and the Humanist Architect in Alberti's *de re aedificatoria* ", *Studies in the Renaissance*, 16 (1969), p. 78.

29 Krautheimer, " Vitruvius and Alberti ", p. 52.

30 Antonio Averlino Filarete, *Trattati di architettura*, A.M. Finoli, ed., L. Grassi, notes, 2 vols. (Milan, 1972), bk. IX, pp. 112-121, bk. XIV, p. 186.

reconstruction of their layout. Filarete actually made drawings to accompany his text whereas it becomes difficult to follow Cortesi's account beyond a certain point. His descriptions seem to be based in part on existing palaces such as the Cancelleria, Palazzo Venezia and the Vatican, on plans for Palazzo Giraud, and partly on an abstract ideal based on the antique.[31]

The connections with Francesco di Giorgio's treatise (1482) on architecture are also tenuous. Common themes, such as the discussion of hidden speaking tubes, seem to derive from Alberti although Cortesi and Francesco resemble each other more than they do their model in the degree of practical emphasis given this subject. Contact between the two men cannot be demonstrated, but they might have met in Rome for Francesco was there in 1486 when Sulpizio published his Vitruvius.[32] Cortesi's long residence in San Gimignano and its proximity to Siena might have provided him with opportunities to read Francesco's treatise or to meet its author.

The most direct counterpart for Cortesi's ideas on *magnificentia* is to be found in the writings of the Neapolitan humanist, Giovanni Pontano (1426-1503). Pontano's two short treatises, *De magnificentia* and *De splendore* (1494) prescribe the same grand style of life Cortesi advocates. Both men see money as the necessary prerequisite for magnificence and a sumptuous palace as one of its most conspicuous manifestations. Both men count libraries as important signs of magnificence and are supporters of the new classical architecture. They both praise Cosimo de' Medici for his revival of the "pervetustem atque obliteratum iam structurae morem...." Pontano advocated public games while Cortesi actually put them on at his villa in San Gimignano. Both authors emphasize the virtue of hospitality. They hold the Aristotelian view that *magnificentia* represents the just mean between miserliness and extravagance and they are aware of the wordly advantage to be had from the judicious display of this quality.[33]

De Cardinalatu represents a liberalization of Cortesi's earlier Ciceronian sentence structure but his vocabulary remains closely imitative of ancient Latin models. A similar but even freer approach governs his relationship to the sources of his ideas in the chapter on palaces. In the traditional way Cortesi uses sources without identifying them. It is instructive that the names of Vitruvius and Alberti are

31 Christoph Luitpold Frommel, *Der römische Palastbau der Hochrenaissance*, 3 vols. (Tübingen, 1973), I p. 53, points this out.

32 Francesco di Giorgio Martini, *Trattati di architettura, ingegneria e arte militare*, ed. Corrado Maltese, (Milan, 1967), p. XLVI.

33 Giovanni Pontano, *I trattati delle virtù sociali*, pp. 99, 234, 235, 245. On Pontano see Francesco Tateo, ed. and trans., (Rome, 1965) and *Umanesimo etico di Giovanni Pontano* (Lecce, 1972).

never mentioned. Aristotle is named only once and then not in order to confer prestige but, quite naturally, in the context of a philosophical discussion of the moral function of painting.

In part, of course, Cortesi simply expected that his cultivated readers would notice his learned references. Nonetheless, it appears that Paolo had actually become willing to transform his sources to the point where they were no longer recognizable because he had become more interested in exploiting them for his own purposes than in making a display of learning. This is an example of his *imitàzione* in its most creative aspect. The model is followed, not only for its own sake, but for its potential in helping to recognize, clarify and beautify the material that the modern author wishes to discuss. The model is neither a preexisting definition nor a limitation of what is possible and permissible. It is, rather, a pattern for new invention. It need hardly be stressed that this attitude also has many equivalents in the liberal classicism of the visual arts in early sixteenth century Rome. For instance, a similar emphasis on the disciplines of antique form, combined with a free approach to the transformation of sources for the sake of function, can be seen in artists as diverse as Bramante, Raphael and Andrea Sansovino.

Literary models were not, however, the only influence on the genesis of Cortesi's chapter on palaces. Because of his place in the Curia and his literary activities, he was closely associated, throughout his life, with the cultural elite of Rome and perhaps, through them, with artists. Indeed, although Cortesi withdrew to San Gimignano as early as 1503, he obviously remained in intimate touch with the most current events and ideas in Rome; an interesting sidelight on the speed and accuracy of communications in Renaissance Italy.

Cortesi's circle was not, in any special way, devoted to the visual arts. We have seen, however, that he was predisposed to Vitruvian studies and that Cortesi's Roman academy attracted poets like Calmeta and L'Unico Aretino who had some interest in artists.[34] Cortesi's closest and most important humanist connections, from our point of view, were with the Maffei family. Mario became overseer to the *fabbrica* of St. Peter's in 1507 [35] and had many other artistic interests whereas Raffaele also had some focused awareness of art as we can see from the long list

34 Vincenzo Colli Calmeta, *Prose e lettere edite e inedite*, Cecil Grayson, ed., (Bologna, 1959), pp. 63-64.

35 On Mario Maffei see in general Luigi Pescetti, "Mario Maffei (1463-1537)", *Rassegna volterrana*, 6 (1932), pp. 65-91; on Mario and his connections with building in Rome, see Renato Lefevre, "Un prelato del '500, Mario Maffei e la costruzione di Villa Madama", *L'Urbe*, 33/3 (1969), pp. 1-11. Cortesi defended the building of St. Peter's in *De Card.*, fol. G 5v.

he made of contemporary artists and from his inclusion of artists among the important men of his time (see text note 67). Raffaele Maffei's *Commentaria urbana* of 1506 also mentions art and architecture, as does Pontano.

Cortesi's relations with the various cardinals are detailed in our notes but Ascanio Sforza, who also frequented Cortesi's academy, was of special significance. It may be that the arrangement and decoration of the Sforza-Cesarini palace were thus also of importance in shaping Cortesi's ideas. Sforza's strongest artistic interest were, however, directed toward music and the Cardinal may have influenced Cortesi's treatise in this way as well. Cardinal Adriano Castellesi was also close to the author and, like him, belonged to the party of the strict Ciceronians among the Curial humanists. As the builder of a great palace at the time Cortesi was writing and, as Bramante's patron, he must also have helped to shape Cortesi's ideas. A lost poem by Castellesi, describing his palace, may have constituted a further link with *De Cardinalatu*.[36] Indeed, such palaces were, themselves, important as the meeting ground where the disparate elements of Roman culture could communicate. Speaking of the Palazzo Riario, the humanist Cleophilus described how architects, painters, singers, physicians, mathematicians, astrologers, as well as orators and poets could all be found gathered there.[37] There too, humanist, patron and artist could interact.

The significance of Cortesi's milieu for *De Cardinalatu* was, therefore, manifold. The great houses he frequented[38] appear in the text as examples of ideal palaces whereas his friends provided first hand information about palace life. In their various ways, many of them helped to shape taste and thus, ultimately, to affect decisions about art patronage.

Cortesi's own attitudes toward the visual arts were typical of his circle. For instance, a discussion of Pisanello which took place in his Roman academy (before 1503) was part of a general discussion of decorum, not concerned with his painting as such.[39] Yet Cortesi was himself a patron of art and architecture. He built a great villa in which he took deep and sustained interest and he recorded with pride that he had a medal made depicting it.[40] The fact remains, however, that the arts

36 Frommel, *Palastbau*, II, p. 212.

37 See Octavius Cleophilus, *Octavius Cleophilus Baptistae Guarino, Antonio Citadino, Nicholae Leniceno, Petro Bono, Ludovico Carboni, Lucae Ripae, Aristophilo Manphredo, Betramo Constabili, Ludovico Pictorio, amicis iocundissimis, S.P.D.* (Rome, 1498-1500), fols. 6v-7r.

38 *De Card.* fol. Q 3v.

39 Calmeta, *Prose e lettere*, p. 34. Praise of Pisanello was a humanist convention, see Michael Baxandall, *Giotto and the Orators* (Oxford, 1971), pp. 78 ff.

40 *De Card.*, fol. H 7v.

play only a modest part in the total scheme of the treatise. References to them are limited to our chapter and to a few other mentions of painters of the older generation such as Filippino Lippi, Signorelli, Mantegna, Perugino and Leonardo. Bramante and Michelangelo are named appear only once whereas Raphael is not mentioned.[41] Apparently, Cortesi's taste was formed at an early moment in his

41 Cortesi makes few references to art or artists. All are given here. For Bramante, text note 47. For Leonardo, *De Card.*, fols. A 1v-2r, " Eodemque modo ex uno ad aliud perueniri imagine docente potest, ut si Mediolani ab aliquo dicatur eius cretacei equi spectari typus, qui sit a Leonardo Vincio thuscanica ratione factus, facile affirmetur ei, Francisci Sfortiae in mentem uenire posse, cui erat eiusmodi equestris statuae decretus honos, quae esset ad famam uirtutis sempiternae testis, ad posteriorum hominum imitationem uita memoriae ". *De Card.*, fol. B 7v for Leonardo and Filippo Lippi, " At uero principatus congruere cum altitudinis mensione debet. Vt quo quis est fortunae potestate maior eo cumulatius scientiarum dignitate praetest. Nec enim inscitia defendi potestatis excusatione potest: quandoquidem magnitudo non in loco, sed in expletionis absolutione consistat, quo sit uirtus praestantiae commendatione prior: ut in picturis pluris aestimari debent Leonardi Vincii aut Philippi Florentini tabulae, quam Renati regis qui pingendi studio tenebatur, cum ab illis tanto interuallo superetur ". *De Card.*, fols. C 4r-v, Michelangelo and Perugino, " Quin etiam intelligendum est, homines non modo praesentium amicorum assiduitate, sed etiam absentium recordatione delectari, quandoquidem absentes amantes specie meditata adsint: ob eamque causam ars, quae est rerum naturae imitatrix iucunda esse solet: ut facile ex his iudicari potest, quae fingendi aut pingendi ratione constant. In quibus quamquam saepe multa minus suapte natura placeant grata tamen esse repraesentata solent: ut uipera, quae quamquam multum per se sit ad aspectum habitura tetri, si tamen aut ex aere sit, a M. Angelo statuario florentino facta, aut manu cernatur P. Perusini picta, nihil dubitationis habeat, quin multum spectantes delectatura sit ". *De Card.*, fol. L 7v, for Mantegna, " Nam cum sacellum in suburbano palatino picturis ornare [Innocentius VIII] decreuisset, Andreamque Mantegnam, qui tum maxime frugi ac uerecundus naturae imitator in pingendo putaretur, sponte conductum adhibuisset atque is cum primo quoque tempore ad eum uenisset, bienniique propre spatium pinxisset, nec assem quidem ab eo accepisset statuissetque pro eo quod erat ingeniosus et pictor, aliqua ei interpunctione salis tenacem remunerandi procrastinationem exprobrare simulachrum muliebri specie adultaque aetate inchoasse dicitur, quod cum Innocentius aspexisset, quaesissetque ex eo, quae nam esset illa tam decursa aetate anus. Atque is ingratitudinem esse respondisset, commode inquit, prope posset patientia pingi ". *De Card.* fol. q 1r for Signorelli, " Horum quoque generi pictores adiungi possunt, quorum muta sedulitas quamquam sit uim habitura loquentem, eodem tamen continetur iussu, quo cautum sit, ne quis feriis pingere inchoata audeat, nisi cum haec sunt diuorum imagines in delubris absolundae, quae admonendo sint ei aduenarum generi profuturae, qui in urbem eulabiae causa aduentare uideantur, ut si his Laurentaliis idem Iulius Secundus Lucae Cortonnensi homini pingendo frugi et naturam uerecunde imitanti diuorum imagines pingere in cella Vaticana iubeat, quo praesens commonitio sit, hominum memoriam alitura, et ad factorum imitationem excitatura mentem, cum apertum sit nihil magis in animo hominum influere solere, quam quod sit aurium admonitu et oculorum aspectu confirmatum ". *De Card.*, fol. Q 14v, for the arts as having been invented in imitation of nature, " Siquidem quemadmodum his rebus quibus extrinsecus noceri potest, naturae cernuntur integumenta dari, ut truncos cortice obduci equos pilis, oues lana, pluma uolucres, pisces squama tegi et uestiri uidemus, sic confidentum est ab hominum genere naturae imitatione uestus, primo repertum esse usum, quo uita esset a frigore et calore, munitior, ex eoque tot genera artium operosa nata, quae essent necessitati subuentura uitae: cum autem uarius sit artium inuentus usus, sciri debet illud primum artium genus debere nominari, quod maxime hominum uictum suppeditaturum sit ". *De Card.*, fol. Q 16v, on work rules for architects and the building trades, " At cum in feriis seruandis lex est his praescribenda, qui sunt instituti ad domorum genera aedificanda fabri, quorum in numero architecti, tignarii, cementarii, scalptores, et lignarii uersan-

career and remained fixed. No doubt his retirement also contributed to this attitude.

For Cortesi, the ultimate significance of architecture is aesthetic only to the degree that beauty " calms the citizens and persuades the unruly to seek order ".[42] The value of the palace lies in its usefulness in fostering an orderly and virtuous life. Its sumptuousness is appropriate to such high official station: the cardinal's magnificence is less a pleasure than a duty and architecture serves, above all, as a political instrument to maintain and strengthen the power of the inhabitants and of the institutions which they represent. This attitude, based on Aristotle, has its Renaissance roots in the work of authors like Vespasiano da Bisticci. It appears in Alberti and Pontano and is, perhaps, most forcefully articulated in the famous statement attributed to Nicholas V by his biographer, Manetti.[43] It was certainly one motivation for the architectural patronage of Cortesi's own time.

In Cortesi's chapter on palaces, painting is seen primarily as a form of architectural embellishment; albeit, one that may have genuine value as a spur to virtue. This effect is to be achieved, however, by means of specifically Christian subject matter. Pagan mythology, so often favored in narrative painted decorations, is to be shunned. This is a rare instance in the treatise when antiquity is not the best model and where the tastes of the ecclesiastical prince should differ from those of his secular counterpart. The reason is, of course, that painting is too effective a means of communication and stimulation to be used lightly. (By the same token, Cortesi insists that music should be used only for moral ends.)[44] Cortesi's position is based on Aristotle's definition of the purpose of poetry which is to " communicate knowledge and moral instruction "[45] and on the tradition of antique rhetoric exemplified by Cicero and Quintilian. Cortesi thus naturally transfers this view to the art of painting. Its aim is to move men to imitate the virtuous actions and

tur, sciendum est semper his ferias in construendo obstare, nisi temporis causa aedificandum sit, cum scilicet belli repentini metu sunt aut moenia reconcinnanda aut muri aedificandi noui quo sit munitior ad hostium impetum repellendum urbs ".

42 Cf. Jan Bialostocki, " The Power of Beauty ", in L. L. Möller and W. Lotz, eds., *Studien zur toskanischen Kunst. Festschrift für L. H. Heydenreich* (Munich, 1964), pp. 13-19. See also text note 89.

43 The basis for this view is Aristotle, *Nichomachean Ethics*, H. Rackham trans. (New York, 1926), bk. IV, 2, 1122a, 1123a, pp. 205-211. See A. D. Fraser-Jenkins, " Cosimo de' Medici's Patronage of Architecture and the Theory of Magnificence ", *Journal of the Warburg and Courtauld Institutes*, XXXIII (1970), pp. 162-170. See Giannozzo Manetti's summary of this attitude in Peter Partner, *Rome in the Renaissance*, (Berkeley, 1967), p. 16.

44 Nino Pirotta, " Musical and Cultural Tendencies in Fifteenth Century Italy ", *Journal of the American Musicological Society* 19 (1966), pp. 152-153.

45 Aristotle, *The Poetics*, W. Hamilton Fyfe trans. (Cambridge Mass., 1965), pp. 9, 35-39.

feelings it depicts. Thus Cortesi follows Alberti in making history painting the most important genre because it imitates life most variously and convincingly and is therefore the most persuasive.[46] The virtues taught by the histories Cortesi describes are, however, most often those of obedience to the papacy while the virtue exemplified by Cortesi's ideal palace tends to be prudence, interpreted as a proper care for self-preservation. Sculpture, curiously, is not discussed at all. It is only mentioned in passing as being more expensive and less appropriate to the cardinal's palace than painted decoration. This attitude is particularly noteworthy when we remember the passion for antique sculpture which gripped Rome at this time. It may be that Cortesi rejects sculpture because of its lack of Albertian *historia* and that he takes the position, articulated by Leonardo and Castiglione, that painting can do everything that sculpture does and more.

In sum, the visual arts are not specially privileged but make up one of the many areas of which the modern cardinal must have some competent acquaintance. Art is to be valued by reason of its utility, its power for moral suasion and its propaganda value. In the same way, music is discussed in *De Cardinalatu* as a subcategory of healthcare (an antique idea) and because, like painting, it has the power to encourage harmony and virtue. More detailed knowledge of the arts is desired only in as far as it aids the implementation of these goals. For architecture, this means an understanding, primarily, of the disposition and function of the parts of the house. The craft of the architect and technical matters are discussed only in this context and, even then, from the strictly lay standpoint of the humanist. There is no mention of wells, cisterns, fountains or conduits for water or privies, of fireplaces or chimneys. The humanist maintains a sovereign disregard for those elements of the palace which helped to make it habitable. Building materials, by the same token, are treated only in passing and then almost as a form of ornamental afterthought.

At the same time, however, Cortesi recognizes the importance of architectural styles, if only as a special case of the general question of decorum. He is uninterested in defining antique style, its orders or systems of proportion. Indeed, he used the Vitruvian word "symmetria" ambiguously and loosely. In any event, however, the ancient "symmetria" is to be preferred to foreign Gothic manners. Here again, Cortesi follows Alberti and seconds the traditional opinions of earlier and later Italian historians. Like them, he sees Gothic architecture as a perverse inter-

46 See Alberti *On Painting*, pp. 71, 103, for history paintings.

polation between the style of the ancients and its revival in good modern buildings. What is unusual, however, is that Cortesi seems to object to the Gothic "symmetria," not as something old and now discredited, but on the grounds of its licentuous novelty which may still tempt contemporary patrons of architecture.[47]

As one would expect, Cortesi champions an architecture whose modernity lies in its renewed adherence to ancient norms; that is, he takes the same attitude toward architecture that he takes toward language. Indeed, for Cortesi, the antique provides the models and standards that should be applied, by means of imitation, to the solution of all modern problems. Thus Cortesi's rather vague discussion of architectural styles is, in fact, still another expression of his fundamental critical approach to all aspects of the cardinal's existence. Whether he discusses architecture or behavior, Cortesi's goal in *De Cardinalatu* is the rationalization of the prelate's mode of life according to the order and rule to be found only in the golden age. In the exaltation of antique norms, in the integration both of details and of the ensemble of his thought through the application of a single standard, in the high ambition of his enterprise, Cortesi is a typical participant in the Roman High Renaissance.

Cortesi's account of the history of architectural styles implies that good style means conformity with antique standards but that style, or indeed the aesthetic dimension, have little independent value. For Cortesi, the work of art is to be judged ultimately on the efficacy of its moral and social function. This attitude has a venerable history dating back to Aristotle (see our text note 97). Alberti had also declared that all the visual arts could move the spectator to forsake vice for virtue,[48] but Cortesi states far more explicitly and emphatically that painting can have powerful, direct effect on the actions as well as the thoughts of men. He saw painting as a genuine, practical means of making people do what one wants and what one thinks best for them. In this sense painting, like architecture, is at least potentially a form of political and social control.[49] (Here Cortesi's position may be very relevant to motives that gave impetus to the decoration of the Vatican by Renaissance popes). Yet, whereas architecture addresses itself to all society [50] — including the rabble — the message of painting (like that of Latin culture) may

[47] Antonio di Tuccio Manetti, *The Life of Brunelleschi.* For an analogous view of the Gothic see Catherine Enggass, trans., Howard Saalman, ed., (University Park, Pa., 1970), pp. 34, 60, 62.

[48] Westfall, " Alberti ", p. 72.

[49] Compare also Westfall, *In This Most Perfect Paradise* (University Park, Pa., 1974), passim. See also, L. D. Ettlinger, *The Sistine Chapel before Michelangelo* (London, 1965), pp. 104-119.

[50] Westfall, " Alberti ", p. 72, n. 47.

be extremely subtle and is best understood by those few with the most fully developed and cultivated minds. On the other hand, the challenge presented by paintings with arcane subject matter and significance, itself stimulates the growth of intellectual and moral faculties in the beholder (see text note 101).

Cortesi's interest for art historians lies partly in his ideas but perhaps even more in the easy authority with which he represents his milieu and projects its intellectual style. He tells us about the role of the visual arts in culture. He sheds light on the Renaissance interpretation of Vitruvius and Alberti and, although Cortesi was neither an architect nor an art-theoretician, he sometimes articulated ideas about architecture and painting that were only just beginning to find expression in actual works of art. He mentions, for instance, subjects for paintings subsequently executed in the Vatican or the Villa Madama. By virtue of his position in time and society, Cortesi also provides specific information about Roman palaces and city life. *De Cardinalatu* thus allows useful comparisons to be made with better-known sources such as Burchardus's *Diarium* or, particularly, with Albertini's *Opusculum* which is exactly contemporary with Cortesi's work in composition, date of publication, and is also dedicated to Julius II.[51]

Cortesi's chapter on palaces looks forward in some ways to Raphael's description of the Villa Madama (before March of 1519). We have compared the two texts both for the attitudes expressed by their authors and for the names assigned to the various parts of the residence. We have referred to Cesariano's Vitruvius commentary of 1521 in the same manner, using his glosses to check our own interpretation of Cortesi's slightly earlier use of Vitruvian words and ideas.[52] Finally, *De Cardinalatu* can be seen as a forerunner of Castiglione's *Il Cortegiano* (composed c. 1513-21) and of Machiavelli's *Il Principe* (composed 1513). Despite the fact that both are written in the vernacular, they share Cortesi's goal to develop a norm of conduct for a specific element of the ruling class; a norm based both on antique principles and on modern experience. Indeed the role assigned to the visual arts is not so different in Cortesi and Castiglione.

Unlike the works of his two great contemporaries, Cortesi's treatise and his views on art had little historical influence. The impact of *De Cardinalatu* was blunted, initially by its author's early death and then by the advent of the Reformation.

[51] Albertini's text was finished on 3 June, 1509, but published Feb. 4 of the following year (Shearman, " Stanze ", p. 25, n. 5) but the colophon of the published text reads Feb. 4, 1510.

[52] See Lucia A. Ciapponi, " Vitruvius " in *Catalogus Translationum et Commentariorum* (Washington, D.C., 1976), vol. III, pp. 401-402 and C. Herselle Krinsky, " Seventy-eight Vitruvius Manuscripts ", *Journal of the*

Cortesi's conception of the cardinal as a figure of wordly magnificence now seemed imprudent and inappropriate. Nonetheless, Cortesi's intellectual influence was propagated to some extent through his pupils and followers among whom the future Cardinal Bembo and Pope Paul III were to be numbered.

In modern times, *De Cardinalatu* has been used by scholars primarily as a source of anecdote. Certain Renaissance scholars since World War II have, however, given various parts of the treatise analytical consideration.[53] Parts of the text have also been published. In 1966 Nino Pirotta, motivated by interests similar to ours, published Cortesi's discussion of music, and, in 1968, Dionisotti studied the chapter *de sermone* from the standpoint of language.[54] The chapter on palaces has also been used by scholars in a variety of ways. As early as 1912, Rodocanachi had given color to his account of Curial life in Renaissance Rome with rather sketchy references to Cortesi's chapter. Dickinson in her *Du Bellay in Rome* (1960) outlines the chapter by way of background to her subject. More recently, however, John Shearman found Cortesi's chapter useful in his study of Raphael's Tapestry Cartoons (1972) and, finally, C. L. Frommel used parts of the chapter systematically in his masterly discussion of the functions of the various parts of Roman cinquecento palaces (1973). Cortesi's chapter can, moreover, be read with benefit as an accompaniment to Frommel's introduction (*Palastbau*, I, pp. 1-25).[55] There has been no previous attempt, however, to present Cortesi's material on the arts in coherent form and we hope that its publication may contribute to the interest in Renaissance palaces that has been generated by the recent work of those mentioned above as well as by scholars such as Goldthwaite, Chambers and Kent.[56]

The Date of De Cardinalatu

Although *De Cardinalatu* was published in 1510 we know neither the dates of its inception or completion, nor can we trace its various transformations with

Warburg and Courtauld Institutes, 30 (1967), pp. 36-70.

53 Full bibliographical details can be found in Jedin, *Chiesa della fede*, Paschini, "I Cortesi" (1957), Cantimori, "Questioncine" (1964), Chambers, "Economic Predicament" (1966), Dionisotti, *Geografia* (1967), Gracci, "Studi sul Paolo Cortesi" (1967), D'Amico, "Humanism and Theology" (1977).

54 Full bibliographical details can be found in Pirotta, "Cultural Tendencies" (1966), Dionisotti, *Gli Umanisti* (1968).

55 See our bibliography for the works listed above.

56 Goldthwaite, "Florentine Palace" (1972), Chambers, "Housing Problems" (1976), F. W. Kent, "'Più superba de quella de Lorenzo', Courtly and Family Interest in the Building of Filippo Strozzi's Palace", *Renaissance Quarterly*, XXX/3 (1977), pp. 311-323.

assurance. In the dedication of his *Liber sententiarum* (1504) Cortesi stated his intention to write a treatise entitled *De principe*.[57] At the end of the work, however, he announced plans for a *De potestate papae*.[58] We cannot tell whether Cortesi's interest had shifted from one topic to the other during the composition of the *Liber* or whether he planned to undertake both tasks. In a letter which prefaces Cortesi's *De Cardinalatu*, the monk Severo Piacentino refers to the planned *De principe* and says that it was Cardinal Ascanio Sforza who persuaded Cortesi to turn his attention from secular princes to princes of the Church.[59] Severo concludes that the result was *De Cardinalatu*.

Recently, however, Delio Cantimori has proposed that Sforza might not have specified whether the ecclesiastical prince was to be the cardinal or the pontiff himself.[60] Perhaps the treatise on the pope, mentioned in the *Liber*, already reflects Sforza's suggestion. It seems more likely to us, however, that — like many authors — Cortesi had several projects in mind at once.

Evidence for Cortesi's actual work on *De Cardinalatu* can be found in a series of letters preserved in the Biblioteca Nazionale in Florence.[61] Apparently Cortesi sent out a number of chapters or drafts of *De Cardinalatu* to influential humanists, princes and prelates, perhaps in the hope of securing patronage or at least in order to court fame and approval for his treatise by asking for advice. It seems as though Cortesi

57 *Pauli Cortesii Protonotarii Apostolici in quattuor Libros Sententiarum argutae Romanoque eloquio disputationes.* It was first published in Rome, 1504 and there were three subsequent sixteenth century editions; see Friedrich Stegmueller, *Repertorium Commentariorum in Sententias Petri Lombardi* (Würzburg, 1947), pp. 298-299. We cite from the Paris, 1513 edition. The text reads " Itaque quamquam separatim a nobis de principe tres scripti sint libri, multaque praeclara in philosophia sint quae illustrioribus litteris potuissent et explicari; mea sum tamen magis interesse ratus, Theologiam christianam ex intima sententiarum aurifodina ad expolitiones reuocare. Nam cum finis bonorum principis veritatis contemplatio sit, facile intelligi potest, eam caeteris praestantiorem uideri, quandoquidem eius hypothesis princeps veritas dicatur, quae sit Deus supra naturae complexum notus ". (fols. A 4v-5r). See above note 10.

58 Cortesi, *Liber sententiarum*, fol. F 5v, " Nos enim interim Pont. Max. minime eiusmodi copulandi munus intermittemus, siquidem et de potestate Pontificis iam quasi superfetantes ingressi sumus, quos sane libros arbitror tibi Senatuique non iniucundos futuros..." See also Cantimori, " Questioncine ", p. 276, n. 1.

59 The text reads " Superant reliqua quae ad instituendum Principem excogitauerat, et iam magna ex parte peregerat de quibus edendis ut ne perirent sui labores, dum forte cum Ascanio Sforza in sermonem incidisset, eius hortatu ac monitu ea quae ad profanum Principem (si tamen profanus Princeps dici potest) erudiendum inchoauerat, ad sacros Principes quos alii Cardinales, ipse Senatores uocat accomodauit ". Paschini gives an Italian translation, " I Cortesi ", pp. 41-42. See above note 11.

60 Cantimori, " Questioncine ", p. 276, note 7.

61 Florence, Biblioteca Nazionale Centrale, Naz. II/III/3. The letters are discussed in Giovanni Targioni-Tozzetti, *Relazioni d'alcuni viaggi fatti in diverse parti della Toscana*, vol. VIII (Florence, 1775), pp. 237-267.

sent correspondents that part of the work in which their names were mentioned; a device still guaranteed to arouse the interest of readers today. On August 28, 1506, Guidobaldo da Montefeltro, Duke of Urbino and *Capitano della Chiesa*, wrote to express appreciation for the mention made of him in the treatise. He promised to use his influence on the author's behalf at the Vatican.[62] Cardinals Isvalies and Federigo Sanseverino (both mentioned in the chapter on palaces) saw part of the manuscript in 1507-08. Indeed, from Isvalies's letter of April 1507, it would seem that publication was thought to be imminent.[63]

At the same time, Cortesi also made persistent efforts to bring the manuscript to the attention of Julius II. On January 25, 1508, Teodoro Gaza wrote Cortesi that the Pope had received a chapter but had not yet looked at it, although Cardinal Trivulzio had it in hand.[64] By March 8, 1508, Cardinal Vigerio had answered Cortesi's anxious queries to say that the Pope had still not examined the work and, thus, Vigerio was hesitant to ask the Pope's opinion of it.[65] The Pontiff's attitude on this occasion seems not to have been unusual, for Raffaele Maffei, the editor of *De Cardinalatu*, was later to comment with acerbity that Julius was so indifferent to scholarship that he did not even read the titles of works dedicated to him.[66] In a letter of July 12, 1509, Cardinal Soderini speaks of the treatise as being " in mano delli impressori ",[67] yet Cortesi must have continued to revise the work since its text still includes mentions of visits made to the author by Cardinals Sanseverino and Soderini in September 1509, as well as the victory of Ferdinand of Spain in Africa in 1510.[68]

Cortesi died sometime in 1510. It is possible that the treatise was still being revised at the time of the author's death, for the task of editing seems not to have been entirely simple. Cortesi's humanist brother, Lattanzio, called upon Raffaele Maffei for assistance in editing the work. The bulk of the *De Cardinalatu* was

[62] Florence, Biblioteca Nazionale Centrale, Naz. II/III/3, fols. 132r-v, dated Urbino, January 18, 1506, " A questo Octobre proximo credo deo dante retrovarmi a Roma, dove me offero paratissimo ad omne uostro beneficio et patemente in omni altro loco dove mi retrovarmi ". See Targioni-Tozzetti, *Relazioni*, p. 260.

[63] Naz. II/III/3, fols. 130r and fol. 130v. Graziosi, in her introduction to *De hominibus doctis*, p. XII, seems wrong when she attributes a letter of 1501 to Farnese.

[64] Naz. II/III/3, fols. 133r-v.

[65] *Ibid.*, fols. 130v-131r; part is transcribed in Targioni-Tozzetti, *Relazioni*, pp. 258-259.

[66] Vatican Library, Ottob. Lat. 2377, Raffaele Maffei, " Breuis Historia Iulii Leonisque ", fol. 235v, " Studiis et litteris omnino alienus. Doctosque propterea omnino negligebat, libros ei dicatos ne titulo quidem tenus legebat, sed statim ut rem superuacuam a se reieciebat ".

[67] Naz. II/III/3, fol. 129r.

[68] *De Card.*, fols. I 9r - I 14v for the visits and fols. Q 14r, q 2r. There are two further glosses lamenting the events of the year 1510, fol. T 5v, V 3v.

printed by November 1510, and finished on December 1 of that year, by the Sienese printer Simone di Nicolò di Nardo, "il Rosso," on a press brought from Siena to the author's villa near San Gimignano specifically for the purpose.[69] The treatise was dedicated to Julius II in a letter written by Maffei and was accompanied by two other introductions: one by the monk Severo, and the other by the humanist Dominican preacher, Vincenzo Mainardo, a close family friend. Mainardo's letter is dated December 20, 1510, and it must have been printed after the rest of the text.[70] It is impossible to say if the Pope ever read the work dedicated to him.

The dating of the chapter *De domo*, devoted to the cardinal's palace, is equally uncertain but the question is of particular consequence for art historians who wish to establish which works of art the author could have known and to what extent his descriptions of architecture and painting preceeded actual works done in Rome. *De Cardinalatu* consists of three books and *De domo* is the second chapter of Book II. We have no indication, however, that Cortesi wrote the treatise in the present order of chapters. Internal evidence for chronology is scant. Cardinal Girolamo Basso della Rovere, who died on September 1, 1507, is discussed as though he were still alive.[71] This is the earliest *terminus ante quem* we have found. The Cardinal of Lisbon is said recently to have owned the Palazzo S. Lorenzo in Lucina; hence it is likely that Cortesi is writing after the Cardinal's death in September 1508.[72] It is most likely, however, that revision of *De domo* continued into 1510 as well.

The Translation

Raffaele Maffei described Cortesi's Latin as "almost Apuleian"[73] and that is certainly the politest description for Cortesi's relentless dedication to classical rhetorical formulae, circumlocutions and word order. For that matter, when the

69 See Jacometti, "Il primo stampatore senese Simone di Nicolò di Nardo", pp. 3, 11.

70 "Vicentius Maynardus Geminianensis Or. Prae. Lactantio Cortesio Equiti", without pagination. For him see Jacques Quétif and Jacques Echard, *Scriptores Ordinis Praedicatorum...* vol. II (Paris, 1771), p. 75.

71 See text note 21.

72 See text note 13.

73 Maffei's letter introduces the entire text but lacks pagination. See also Vatican Library, Barb. Lat. 2517, fol. 11r where Maffei discusses with Cortesi his style and makes the same criticism. Maffei and Severo discussed Cortesi and his retreat, see Barb. Lat. 2517, fols. 11 v-12 r. These last letters seem to have been written after Cortesi's death, but they lack year dates.

manuscript was being edited for publication, shortly after its author's death in 1510 his brother, Lattanzio, already found it necessary to make a series of emendations to the most obscure words and to enlist the aid of Maffei, the learned curialist who had been such a good friend to Paolo.[74] The text was provided with a dense apparatus of marginal glosses which are often interpretative in content.[75] Cortesi's convoluted style originally gave authority and stature to the work and its contents, but it makes the text difficult to comprehend for most modern readers. Like Nino Pirotta, who translated Cortesi's chapter on music,[76] we found that a strict translation was impractical. We have, however, gone further than he did in the direction of a close English paraphrase which seeks to retain something of the original rhetorical flavor while eliding some of the text's more defeating encumbrances. The Latin text faces the English translation but problematic Latin words are inserted in parentheses to help the reader check our interpretations. Punctuation, paragraphing, and spelling have been standardized, abbreviations expanded and misprints have been silently corrected.

In its use of a strictly classical vocabulary to deal with modern and practical matters, Cortesi's Latin is at once highly technical and ambiguous while the confusion is only compounded by his reliance on literary models like Vitruvius and Alberti. This is particularly noticeable in Cortesi's treatment of the aesthetic or theoretical aspects of architecture and in his use of words like *ratio* and *symmetria*. It has seemed preferable to translate these words with a certain flexibility, depending on their context for their meaning, as we believe Cortesi did. We have included all the glosses and annotations made by Cortesi's cinquecento editors. They are very helpful to the modern translator and annotator and we have made the assumption that they are, with certain exceptions, generally correct in what they say. In any event, they tell us what his contemporaries and close friends thought Cortesi was trying to say.

[74] Besides their intellectual relationship, Cortesi and Maffei were related by marriage. Cortesi's sister was married to Maffei's older brother, Antonio, who was executed because of his involvement in the Pazzi Conspiracy against the Medici in Florence. See Pio Paschini, " Una famiglia di curiali: i Maffei di Volterra ", *Rivista di storia della chiesa in Italia*, 7 (1953), pp. 342–343.

[75] Authorship of the glosses is uncertain, but Raffaele Maffei is the most likely candidate, see Pirotta, " Cultural Tendencies ", p. 156. It is possible Cortesi himself planned the glosses.

[76] See Pirotta, " Cultural Tendencies ", p. 156 for his translation principles.

PAULI CORTESII

DE CARDINALATU LIBRI TRES

Liber II Capitulum 2

DE DOMO CARDINALIS

PAOLO CORTESI

THREE BOOKS ON THE CARDINALATE

Book II Chapter 2

ON THE CARDINAL'S PALACE

QUALIS ESSE DEBEAT DOMUS CARDINALIS

Sed quoniam satis de uectigalium aequandorum ratione disputatum est, deinceps sequitur ut de senatoria domo dicendum sit quae maxime uiuendi rationi seruit. In quo quidem illud primum a multis quaeri disputando solet, quo nam maxime urbis loco senatoria domus statuenda sit. Siquidem multi cum patritiam uitam putent in humanorum commodorum genere tuendo uersari, facile affirmant eius domum in urbis oculis esse debere sitam, quo negocia gerentibus facultas commodior adeundi sit. Contra autem alii cum eorum studium contineri maximarum artium cognitione statuant, eos illius domus uolunt commoditate frui, quae longe ab hominum frequentia quotidiana absit, quo in genere eam esse dicunt quae ad aquam uirgineam a Iulio secundo est aedificata summa dignitate domus.

In quo loco sit locanda domus

Domus S. Apostoli

Iulius II

Nos uero cum senatoriae domus extruendae locum palatinarum aedium ratione metiamur, facile confiteri cogimur eam non ita a Vaticano abesse debere longe ut, cum legitimo Senatus die aut flaminialibus comitiis uel palatinis feriis siue extraordinario euocatorum accitu Rei publicae constituendae causa in Senatum ueniendum sit, magna temporis iactura eundo et remigrando fiat, qualem Sixti quarti domum fuisse in cliuo Exquilino dicunt. At uero cum senatoribus est proprii magistratus utendi ius, nihil causae esse potest quin affirmandum sit in urbis oculis eorum statui debere domum, quo locus commodior negotiantium frequentiae adeundi sit; quales modo aut Sixti Ruerae Pontificii Proscribae aut Raphaelis Riarii praefecti aerarii domus uideri possunt, quorum alteram in Via Florida, alteram in Theatro Pompeii constitutam esse cernimus, quibus in locis maxime quotidiana hominum frequentia uersari negociando solet.

Quod Car. qui habent officia debent habere domum in loco celebriori. 1.

Domus S. Petri ad uincula

Sixtus IIII

Domus Vicecancellarii

Sixtus Vicecancellarius

Domus S. Laurentii in Damaso

Raphael Riarius camerarius

Quod idem est de eorum senatorum domo dicendum quibus ex Senatus Consulto est aut causarum noscendarum ius aut arbitria priuata extra duodecimuirale iudicium Pontificis Maximi permissu dantur, ut ea Petri Rhegyni Senatoris conficientissimi hominis domus numerari potest quae est in celeberrimo eiusdem Pompeii Theatri constituta loco. At eorum domus quibus

Quod Car. qui tractant negocia debent habere domum in loco celebriori. 2.

Petrus Reginus Car.

HOW THE CARDINAL SHOULD BE HOUSED [1]

Now that we have sufficiently discussed the equitable distribution of the [cardinal's] income,[2] we should next consider his residence since it relates to his manner of life. It is usual first to discuss where in Rome the cardinal's palace should be located. Many believe that his Roman residence should be situated in the heart of town (*in urbis oculis*) to facilitate the transaction of business, for they think that patrician life involves the cultivation of such human comforts. Others think, however, that the cardinal should enjoy the amenities of a residence which is far away from crowds so that he can devote his energy to study of the highest arts and sciences.[3] The most noble palace which Julius II built at the Acqua Vergine [4] belongs to this type.

Where the palace should be located

The palace of SS. Apostoli

Julius II

When, however, we bear in mind the importance of the Vatican, it becomes clear that the cardinal's palace should not be so far from it that time will be wasted in coming and going when the College of Cardinals meets for ecclesiastical ceremonies such as secret consistories or consistorial promotions or celebrations of feast days at the Vatican or special councils of war.[5] This was said of Sixtus IV's palace on the Esquiline hill.[6] However, cardinals also have public functions (*magistratus*) of their own to perform appertaining to their office and for this reason, too, their palaces should be built in the center of Rome in order to make them more accessible to the many people who have business with the cardinal.[7] Such houses belong to Sisto della Rovere the Papal Vice-chancellor or Raffaele Riario the Papal Chamberlain. The palace of the former is located on the Via Florida, that of the latter in the Theater of Pompey, both parts of town where there is great activity.[8]

That cardinals who have duties should have a palace in areas of great activity. 1.

The palace of S. Pietro in Vincoli

Sixtus IV

The palace of the Vice-chancellor

Sisto Vice-chancellor

The palace of S. Lorenzo in Damaso

Raffaele Riario Chamberlain

The same can be said of the residence of those cardinals who by the decision of the College are given judicial powers or by papal consent rights of private arbitration (*priuata arbitraria*) outside the jurisdiction of the Rota.[9] Cardinal Pietro of Reggio [Calabria], a most learned man, has such a residence which is located in the most frequented area of the Theater of Pompey.[10] Yet even the residence of those who need

The cardinals who are engaged in business should have a palace in areas of great activity. 2.

Cardinal Pietro of Reggio [Calabria]

Quod Car. qui non tractant negocia debent habere domum in loco remotiori. 3.

Domus S. Laurentii in Lucina

Georgius Por. Car.

non sit aut libellorum | (G iv) obsignandorum aut noscendarum causarum siue proprii magistratus cura gerendi data, dubitationem non habet quin sit ad eam situs reuocanda partem quae nec longe a Senatu nec a quotidiana hominum assiduitate distet, quo non modo liberior ratio uacandi sed etiam locus sit aedificandi laxior; qualis ea domus uideri potest quae modo in Via Flaminia Georgii Vlysponensis Senatoris fuit.

Quod Car. debent esse directores familiae. 4.

Quod domus Car. debet abesse ab inuitamentis gulae et luxuriae. 5.

Idque eo fieri utilius probari ratione potest, quo certius ultimi ratione constituitur. Nam cum perspicuum sit Senatores principes familiae in ultimum dirigendae dari, abesse nullo modo potest quin fatendum sit ab his ea in domus statuendae ratione adimi debere prouidendo quae maxime sint praestitutum impeditura finem. Atqui cum apertum sit animam sensuum perceptione in intelligendo uti, satis sciri potest ea esse a familiae conspectu remouenda quae sensus sint ad eos turbidos impulsura motus quibus constitutus finis interuersum iri potest; quare iure dicendum est senatoriam domum non modo ab eo inuitamentorum genere distare debere longe quae sint gulae et ueneris excitatura malum, sed etiam ab earum esse rerum auditione semotam qua et obscenarum rerum memoria euocatur et libera animi uacatio impediri obstrependo soleat. Quo in genere ea maxime improbari debent in quibus malum utrumque soleat finitima contagione nasci, in quorum altero unguentarii, cupedinarii, fartores, mellarii, dulciarii, pulmentarii, coci, in altero ferrarii, lignarii, argentarii, loricarii et id genus nominari possunt, quorum maxime strepitu uidemus auditus obtundi solere sensum qui praeter caeteros disciplinae in intelligendo seruit.

RATIO ASPECTUS COELI

Quod in domo collocanda debet attendi ratio coeli et uentorum. 1.

Sed cum maxime habenda sit domus statuendae ratio quo hominum incolumitas seruari uiuendo possit, intelligendum est duplex esse in urbe domus collocandae genus: unum quod coeli natura, alterum quod uentorum uarietate

neither sign petitions [in the Vatican] (*libelli obsignandi*) [11] nor examine cases nor perform an office of their own undoubtedly should not be [too] distant from the Curia (*Senatus*) nor from centers of activity; [their residences] [12] should, however, be enough removed to allow greater opportunity for relaxation and more open space for building. An example is the palace which lately belonged to Cardinal George of Lisbon on the Via Flaminia.[13]

That cardinals who do not have these duties should have their palaces in a more remote place. 3.

Palace of S. Lorenzo in Lucina

Cardinal George of Portugal

Reason shows us that the utility of a building depends on the degree to which it serves the purpose for which it was intended.[14] Since cardinals as heads of households are obviously responsible for guiding them to the achievement of their aims [i.e. an orderly, virtuous life],[15] it follows that care should be taken in planning the building of the house to avoid those things most likely to interfere with these goals,[16] and, since we know that the soul uses sense perceptions to form understanding,[17] it follows that those things which are likely to throw the senses into those turbulent motions, which divert the soul from its proper goals should be removed from the sight of the cardinal's household. Therefore, it may rightly be said that the cardinal's household should be far removed from those attractions likely to excite the evils of gluttony and of lust, but also from the sounds of things which invoke improper memories and which hinder the free play of the mind because of noise. Places in which both types of diversion occur together are to be avoided above all. Gluttony and lust are fostered by perfumers, venders of delicacies, poulterers, honey venders and cooks of sweet and savory foods. On the other hand blacksmiths, carpenters, silversmiths, armorers and the like make noisy neighbors. Their clamor usually blunts the sense of hearing which beyond all others serves the understanding.[18]

That cardinals should be directors of their households. 4.

That the cardinal's palace should be distant from inducements to gluttony and luxury. 5.

[*SITUATING THE RESIDENCE*] *ACCORDING TO THE* (*RATIO*) *QUARTERS OF THE HEAVENS*

Since a house should be planned with special care to protect the health and well-being of men,[19] it should be understood that there there are two ways of situating a residence in Rome: one which is

That in situating a house the sky and winds should be considered. 1.

Quod domus meridionales minus sunt sanae. 2.

Quod domus occidentales non sunt multum sanae. 3.

Hieronymus de Ruere Car.

Quod domus orientales sunt saniores. 4.

Domus Millina

Bernardinus Caruagiallus Car.

Quod attendi debet usus habitantium. 5.

Domus Federici Car. de S. Seuerino

expendatur. Itaque cum urbs haud quaquam multum sit ab infero disiuncta mari, facile probari potest eas aedes quae sint ad meridianum solem constitutae minus uideri debere salutares, cum minus matutino sole illuminatae caleant et meridie constanti diuturnoque torreri solis ardore soleant. Eodemque modo ea aedium genera quae ad obeuntem solem locata cernimus, quales Hieronymi Ruerae Senatoris in Pratis Flaminiis sitae uideri possunt, cum matutino tepescant aduentu solis et meridianis uespertinisque temporibus solis flagrantia collustratae ferueant, minus / (G ii^r^) *probari seligendo possunt. At uero si sint ad nascentem constitutae solem, ut ea est Millinorum domus quae modo a Bernardino Caruagiallo Senatore habitatur, cum mitigetur caloris moderatione temperatius nec meridiano uespertinoque calore torreri possit, dubitationem non habet quin praeter caeteros ad incolumitatis conseruationem aptior iudicari debeat, in quo tamen intelligi potest aedium collocationem non solis aspectu sed incolentium usu esse metiendam, quo familiae incolumitati consulatur. Nec enim modo Federici Sanctoseuerinatis Senatoris domus ob id pestilentior uideri debet propterea quod sit ad meridianum collocata solem, cum ab ea coeli parte maxime sit aduersus omnium prope membrorum constitutus usus.*

RATIO VENTORUM

Quod uentus auster est pestilens

Quod uentus auster est fugiendus

Quod Roma offenditur austro

Eademque est uentorum considerandorum ratio, in quo quidem cum satis notum sit austrum unum e multis afflare solere pestilentius, propterea quod multo caeteris sit meridionalis natura calidior contortoque spiritu soleat cogere perflando nubes, ex qua crassa concretaque coeli natura soleant hominum corpora tabefactata mori. Nihil causae esse debet quin senatoria domicilia sint ab ea coeli remouenda parte quae maxime feriri austro perflante solet, quod cum in caeteris Italiae ciuitatibus tum maxime est in urbis natura fugiendum quae fere tota austro saucianti euelata et nudata patet, ex quo maxime possit tabificum morbi excitari genus.

determined by the nature of the heavens, [i.e. direction of the sun], the other by the variety of the winds.[20] Therefore, since Rome is not far above sea level it is easy to see why those buildings which face south would appear to be less healthy [than others] since they receive less morning light and are generally scorched at midday by the constant, daily heat of the sun. Likewise, those buildings which face west, such as [the palace] of Cardinal Girolamo della Rovere in the Campo Flaminio,[21] cannot be recommended since, warmed by the morning sun and exposed to the glare (*collustrae*) of the burning sun [at noon], they bake throughout the afternoon and evening as well. There is no doubt, however, that houses facing the rising sun, like the palace of the Mellini presently inhabited by Cardinal Bernardino Carvajal,[22] should be judged the healthiest of all since they are cooler because they receive less intense heat and are not scorched by the afternoon and evening [setting] sun.[23] Nevertheless, the health of a household is determined not by the sun's direction but by the habits of the residents.[24] Thus the palace of Cardinal Federigo Sanseverino [25] need not be thought more pestilential because it faces the afternoon sun, since practically all the rooms actually in use face away from that quarter.

That houses facing south are less healthy. 2.

That houses facing west are not very healthy. 3.

Cardinal Girolamo della Rovere

That houses facing east are healthier. 4.

Palace of the Mellini

Cardinal Bernardino Carvajal

That habits of the residents should be taken into consideration. 5.

Palace of Cardinal Federigo Sanseverino

[*SITUATING THE RESIDENCE*] *ACCORDING TO* (*RATIO*) *THE WINDS*

The same consideration (*ratio*) applies in considering the winds since it is certainly well known that the south wind, above all, usually blows more pestilentially. Because of its southern nature, this wind is much hotter than the others and, blowing with vehement force, it drives the clouds together making a thick and heavy atmosphere which causes men's bodies to waste away and usually to die. For no reason should the cardinal's dwellings be exposed to the blast of the south wind, and this is true for other cities of Italy but especially for Rome, which is almost completely defenseless and exposed to the destructive south wind which is especially conducive to the wasting kind of sickness [malaria?].[26]

That the south wind is pestilential.

That the south wind should be avoided.

That Rome is struck by the south wind.

DESCRIPTIO DOMUS

Quod modus describendae domus uariatur secundum aetates et secula

Graeci

Romani

Federicus II

Castrum Capuanum

Martinus quartus

Descriptio autem domus duplex uideri debet: una quae in membrorum partitione consistit, altera quae in ornamentorum genere uersatur. Partitio enim mutari temporum conditione solet, nec enim dubitari debet quin perspicuum sit non modo dispari ratione temporum alium apud Graecos et alium apud Romanos fuisse aedificandi modum, sed etiam illos ipsos inter se uno tempore dissimiles in aedificandi ratione extitisse, cum ex his alii Ionico, alii Corinthio, alii Dorico, alii Thuscanico construendi genere uterentur. Postea uero temporibus ita flagitantibus non modo est ex prisca symmetriae ratione deflexum, sed etiam ratio est aedificandi importata noua, siquidem Federicus secundus parthenope est germanica symmetria in campana domo describenda usus. Eademque nouitatis ratione a Martino quarto domum in phaliscis gallico genere aedificatam ferunt; quod idem a multis uidemus extraordinaria cupiditate factum, quo aut aduentitiae symmetriae usurpatione aut commenti nouitate placere aedificando pos- / (G 11^{v}) *sent. Nos autem cum modo uidemus instauratitia sedulitate priscae symmetriae renouari genus, facile affirmamus id senatores debere in domo partienda sequi quod maxime priscorum descriptioni temporumque rationi congruat.*

Quod cubiculum palafernariorum debet esse in uestibulo. 1.

Quod munitio armorum debet esse in uestibulo. 2.

Itaque in senatoria domo constituenda is est describendus partiendi modus, ex quo intelligi possit eam aedium partem quae sit ad solem nascentem constituta partiri solere aptius si id cubiculum sit in adeundo primum quod circumpedum generi in describendo datur, quo priuatim seruari aut britannici senatorii equi aut tullutariae mulae ephippia dorsualiaque ornamenta possint sitque commodior excubandi locus; eique tantum spacii adiungi triclinii fornicati debet, quod satis sit armamentario faciendo loci, ut siquid periculi

PLAN (DESCRIPTIO) OF THE RESIDENCE

The plan (*descriptio*) of the house ought, moreover, to be considered in two ways: one according to the distribution of rooms (*membra*) and the other according to the variety of ornamentation. Now the way in which a house is disposed (*partitio*) usually changes according to the condition of the times (*temporum conditio*). There is no doubt that the differences between the Greek and Roman modes (*modum*) of building reflects changes in the fashion of the times (*ratio temporum*).[27] Indeed, even the Greeks differed among themselves at one and the same time in the manner (*ratio*) of building while the Romans employed some, the Ionic, others the Corinthian, others the Doric and yet others the Tuscan type (*genus*) of construction. Later, due to the times, there was not only a turning away from the ancient system of design (*ratio symmetriae*),[28] but a new manner (*ratio*) of building was introduced as well. Thus, Frederick II of Naples used the German [Gothic] system (*symmetria*) in planning his Campanian house.[29] And it is said that Martin IV was guided by the same regard (*ratio*) for novelty when he built his Faliscan house in the French manner (*genus*).[30] And we see the same thing done by many people who, out of an abnormal passion [31] [for novelty], take delight either in the use of foreign modes (*symmetriae*) or in new contrivances (*commenti*) in building. Nowadays, however, when we see that type [of architecture] which is being revived by the fervent application of the ancient standard of design (*prisca symmetria*) we warmly recommend that in planning their residences the cardinals should turn to this mode [of architecture] because it conforms well both to the design (*descriptio*) and system (*ratio*) used in ancient times.[32]

That the mode of planning the residence varies according to epochs and centuries.

The Greeks

The Romans

Frederick II

Capuan castle

Martin IV

In building the cardinal's palace, care should be taken to arrange (*describendus partiendi modus*) the plan so that the building faces the rising sun and that, upon entering [the vestibule],[33] we encounter a room housing the grooms. Thus the saddles and harnesses of the cardinal's British horse or trotting mule [34] can be kept apart there and this also makes a more convenient place for standing watch.[35] And to this a vaulted room ought to be added large enough for use as an armory.[36] Therefore, if any danger or disturbance should seem

That the grooms' room should be in the vestibule (*vestibulum*). 1.

aut motus nasciturum uideatur, temporis causa arma sint prouisa et descripta ratione promptiora domusque in aditu sit in obsistendo et repellendo tutior.

Atrium. 3.

Quod cubicula hospitum debent esse in porticu atrii propter commoditatem. 4.

Cubicula hospitum.

Eademque ratione ex uestibulo aditus est in atrium tamquam in forum statuendus, cuius mensio quoquouersus ad compluuium quadrata pateat porticusque transitoria ambulatione cingatur. Ex quo causa affirmandi sit hospitalia cubicula sub porticu in eadem esse domus collocanda parte, quo a senatoriae familiae usu secretior libertas hospitibus degendi sit et quo locus ianuae uicinior eundi et redeundi detur. In quo eo solet laudari mensio considerata magis, quo commodius et honorificentius ab hospitum genere habitari potest et quo saepe senatori esse potest occasio gratificandi maior, ut munificentissimum hominem Federicum Sanctoseuerinatem Senatorem fecisse uidimus, a quo sunt ducenteni uiceni quini parthenopei hospites lyriana clade recepti, et a quo est tantum opis profugorum egestati latum, quantum ab homine praestari in illa temporum asperitate posset.

Federicus Car. de S. Seuerino.

Clades ad Garilianum

Quod bibliotheca debet esse in porticu propter comunem utilitatem et commoditatem. 5.

Quod schola legendi debet esse in porticu propter commoditatem. 6.

Quod schola debet esse fornicata et rotunda propter uocem. 7.

Quod cubicula aestiua debent esse ad septemtriones. 8.

Quod cubiculum musicae debet esse fornicatum et rotundum propter vocem. 9.

Quod cubiculum musicae debet habere uasa musica in pariete collocata ad consonantiam. 10.

In eademque ambulatione ob eam causam his est senatoria bibliotheca adiungenda, ut et legentibus matutino sole illuminata seruiat et cuiusque generis litteratae multitudini a ianua pateat in bibliothecam gratuitam uia, quo nihil excogitari potest ad eruditorum hominum egentem auiditatem maius. Nihiloque disiunctius domesticum auditorium esse debet. Idque est rotundum ad circinum testudinea ratione faciendum, ne diffusa uox in legendo elabatur neue uaria incisione angulorum lacunosoque conspectu possit uidendi abalienari sensus. At in ea domus parte, quae est ad septemtrionum plagam con- | (G iii^{r}) stituta, nulla causa dubitandi datur quin aestiua cubicula musicaque triclinia collocanda sint, in quorum alteris cum meridiandi locus tum maxime coclearius pseudotirus constitutus sit, in alteris etiam fornix rotunda concameratione statuatur, ne causa uoci errandi et elabendi sit, ideoque multis curae fuisse legimus, ut in eiusmodi tricliniorum cellis aenea uasa aut fictilia dolia musica ratione collocarent, ex quibus uox tamquam e medio nata commeans uasaque caua feriens multo fieret canendo et sonando dulcior.

likely to arise, time will be saved, arms will be ready to hand for the reason described, and the entrance of the house will be safer and easier to defend. And, accordingly, from the vestibule (*vestibulum*) an entrance (*aditus*) leads into the courtyard (*atrium*) which should be arranged like a forum. It should be square in plan, open on each side onto a compluvium [open court] [37] and should be surrounded by loggias (*porticus transitoria ambulatio*). The guest rooms should be located behind the loggias (*sub porticu*) in order to allow the guests privacy and freedom of action apart from the cardinal's household, and to place them in that part of the house which is closer to the door for greater ease in coming and going.[38] This judicious arrangement is the more laudable because the guests can be more comfortably and honorably housed and the cardinal is given the greater opportunity to show hospitality to his guests. Thus we have seen Federigo Sanseverino, a most munificent man, who received two hundred and twenty-five Neapolitan guests after the battle of the Garigliano [39] and offered as much aid for the needs of the refugees as could be given by a man in those difficult times.

That the armory should be in the vestibule (*vestibulum*). 2.

The Atrium 3.

That the guest-rooms should open onto the loggia (*porticus*) for convenience. 4.

Guest-rooms.

Cardinal Federigo Sanseverino

Battle of Garigliano.

For this reason the cardinal's library ought also to be in the same loggia (*ambulatio*), since it is lighted by the morning sun, which is so good for reading, and provides free access from outside to the library — something of the greatest possible service to learned men.[40] Neither should the auditorium of the palace be more distant [than the library from the loggia].[41] It should be made round in circumference and valuted lest the voice be lost and the view be cut off by corners or by too great a distance across the room.[42] Yet there is no reason why the summer apartments and the music rooms should not be placed in the northern part of the palace.[43] In the summer apartments, both a place for taking an afternoon rest and also a spiral private staircase have been built.[44] The music rooms have been given a round vaulted ceiling lest the voice wander or be lost. And hence we read that bronze vases or earthenware jars are often put into niches (*cellae*) in the walls of the music room. This is done for the sake of the music, so that sound coming from the middle of the room strikes against the empty vessels, making both singing and playing sound much sweeter.[45]

That the library should be in the loggia (*porticus*) for common use and convenience. 5.

That the reading room (*schola legendi*) should be in the loggia (*porticus*) for convenience. 6.

That the reading room should be vaulted and round for hearing. 7.

That the summer apartment ought be in the north. 8.

That the music room should be vaulted and round for hearing. 9.

That the music room should have music vases placed in the wall for the sake of resonance. 10.

Quod scalae debent nasci in porticu ad aquilonem. 11.

Quod scalae debent habere inflexu spatia quietiora. 12.

Atque ex hoc intelligendum est etiam in eiusdem transitoriae ambulationis angulo ad aquilonem scalarum statui debere gradus, ex quibus ab interiori aedium parte facultas in tectum ascendendi sit, in quo quidem genere ad commoditatis diligentiam hae maxime probari construendo solent quae flexuosa ascendendi ratione constant. Quales maxime iudicari possunt quae modo sunt a Iulio II in suburbano palatino uia fornicata factae, in quibus ita sunt gradationis areae, rata interualli ratione constitutae, ut non modo in his causa commodior interquiescendi detur, sed etiam maxime decipi soleat uidendi in ascendendo sensus, ne uno aspectu scalarum altitudine deterreri possit. Quod contra in his scalis usu nobis uenire cernimus quae sunt ad Deae Matris aedem in cliuo Capitolino constitutae, in quibus perspicua altitudo tota ascendendi patet. Idque maxime fieri ratione scimus, cum satis apertum esse possit homines ad ea moueri solere tardius quae natura aduersante fiunt, atqui cum corporum genus superiora natura repugnante capessat, facile cognosci potest homines, quo difficiliorem scalarum gradationem oculorum terminatione metiuntur, eo ad ascendendum moueri solere lentius.

Scalae S. Mariae in Aracoeli

Ratio naturalis

Quod cubiculum magistri domus debet esse in calce scalarum. 13.

Quod cubiculum architriclinii debet esse iunctum cum cubiculo magistri domus propter conformitatem magistrii. 14.

Quod colina cella dispensatoria et cella cenatoria debent esse in porticu. 15.

Quod ista tria membra debent esse in porticu propter proximitatem magistri domus et architriclinii. 16.

Quo circa uidendum est ut his finitimum decurionis domus cubiculum statuatur, quo sit multitudini adeunti notius et quo tamquam quidam sit constitutus iuris dicendi locus, ad quem a famulantium genere sit in litium disceptatione corrependum, in eoque quasi lex sit contubernalium descripta uitae, qua non modo sonti iurgiorum poena sed etiam discubitoria mulcta irrogetur, quo in senatoria domo possit tranquilla ratione uiui. Quod idem fere dici de praefecti popinarii cubiculi descriptione potest, qui ei prope est muneris cognatione in domo administranda par. Itaque iure affirmari potest, in eadem ambulatione porticus his tricliniis non modo cellae obsonariae sed etiam colinae delibatoriique mem- / (G iii^{v}) bra esse uincienda, ut si quippiam euenturum sit, cui occurri tempestiua medicina debeat, eorum alter amboue ita proximi tricliniorum uicinitate sint, ut repente nascenti malo mederi explorata remediorum ratione possint.

Quod aula debet esse magna. 17.

Eodemque modo hisdem scalis in superius peristylium ascendi debet, ex quo maxime ducta et directa pateat in publicam aulam eundi uia. In aula

The staircase of the palace should also be located in a corner of the north loggia of the courtyard (*transitoria ambulatio*) and should lead up through the house to the roof. A staircase broken up into flights (*flexuosa ascendendi ratio*) is the most convenient for this purpose.[46] Such stairs were recently built by Julius II in his villa palace [Belvedere] with its vaulted passageway (*via fornicata*).[47] In these stairs are landings at set intervals to break the ascent and to make it more comfortable by allowing for pauses. Moreover, by breaking the stairs into flights with landings [at the turns], the sense of sight is especially deceived for, in ascending, the visitor is not discouraged by seeing the full height of the stairs in a single glance.[48] This is just what happens at the church of the Mother Goddess on the Capitoline Hill [S. Maria in Aracoeli] where the entire steep ascent is made by a continuous flight of stairs. Indeed, reason tells us why this should be so, for men are clearly moved much more slowly to do those things which contradict nature.[49] And it is, in fact, against nature for bodies to strive to reach high places, thus it is natural that men are less eager to ascend those stairs which their eyes tell them to be the steepest.

That the stairs should be in the loggia (*porticus*) to the north. 11.

That the stairs should have landings at the turns. 12.

Stairs of S. Maria in Aracoeli

Natural law

Hence the room of the major-domo should be situated close to the [main] stairs,[50] so that it may be the more visible to people as they enter. There should be a certain place designed as a courtroom (*iuris dicendi locus*) in which members of the household may seek a hearing,[51] and where the law governing the servants' lives is laid down, punishment is meted out to those guilty of quarrels, and servants are penalized by being deprived of meals, so that peace (*ratio tranquilla*) may reign in the cardinal's house. The room of the steward should adjoin that of the major-domo because these two are practically equals in running the palace.[52] The same loggia (*ambulatio*) should also contain the pantry, the kitchen and breakfast room and they should adjoin the [small?] dining room. This arrangement will allow either the major-domo or the steward or both to provide a timely and fitting remedy for any problem that may unexpectedly arise.

That the major-domo's room should be at the foot of the stairs. 13.

That the steward's room should be joined to that of the major-domo because of similarity of their duties. 14.

That the pantry, kitchen and breakfast room should be in the loggia (*porticus*). 15.

That these three rooms should be in the loggia (*porticus*) to be close to the major-domo and steward. 16.

And, in the same manner, one may ascend by the same staircase to the next loggia (*peristylium*) which leads us directly to the great hall [sala grande]. It should be spacious enough to seem built for the meeting and gathering of men rather than for private comfort.[53] In this hall,

That the hall should be large. 17.

Quod cappella debet esse in aula et aperta propter audientes missam. 18.

autem ea est laxitatis adhibenda cura, ut non ad priuatae commoditatis diligentiam sed ad hominum celebritatem et conuentum facta esse uideatur. In ea ad hybernum nascentem solem sacellum est imprimis penatium diuorum statuendum, quo nihil in ea prius adeuntium multitudini occursurum sit memoriaque euocetur salutandi diuos. Ideoque non sine causa intelligendum est id ita fenestrarum dispertita ratione patere debere palam, ut facile ex his a uentitantium genere spectari possit flamen in ara litans.

Quod cubiculum audientiae debet esse in aula. 19.

Quod cubiculum audientiae Car. debet habere portas fallaces propter nuntios extraordinarios. 20.

Quod in cubiculo audientiae non debent esse fenestrae cancellatae, quemadmodum utebatur Paulus II. 21.

Nihiloque dicendum est de salutatorii descriptione secius, quod quidem ea est symmetriae ratione faciendum, ut non modo clandestinum hostium perystilio adiunctum habeat, quo temporis causa tabellarii internuntiique commeare extraordinario ingressu possint, sed etiam in eo quidam sint abstrusi constituti loci, ex quibus maxime causa hominum pernoscendorum detur. Ideoque multos in hoc salutatorii genere exploratoriis fenestris usos fuisse cernimus, quo apertius non modo hominum sermonem sed etiam gestum et uultum notare animaduertendo possent. Quales in tricliniorum palatinorum descriptione cernuntur quae sunt a Paulo secundo germanica ratione factae. Quod quidem ob id minus a multis probari solere scimus, properteaquod in his nimis perspicuus sit fallaciae meditatae dolus intellectoque astu causa salutantium generi ab habitu naturae discedendi sit, ex quo ratio detur hominum naturae pernoscendae difficilior, cum satis in promptu esse possit homines, cum se occulte a principum oculis obseruari suspicantur, non modo uocem et uultum sed callide etiam mutare solere dissimulando mores. Quare in hoc genere honestiori fallacia parietum structurae aut spectatoriae fistulae collocantur aut auscultatorii includuntur tubi, ex quibus ante salutationem senatori causa hominum naturae explorandae sit. Idque tum minus fieri suspitiose potest, cum earum ora solent peripetasmatum operimento tegi, nequa appareat in obstructa calliditate fraus.

Quod melius in cubiculo audientiae collocantur fistulae uisoriae et auditoriae. 22.

Quod cella cenatoria debet esse supra uiridarium. 23.

Quod cella repositoria argenti debet esse propinqua cenatoriae. 24.

Huic au- (*G iiii*^{r}) *tem cenationem et cellam argentariam adiunctum iri debere dicimus, quarum altera xystum et topiarium subiectum spectet quo eorum iucundo aspectu sit accubatio futura laetior, altera ita dispertita abaci ratione constet, ut uno conspectu possint argentea exposita uasa cerni facultasque harum rerum studiosis emblematum considerandorum argentique trac-*

facing toward the rising winter sun,[54] the chapel of the patron saints (*penates diui*) ought to be situated so that visitors will come to it first and will be reminded of their religious duties. And, by the same token, the chapel should be opened [to the hall] by means of windows so that, through them, the priest saying Mass (*flamen in ara litans*) can easily be observed by those who frequent the hall.[55]

That the chapel should be in the hall and open [onto it] for hearing Mass. 18.

The same applies to the way (*ratio symmetriae*) the audience chamber (*salutatorium*)[56] is to be arranged. It should have both a secret door and certain hiding places. The hidden entrance is connected to the loggia (*peristylium*) so that couriers and messengers can save time in their frequent comings and goings, while the concealed places provide the opportunity to examine visitors with care.[57] And thus, spy-windows [with grills] are often used in this type of audience chamber so that men's speech, gestures and expressions can be more clearly studied by means of observation. We see this in the arrangement (*descriptio*) of the palace rooms done by Paul II in the German manner (*ratio*).[58] In general this device is not much favored because it is too obvious in its intention to deceive and, once the trick is understood, those who come to pay their court are moved to abandon their natural behavior because of it. As a result the scrutiny of men becomes more difficult since it is evident that, when they suspect themselves to be secretly observed by the eyes of princes, men are inclined to alter not only their voices and faces but also cunningly to disguise their demeanor (*mores*). Wherefore it is preferable to install such contrivances as viewing or listening tubes in [the thickness of] the walls. By this means the cardinal may examine the nature of his visitors before receiving them. Such openings arouse least suspicion when they are kept covered by tapestries and the deception thus goes unnoticed.[59]

That the audience chamber should be in the hall. 19.

That the cardinal's audience hall should have hidden doors for special communications. 20.

That in the audience hall there should be no grilled windows such as those used by Paul II. 21.

That it is better to have viewing and listening tubes in the audience chamber. 22.

The dining room and silver closet (*cella argentaria*) ought to be adjacent to the audience chamber. The main dining room overlooks a covered walk (*xystus*) and a garden (*topiarium*) so that their cheerful aspect will make dining (*accubatio*) the more pleasant.[60] The silver closet (*cella argentaria*), on the other hand, is arranged with cabinets (*dispertita*)[61] so that, in a single glance, the display of silver vases can be seen and connoisseurs are enabled to examine its ornament (*emble-*

That the dining room should be above the garden. 23.

That the silver should be stored near the dining room. 24.

Quod cella lucubratoria et dormitoria debent esse propinquae propter alternationem studii et soni. 25.

Quod istae cellae debent habere scalas quae descendant in bibliothecam et scholam. 26.

Quod scalae debent habere fistulas auditorias ex quibus audiantur dispuntantes in schola. 27.

tandi sit. Idemque prope est de lucubratorii dormitoriique cubiculi ratione dicendum quae quidem triclinia, eo quod in his sit coniunctus uitae partiendae usus, recte erunt finitima propinquitate nexa, et quod utrorumque usus maxime esse debeat ab interuentorum interpellatione liber, non sine causa utrumque triclinii genus erit in intermedia domus descriptione situm. Itaque iure in lucubratorio non modo tubulos auscultatorios sed etiam coclearias scalas esse debere censemus, ex quorum alteris in auditorio disputantes audiantur, ex alteris intestinum sit descendendi in bibliothecam iter.

Quod his debet esse propinqua cella gemmarum. 28.

Quod cellae secretarii et scriptoris debent esse ad septemtriones propter aequalitatem luminis. 29.

Quod cella rationarii et pictoris debent esse ad eandem coeli partem propter eandem rationem. 30.

Caradoxus Mediolanensis aurifex.

Quod cubicula cappellanorum, scutiferorum et similum debent esse in peristylio propter propinquitatem aulae. 31.

Quod cubicula reliquae familiae debent esse supra propter defensionem domus. 32.

Eademque ratione paulo supra annecti dactylotheca debet in eaque ita sunt gemmarum arculae descripta ratione statuendae, ut in his commode possint aut aurei seruari nummi aut gemmarum genera signata et anaglypta condi. Quales eas tabulas in Federici Sanctoseuerinatis Senatoris dactylotheca esse cernimus, quas tricies mille uenisse auctionaria licitatione ferunt. In peristylio autem ad septemtriones dubitari nullo modo potest quin librarii senatoriique scribae triclinia collocanda sint. Nam cum ea domus pars maxime sit a solis auersa cursu, commodius uti constanti luminis aequalitate potest, quocirca iure his adiunctum iri ratiocinarium artificumque officina debent: quorum alterum ea est armariorum descriptione construendum, ut facile modus ex his codices et aduersaria inspiciundi sit, ex quibus celeriter deduci menstrua accepti expensique summa possit, altera pictorum, graphidum, encaustuum toreutuumque officina sit. Qualis nobis pueris ea uideri potuit quae in Ioannis Aragonis Senatoris domo erudita fuit, in qua a Caradoxo Mediolanense anaglyptum atramentarium antiquo opere ex argento caelari uidimus. Quin etiam in eadem peristylii ambulatione ad aquilonem, eorum sunt triclinia statuenda qui maiorum gentium in familiam conscripti uideantur: quales flamines, admissionales, anteambulones, archiatri et id genus nominari possunt. Quod idem est de superiorum tricliniorum ratione affirmandum quae sic quoquouersus de- / (G iiii^{v}) bent transitoria ambulatione necti, ut facile ex ea facultas familiae sit aut in seditione tuendae domus aut in interregni tempestate repugnandi.

matum) and handle the silver. The same should be said about the arrangement of the room used for study at night (*cubiculum lucubratorium*) and the bedroom,[62] the which should be very near to each other; because they serve closely related activities [i.e. the alternation of work and sleep]. Both these rooms should be especially safe from intrusion and so we see why they should be placed in the inner parts of the house. We also think there should be listening devices in the night study through which disputants in the auditorium can be heard, as well as a spiral staircase which provides an inside passage down into the library.[63]

That the night study and bedroom should be near each other because of alternation between study and sleep. 25.

That these rooms should have stairs which descend intc the library and reading room. 26.

That the stairs should have hearing tubes by which the discussion in the reading room may be heard. 27.

A gem room (*dactylotheca*) should be added a little above.[64] In it, small cases of gems should be set out in an orderly fashion (*descripta ratio*) so that gold coins can be displayed or that gems, both intaglios (*signata*) and those carved with bas-reliefs (*anaglypta*), can conveniently be kept. Such tables for display can be seen in the gem room of Cardinal Federigo Sanseverino, whose collection is said to have brought 30,000 (ducats) at auction.[65] In the loggia (*perystilium*) to the north [on the piano nobile] the rooms of the cardinal's secretaries and scribes should be located, for this part of the palace is least affected by the course of the sun and receives the most constant and equal light.[66] Therefore, it is fitting that the offices of the accountants and artists (*artifices*) [67] should be located nearby. The rooms of the former should be disposed like a storeroom with shelves so that it is easy to inspect the various account books and ledgers from which the monthly statement of receipts and disbursements can quickly be drawn up.[68] The latter room is a workshop for painters (*pictores*), draughtsmen (*graphides*),[69] and workers in encaustic and repoussé [70] such as we saw as a child in the cultivated household of Cardinal Giovanni of Aragon, where we saw an inkstand cast in silver with relief work done in the antique fashion by Caradosso of Milan.[71] In fact, the rooms of those in the service of great households, such as the clergy, ushers (*admissionales*), heralds (*anteambulones*), house physicians [72] and the like, should also be located in the same loggia [floor] to the north (*in eadem peristylii ambulatione*) [for the sake of proximity to the great hall]. In the same way,[73] the upper rooms [on the third floor] ought to be connected by a continuous corridor (*transitoria ambulatio*) [74] so that

That the gem room should be near the stairs. 28.

That the rooms of the secretaries and scribes should be in the north for even light. 29.

That the rooms of the accountants and painters should be in the same place for the same reason. 30.

Caradosso of Milan Artist

That the chaplains, pages and the like should be in the loggia (*peristylium*) for proximity to the great hall. 31.

That the rooms of the rest of the household should be above for the defense of the palace. 32.

DE ORNAMENTO DOMUS

Quod duplex debet esse genus ornamentorum.

Ornamentorum autem genus duplex esse potest: unum quod extrinsecus in excolendorum ratione uersatur, alterum quod in interiori ornandi descriptione consistit. Ornamenta enim quae extrinsecus adhiberi solent temporum conditione discendique progressione mutantur. Siquidem patrum memoria Cosmus Medices, qui auctor Florentiae priscorum symmetriae renouandae fuit, primus Traiani fori modulo est in ornandorum parietum descriptione usus. Postea uero a magno homine Federico Vrbinate ex manubiis bellorum multa sunt renouata solertius, quod idem est a Sixto quarto in libellionum plumbariorumque tricliniorum descriptione factum. Nec multo quidem longe Robertum Salernitanum ab ea symmetriae ratione discessisse in parthenopea domo aedificanda ferunt. At hodie plura praestantius a Iulio secundo in Vaticano palatinoque suburbano constituta cernimus, eoque uidemus aedificandi descriptionem artificiosius absolutum iri, quo fit ingeniorum sedulitas temporis progressione maior. Itaque cum in hoc genere uarius celebretur aedificandi modus multumque sit ratio in ornando dispar, facile intellectu esse potest alios ad amphitheatri symmetriam tiburtino lapide solere in parietum structura uti, quales aedes Raphaelis Riarii in Theatro Pompei et Hadriani Senatoris in Vaticano numerari possunt, nonnullos qui laudem in aedificandi frugalitate ponunt intercolumniis lateritiis addere mutulos epistyliaque tiburtina uelle, quosdam etiam qui cementitia structura delectentur, tectorio uti scalpturato malle, qualis modo est Francisci Alidosii Ticinensis Senatoris, artificio concinna magis quam marmorum copia sumptuosa domus.

Cosmus Medices

Federicus Vrbinas

Sixtus IIII

Robertus dux Salernitanus

Iulius II

Ornamentum ex lapide tiburtino.

Raphael Riarius Car. t.[i]t. S. Georgii [et] Sabinensis.

Hadrianus Car. t.[i]t. S. Grisogoni Bathoniensis.

Ornamentum ex lateribus

Franciscus Alidosius Car. Papiensis.

the members of the household can move about freely to protect the palace in periods of civil strife or to defend it during an interregnum [*sede vacante*].[75]

ON THE DECORATION OF THE PALACE

The palace can be decorated in two ways; the one which ennobles the exterior, the other which decorates the interior of the palace. In fact, exterior ornaments change according to the fashion of the times (*temporum conditio*) and the progress of learning.[76] Thus, indeed, in our fathers' time, Cosimo de' Medici,[77] who initiated the revival of the manner (*symmetria*) of the ancients in Florence, first used the example of Trajan's forum in planning the decorations of the walls.[78] Afterwards Federico of Urbino,[79] who was a great man, used monies gained through the spoils of war for many skillful renovations [of architecture]. The same thing was done by Sixtus IV in the disposition (*descriptio*) of the rooms of the notaries (*libelli*) and the papal seal (*plumbarii*).[80] Neither did Robert of Salerno,[81] it is said, depart far from this system of design (*ratio symmetriae*) in building his Neapolitan residence. Nowadays, however, we see that Julius II built things greater, both in number and in excellence, at the Vatican Palace and the Belvedere (*in Vaticano palatinoque suburbano*).[82] Thus we see that the manner of building (*descriptio aedificandi*) improves in skill and artfulness (*artificiosius*) as talents are increasingly dedicated to it with the progress of time.[83] And since, in exterior decoration, many modes of building are in favor and since the system (*ratio*) of ornament used is most varied, it is easy to see why some habitually use travertine in building walls in the manner (*symmetria*) of an amphitheater.[84] We can see this in such palaces as those of Cardinal Raffaele Riario in the Theater of Pompey and of Cardinal Adriano [Castellesi] near the Vatican.[85] On the other hand, those who favor frugal building prefer to use brick for the walls between the columns reserving the use of travertine only for consoles (*mutuli*) and architraves (*epistylia*).[86] Others favor the use of concrete for building walls,[87] preferring to face them with incised stucco (*tectorium scalpturatum*)

That there should be two types of decoration

Cosimo de' Medici

Federico of Urbino

Sixtus IV

Robert Lord of Salerno

Julius II

Travertine decorations

Raffaele Riario Cardinal of S. Giorgio [in Velabro] and Cardinal bishop of Sabina

Adriano Cardinal of S. Crisogono, Bishop of Bath

Wall decorations

Quod domu Car. debent esse sumptuosae

Quare haec ornamentorum genera ad eam sunt prudentiae terminationem reuocanda, in qua non modo quidam insit descriptioni lepos sed etiam is sumptus in aedificando fiat qui imperitam multitudinem, quae ad senatorum caedem aut ad eorum bona diripienda imminere uideantur, potentiae magnitudine opumque admiratione deterreat. Nam cum perspicuum sit indoctam hominum multitudinem sensu solere magis quam ra- / (G v[r]*) tione meditata duci, satis sciri potest eam cum sumptuosas senatorum aedes spectando admiratur perfacile solere ab iniuria inferenda reuocari, cum senatoriam potentiam aestimet sensus imbecillitate tanti, ut nullo modo locum sibi putet ad eos pellendos aut ad eorum bona diripienda dari. At uero cum homines a senatorum genere cernunt modicas habitari aedes, easque subito credunt oppugnatum et disturbatum iri posse, facile praedae peruersaeque libertatis spe de eorum statu conuellendo et labefactando cogitant; ut patrum memoria Eugenio quarto contigisse legimus, qui, cum in domo transtyberina habitaret, propter contemptum non modo est ex domo deiectus a plebe, sed etiam ex urbe est tribunitia seditione pulsus. Quod si hoc Pontifici Maximo plebis aspernatione contigit, quid putandum est senatorum generi euenturum, qui sine fascium metu sineque stipatorum custodia armata uiuant? Itaque si in alterutrum incidendum est, dubitari nullo modo debet quin magis sit optanda in senatoria domo ornanda ratio, quae dignitate sit oculos praestrinctura plebis quam quae contemptum mediocritate paritura uideatur.*

Quod plebes insurgit contra Car. propter contemptum

Eugenius IIII

thus rendering a house more elegant through skill than sumptuous through the abundant use of marble. The palace of Cardinal Francesco Alidosi of Pavia is such a residence.[88]

Cardinal Francesco Alidosi of Pavia

Such [external] decorations of palaces which make them appear attractively designed and sumptuously executed are also to be recommended for reasons of prudence. Thus the ignorant mob will be deterred from threatening the cardinals with harm and from plundering their goods by the mightiness of the building and through admiration for its opulence.[89] Since it is clear that the uneducated multitude is usually led by its sense[s] (*sensus*) rather than by rational reflection, we can see why the sight of the sumptuous cardinals' palaces easily restrains the admiring multitude from doing harm;[90] for, since the multitude is guided by the feeble [judgment] (*imbecillitas*) of the sense[s], it believes the cardinals' power to be so great as to prevent the mob from expelling the cardinals or from plundering their goods. On the other hand, when men see cardinals housed modestly, they immediately believe that the palaces are vulnerable to attack and so they think readily of overturning and destroying the cardinals' position in the hope of loot and from [the desire] for perverse liberty. We read that this happened to Eugenius IV in our fathers' time when he was living in his palace in Trastevere.[91] Not only was he thrown out of his house by the people because of their contempt for him, but he was also driven from Rome by a revolt of the municipal officials (*tribunes*). If even a Pontifex Maximus could be struck by such misfortunes because of the people's contempt for him, how easily might still worse things befall cardinals who are unable to inspire the fear due to a higher authority (*fasces*) and who live unattended by armed guards.[92] And so we conclude that, in choosing the manner of exterior decoration of the cardinals' palaces, that type should be chosen which will dazzle the eyes of the people by its dignified splendor, rather than one which will tend to inspire contempt by its modest appearance (*mediocritas*).

That the cardinal's palaces should be sumptuous.

That the people rise up against cardinals through contempt.

Eugenius IV

ORNAMENTA INTERIORA

Interiorum autem ornamentorum genus multiplex adhiberi solet, siquidem multi plastices ratione, nonnulli statuaria, quidam etiam gypseo uti ornamento malunt. Nobis uero frugalius et utilius id genus uideri in senatoria domo ornanda debet quod pingendi ratione constat; nec enim dubium esse potest, cum homines aliquo picturae genere teneantur quo possint tamquam praesenti historiae eruditione frui, quin in his ex uehementi imaginum similitudine aut animi appetitio praeparetur aut motrix euocetur uirtus, quandoquidem Aristotele auctore imaginatione et intelligentia rerum dicatur contineri uis. Quocirca in atrio, quod est in hominum conspectu constitutum, ea debent rata intercolumnii mensione pingi quae maxime sunt a nostrorum imperatorum genere christiana ratione gesta. Quid enim est aut tam admirabile quam spectare pontificiae maiestatis uerecundiae [*sic*] *Constantino Caesari causam fuisse urbis omnium gentium principis deserendae Imperiique in Thraciam transferendi datam? Aut tam iocundum cognitu quam Carolum Magnum Senatus Consulto ac -* / (G *v*^{v}) *cersitum cernere ad Longobardos Italiae possessione pellendos hostesque ab eo fugatos et Italiam diuturna barbarorum uexatione liberatam, eumque deinde ex Senatus Consulto terrarum orbe partito imperatorem fuisse Pontifice Maximo referente factum?*

Quod triclinia debent magis pingi.

Aristoteles de motu animalium.

Quod in atrio debent pingi gesta Imperatorum Christianorum et Ducum. I.

Constantinus Caesar

Carolus Magnus

In peristyliis autem et ambulationibus ea exprimi pingendo possunt quae uatum nostrorum consignata traditione constant, non quae priscarum fabellarum narratione pingi fingendo solent. At uero in aula eorum est species pingenda notatior qui cum imperium Pontificis Maximi Senatusque delere conati essent graues iustasque Rei publicae dedere poenas, qualis ex eo genere Federicus secundus numerari potest, qui cum diu maxime acerbus in Re publica uexanda fuisset a Manfredo filio est propter fruendi regni cupiditatem interfectus. Nec item minus homines in eo picturae genere admoneri admi-

Quod in ambulatione debet representari historia et scriptura. 2.

Quod in aula debent pingi principes qui fuerunt rebelles ecclesiae et domiti sunt. 3.

Federicus II

Manfredus Rex Neapolitanorum

INTERIOR DECORATIONS

Many types of interior ornaments are used in palaces.[93] Whereas indeed, many prefer to use terracotta decorations,[94] others prefer statuary, and certain others plaster ornament [stucco]. It seems to us, however, that painting would be a more frugal and advantageous manner of decoration, for the cardinal's palace than these,[95] since men are fascinated by that type of painting by which they may benefit from the lessons of history brought to life.[96] For [by the sight of these paintings] either the appetite of the soul is aroused or the capacity for motion — the which consists, according to Aristotle, in the combination of imagination (*imaginatio*) and the intellectual understanding of things (*intelligentia*) — may be prompted by the striking lifelike imitation, in the painting, of the thing represented.[97] For which reason in the courtyard (*in atrio*) where all visitors can see it, in the spaces between the columns [on the loggia wall] those scenes ought to be painted which show deeds performed by emperors in a Christian manner.[98] For what is more admirable than to see how Constantine showed his deference to papal authority (*pontificia maiestas*) when he gave up Rome, which is the leader of all nations, and transferred the seat of the empire to Thrace?[99] Or what is more pleasing than to see how Charlemagne was summoned by the advice of the College of Cardinals (*Senatus Consultus*)[100] to wrest from the Lombards their possession of Italy, and how he put the enemy to flight and freed Italy from constant oppression by the barbarians, and thereupon, through the partition of the world by the College, he was made Emperor on the advice of the Pope?[101]

That rooms should be painted

Aristotle on the motion of animals

That in the atrium the acts of Christian emperors and leaders should be painted. 1.

The Emperor Constantine

Charlemagne

In the loggias and passages [in the upper floor] (*in peristyliis et ambulationibus*) moreover, scenes depicting the teachings of our prophets [Old Testament scenes should be shown] and not mythological narrations such as are often depicted in painting.[102] The great hall (*aula*) should be painted with the better-known examples of those who paid severe and just penalties to the Church (*Res publica*) when they tried to overthrow the rule of the Pontifex Maximus and the cardinals.[103] Among these can be numbered Frederick II since he was especially persistently bitter in harassing the Church. He was

That in the passageway (*ambulatio*) histories and scripture should be represented. 2.

That in the hall princes who were rebels against the Church and were conquered should be represented. 3.

Frederick II

Manfred King of the Neapolitans

rando possunt in quo eorum solent representari casus qui cum saepe Rem publicam labefactando aflixissent, animi postea morsu scelerumque recordatione fracti ad Pontificis Maximi Senatusque potestatem compressa superbia redierunt, ut Henricum tertium [*sic*] *fecisse in Gregorii septimi fide imploranda ferunt. Nam cum ad eum gratiae reconciliandae causa in Canosum Galliae oppidum uenisset intellexissetque se ab eo reiectum et repudiatum iri, triduo dicitur piaculi causa extra pomerium nudis pedibus mansisse penulatus. Quo quid potest esse in superba felicitate maius? quid admirabilius quam Imperatorem Pontifice Romano maximo exercitu summaque belli disciplina praestantem eius se subicere potestati uelle qui sine ullo armorum militumque praesidio, execraria tantum potestate niteretur?*

Quod in aula debent pingi principes qui humiliati uenerunt ad misericordiam ecclesiae. 4.

Henricus III [sic]

Canosum oppidum

Gregorius VII

In sacello autem id picturae genus maxime probari debet, in quo aut Deae hospitalis imago aut diuorum potest representari uita. Quid enim uel splendidae fortunae contemptu uel domitae superbiae exemplo tam admirabile spectatu esse potest, quam in sodalitiorum conturbernio aut Lodouicum Neapolitanorum regis filium cernere colinaria lauare uasa, aut Diuum Thomam theologorum ducem olera spectare sarrientem? Ex quo quidem intelligi potest senatorium sacellum eo pictum esse debere eruditius, quo facilius animi oculorum admonitu ad factorum imitationem excitari spectando possunt. Quale illud uotiuum sacellum historiae ratione iudicari potest quod est a clarissimo homine / (G *vi*r) *Sixto quarto in aede palatina constitutum, aut quale illud Oliuerii Carraphae Senatoris uideri debet quod est in Mineruae delubro ingeniosa argumentorum ratione pictum.*

Quod in cappella debent pingi principes qui professi sunt religionem mendicantum et seruilibus officiis functi sunt. 5.

S. Lodouicus

S. Thomas

Sixtus IIII

Oliuerius Carrapha Car. Ostensis

In salutatorio uero id maxime solet picturae probari genus quo principum dissimilitudo in postulantium genere audiendo ostenditur, ut si modo Petrus Soderinus Florentinus dictator cernatur assidere solere semper, quotiens uideat salutatorem aduentare senem quo ei honorificentior causa sit senem recipiendi

Quod in cubiculo audientiae debent pingi principes diuersimode dantes audientiam. 6.

Petrus Soderinus

killed by his son Manfred who desired to rule the kingdom in his father's stead.[104] And, likewise, men can be admonished [by the sight of these paintings] representing the fates of those whose attacks often vexed the Church (*Res publica*), but who afterwards appealed once more to the rule of the Pontifex Maximus and cardinals, their arrogance curbed by the remorseful recollection of their crimes. It is said that Henry III [sic] acted in this way in begging Gregory VII for protection. He came to the Cisalpine city of Canossa in order to be reconciled with the Pope but realized that Gregory would reject and repudiate him. As a sign of atonement, it is said, that Henry remained for three days outside the city walls wearing his traveling cloak and with his feet bare.[105] And what could be greater or more admirable than this: that a proud and prosperous emperor of the Roman people, outstanding because of his great army and consummate skill in war, should want to subject himself to the power of him who relies solely upon the power of condemnation without any help of arms or soldiers?[106]

That in the hall princes who having been humiliated submitted to the mercy of the Church. 4.

Henry III [sic]

Canossa

Gregory VII

In the chapel, moreover, pictures such as images of the Virgin (*Dea hospitalis*)[107] or of the lives of the saints (*diui*) can be represented. When the faithful are met together what could be more admirable than to see examples of contempt for high station or of pride tamed: to see Louis, son of the king of the Neapolitans, washing the kitchen pots, or to see Saint Thomas, the prince of theologians, hoeing vegetables?[108] Now it should be understood that the more erudite are the paintings in a cardinal's chapel, the more easily the soul can be excited by the admonishment of the eyes to the imitation (*imitatio*) of acts, by looking at [painted representations of] them.[109] The truth of this can be judged by the histories painted in the votive chapel built by the most illustrious Sixtus IV in the Vatican (*in aede palatina*),[110] or seen in the ingenious subjects (*argumenta*) represented in the paintings of Cardinal Oliviero Carafa's chapel in S. Maria sopra Minerva.[111]

That in the chapel princes who entered mendicant orders and performed servile work should be represented. 5.

Saint Louis

Saint Thomas

Sixtus IV

Oliviero Carafa Cardinal of Ostia

Pictures showing the different ways princes give audiences are particularly to be recommended for the decoration of audience chambers.[112] Now Piero Soderini,[113] the Florentine Dictator, would usually be seen to receive visitors while seated. His reasons for this do him

That in the audience chamber princes ought to be painted giving audiences in different ways. 6.

Piero Soderini

Paulus II

sessum, uel contra spectaretur Paulus secundus homo urbana calliditate afer eum postulantem audire solere ambulando quem id esse petiturum iudicaret quod ei esset priuata utilitate negaturus, quo causa oculorum obtutus fugiendi esset negandique pudor posset ambulando dilui; aut rursus Lodovicus Sfortia cernatur a lumine auersus audire consuesse postulantes, quo lucidius et certius hominum naturam ex oculorum motu notare iudicando posset, siue Ioannem Medicem Senatorem cernamus hoc auditorio tempore in aulam aut xistum uenire solere semper, quo omnibus sine ianitore pateat adeundi uia. Eodemque modo de dormitorii cubiculi descriptione dicendum est, in quo ea maxime esse debent uirtutum expressa signa, quibus animi ad similitudinem factorum matutina commonitione excitentur, ut si Franciscum Sfortiam spectari debere dicamus quotidie collimare solere iaculantem, quod maxime sit in bellorum exitu praesentiendo prudentiae cogitatae signum, in quo quidem multa eius generis inueniri possunt quae domestica senatori sint proposita exempla ad imitandum domi.

Ioannes Medices diaconus Car. S. Mariae in Domnica

Quod in cubiculo dormitorio debent pingi principes cum actibus diuersimode significantibus uirtutes. 7.

Franciscus Sfortia

Atque idem fere est aestiuorum tricliniorum describendorum modus, in quo genere eo est pictura putanda litteratior quo subtiliori mathematica ratione constat, ut siquid modo spectetur hydraulica aut cthesibica machinatione pictum in quo ratio subtilior considerandi sit. Quod idem est de ductaria, tractoria, oppugnatoria siue corriuatoria ratione dicendum, ut nos apud Ianenses sumus in Cortesii Oppidi lacu construendo commenti, ex quo humum scrobibus aqua corriuata eduximus. Nec item minus eruditae iucunditatis habet aut mundi depicti pinax aut eorum descriptio locorum quae nuper sit nostrorum hominum audaci circumuectione nota, qualis ea modo iudicari potest quae est ab / (G vi^{v}) *Emanuele Lusitanorum Rege de Indiae peruaga-*

Quod in cubiculis aestiuis debent pingi instrumenta mathematica. 8.

Oppidum Cortesium

Quod in his debent pingi mappa mundi et descriptio terrae nouiter inuentae. 9.

Emanuel Rex Portugallensium

honor; namely, when he receives an aged caller the old man may be seated as well. On the other hand Paul II,[114] a master of urbane shrewdness, might be seen as he used to listen, while walking about, to a petitioner whom he judged should be denied because he asked a favor for selfish motives. By walking about, the Pope could avoid his visitor's gaze and the embarrassment produced by denying the request. Or again, Ludovico Sforza [115] might be seen turned away from the light as was his habit when listening to a petitioner so that the Duke could more clearly and surely observe the nature of men by judging the motion of their eyes. Or we might see [116] how Cardinal Giovanni de' Medici [117] always holds audience today in the great hall (*aula*) or in a garden loggia (*xystus*) [118] where the way is open to all and where no one guards the door. And it ought to be said in the same way about bedrooms that the pictures should be symbols of virtue so that by this matutinal reminder, the soul will be excited to similarly virtuous acts [throughout the day].[119] Thus Francesco Sforza should be represented practicing, as he did daily, his aim with the javelin which is a symbol of prudent judgment in foretelling the outcome of wars.[120] His life certainly also offers examples of domestic virtues which a cardinal can imitate at home.

Paul II

Cardinal Giovanni de' Medici Cardinal Deacon of S. Maria in Domnica

That in the bedroom princes should be painted doing acts signifying virtue in various ways. 7.

Francesco Sforza

The summer rooms should be decorated in almost the same way. The more subtle a mathematical concept (*subtilior mathematica ratio*) [121] a painting displays, the more learned (*litteratior*) the picture will appear. For instance there could be a painting something like a hydraulic or cthesibian machine the which [representation] permits more subtle reasoning [by the viewer].[122] The same thing should be said about systems of drawing water, hoisting, laying seige or channeling streams [123] of water such as we contrived at San Gimignano to build the lake on the Cortesi family estate.[124] We removed the earth by means of water gathered together in streams through ditches.[125] And likewise there is no less delight to the learned in a painted picture of the world (*pinax*) [126] or the depiction (*descriptio*) of its parts which have recently become known through the daring circumnavigation[s] accomplished by our people, such as the exploration[s] (*peruagatio*) of Manuel King of the Portugese [127] around India. And the same holds true for paintings done from life (*zographiae describendae ratio*) [128]

That in the summer rooms mathematical instruments should be painted. 8.

Villa Cortesi

That in these rooms a map of the world and a chart of newly discovered lands should be painted. 9.

Manuel King of the Portugese

tione facta. Eademque est zographiae describendae ratio qua diuersorum exprimitur animantium natura notatior, in qua eo est commenti sedulitas laudanda magis quo minus nota animantium genera exprimi pingendo solent. Eodemque modo in hoc genere aenigmatum apologorumque descriptio probatur qua ingenium interpretando acuitur fitque mens litterata descriptione eruditior.

which show the different characteristics of various creatures. The rarer the creature shown in the painting, the more the zeal for novelty should be praised. And in this genre we recommend the depiction of riddles (*aenigmata*) and fables (*apologi*). Their interpretation sharpens the intelligence and [inspection of] their learned representation fosters the cultivation of the mind.[129]

NOTES

1 Cortesi's use of classical terminology required occasional arbitrary decisions on our part. Generally we have rendered classical Roman terms into their appropriate Renaissance or modern equivalents. "Senator" is always rendered cardinal: "urbs" is usually simply translated as Rome. "Domus" presents special problems. Generally it is translated simply as palace which is in keeping with contemporary usage, cf. C.L. Frommel, *Der römische Palastbau der Hochrenaissance*, 3 vols. (Tübingen, 1973), II, p. 212, "Palatium seu domum". Sometimes, however, the more general term residence seemed more appropriate. We have tended to avoid the word style, as well as the English word portico, because of their ambiguity. Literary classicism was defended by Flavio Biondo, in his *Roma instaurata*, of 1466, in *Codice topografico della città di Roma*, vol. 4 (Rome, 1953), p. 318, for Rome's "dictator perpetuus" was no longer Caesar but the pontiff. By the same token, "senatores sunt cardinales: Senatum praesentis Romae, cardinales ecclesiae, post pontificem orbis veneratur". Biographies of cardinals are based on C. Eubel, *Hierarchia Catholica Medii Aevi*, (Regensburg, 1914-29) vols. 2-3.

2 In the previous chapter of *De Card.*, bk. 2, ch. 1, Cortesi discusses the financial needs and resources of the cardinal. Cortesi argues that money is the proper pay for a cardinal since other forms of payment, such as land, would bind him to cares outside the Church. A cardinal's income should come from the common revenues of the College and be distributed equally to all. Cortesi sees no evil in money, but rather argues in Aristotelian manner, that it is necessary for virtue. Money allows the cardinal to dispense charity as well as to live in a manner becoming his dignity. Furthermore, adequate payments prevent the cardinal from borrowing money which could compromise his first duty to the pope and the Church. Cortesi estimates the common revenues of the Sacred College to be 490,000 gold ducats which, when divided among the 40 cardinals (the number Cortesi feels is ideal for the College) yields a standard income of 12,000 gold pieces. In fact there were only about twenty cardinals resident in Rome and their actual income was usually lower. Cardinal Adriano Castellesi who built a palace Cortesi admired had an estimated income in 1517 of 10,000 ducats. An average cardinal's income around 1500 was nearer to 6,000 ducats. Cardinals often rented their residences, received them with their titular churches or through papal loan or gift. Other "Palatine cardinals" lived in the Vatican. See D.S. Chambers, "The Economic Predicament of Renaissance Cardinals", in *Studies in Medieval and Renaissance History*, 3 (1966), pp. 289-313, and more recently, F.R. Hausmann, "Die Benefizien des Kardinals Jacopo Ammanati Piccolomini: Ein Beitrag zur ökonomischen Situation des Kardinals im Quattrocento", in *Römische Historische Mitteilungen*, vol. XIII (1971), pp. 27-68 and appendices. See P. Partner, *Rome in the Renaissance*, chapter V.

3 See Leon Battista Alberti, *Ten Books on Architecture*, J. Leoni, trans., J. Rykwert, ed., (London, 1955), bk. V, ch. VI, ch. XIV, and bk. IX, ch. II.

4 The annotation (fol. X 1 *recto*) reads, "Ad aquam uirgineam, aqua uiriginea erat ubi nunc Palatium S. Apostoli sub Quirinali". Julius II lived in the palace at S. Apostoli while he was a cardinal as early as the 1480's and was responsible for building and restorations there. The Acqua Vergine is displayed at the Trevi Fountain. See T. Magnuson, *Studies in Quattrocento Architecture* (Rome, 1958), pp. 316-327, and Francesco Albertini, "*Opusculum de mirabilibus novae et veteris urbis Romae*" in *Codice topografico della città di Roma*, vol. 4, (Rome, 1953), pp. 513 and 546.

5 "Legitimo Senatus die" would seem to be the day regularly set for secret consistories of cardinals. See Agostino Patrizi Piccolomini, *Caeremoniale Romanum* [1488] (Venice, 1516; rpt. Gregg Press, Ridgewood N.J., 1965), fol. 45 *verso*, ff. The secret consistories met twice weekly. "Flaminialibus comitiis" probably refers to the forwarding of episcopal candidates. However, annotation (fol. X 7 *recto*) reads "Sacerdotiis comitiis, sacerdotitia comitia hic accipiuntur pro conuentibus episcopalibus, qui fiunt quando clerici ordinantur ad sacerdotia". Erasmus, in his attack on such classical usage, however, glossed "flamen dialis" as the pope and the "comitia" as "pro electione episcoporum". Erasmus, *Ciceronianus*, A. Gambaro, ed., (Brescia, 1965), p. 140. On forwarding of bishops; see A.V. Antonovics, "A Late Fifteenth Century Division Register of the College of Cardinals", *Papers of the British School at Rome*, XXXV, (N.S.)

XXII (1967), pp. 87-105. " Palatinis feriis " would seem to refer to any papal mass which cardinals were expected to attend or perhaps any celebration involving the pope and cardinals. " Extraordinario evocatorum accitu Rei publicae constituendae " refers to a special summoning of councils of war when the State was endangered in classical Rome; see Cicero, *The Verrine Orations*, L. H. G. Greenwood, trans., (Cambridge, Mass. 1935), vol. II, p. 80. Under Julius II the term may be used merely to denote a special consistory, as distinct from the " legitimo Senatus die ", however, the phrase has a military ring in Cicero which we have retained in the translation. Indeed Cortesi joins other apologists for Julian military ventures with a defense of legitimate wars in *De Card.* (fol. X 7 *recto*). See also J. Shearman, " The Vatican Stanze: Function and Decorations ", *Proceedings of the British Academy*, 57 (1971), p. 52, n. 119.

6 The palace at S. Pietro in Vincoli underwent a long series of restorations and amplifications. These were done, however, under the aegis of Cardinal Giuliano della Rovere but may have begun as early as 1481 during the reign of his uncle, Sixtus IV (d. 1483). Compare, Albertini, *Opusculum* p. 513 and p. 513, n. 3, with Magnuson, *Quattrocento*, p. 330. Perhaps Cortesi is confused since Sixtus undertook work in the adjoining cloister of the church or he may actually provide early evidence for the Pope's concern with the palace as well.

7 It should be noted that Cortesi expresses no interest in having the cardinal build his palace near his titular church, although the della Rovere cardinals built palaces near their tituli. However, an address in the Rione Ponte near the Vatican and the banking quarter was important. Cortesi, (fol. Q 8 *recto*), discusses the desirability of renting palaces in various areas of Rome. Not all cardinals could or did build their own palace, see D. S. Chambers, " The Housing Problems of Cardinal Francesco Gonzaga ", *Journal of the Warburg and Courtauld Institutes*, vol. XXXIX, (1976), pp. 21-58.

8 The annotation (fol. X 6 *recto*) reads, " Pontificii proscribae, a scribo, scriba, proscriba. Proscriba enim est loco scribae. Hic accipitur pro Vicecancellario S. R. C. [sic] qui gerit uices S. Laurentii qui fuit scriba seu cancellarius Pontificis ". Cardinal Sisto Franciotto della Rovere (1507-1517) was Vice-chancellor of the Church. He was a nephew of Julius II and was given the Pope's old titulus of S. Pietro in Vincoli succeeding his brother Galeazzo. The palace mentioned is the Cancelleria Vecchia: the present Palazzo Sforza-Cesarini built by Cardinal Roderigo Borgia. It was inhabited successively by Ascanio Sforza (1492) and Galeazzo della Rovere, both Vice-chancellors. In the quattrocento the palace was praised for its sumptuous exterior and interior decorations and was compared to the Golden House of Nero (cf. Albertini, *Opusculum*, p. 517). The Via Florida is the Via Florea opened in 1493, today the Via dei Banchi Vecchi; see Frommel, *Palastbau*, vol. II, pp. 332-333, and Magnuson, *Quattrocento*, pp. 230-240. In 1508-09, when Cortesi was completing the *De Card.*, Pope Julius and his architect Bramante were planning the Palazzo dei Tribunali and a large piazza in relation to this palace. Thus the Cancelleria Vecchia was a highly topical example of a palace built at the center of urban and administrative activity.

Raffaele Riario was created Cardinal on Dec. 10, 1477. His titular churches were S. Giorgio, then S. Lorenzo in Damaso. He died July 9, 1521 as Card. Bishop of Sabina. He was Papal Chamberlain and Prefect of the Papal Treasury and inhabited the Cancelleria Nuova. Albertini, *Opusculum*, pp. 490, 516, like his contemporaries, comments on the lavishness of the antiquities and of the new decorations. See A. Schiavo, *Il Palazzo della Cancelleria* (Rome, 1964).

9 This is derived from Vitruvius Pollio, *De Architectura*, F. Granger, trans., 2 vols., (New York, 1931-1934), *Ten Books*, bk. VI, ch. V, pp. 37, 39, on housing for persons of high rank who hold offices and magistracies and on palaces where trials and judgments take place.

Judicial activities were an important part of a cardinal's duties. Cardinals were placed in charge of cases which came to the Holy See and which the pope specifically delegated to one or more cardinals for a decision or an opinion. See G. Mollat, " Contribution à l'Histoire du Sacre College de Clement V à Eugene IV ", *Revue d'Histoire Ecclésiastique*, (1951), p. 81. The phrase " arbitraria privata " refers to " decisions concerning the private interests of individuals "; see A. Berger, *Encyclopedic Dictionary of Roman Law*, (Phila., 1953). The annotation (fol. X 3 *recto*) reads, " Duodecimuirale iudicium hic sumitur pro iudicio Rotae ". The Rota, the Curia's major court, was given a complement of twelve men in 1472 by Sixtus IV. *Dictionnaire du droit canonique*, vol. II (Paris, 1937), cols. 1310-1339, summarizes the modern duties of cardinals.

10 Pietro Isvalies, Bishop of Reggio Calabria, created Sept. 28, 1500, d. 1511, was titular Cardinal of S. Ciriaco, then of S. Pudenziana. The famous jurist lived in the Palazzo dell'Orologio begun by Cardinal Francesco Condulmer, nephew of Eugenius IV, and located at the eastern end of Campo dei Fiori. It became the Palazzo Orsini, where the Medici also lived for a time, and, later, was owned by Alberto Pio da Carpi. It was built over the ruins of the Theater of Pompey: Magnuson, *Quattrocento*, p. 229. Albertini, *Opusculum*, p. 516, praises its elegant exterior, statues and pictures. L. von Pastor, *The History of the Popes*, F.I. Antrobus, ed., 4th ed., (London, 1923), VI, p. 342, says Julius II moved into this house during his illness, January 1511. In a letter dated Rome, April 17, 1507, Isvalies informs Cortesi that he is " avide " for the appearance of the *De Card.* (Florence, Biblioteca Nazionale Centrale, Naz. II/III/3, fols. 130 and G. Targioni-Tozzetti, *Relazioni d'alcuni viaggi fatti in diverse parti della Toscana*, vol. 8, (Florence, 1775), p. 264).

11 The annotation (fol. X 5 *verso*) reads, " Obsignatores, hic accipiuntur pro referendaris et dataris Pont. Max. qui obsignant libellos ". The referendaries were officials who signed supplications in the Signatura, the highest tribunal of the Curia. It had two divisions: the Signatura justitiae and the Signatura gratiae. A cardinal was in charge of the former, the pope of the latter. Supplications could be signed only in the Vatican. The Apostolic Signatura, unlike the Rota, was not an appeals court. See B. Katterbach, O. F. M., *Referendarii utriusque signaturae a Martino V ad Clementem XI*, Sussidia per la Consultazione del Archivio Vaticano, (Vatican City, 1931), vol. II, p. xii; Shearman, " Stanze ", pp. 11-12.

12 This is related to Alberti, *Ten Books*, bk. V, ch. IX, p. 92 which deals with the activity of secular " senators ".

13 Jorge da Costa of Portugal, nominated Dec. 18, 1476, d. Sept. 1508, was titular Card. of SS. Marcellino e Pietro, then of S. Maria in Trastevere. He lived in the Palazzo S. Lorenzo in Lucina (site of the present Palazzo Fiano) near the Arco di Portogallo, on the extension of the Corso then known as the Via Flaminia. (Albertini, *Opusculum*, p. 517, 517 n. 3). Cardinal Fazio Santoro of Viterbo, builder of the Palazzo Doria-Pamphili, moved to the Palazzo di Portogallo upon da Costa's death in 1508, dying there himself in March of 1510. (Frommel, *Palastbau*, vol. II, p. 95).

14 Alberti, *Ten Books*, bk. V, ch. XIV, p. 100. " A private house is manifestly designed for the use of the family ", but later in the same chapter he states that the houses of the rich should also serve pleasure and delight. Cortesi stresses the utilitarian ideal in line with his general Aristotelian bent. Utility is part of excellence. It is also a suitably moral criterion for the palace of a cardinal.

15 For Cortesi the two most important functions of a cardinal are the administration of the household and of the Church. The following chapter in *De Card.*, bk. II, ch. 3, amplifies the responsibility of the cardinal for the just administration of his own household. On fols. G 8 *verso* - H 1 *recto* Cortesi specifies " Itaque iure ex famiulantibus sexagenos in maiorum et octogenos in minorum gentium numerum conscribi debere censemus... "; however, the gloss to this reads " Quod numerus debet esse 120 ". Such a large number is necessary " propter rationem temporum " and " propter perfectionem (familiae) ". Francesco Priscianese, *Del governo della corte d'un signore in Roma*, L. Bartolucci, ed., (Città di Castello, 1883), p. 4, a generation later, recommends only 107 retainers for a lord. Cortesi also lays down the rules for the treatment of the " familia ". He argues that servants should be paid well for the good of the household, the employer's reputation and to prevent servants from getting involved in evils. He specifies 50 " auri annuatim " for " cappelani " and " scutiferes ", and benefices for those members of the household who qualify. He prefers Germans and Frenchmen as servants to Italians whom he finds either too violent or too imperious to serve well, (G 7v). The cardinal's palace, when properly run, is not only a place of " magnarum artium studia " but also for cultivating virtue and where " turbida animorum appetitia " is mitigated. See also fol. H 2 *recto*. For Alberti's account of the ecclesiastic's household see his *Pontifex* in L.B. Alberti, *Opera inedita et pauca separatim impresa*, G. Mancini, ed., (Florence, 1890), pp. 75-80. For the development of the " familia "; see G. Moroni, *Dizionario di erudizione storico-ecclesiastica*, vol. XXIII, (Venice, 1843), pp. 126-146.

16 In the *Ten Books*, bk. V, ch. VI, p. 89, Alberti declares that the houses of men of high station should be " in a private part of the city, shaded with trees...

remote from the concourse of the vulgar and from the noise of trades... [so that the family] may not lie in the way to be corrupted and debauched by an ill neighborhood". Cortesi is more literal, basing his opinions on the actual location of cardinal's palaces both in and outside the city.

17 In his letter in defense of imitation to Angelo Poliziano, Cortesi laid down the same Aristotelian-Scholastic principles: "I maintain that imitation is necessary, not only in eloquence but in all other arts as well; for all knowledge is obtained from antecedent knowledge and nothing is in the mind which is not previously perceived in the senses". E. Garin, ed., *Prosatori latini del quattrocento* (Milan, 1958), p. 908.

18 Aristotle, *On the Soul, Parva Naturalia, On Breath*, W.S. Hett, ed., (Cambridge, Mass., 1964), p. 219. "The faculty of seeing, thanks to the fact that all bodies are colored brings tidings of multitudes of distinctive qualities of all sorts; ... while hearing announces only the distinctive qualities of sound and to some few animals, those also of voice. Indirectly, however, it is hearing that contributes most to the growth of intelligence. For rational discourse is a cause of instruction in virtue of its being audible". Cortesi also warns against visual distractions (fols. Q 13 *recto* and *verso*). Alberti, *Ten Books*, bk. V, ch. I, p. 83 and bk. VII, ch. I, p. 134, believes that patricians should leave the center of town to "cooks, victuallers, and other such trades, and all the scoundrel rabble belonging to Terence's Parasites". Cooks, bakers, butchers and the like are also seen as dangerous and disagreeable neighbors but without the high-toned explanation given by Cortesi.

19 Cicero, *De inventione*, H. M. Hubbell, trans., (Cambridge, Mass., 1949), p. 336, "Incolumitas est salutis rata atque integra conservatio".

20 This phrase and the passage that follows are closely modeled on Vitruvius's considerations on the sites of cities (*Ten Books*, bk. I, ch. I, p. 15 and chs. IV, p. 37, VI, p. 53-55; also bk. VI, ch. III, p. 33, IV, p. 35, and bk. VIII, ch. II, pp. 145-147). In some respects, Cortesi is closer to Alberti, *Ten Books*, bk. I, ch. III. In no case, however, is there a direct paraphrase. South wind is condemned by Francesco di Giorgio Martini, *Trattati di architettura, ingegneria e arte militare*, C. Maltese, ed., (Milan, 1967), vol. II, p. 308. Raphael, however, says that he sited the Villa Madama north-south (maestro-scirocco) for the sake of "venti più sani". P. Foster, "Raphael on the Villa Madama: the Text of a Lost Letter", in *Römisches Jahrbuch für Kunstgeschichte*, vol. XI (1967), p. 309.

21 Girolamo Basso della Rovere, bishop of Recanati, received the red hat from Sixtus IV on Dec. 10, 1477. His titular churches were first Sta. Balbina, then S. Crisogono. He died as Card. Bishop of Palestrina on Sept. 1, 1507 and was buried in the della Rovere church of S. Maria del Popolo at the expense of Julius II in the famous tomb designed by Andrea Sansovino. Cardinal Girolamo lived until 1480 in the palace of Cardinal Ammanati on the shore of the Tiber across from Castel S. Angelo and thereafter near S. Agostino in the Palazzo S. Apollinare of Cardinal Guillaume d'Estouteville then under construction. The palace no longer exists but was located on the Via Recta just across from the Piazza Navona. See Albertini, *Opusculum*, p. 520; and Magnuson, *Quattrocento*, map of fifteenth century Rome.

Cortesi locates the Palazzo S. Apollinare as "in Campo Flaminio". This cannot be the Circus Flaminius on the site of the present Via delle Botteghe Oscure. Several other regions are sometimes associated with the Campus Flaminius, but these are not close by either. Cortesi here follows Flavio Biondo and other contemporaries in his belief that the piazza Navona (Campus Agonis) was the Circus Flaminius. See Flavio Biondo, *Roma instaurata*, pp. 311, 473-4; Albertini, *Opusculum*, pp. 473-4, calls the "(circus) Flaminius sive Apollinaris in Campo Martio...".

22 Bernardino Lopez de' Carvajal, bishop of Cartagena, made Cardinal Sept. 20, 1493, with title of SS. Marcellino e Pietro, was expelled from office by Julius II for his part in the Council of Pisa but was reinstated by Leo X. He was famous for his learning, and Cortesi relates that the Cardinal was unable to sleep after reading Scotus because of agitation (*De Card.*, fol. I 6 v). The Mellini family palace was on the Piazza Navona to the right of S. Agnese and opened onto the Via dell'Anima. See Albertini, *Opusculum*, p. 524.

23 We have interpreted the virtues attributed solely to the Mellini's house to apply to all the palaces. Vitruvius, *Ten Books*, bk. I, ch. IV, p. 37, comments on the unhealthiness of southern and western sitings. Alberti, *Ten Books*, bk. V, ch. VI, p. 89, says that temples in ancient times according to "Nigregeneus" were to face west but later it was preferred that they

face east. J. Rykwert in Alberti, *Ten Books*, pp. 244-245, n. 95, also cites from Hyginus, *De limitibus*. Raffaele Maffei, *Commentariorum urbanorum libri* 38, (Rome, 1506), CCCXCVIII *recto*, quotes Xenophon's *Economist* where buildings facing south are especially recommended. However, Alberti, *Ten Books*, bk. V, ch. XIV, p. 101, disapproves of the rule that houses should always face east and never south. A similar skepticism is reflected by Cortesi on the basis, not of theory, but of actual houses known to him in Rome.

24 This attitude contrasts with Vitruvius who emphasizes the direction of siting as a dominant factor determining the healthiness of sites. Alberti, *Ten Books*, bk. V, ch. XIV, XVII, is more flexible, believing that rules about site should vary with the climate. Cortesi emphasizes the utility of the house while Alberti, *Ten Books*, bk. I, ch. IX, sees the utility of the building as an aspect of its beauty and decorum, rather than of health, but see bk. V, ch. XIV, p. 100.

25 Federigo Sanseverino, nominated March 9, 1498, d. Aug. 7, 1516, was titular Cardinal of S. Teodoro. His palace was at S. Agata dei Goti near the Quirinal. Albertini, *Opusculum*, p. 519, mentions its " hortulus ". The palace had formerly belonged to Cardinal Francesco Gonzaga and was located near the vigna of Cardinal Giovanni de' Medici. See D. S. Chambers, " Gonzaga ", pp. 32-33. However, see below, n. 39. Paride de Grassis says that the Cardinal was a great soul, extremely tall of stature, very rich, with an income of 26,000 scudi yearly from benefices, and liberal beyond measure. See, Moroni, *Dizionario di erudizione storico-ecclesiastica*, (Venice, 1853), vol. LXI, pp. 51-52. On January 25, 1508, Sanseverino wrote from Rome to Cortesi thanking him for his treatise and for the kind mention the author makes of him (published in M. T. Graziosi, ed. and trans., *De hominibus doctis dialogus*, (Rome, 1973). See our introduction and below n. 113.

26 Unlike Vitruvius, Cortesi seems to have a low opinion of the healthiness of the Roman climate. He seems to be referring to the scirocco and malaria. Vitruvius was, however, speaking about the temperate climate of Italy as a whole. The south wind is only dangerous to health in some places. (Vitruvius, *Ten Books*, bk. VI, chs. I, V, VI, pp. 19, 53). See also Hippocrates, *Airs, Waters, Places*, in W. H. S. Jones, ed. and trans., (London-New York, 1923), vol. I, pp. 79-83. Alberti, however, quotes Galen as saying that Rome is always subject to agues. He also finds the south wind heavy and oppressive (Alberti, *Ten Books*, bk. IV, ch. II, p. 70). Cortesi's description of the action of clouds is also related to Vitruvius, *Ten Books*, bk. VIII, ch. II, p. 145. Leonardo da Vinci was, only a few years later, to be involved briefly in a project to drain the Pontine marshes to counteract malaria. L. H. Heydenreich, *Leonardo da Vinci* (New York, 1954), p. 145.

27 " Conditio [sic] temporum " would refer to political, economic and social conditions. This position is quintessentially Albertian as defined by R. Krautheimer in " The Beginnings of Art Historical Writing in Italy ", (1929) trans. in *Studies in Early Christian, Medieval and Renaissance Art*, (New York, 1969), p. 267. On the other hand, " ratio temporum " and use of the term suggests Cortesi is thinking more in terms of modes or tastes. R. Maffei, in his *Comm. urb.*, (fol. CLXX, *recto*), however, seemingly uses the term neutrally to mean the passage of time.

28 The annotation (fol. X 7 *recto*) reads, " Symmetria est commensuratio, non habet nomen latinum: ut ait Plinius, hoc utitur sequentur uictruius [sic] ". See Vitruvius, *Ten Books*, bk. I, ch. II, p. 27, bk. VI, ch. II, pp. 20-21. For the meaning of " symmetria " and " ratio symmetriae " in antiquity see J. J. Pollitt, *The Ancient View of Greek Art: Criticism, History and Terminology* (New Haven, 1974), ch. I and pp. 256-258. In all cases, " symmetria " means the " commensurability of parts " in a work of art. For a similar interpretation see Maffei, *Comm. urb.*, fol. CCCXCVII *verso* and Cesare Cesariano, *Vitruvius, De architectura*, (Como, 1521: rpt. New York, 1968), bk. I, ch. II, fol. XIII. Bernardino Baldi, *De verborum vitruvianorum significatione sive perpetuus in M. Vitruvium Pollione commentarius* (Augsburg, 1602), p. 164 summarizes sixteenth century Vitruvius commentators. Alberti's " concinnitas " has similar connotations. However, Cortesi's uses of both " ratio " and " symmetria " cannot always be rendered in this way or as systems of proportions but sometimes approach modern ideas of an historical style, manner, or of an architectural order such as Gothic symmetria. " Ratio symmetriae " seems to refer to principles or values belonging to a given type of rule or order as in Vitruvius, *Ten Books*, bk. III, ch. I, p. 159, which Granger translates as " method of symmetry ".

29 Frederick II Hohenstaufen (1194-1250) was Holy Roman Emperor. Cortesi is correct in seeing Frederick's building activity as important in the introduction of

German and French Gothic styles into Italy. The special place the Cistercians enjoyed under Frederick, the Emperor's trips to Germany and the Latin East during his short crusade (1228) brought him into contact with Gothic style. He built numerous buildings, of considerable size, throughout southern Italy and Sicily that often combine Gothic and Classical elements. The gloss " castrum capuanum " explicates the phrase " Campanian palace " in the text. This is probably the Hohenstaufen citadel in Naples which was Duke Alfonso's official residence and was transformed in the 1530's into the Palazzo dei Tribunali. It is just possible, however, that the gloss refers to the famous gateway at Capua (Campania). If the glossator is mistaken and Cortesi's " in campana domo " simply means southern Italy, Cortesi may be referring to Frederick's Castel del Monte in Apulia. For bibliography see L.H. Heydenreich, W. Lotz, *Architecture in Italy: 1400-1600* (Harmondsworth, 1974), pp. 354-356.

30 Martin IV (1281-1285), a Frenchman, Simon de Brion (Brie) was elected Pope at Viterbo, spent most of his reign at Orvieto and never lived in Rome. The " Falisci " were a South Etruscan tribe. Vitruvius, *Ten Books*, bk. VIII, ch. 3, p. 167, speaks of " Faliscus ager " as being on the Via Campana in the neighborhood of Corneto (Tarquinia). Falerii Veteres, capital of the Falisci and reconstructed nearby after 241 AD by the Romans as Falerii Novi, is present day Città Castellana, nearer Viterbo than Orvieto. Cortesi seems, however, to use the term " Faliscan " in a more general sense that would fit both cities. He may be referring to the Gothic papal palace at Orvieto, sometimes thought to have been begun under Martin IV (D. A. Valentino, " Il restauro del palazzo papale di Orvieto ", *Bollettino d'arte*, Anno LX, 1975, nos. 3-4, p. 209).

31 Cicero, *The Verrine Orations*, vol. II, p. 509, translates " extraordinariis cupiditatibus " as " abnormal passions ". It seems highly likely that Cortesi has already done what Gombrich attributes to Vasari (" Norm and Form " in *Norm and Form*, (London, 1966), p. 83). Cortesi models his attitude towards the Gothic style on Vitruvius's description of the licentious and unnatural decoration fashionable in his own day (Vitruvius, *Ten Books*, bk. VII, ch. V, p. 105). Cortesi's " extraordinaria cupiditas " also parallels the Vitruvian " iniquis moribus " or improper taste of the present. There is also a closely related parallel to Alberti, *Ten Books*, bk. VI, ch. I, p. 111, who laments that those who undertake new buildings run after the whims of the moderns. The original Latin is much stronger, " et qui forte per haec tempora aedificarent, novis ineptiarum deliramentis potius quam probatissimis laudatissimorum operum rationibus delectari ". Leon Battista Alberti, *L'architettura* (*De re aedificatoria*), G. Orlandi, ed. and trans., P. Portoghesi, notes, 2 vols., (Milan, 1966), p. 443. See also Manetti's definition of the German or modern style which flourished until Brunelleschi put an end to it, in Antonio di Tuccio Manetti, *The Life of Brunelleschi*, G. Enggass, trans., H. Saalman, intro. and notes, (University Park, Pa., 1970), lines 18, 530.

32 We have interpreted this text as a reference to the new Renaissance architecture as exemplified by Alberti and Bramante with its claim to authority based on its new truth to the standards of ancient art. Note, however, that Cortesi the Ciceronian is not content with this appeal to tradition alone, but praises the new architecture on grounds of utility, the Aristotelian argument in justification of art which permeates Cortesi's entire chapter and treatise.

33 Here " vestibulum " appears to be an " andito ", a room, passage or corridor connecting the front entrance of the palace with the courtyard and perpendicular to the facade. See Frommel, *Palastbau*, vol. I, p. 54. For a masterly discussion of the parts of the Roman palace and their names, see Frommel, *Palastbau*, vol. I, pp. 53-94, and further V. Fontana, P. Morachiello, *Vitruvio e Raffaello: Il ' De Architectura ' di Vitruvio nella traduzione inedita di Fabio Calvo Ravennate* (Rome, 1975), pp. 40-44.

34 The annotations (fol. X 2 *verso*) read " Circumpedes, qui circum pedes eunt; uulgo stapherii uocantur; Cic. in Verrem "; (fol. X 3 *verso*) " Ephippium est sella uel stratum equorum ornamentum ἀπὸ τοῦ ἐπὶ καὶ ἵππον Graeci equum dicunt: unde ephippiarii qui faciunt ephippa ". In bk. II, ch. 6 of *De Card.* Cortesi discusses the various types of horses a cardinal should use as well as their gaits. Cortesi advocates the Italian style of horseback riding over the Spanish and French. Priscianese, *Governo*, p. 4, suggests 40 horses are needed. British horses have the most pleasing, natural walking gait (*gradiundi genus*). Experience is, finally, the best judge of the type to be used. When Cardinal Lang entered Rome in 1511 after the alliance between Julius II and the Emperor Maximilian, the Pope according to Paride de Grassis, the papal master

of Ceremonies, " ... misit eius [Lang's] domum unam mulam phaleratam et ornatam sicut Cardinales solent habere..." (see text in C. O'Reilly, " ' Maximus Caesar et Pontifex Maximus ': Giles of Viterbo proclaims the alliance between Emperor Maximilian and Pope Julius II ", in *Augustiniana*, XXII (1972), pp. 80-117; at p. 113.

35 This corresponds to the entrance of the Greek house in Vitruvius, *Ten Books*, bk. VI, ch. VII, pp. 45-47.

36 The annotation (fol. X 1 *recto*) reads, " Armamentarium est repositorium armorum, ex quo miror quod in scalis palatinis inscriptum sit munitio armorum pro armamentario ". A similar room, used as an armory, is described by Baldi in the palace at Urbino (Bernardino Baldi, " Descrizione del palazzo ducale d'Urbino " in *Versi e prose scelte di Bernardino Baldi*, (Florence, 1859), *Descrizione*, p. 552). See Frommel, *Palastbau*, vol. I, pp. 4 ff. Rooms on the ground floor are often vaulted to give additional support to the structures built over them, but it is likely that the armory is vaulted to give it greater strength in the event of an explosion of gun powder. From this point on, the discussion of the palace is loosely modeled on Alberti, *Ten Books*, bk. V, chs. II, III, pp. 84 ff., but Cortesi's description is far more explicit and the disposition of rooms could be reconstructed; something that is not true of Alberti's description.

37 Alberti, *Ten Books*, bk. V, ch. II, p. 84, " Vestibules, halls, and the like places or publick receptions in houses ought to be like squares and other open places in Cities, not in remote private corners, but in the center and most publick places ".

" Atrium " seems to refer to the courtyard as a whole. It is like a forum since it is an arcaded open space for public use. The compluvium is the open center of the court. This is a modernization of Vitruvius, *Ten Books*, bk. VI, ch. III, pp. 24-29. See Frommel, *Palastbau*, vol. I, pp. 54-58. Cesariano, *Vitruvius*, bk. VII, fol. CXVII *recto*, uses " ambulatione " as Cortesi does: " cioè portico aperto ". We have, however, avoided the use of the English word " portico " as ambiguous and use " loggia " wherever possible. The confusion generated by this passage in Vitruvius is reflected in Fra Giocondo's illustration of the noble's house in his edition of Vitruvius, *M. Vitruvii de Architectura* (Florence, F. Giunta, 1522), p. 110 *verso*, where a " vestibolo " and " atrio " in the facade wing open onto a " cavaedio " (or atrium). Raphael, on the other hand, was convinced that Vitruvius intended a two-part arrangement consisting of vestibule and atrium (courtyard). See Frommel, *Palastbau*, vol. I, pp. 54-56 and Fontana and Morachiello, *Vitruvio e Raffaello*, pp. 40-43.

38 The guest-rooms are apparently located primarily in the east wing as at Urbino (Baldi, *Descrizione*, p. 559). This corresponds to Vitruvius, *Ten Books*, bk. VI, ch. VII, p. 49; on the Greek house also, Cicero, *De officiis*, W. Miller, trans., (Cambridge, Mass., 1913), vol. I, pp. 142-145 and Frommel, *Palastbau*, vol. I, p. 80. Alberti, *Ten Books*, bk. V, ch. XVII, pp. 105, 107.

39 Neapolitan troops lost the battle against the Spanish on the banks of the river Garigliano on Dec. 27, 1502. The battle and the Cardinal's generosity are also mentioned in *De Card.*, (fol. NN 5 *recto*). See also P. Pieri, *La Battaglia del Garigliano del 1503* (Rome, 1938). The hospitality of the Cardinal fits with the ideal of " magnificenzia " and " liberalità " elaborated in Pontano's, *I trattati delle virtù sociali*, [1498], F. Tateo, ed. and trans., (Rome, 1965), specially pp. 146, 184 ff. Possibly Cortesi refers to the family palace in Naples (see note 81). The Roman Sanseverino palace as described in the time of Cardinal Francesco Gonzaga (D. S. Chambers, " Gonzaga ", pp. 32-33) was far too small for so many guests, although (p. 38, n. 122) it did once house 50 guests. Cardinal Sanseverino enlarged the residence or had another one. However, in 1510 Albertini mentions only the Sant'Agata palace. Cortesi's description of the Cardinal's gem room (p. 108, note 65) also seems to imply an elaborate residence.

40 In the Latin text, " gratuitam " refers to the library and suggests its use was free of charge. The gloss, however, implies that access was unimpeded. Cortesi locates the library in the east wing and, like the guest rooms, near the entrance to the palace. Vitruvius, *Ten Books*, bk. VI, ch. IV, p. 35, recommends that libraries should look to the east for the sake of the morning light and to preserve the books from dampness. (In this section, Vitruvius also prescribes the siting of a number of other rooms as does Cortesi). Baldi, *Descrizione*, p. 561, however, praises the siting of the library at Urbino which faces west. Pliny, *Letters and Panegyricus*, B. Radice, trans., (Cambridge, Mass., 1969), vol. I, bk. II, ch. XVII, p. 133 describes a room in his villa as " built round in an apse to let in the sun as it moves round... and with one wall fitted with shelves like a library to hold the books which I read... ". For the great libraries of fifteenth

century Rome, see Frommel, *Palastbau*, vol. I, p. 90, such as those in the Palazzo Medici and the Vatican, and Albertini, *Opusculum*, pp. 529-532. He says that it was possible for visitors to study in the Medici library even when the Cardinal was there. The creation of libraries and generosity in allowing scholars to use them had become expressions of private and public virtue in a ruler and laudible examples of " magnificentia ". See Cortesi, *De Card.* (fol. NN 2 *recto*) where Nicholas V, Cosimo de' Medici, Matthias Corvinus, Federico of Urbino, Lorenzo il Magnifico and Cardinal Giovanni of Aragon are mentioned to illustrate this point. Pontano in his *De magnificentia*, p. 101, singles out Cosimo de' Medici as reviving antiquity in this respect. See below, note 77.

41 The annotation (fol. X 1 *recto*) reads, "Auditorium, locus ubi auditur, et hic accipitur pro loco audientiae in domo ". However, " auditorium " is particularly Ciceronian and hence a natural choice for Cortesi. What is more, as the gloss makes clear, this is not a music but a reading room. The note also indicates that reading aloud is the norm. Undoubtedly lectures were also given here. See below, note 63. For the music room see below, note 45. Cortesi continued the discussion of magnificence mentioned in the preceding note by urging upon the cardinal the encouragement of public study. Such activity, Cortesi felt, was fitting to the cardinal's dignity since patronage of learning is one of the great features of Cortesi's picture of the cardinal. Further, Cortesi wants his cardinals to build " national seminaries " (" domus sapientiae ") which in Rome were paid for by Jewish taxes. Cortesi contrasts the public " studium " (university) of Rome which is run for the glory of the city with such seminaries run for the glory of the Church, (fols. NN 2 *recto*, *verso*).

42 This passage bears some resemblance to Vitruvius's description of the acoustics of theaters in *Ten Books*, bk. V, ch. VIII, p. 293, but the round form of the room is not mentioned. However, a room proposed by Raphael in his designs for the Villa Madama was to have a cupola over a square plan. (Foster, " Raphael ", p. 310). Interestingly enough, however, Cortesi's account is close to Alberti's description of " curiae "; particularly of the " priest's court " which may have a vaulted roof and where " something [must be done] to prevent the voice from ascending too high and being lost " (Alberti, *Ten Books*, bk. VIII, ch. IX, p. 182). See below, note 43.

43 See Vitruvius, *Ten Books*. bk. VI, ch. IV, p. 35. Under Leo X, the Stanza della Segnatura may have served both as a music room and summer apartment. It is indeed in the north wing of the Vatican palace. (Shearman, " Stanze ", p. 21). On the other hand, Alberti specifically prescribes a flat ceiling supported on beams, instead of vaults, for any room in which the human voice is to be heard (*Ten Books*, bk. I, ch. IX, p. 93).

44 " Coclearae " is annotated as " Cochlearius pseudothyrus, pseudothyrus est quasi falsum hostium et sumitur pro postico, hic accipitur pro scalis posticalis quae uulgo limaces dicuntur (fol. X 2 *recto*) ". Frommel, *Palastbau*, vol. I, p. 65, vol. III, pl. 85 c, also notes that spiral staircases are used for private or service stairs as in the Palazzo Giraud.

45 See also Pirotta, " Music and Cultural Tendencies ", p. 156. He seems mistaken in his rejection of the function of the " musica triclinia ". Vitruvius, *Ten Books*, bk. V, ch. V, pp. 277, 281, 283, and ch. VIII, p. 293, discusses these resounding vessels usually made of bronze but sometimes, for the sake of economy, of earthenware, and used in theaters. See above note 23. This is picked up by Alberti, *Ten Books*, bk. VIII, ch. VII, p. 179. For other round rooms see above, note 23. Frommel, *Palastbau*, vol. I, p. 53, believes this room is a fantasy " all'antica ", not based on an actual room.

46 It is actually rather rare for the staircase to be located in the north wing of a Roman palace. See the Cancelleria, Palazzo Giraud and the Ducal palace at Urbino. Frommel, *Palastbau*, vol. I, pp. 61, 62, n. 38. Baldi, *Descrizione*, p. 553, says that such stairs are preferable because the visitor turns to the left as he ascends; a " natural " arrangement because the right half of the body moves with greater ease than the left. The main stairs of the Palazzo Farnese originally (before 1534) faced northeast. This siting protected the visitor from getting the sun in his eyes as he climbed (C. L. Frommel, verbal communication). Cortesi described not a winding stair but rather a dogleg stair without a well. See the Palazzo Giraud and the Cancelleria. (Frommel, *Palastbau*, vol. I, p. 60-64). See also, N. Pevsner, et al., *A Dictionary of Architecture* (London, 1975), pp. 482-483.

47 Cortesi refers to stairs in the Cortile del Belvedere. The annotation (fol. X 3 *verso*) reads, " Fornicata via, fornix est arcus in aedificiis et concameratio,

hic accipitur pro illa uia concamerata facta a Julio II Bramante architecto quae a palatio ad suburbanum ducit ". Cortesi's use of the term " via fornicata " for these Belvedere stairs is a reminder of the degree to which contemporaries saw the functional aspect of stairways. Cf. Shearman, " Stanze ", p. 25, n. 6. Cortesi's annotator misunderstands the text for he describes a vaulted tract of the Belvedere courtyard rather than a staircase with landings. Cortesi seems to refer to the stairs at the eastern wall of the intermediate (grotto) court. See J. S. Ackerman, *The Cortile del Belvedere* (Vatican, 1954), pl. 1, location no. 12. See also Frommel's forthcoming book on the Vatican under Popes Julius II and Leo X.

48 In other words, the flights double back over each other as they do in the Palazzo Giraud - Torlonia. In this way only one flight at a time can be seen and the total distance cannot be judged. Alberti, *Ten Books*, bk. I, ch. 13, p. 19, advocates many landings to prevent fatigue.

49 According to Aristotle an unnatural movement would be a light thing, such as fire, moving downwards or a heavy body, such as an earthly body, moving upwards. For Cortesi, since man is an earthly body, upward motion is, in him, unnatural. See Aristotle, *The Physics*, P. H. Wicksteed and F.M. Cornford, trans., (Cambridge, Mass., 1935), vol. II, p. 309; and *On the Soul, etc.*, pp. 33-34.

50 As in the Palazzo Giraud-Torlonia, see Frommel, *Palastbau*, vol. III, pl. 85 d. The world " calce " in the gloss means " foot " of the stairs, but both Rodocanachi, *Rome au temps de Jules II et Léon X*, p. 22 and Frommel, *Palastbau*, vol. I, p. 53, conclude that the head of the stairs on the first floor or piano nobile is meant. The text suggests, however, that Cortesi envisages the major-domo's room on the ground floor. In the Vatican, it is near the Scala Regia (Frommel, verbal communication).

51 Frommel, *Palastbau*, vol. I, p. 53 sees this " iuris dicendi locus " as a separate room but it may also simply be another function of the major-domo's room. A cardinal's judicial duties included his own household. He was expected to maintain a tribunal to settle problems within the " familia ". Usually an auditor (here, for Cortesi, the major-domo) would have jurisdiction over all the personnel of the palace; see Mollat, " Contribution ", p. 80. The annotation (fol. X 2 *verso* and 3 *recto*) reads, " Discubitoria multa, accumbo, recumbo, et discumbo, hinc discubitus et discubitorius: hic accipitur pro poena, qua familiaribus Car. pro delicto interdicitur caena uel prandio ".

52 Frommel, *Palastbau*, vol. I, p. 53, seems to read " domus architriclinii " as a sort of pantry, but " chief-steward " corresponds to C. T. Lewis and C. Short, *A Latin Dictionary* (Oxford, 1969), p. 154. See also Baldi, *Commentarius*, pp. 127-128. The annotation (fol X 2 *recto*) reads, " Cellae obsonariae, obsonium Graeca uox est, et est quicquid praeter panem et uinum additur cibo: hic accipitur obsonaria cella pro repositorio rerum pertinentium ad conuiuium ". The annotation (fol. X 3 *recto*) reads, " Delibatorii, a libo, delibo, praelibo, prolibo unde libatio et libatorius: hic accipitur pro cella ientatoria ".

53 This is the first specific indication in the text that we are ascending to another storey. Compare Rodocanachi, *Rome au Temps de Jules II et Léon X*, pp. 22-23, and Frommel, *Palastbau*, vol. I, p. 53. Note that the term " peristylium " is used to describe the upper storey. Apparently Cortesi's ideal palace also had colonnades on the upper storey which overlooked the cortile. See F.M. Grapaldi, *De partibus aedium, lexicon utilissimum* (Basel, 1533), p. 9. The " sala grande " or " aula magna " is a traditional feature of the palace. See Frommel, *Palastbau*, vol. I, pp. 66-70. In the Vatican the Sala Regia had this title and function. See Shearman, " Stanze ", p. 26, n. 6. Cortesi's description of the " Sala " alludes to the distinction between palaces and private houses, as in Alberti, *Ten Books*, bk. V, ch. II, pp. 84-85. This seems to be a commonplace.

54 Cortesi's " sala grande " receives light both from the east and west since it is located in the east or facade wing of the palace. The winter sun rises east-southeast so, in order to receive its direct light, the chapel must be located on the east wall of the " Sala ". Vitruvius, *Ten Books*, bk. VI, ch. IV, p. 35, says rooms used in autumn should look east while western light is best for winter rooms. Thus, Cortesi's " sala grande " is designed to be used all year round. Interest in the " winter rising sun " seems to come, however, from Hippocrates, *Air, Waters, Places*, p. 69. See also Alberti, *Ten Books*, bk. V, ch. XVII, p. 104. For the seasonal use of rooms in the Vatican palace; see G. Dehio, *Bauprojecte*, p. 246 as cited by Shearman, " Stanze ", p. 26, n. 7. The Papal " Sala " in Palazzo Farnese

faces southeast. The idea that it should be possible to hear Mass from a room adjacent to the chapel is reflected in the arrangements of several Roman palaces and in the Vatican. We have not, however, been able to find an example just like Cortesi's, although there was a connection between the " sala grande " of the Cancelleria and the church of S. Lorenzo in Damaso. See also, L. Partridge, " Divinity and Dynasty at Caprarola ", *Art Bulletin* LX, Sept. 1978, pp. 494-530, p. 495, fig. 1, for the audience chamber connected with a chapel and a side room for hearing Mass unobserved.

55 The " penates " or " penates diui " were the Roman gods of the hearth. Compare with Maffei, *Comm. urb.*, fol. CCCXCVIII *recto*. This passage is a variant on Alberti, *Ten Books*, bk. V, ch. XVII, p. 105 on the country house.

56 The annotation (fol. X 7 *recto*) reads, " Salutatoris, a saluto, salutaris, salutatio, salutiger, salutator et salutatorium: quod locus in quem salutantes introducuntur ". Note that the gloss indicates that the chamber or alcove where audiences are held is actually within the great hall. An arrangement of this sort would seem to be used in the Palazzo Vecchio in Florence where the " udienza " forms a platform across one end of the " sala grande ". Cortesi's " udienza " is, however, closed off. Cf. Frommel, *Palastbau*, vol. I, pp. 66 ff. on " sale grandi " known to Cortesi. For audience halls and other large reception rooms in the Vatican, see Shearman, " Stanze ", pp. 5, 17 *et passim*. The Stanza d'Eliodoro may have served at one time as " udienza ".

57 Alberti, *Ten Books*, bk. V, ch. II, p. 84.

58 That is, the Palazzo Venezia. Rodocanachi, *Rome au Temps de Jules II et Léon X*, p. 22, believes that these rooms imitate those in German palaces, but it seems more likely that Cortesi is simply referring to rooms in Gothic style.

59 Rodocanachi, *Rome au Temps de Jules II et Léon X*, p. 22, gives a confused reading here. A peephole of a similar kind was provided for Julius II in the wall of the Sistine Chapel so that he could look at the cardinals assembled for prayers. Alberti, *Ten Books*, bk. V, ch. II, III, pp. 84, 86, mentions such contrivances for hearing and approves of their use, although he specifies that they are suitable for the houses of tyrants. See also our note 63. The annotation (fol. X 7 *recto*) reads, " Spectatoriae fistulae, specto frequentatium signat saepe seu fixe intucror [sic — intueor] hinc spectacula et spectatorius ". The next (fol. X 1 *recto*) reads, "Auscultatorii tubi, auscultatorius, -a, -um, ab ausculto: quod significat audio: uide Cicero in Topicis " [sic] cf. *De partitione oratoria*, 3, 10. Cortesi (fol. N 3 *recto*) tells that Cardinal Raffaele Riario wished to build " a bigger " audience hall in order to have greater opportunity to watch his visitors walking and thereby to judge their character.

60 The dining room is thus in the west wing overlooking the gardens in back of the palace. For " dining " Cortesi uses " accubatio " that is, dining in a reclining position in the antique fashion. The annotation (fol. X 7 *verso*) reads, " Topiarium est opus ex frutice [sic] factum, et dicitur απὸ τόν τòπον uide Pli. Cecilium ". " Xystus " has a variety of related meanings. It is most often a covered walk or portico, cf. Baldi, *Commentarius*, p. 11. However, Cortesi may be using it in the sense given it by Cesariano, *Vitruvius*, bk. V, fol. LXXXVIII *verso*, as two " portici " between which trees are planted where one can walk. Cesariano also goes on to discuss the use of topiary work. For " xystus ", see Vitruvius, *Ten Books*, bk. V, ch. XI, p. 311, a tree-lined walk and bk. VI, ch. VII, p. 49; also Alberti, *Ten Books*, bk. IX, ch. IV, p. 193, in his description of the gardens of a private house. Raphael also describes the " xysto " of the Villa Madama in the same way (Foster, " Raphael ", p. 310). Pliny, however, writing in the *Letters*, vol. I, bk. II, ch. XVII, pp. 138-39 uses " xystus " to mean a terrace. Most recently, J. J. Pollitt, *Sources and Documents in the History of Art. The Art of Rome* c. 753 B.C.-337 A.D. (Englewood Cliffs, N.J., 1966), p. 173, translates " xystus " as " open walk ".

For the pleasantness of dining, compare Alberti, *Ten Books*, bk. V, ch. II, p. 85, " The apartments where princes eat should be in the noblest part of the palace; it should stand high and command a fine prospect of sea, hills, and wide views, which gives it an air of greatness ". Vitruvius, *Ten Books*, bk. VI, ch. III, p. 33 describes the Greek dining room which is arranged so that " the guests, under cover, may have a view of the garden " " viridia ", not " xystus "). For dining rooms in Roman palaces, see Frommel, *Palastbau*, vol. I, pp. 82-85. In the Vatican, the Stanza dell'Incendio probably served as dining room for Leo X, if not before. See Shearman, " Stanze ", pp. 22-23.

[61] The annotation (fol. X 2 *recto*) reads, " Cellam argentarium accipitur pro repositorio uasorum ex argento: uulgo credentia dicitur ". Frommel, *Palastbau*, vol. I, p. 70, interprets this as a credenza-like piece of furniture, but Cortesi may mean that the cabinets are built in (see below, note 65). For a similar arrangement in the Palazzo Venezia see Magnuson, *Quattrocento*, p. 285. Ascanio Sforza in a letter to his brother Lodovico, Oct. 22, 1484, wrote of the Borgia palace " ... haveva una credenza tutta piena de vasi de argento et oro molto ben lavorati ultra li altri piati... ". (Text in Pastor, *History*, vol. V, p. 529, in Magnuson, *Quattrocento*, p. 240.

In the Vatican, silver was stored in a guardaroba in the Torre Borgia which was a logical place for safekeeping and was located next to the dining room (probably the Stanza dell'Incendio, during Leo's pontificate). See Shearman, " Stanze ", p. 22 ff.

[62] The text is annotated, " Lucubratorio, a lucubro quod est uigilo lucubratorium " (fol. X 4 *verso*). Maffei, *Comm. urb.*, fol. CCCXCVIII *verso*, traces the word to Suetonius and testifies to its frequent modern use. These rooms lie on the south side of the east wing of the second floor. Alberti, *Ten Books*, bk. V, ch. XVII, p. 107, says that a man of elegance uses several parlors and bedrooms and thus, presumably, also several studies.

[63] The gloss indicates that the stairs should have hearing devices while the text locates them in the night study. Alberti, *Ten Books*, bk. V, ch. XVII, p. 107, says that the master's bedroom should open into the library and be near the gem room. This is substantially Cortesi's arrangement as well. Alberti advocated the use of hearing tubes in the aula (see our note 59). Francesco di Giorgio, however, says that these devices may be anywhere in the house. He recommends them so that the master can know what is going on everywhere and so that the servants will remember this. Francesco illustrates such a tube in a drawing of " case di principi " (Francesco di Giorgio, *Trattati*, vol. II, p. 559, pl. 207). Cortesi gives a more elevated rationale for the same technique.

[64] The annotation: " Dactylotheca, Graeci anulum dactylion uocant, unde dactylotheca, quae est repositorium gemmarum ". (fol. X 2 *verso*). See Pliny, *Natural History*, Bks. XXXVI-XXXVII, D.E. Eichholz, ed. and trans., (Cambridge, Mass., 1962) bk. XXXVII, p. 170 and Maffei, *Comm. urb.*, fol. CCCXCVI *recto*. This room may be located further up on the same staircase or, conceivably, just slightly further along the corridor on the same floor. In the Palazzo Vecchio in Florence, the " tesoro " is, in fact, a short flight up from the " studiolo ". For the gem room in the Palazzo Venezia, see Magnuson, *Quattrocento*, p. 285 and Frommel, *Palastbau*, vol. I, p. 90.

[65] These gems and valuables were largely collections of antiquities and antique imitations. They provided a great thesaurus of motifs which were also used in the monumental arts. The famous Medici gem collection was originally acquired from Paul II and provides an excellent example of what Cortesi meant. See N. Dacos, A. Giuliano and U. Pannuti, *Le Gemme*, vol. I of *Il Tesoro di Lorenzo Il Magnifico*, N. Dacos, ed., (Florence, 1973), p. 5; for Barbo's collection see also E. Müntz, *Les Arts à la cour des papes pendant le XVe et le XVIe siècles* (Paris, 1878-1887), vol. II, pp. 181-287 and R. Weiss, *Un Umanista veneziano: Papa Paolo II* (Venice, 1958). Cesariano, *Vitruvius*, bk. VII, fol. CXIII interprets " Sigilatione " as " intagliatura sculpta ". There seem to be differences between the cases or chests (" arcula ") recommended by Cortesi and the " tabula " used for display by Cardinal Sanseverino. The annotation (fol. X 2 *recto*) reads, " Anaglypticum atramentarium, anaglypta accipiunt nomen ab asperitate, quia eminent in rebus caelatis, uulgo releuia dicunt ". In 1505, Sanuto described the collection of Cardinal Grimani in the Palazzo Venezia. It was housed in a credenza (see above, note 61) and was valued at between fifteen and twenty thousand ducats. See M. Sanuto, *I Diarii*, G. Berchet, ed., (Venice, 1881), vol. VI, col. 172.

The annotation (fol. X 1 *recto*) reads, " Auctionaria licitatione, auctio nomen ab augeo, et ponitur pro uenditione quae fit per accrectionem pretii, unde auctionarius, -a, -um. Vide Ciceronem in Rulum [sic] ".

[66] Directly from Vitruvius, *Ten Books*, bk. VI, ch. IV, p. 35. Also Alberti, *Ten Books*, bk. V, ch. XVIII, p. 110.

[67] It is interesting that " artificum ", which can denote either an artist or an artisan, is automatically interpreted here by the glossator in its highest sense as " painter ". Renaissance artists were struggling in precisely these years for a status that could not be confused with that of the artisan. For R. Maf-

fei's appreciation and knowledge of artists of his day see his *Comm. urb.*, fols. CCC *recto-verso* (reprinted in Müntz, *Les Arts à la cour des papes*, pp. 304-305).

68 Apparently Cortesi means "libri mastri" and "libri giornali", with their summaries of "dare" and "avere". A similar interest in the description of musical technique in Cortesi is noted by Pirotta, "Music and Cultural Tendencies", p. 157.

69 It is not clear just who the "graphis" is: a general designer, an engraver, a carver of intaglio? However, in Vitruvius, *Ten Books*, bk. I, ch. 1, p. 18, the word denotes Apelles' skill with a pencil. Workshops of the kind Cortesi recommends also existed at the Vatican in the Belvedere. For the Vitruvian and Albertian sources of this whole passage see above note 66. Cesariano, *Vitruvius*, bk. IV, notes that the term can mean both drawing and engraving. For the importance of Poliziano in defining "graphice" for the Renaissance as "disegno", see V. Jüren, "Politien et la théorie des arts figuratifs", in *Bibliothèque d'Humanisme et Renaissance*, XXXVII (1975), pp. 131-138. Baldi, *Commentarius*, pp. 82-83, unhesitatingly equates "graphein" with "disegno".

70 The following sentences make it clear that Cortesi is not speaking of marble reliefs.

71 Cristoforo Foppa, il Caradosso (c. 1452 - c. 1527). The Milanese goldsmith, medalist and antiquary was in Rome ca. 1477 and resided there in October 1505 and thereafter. The foundation medals of new St. Peter's are attributed to him. He worked for a wide variety of distinguished patrons, both as an artist and as an appraiser. His fame among contemporaries was so great that they compared him with Leonardo. Cellini singles him out for praise both in the autobiography and in his treatise on goldsmithing. See R. Weiss, "The Medals of Pope Julius II (1503-1513)", *Journal of the Warburg and Courtauld Institutes*, vol. XXVIII (1965), pp. 163-182, for information and bibliography. Cardinal Giovanni of Aragon, a son of the King of Naples, was a patron of literary men and artists. See *De Card.* (fol. NN 2 *recto*), where Cortesi praises him for maintaining a library. Raffaele Maffei accompanied the Cardinal on a trip to Hungary in the winter of 1479.

72 The annotations read (fol. X 1 *recto*), "Admissionales, admissionale ab admitto, sunt cubicularii qui introducunt salutantes. Vide Lampridium in uita Alex. Caesaris" and (fol. X 1 *recto*), "Anteambulones, ab ambulo, anteambulo, qui honoris causa aliquem Cardinalem praecedunt comitando". This seems the nearest modern equivalent to the "forerunner", who preceeds the cardinal in procession. "Scutiferro" mentioned in the gloss seems to be a squire or page rather than a man at arms. The annotation (fol. X 1 *verso*) reads, "Archiatri latine princeps medicorum qui et protomedici a conciliatore dicuntur".

73 That is, for similar ease of access to the great hall. Note that Cortesi begins at this point to describe the third floor of the palace.

74 These would now seem to be corridors. Frommel, *Palastbau*, vol. I, p. 91, shows how corridors first developed on upper floors of palaces. In Cortesi's ideal palace, they serve a specifically defensive function. They may, indeed, have been introduced by analogy with corridors in fortifications. Privacy for the inhabitants is certainly not at issue.

75 The annotation (fol. X 4 *recto*) reads, "Interregis, interregnum dicitur id tempus quo regnum Rege uac. i. antequam inde mortui locum nouus Rex creatur, et interrex qui interea locum Regis tenet". Civil disorder and looting were particularly frequent in Rome during those periods of decreased papal authority after a pope's death.

76 See above, note 27, e.g., humanistic learning and the rediscovery of antiquity. The term "progressio" was especially popular in Cicero; see Lewis and Short, *Latin Dictionary*, p. 1461.

77 Cosimo de' Medici (1389-1464) was *de facto* ruler of Florence. The Cortesi were Medici partisans. Both Paolo and his brother, Alessandro, maintained close contact with Florentine circles, and their mother was a Florentine Aldobrandini. Alessandro had hoped to advance in the Church through the patronage of Lorenzo il Magnifico and Paolo dedicated his *De hominibus doctis* to him. Cosimo was one of the great patrons of the revival of art "all'antica"; see E.H. Gombrich, "The Early Medici as Patrons of Art" in *Norm and Form*, (London, 1966), pp. 35-57; A. D. Fraser-Jenkins, "Cosimo de' Medici's Patronage of Architecture and the Theory of Magnificence", *Journal of the Warburg and Courtauld Institutes*, vol. XXXIII, (1970), pp. 162-170, where Maffeo Vegio's defense of Cosimo is discussed. See also Vespasiano da Bisticci's life of Cosimo in *Renais-*

sance Princes, Popes and Prelates (New York, 1963), pp. 213-234. Cortesi parallels Pontano's appreciation of Cosimo, in *De magnificentia* p. 101, and, at p. 103, " Ad Cosmi auctoritatem addidere plurimum tum villae diversis in locis ab ipso aedificatae singulari cum magnificentia, tum domus, in qua condenda pervetustum atque obliteratum iam structurae morem modumque revocavit, qui mihi id videtur egisse, ut discerent posteri qua via aedificarent ".

78 Cortesi refers here to the rusticated facade of the Palazzo Medici in Florence which he derives from the Forum of Trajan. Cortesi seems to be thinking of the rusticated back wall of the Forum of Augustus.

79 Federico da Montefeltro, Duke of Urbino (1422-1484) was one of the great condottieri of the Renaissance. See the biography in Vespasiano, *Renaissance Princes, Popes and Prelates*, pp. 83-114. Among the victories which brought him great spoils was the sack of Volterra, Raffaele Maffei's home town, in 1472. (Cf. *De Card.* fol. T 5 *recto*.) Maffei's brother, Antonio, took part in the Pazzi Conspiracy against the Medici in 1478 as revenge for the Sack of Volterra; see Angelo Poliziano, *Della Congiura dei Pazzi*, A. Perosa, ed., (Padua, 1958), pp. 19-20.

On Federico's building activity see L. H. Heydenreich, " Federico da Montefeltro as a Building Patron ", *Studies in Renaissance and Baroque Art presented to Anthony Blunt on his 65th Birthday* (London, 1967), pp. 1-6; C.H. Clough, " Federico da Montefeltro's Patronage of the Arts, 1468-1482 ", *Journal of the Warburg and Courtauld Institutes*, XXXVI (1973), pp. 129-144, who suggests that Federico's architectural patronage was a spur to papal patronage in the reconstruction of Rome in the early sixteenth century (pp. 142-143). Cortesi may actually be thinking of the drafted marble ashlars on the Urbino palace facade.

80 Cortesi refers to the ground floor of the palace of Innocent VIII (the south wing of the lower palace between the courtyard and the atrium of St. Peter's). This wing housed the Camera Apostolica. Between the large central " audientia rotae " and the staircase to the west, were four rooms housing papal offices including that of the " plumbum ". A drawing by A. Sangallo, the Younger, shows the disposition of the rooms (Uffizi 715 A). See further H. Egger, " Das päpstliche Kanzleigebäude im 15 Jahrhundert ", in *Mitteilungen des österreichischen Staatsarchivs*, II (Vienna, 1951), pp. 487 ff. and Magnuson, *Quattrocento*, p. 146.

Cortesi only mentions buildings that he assumes to be well-known to his readers but the date and attribution of this part of the Vatican palace had become lost to modern scholarship. C.L. Frommel has, however, found the following reference of 1483 which confirms Cortesi's value as an historical source and which now clarifies an important element in the building history of the Vatican under Sixtus IV. Since Cortesi's reference occurs in the section on exterior decoration it may be inferred that he is praising the architecture itself, perhaps including the rooms and logge on the floor above the papal offices. Antonio de Vascho, *Il Diario della Città di Roma, Rerum Italicorum Scriptores*, vol. 23/3 (Città di Castello, 1911), p. 506. " Ricordo come fino dell'anno 1483 fu cominciata a fare la Audientia, cioè l'edificio nuovo del palazzo del papa a mano dritta verso Santo Pietro, dove di sotto deve essere detta Audientia e Rota e di sopra stantie da prelati con loggie e corritori fino alla loggia della beneditione sopra le scale di Santo Pietro, e la fece fare papa Sisto con grande fretta, e li travertini cavati in piazza Giudea furono messi in quello lavoro ".

81 Roberto Sanseverino, Prince of Salerno (1418-1487) was a condottiere in the pay of various Italian princes and governments. He was the nephew of Francesco Sforza. His palace in Naples now forms part of the facade of the church of the Gesù. See Heydenreich and Lotz, *Architecture in Italy: 1400-1600*, pp. 128, 356. Pontano in his *De magnificentia* (1498), in *I Trattati*, pp. 93-95 also mentions this palace and may be Cortesi's source. " Robertus, princeps Salernitanus, cum magnificam Neapoli domum aedificasset, ad caedendam comportandamque e Lucania materiam avare atque impotenter popularibus suis usus dicitur... Robertus, princeps Salernitanus, non mediocriter accusatur, quod in aedibus Neapolitanis multa a lapide ignobili, quae marmor requirerent, fieri passus sit... ".

82 The annotation (fol. X 7 *recto*) reads, " Suburbano palatino, ab urbe, urbicus, suburbium, surbubanum, quod est praedium seu uilla sub urbe ".

83 This is a problematic passage in all respects. " Descriptio aedificandi " is not the same as architecture itself but seems both a style or mode and the skills involved in its practice. " Artificiosius " continues this

double sense of style and skill. "Progressio temporis" also seems to imply a theory of development or improvement in the sense that Ghiberti and Alberti use it. See Krautheimer, "The Beginnings", pp. 257-273. It is not clear, though, that the working of time itself actually causes the application of greater and more numerous talents to architecture. Cortesi's positive and optimistic appreciation of the potential of his own times can be compared with his critique of modern literature in his *De hominibus doctis* (1490) and with the sermon of Giles of Viterbo. See J. O'Malley S.J., "Man's Dignity, God's Love and the Destiny of Rome. A Text of Giles of Viterbo", *Viator*, 3 (1972), pp. 389-416. Cortesi also makes comparable statements about the "revival of lost perfections" in lute playing in his chapter on Music, see Pirotta, "Music and Cultural Tendencies", p. 158.

84 For the building materials of Roman palaces see Frommel, *Palastbau*, vol. I, pp. 8-10. The use of travertine is characteristic of Roman architecture at the turn of the century, e.g. the facade of S. Pietro in Montorio and Bramante's cortile of S. Maria della Pace. Among palaces, the most relevant examples are the facades of the Cancelleria and Cardinal Adriano Castellesi's palace (Giraud-Torlonia). See below, note 85. Significantly, they are also three-storey facades articulated in the manner of the Colosseum. Flavio Biondo mentions "quadri lapides tiburtini" being taken from the Colosseum and burned for lime (Flavio Biondo, "Roma Instaurata", p. 310). Alberti, *Ten Books*, bk. VIII, ch. VII, p. 176, says that amphitheaters were decorated with "quadratus lapis". Alberti, *De re aedificatoria*, vol. II, p. 729 and Flavio Biondo (p. 305) also describe the Theater of Pompey (not an amphitheater) in this way.

85 The first palace mentioned is the Cancelleria located at the corner of the Campo dei Fiori, see above note 8. See A. Schiavo, *Il Palazzo della Cancelleria* (Rome, 1964) and Heydenreich and Lotz, *Architecture in Italy*, pp. 68-78. Built by Cardinal Raffaele Riario as the largest and most costly structure of its kind and time, it was the prime example in Cortesi's mind of the cardinal's palace. Cardinal Adriano Castellesi had just begun to build the present Palazzo Giraud-Torlonia in the Borgo. Frommel, *Palastbau*, vol. II, pp. 207-215, and Cortesi's text suggest that the travertine facade shown in 1516 in a drawing by Hermann Vischer was already under way. Castellesi was called the "rich cardinal" and enjoyed a yearly income of 10,000 ducats. He could afford the expense of a full travertine facade. Both Riario and Castellesi took travertine from various classical monuments (Frommel, *Palastbau*, vol. I, p. 9). Castellesi actually lived in a palace in the Piazza Navona (Frommel, *Palastbau*, vol. II, p. 212). Albertini, *Opusculum*, p. 525.

86 Alberti, *Ten Books*, bk. II, ch. X, p. 34, says that brick is so useful and beautiful that the Ancients made "even their palaces of brick". This derives from Vitruvius, *Ten Books*, bk. II, ch. VIII, pp. 117, 118, 125, 127, who also praises the palace of King Mausolus which had "all parts finished with Proconnesian marble (yet) it has walls made of brick". For similar praise of the brickwork and travertine of the palace at Urbino, see Baldi, *Descrizione*, pp. 549, 581. Brick is advocated as particularly suitable for buildings in Rome. Alberti, *Ten Books*, bk. II, ch. II, p. 24, praises modesty even in the buildings of the great, although he also sees the appropriateness of public magnificence. The use of brick was indeed much favored in Roman palaces as in the Palazzo Baldassini. This material is also occasionally used for columns and pilasters and faced with stucco as at the Villa Madama. Travertine is used for architraves and pilasters, see Frommel, *Palastbau*, vol. I, p. 9. The annotation (fol. X 3 *recto*) reads, "Epistylium est capitellum, quod super columnam ponitur: nam ἐπὶ supra στῦλος columnam quidam id esse dicunt, quod uulgo architrabs dicitur".

87 "Cementitia structura", see Vitruvius, *Ten Books*, bk. II, ch. IV, p. 94. It is clear neither what Vitruvius meant nor how Cortesi understood him. Cortesi, however, evidently uses the term here to designate a form of concrete construction. Alberti, *Ten Books*, bk. III, ch. XI, mentions the use of stone pilasters and of wall faced with plaster but for reasons of function not of decorum or decoration. See also Vitruvius, *Ten Books*, bk. II, ch. VIII, pp. 119-125; the palace of King Mausolus at Halicarnassus survived intact because its brick walls were faced with plaster. This construction was selected for the sake of "firmness" and not for lack of funds.

88 The annotations (fol. X 7 *verso*) read, "Tectorio, a tego, tectorium, quod est crusta ex calce ad murum tegendum et ornandum facta: uulgo tunicatum dicitur"; (fol. X 7 *recto*): "Scalpturato, a scalpo, scalpturio, scalptura, scalptum, scalpelere et scalsuratum

genus in quo albaria tretoria scalpto raduntur in superficie, uulgo sgrafiatum uocant ". For " scalpturo " see Vitruvius, *De Architectura*, bk. III, ch. V, p. 193, bk. IV, ch. I, p. 203 where it means carving. However, the closest parallel is in Pliny, *Natural History*, bk. XXXVII, 7, 30, " graving or cutting in stone ", and *ibid.* bk. XXXVII, 10, 63, para. 173 for the plural form. Cortesi night be thinking not of carved stucco but of sgraffito. Also K. Jex-Blake and E. Sellers, *The Elder Pliny's Chapters on the History of Art* (London, 1896), bk. XXXV, p. 180, n. 3.

Francesco Alidosi became a cardinal November 12, 1505 and was killed in 1511. See *Dizionario biografico degli italiani*, vol. II, (1960) pp. 373-376. He rented the newly built Palazzo S. Clemente (today Palazzo dei Penitenzieri) near the Vatican on the Piazza Scossacavallo built by Domenico della Rovere (Frommel, *Palastbau*, vol. I, pp. 13-14). The Alidosi palace is also mentioned by Albertini, *Opusculum*, p. 526, n. 1. Vasari says the facades were painted in " sgraffito " by Pintoricchio and some traces of the work are still visible. (C. Pericoli Ridolfini, *Le Case romane con facciate sgraffite e dipinte*, (cat.) (Rome, 1960), p. 85: Palazzo dei Penitenzieri). The painter's decorations of a " magnificent series of staterooms " on the piano nobile have vanished (Magnuson, *Quattrocento*, pp. 332-337). There was also a " sgraffito " representation of Vitruvius dressed in a toga and crowned with laurel, which was meant to portray the architect of the palace (D. Redig de Campos, *I Palazzi Vaticani*, (Bologna, 1967), p. 70).

Cortesi contrasts the stucco facade of the Alidosi residence with the use of travertine in the Castellesi palace which was being built directly across the street. The aesthetic preference for precious workmanship over precious materials is an antique theoretical distinction which Cortesi will pick up again later on p. 113, note 95, and which reflects contemporary arguments used in the *paragone* disputes on the relative merits of painting, sculpture and the other arts.

89 This idea is expounded by Alberti in the preface to his *Ten Books*, " Thucydides extremely commends the Prudence of some Ancients, who had so adorned their City with all sorts of fine Structures, that their Power thereby appeared to be much greater than it really was ". Also bk. V, ch. 1, cites the opinion of Euripides that " the multitude is naturally a very powerful enemy and if they added cunning and fraud to their strength, they would be invincible ". The dangers of the rabble are further expounded in this chapter. Compare also Vitruvius, *Ten Books*, bk. VI, ch. VIII, p. 57 and Cicero, *De officiis*, I, 39. This idea is attributed to Nicholas V in Giannozzo Manetti's biography of him. The appropriate Latin text is published by Magnuson, *Quattrocento*, pp. 351-62 and translated by Partner, *Renaissance Rome*, p. 16.

90 It is not quite clear whether admiration itself causes restraint or whether it allows crowds to be restrained more easily. In any event it seems not to be the beauty of the building but the power it represents that has this effect. For the dangers potential in the multitude, see note 89.

91 The house of Eugenius IV, Pope from 1431-1447, was at S. Maria in Trastevere, see Magnuson, *Quattrocento*, p. 223. The palace was not built by the Pope but was his temporary residence, (Pastor, *History*, vol. 1, pp. 294-5). Flavio Biondo gives an account of these events in *Decades*, II, vi. A republic was actually declared on May 29, 1434, and Eugenius fled on June 4, 1434. Aristotle speaks of contempt as a reason for the overthrow of monarchies (Aristotle, *Politics*, H. Rackham, ed. and trans., (London, 1932), p. 449, bk. V, 8, 1312).

92 The argument for sumptuous external decoration of palaces is one of Cortesi's most interesting and most rich in implication. It is clear that throughout this passage Cortesi is thinking both of the physical safety and the basis of political authority of the cardinals. Art and display are seen as instruments of papal control of the latent proletarian and republican sentiments of the Roman people as well as their representatives. The use of the term " tribunes ", probably for *tribunes plebis*, would seem to indicate the *Conservatori* of the City. A republic was established in Rome and Eugenius was expelled. See Pastor, *History*, vol. I, pp. 294-295. The annotation (fol. X 3 *verso*) reads, " Fasces numero pluri accipiuntur pro magistratibus et honoribus ".

93 The following passage is modeled on Alberti, *Ten Books*, bk. IX, ch. IV, on the ornamentation of a private house.

94 " Plastices " is a Greek genetive. In Vitruvius, *Ten Books*, bk. I, ch. 1, pp. 18-19, " rationes plasticae " is translated as " plastic arts " which makes no sense in our context. Indeed, Cesariano, *Vitruvius*,

fols. IX *recto* and *verso*, gives a gloss on the term as including all of sculpture as defined by Pliny. For Pliny, however, (Jex-Blake and Sellers, *Chapters*, bk. XXXIV, p. 28, bk. XXXV, p. 174) "plasticen" means modeling, particularly in clay. Grapaldi, *Lexicon*, p. 138 defines "plasticen" as the making of images in clay. This would seem to be Cortesi's meaning as well. Unlike Cortesi, Alberti generally prefers sculpture to painting for the decoration of churches and public places *Ten Books*, bk. VIII, chs. X, XV, XVII. See also bk. VI, ch. IX for stucco relief and bk. IX, ch. IV, p. 192 for decorations in private houses.

95 Here Cortesi seems to echo the *paragone* arguments so popular in the sixteenth century (see also above, note 88). He prefers painting to sculpture at least initially on utilitarian grounds. Painted decoration is less expensive, as impressive and far more lifelike. For cost as a factor in choosing painted over sculptural decoration later in the century, see B.F. Davidson, "The Decoration of the Sala Regia under Pope Paul III", *Art Bulletin* LVIII, Sept. 1976, p. 421. Cortesi may be the first cinquecento printed source explicitly to take this position. He omits sculpture from the ideal decoration of palaces. Alberti still advocated modesty for the houses of kings, magistrates and the rich (*Ten Books*, bk. IX, ch. I, pp. 186-187 and our notes 90-92) but admired sculptural decor. See J.B. Riess, "The Civic View of Sculpture in Alberti's, *De re aedificatoria*", *Renaissance Quarterly*, XXXII, Spring 1979, pp. 1-17.

96 Imitation of nature as the criterion for excellence in the painter is found in many places, but see Philostratus, *The Life of Apollonius of Tyana*, F.C. Conybeare, trans., (New York, 1921), vol. 1, pp. 173-179. "Historia" means the narrative mode in general. In *Ten Books*, bk. VIII, ch. X, p. 150. Alberti says that paintings and written accounts of history "both indeed are pictures, only the historian paints with words and the painter with his pencil". In *Della Pittura*, Alberti stresses the primacy of "historia" as the great work of the painter (*On Painting and On Sculpture*, p. 71). For the moral power of "historia" see below, notes 109 and 129.

97 Aristotle, *De motu animalium* in E. S. Forster, trans., *Parts of Animals, Progression of Animals*, (Cambridge, Mass., 1961), ch. 6, pp. 457-459, but see also Aristotle, *On the Soul*, bk. III, ch. IV, 427b27-429b8; ch. X, 433a9-433b1. For Aristotle, it is the motion of the soul that causes action in animals and humans. Aristotle's psychology allows for the soul to be moved through the stimulus of imagination coupled with the mental qualities of imagination and intellect. Cortesi does not follow Aristotle's reasoning exactly in this passage but sees art as stimulating all three of the psychological preconditions to action. Art has this effect because of its own power to imitate real things and actions convincingly. Aristotle, *The Politics*, H. Rackham, ed. and trans., (London 1932), bk. VIII, 1340a, pp. 657-659. Aristotle, *The Poetics*, W. Hamilton Fyfe, trans., (Cambridge, Mass., 1965), 1448b, pp. 13-14. The power of art to imitate nature is reiterated in Cortesi's discussions of painters such as Mantegna and Signorelli in *De Card.*, fols. L 7 *verso*, Q 1 *recto*.

Cortesi makes the same argument in favor of music. See Pirotta, "Music and Cultural Tendencies", pp. 152-153. The view that art has the power to move men to virtue is a very old one. Cortesi would have based himself on Cicero and Quintilian, but see Baxandall, *Giotto*, especially pp. 80-83 on early humanist Aristotelian aesthetics.

Alberti, in *Della pittura*, saw "historia" as inciting to "pleasure and emotion" (*voluptate e animi motu*), (Grayson, *On Painting*, pp. 78-9) which parallels Cortesi without his strong ethical emphasis. Elsewhere, however, (p. 62) Alberti observes that painting contributes to piety and that statues of gods "have a very good influence on the morals of the vulgar... (inspiring) love of glory and emulation of their virtue" (*Ten Books*, bk. VIII, ch. XVII, p. 160). See also C. Westfall, "Society, Beauty and the Humanist Architect in Alberti's *de re aedificatoria*", in *Studies in the Renaissance* 16 (1969), pp. 61-79, especially pp. 70-72 and, by the same author, *In This Most Perfect Paradise*, (Univ. Park, Pa., 1974). For the continued life of the medieval tradition of the power of sacred histories in Churches to incite virtue see J. Shearman, *Raphael's Cartoons in the Royal Collection* (London, 1965), p. 45, n. 1. Cortesi applies the same principles to private palaces. See below, notes 105 and 109 and our introduction.

98 Cesariano, *Vitruvius*, bk. VII, ch. 5, fol. CXVIII *recto* and CXLI *verso* on subjects. Alberti, *Ten Books*, bk. VII, ch. X, p. 149, recommends "representations of great actions" in pictures for the portico. In bk. IX, ch. IV, on the private house, he emphasizes the discussion of portico decoration concluding that "the brave and memorable actions of one's countrymen and their effigies are ornaments extremely suit-

able both to Porticos and Halls. Caius Caesar embellished his Portico with the statues of all those that had enlarged the confines of the republic... ". For Cortesi, the republic is the Church and the deeds of Constantine and Charlemagne are the political equivalents of those of Caesar.

99 i.e. Constantinople. Cortesi seems to accept the long disproved authenticity of the Donation of Constantine of the Western Empire to the papacy. Although Lorenzo Valla had demonstrated in the quattrocento that the Donation was a forgery yet the subject, with its implied guarantee of papal power, was represented in the Vatican Sala di Costantino begun by Raphael in 1520. Since Cortesi belongs to the inner circle of Curial humanists his statement as early as 1508 is of particular interest. Presumably, Cortesi retains the theme of the Donation whether or nor it is historically authentic because it nonetheless serves as a good model for virtuous behavior, from the papal point of view. Indeed, the subject had special personal interest for Cortesi since his father, Antonio, had written a treatise, " Antivalla ", on this very subject. See Giovanni Antonazzi, " Lorenzo Valla e la Donazione di Costantino nel secolo XV con un testo inedito di Antonio Cortesi ", *Rivista di storia della chiesa in Italia*, anno 4/2, (1950), pp. 186-234, esp. p. 226. In Paolo's own *De hominibus doctis*, pp. 40-41, he praises Valla for his language but disagrees with his ideas. Valla's *Donatio* was in fact published only in 1506; see Wolfram Setz, *L. Vallas Schrift gegen die Konstantinische Schenkung: Zur Interpretation und Wirkungsgeschichte*, *Studies in Medieval and Reformation Thought* (Tübingen, 1976). See also Partner, *Renaissance Rome*, pp. 128-130. M. Miglio, " L'umanista Piero Edo e la Polemica sulla donazione di Constantino ", in *Bollettino dell'Istituto Storico-Italiano per il Medioevo e Archivio Muratoriano*, LXXIX, (1968), pp. 167-132. Earlier, writing for a Florentine patron, Lorenzo the Magnificent, Cortesi had deplored the *translatio imperii*, as the beginning of the barbarian age (*De hominibus doctis*, p. 14).

100 " Senatus Consultus " was the advice of the Senate which in Imperial times had the force of law. It is not clear exactly how Cortesi uses the term. Here it would seem to refer to the College of Cardinals.

101 In his *De hominibus doctis*, p. 2, Cortesi used similar terminology, " ex diuturna barbarorum vexatione Italia liberata ". There is a close relationship between Cortesi's rendition of the Charlemagne story and that of Manetti in his *Life of Brunelleschi*, line 516.

The annotation (fol. X 4 *verso*) reads, " Longobardus, Politianus langobardos scribit, quidam lingobardo a lingonibus Germaniae et Bardis Galliarum dicunt, unde mutata " i " in " o " langobardiam ". A related subject, the Donation of Charlemagne, was later painted in the Sala Regia (Davidson, " Sala Regia ", p. 418). Raphael's *Coronation of Charlemagne* in the Stanza dell'Incendio dates from after 1516 (S.J. Freedberg, *Painting in Italy: 1500-1600*, (Harmondsworth, 1971). See L.D. Ettlinger, *The Sistine Chapel Before Michelangelo* (Oxford, 1965), pp. 110-114.

102 These are apparently upstairs corridors (see gloss and, above, note 73); private, not public walkways. Thus the virtue of the family is involved. This idea is to be found in Alberti, *Ten Books*, bk. IX, ch. IV, pp. 192-193, who, however, also welcomes the mythological scenes that Cortesi rejects. Raphael's *Logge* in the Vatican would have corresponded to Cortesi's prescriptions.

103 Such scenes of punishment are not mentioned by Alberti but they belong among his subjects " promoting to good manners " (*Ten Books*, bk. IX, ch. IV, p. 192). See also the fifteenth century frescoes in the Sistine Chapel, particularly Botticelli's *Punishment of the Sons of Corah* (Ettlinger, *Sistine Chapel*, pp. 66-70, 105). Raphael's frescoes in the Stanza d'Eliodoro, particularly the *Expulsion of Heliodorus* and the *Repulse of Attila* fit this category. Work on the Stanza was probably begun by mid-1511 and painting continued into 1514 (Shearman, " Stanze ", pp. 18, 48, n. 94; Freedberg, *Painting in Italy*, p. 35). The frescoes in the Vatican Sala Regia of the 1540's continue this tradition (Davidson, " Sala Regia ", pp. 416-421).

104 Here the antique theme of " enemies of the republic " is adapted to the anti-republican papal regime. For Cortesi's hostile attitude to the Hohenstaufen family see *De Card.*, fols. A 5rv, A 6v, C 5r, I 3v, R 13v, T 6r. Frederick II Hohenstaufen was one of the great enemies of the papacy in the Middle Ages. His son Manfred (1232-1266) succeeded him as King of Sicily. Manfred's patricide is apocryphal as is his murder of this brother, Conrad (fol. I 3v); see Maffei, *Com. urb.*, fol. Y 3v.

[105] i.e. Henry IV (1056-1106). For Canossa see, H. Zimmerman, "Der Canossagang von 1077", *Wirkung und Wirklichkeit*, (Wiesbaden, 1975), also for paintings.

[106] For an earlier example, see Pintoricchio's lost "storie" of Pope Alexander VI in the Castel S. Angelo (Vasari, *Le Vite*, vol. III, p. 279, note 4). The Sala di Costantino (begun 1520) also takes up these themes. Ettlinger, *Sistine Chapel*, p. 118, mentions two earlier painted programs glorifying the papacy in the Lateran: the mosaics of the *Triclinium Lateranense* done for Leo II and the *Chapel of St. Nicholas* done for Calixtus II after the Concordat of Worms. However, neither of these decorations include a narrative cycle.

[107] The standard classical Latin phrase, used by Cicero, was "deus hospitalis" and defined as "...qui hospiti praeses et vindex est, quod in ejus tutela hospites esse credebantur", and always refers to Jove, see E. Forcellini, *Totius Latinitatis Lexicon*, (Padua, 1772) vol. 2, pp. 681-82. The aspect under which Cortesi is invoking the Virgin is unclear. For a fascinating contemporary description of paintings suitable for a chapel; see Grapaldi, *Lexicon*, (1st ed., 1494), pp. 228, 230, who recommends rich ornament, a a painted vault, an altar made of marble or incrusted if made of wood or brick. The altarpiece should represent Christ, the Saints or the Virgin.

[108] Louis of Anjou, Bishop of Toulouse (1274-1297) was the second son of Charles the Lame, King of Naples and Sicily. Louis renounced his claim to the throne of Naples and became a Friar Minor. He was canonized in 1317; his feast day is August 19th. Saint Louis was renowned for his humility and the story Cortesi alludes to is to be found in the medieval "Vita S. Ludovici Episcopi Tolosani conscripta a Iohanne de Orta" in *Analecta Bollandiana* IX (1890), pp. 278-353 at p. 310. The Saint's humility is usually illustrated in art by means of other scenes as in the predella of Simone Martini's Saint Louis altar in Naples. Cortesi's choice of example was particularly apposite, since Saint Louis had originally been a secular ruler. Saint Louis was the patron of the *parte guelfa* in Florence and was therefore closely connected with the papal cause in Tuscany. This might have contributed to Cortesi's interest in the Saint here. Saint Louis was canonized soon after his death, as was, in 1323, Saint Thomas Aquinas (1225-1274), who was also an aristocrat. Cortesi mentions the humility of Saint Thomas again in *De Card.*, fol. V2 *verso* but we have been unable to find representations in art of the Saint as gardener. Elizabeth Beatson suggests that Cortesi may have been thinking of the passage quoted by the Bollandists for the Saint's feast day, March 7th: "Illa sequens vestigia, frontes et fructus facies, in vineam Domini Sabaoth utiles; quamdiu vitam humeris proferes ac produces. Haec si sectatus fueris, ad id attingere poteris quod affectas", (Opuscul. 68) in P. Guerin, ed., *Les Petits Bollandistes* (Paris, 1888), vol. III, p. 245. We also wish to thank Mrs. Beatson for her help at the Index of Christian Art, Princeton University.

[109] This is a fascinating and highly elitist argument, but it makes Aristotelian sense in that the intellect moves the soul to action. The more mental activity, the more stimulation to action and virtue result. This is also an affirmation of the social and moral utility of painting. For Alberti on the utility of painting in moving men to forsake vice for virtue see Westfall, "Alberti", p. 72. Cortesi had already maintained in his earlier *Liber sententiarum* that beauty of language moved men to virtue and was therefore useful. Literary beauty, no matter how sophisticated, remained "natural" since beauty and utility are in nature always joined. This attitude now seems to be transferred to painting. We know of no clearer contemporary statement than Cortesi's of the idea that painting was intended for the learned rather than for the mass of the faithful. Cortesi's admonition should be remembered when historians feel their common sense revolt against the complex programs and layers of symbolism often proposed for Renaissance decorations. Cortesi sees the deciphering of iconography as a form of intellectual and thus ultimately of spiritual exercise.

[110] The paintings on the side walls of the Sistine Chapel were done between 1481 and 1483. The Pope assigned a team of what were considered the best Tuscan and Umbrian artists to paint scenes from the lives of Christ and Moses. For the iconography with its emphasis on the legitimacy and the political power of the papacy, see Ettlinger, *Sistine Chapel*, *passim* and Shearman, *Raphael's Cartoons*, pp. 47 ff.

[111] Cardinal Oliviero Carafa was one of the great Maecenases of his time. The chapel was decorated in several phases between 1487-1502 by Filippino Lippi and depicts the Triumph of Saint Thomas, the

Assumption of the Virgin, and, on the altar wall, the Annunciation with Saint Thomas and Cardinal Carafa. See C. Bertelli, " Appunti sugli affreschi nella cappella Carafa alla Minerva ", in *Archivum Fratrum Praedicatorum* XXV, 1965, pp. 116-130 and G. Geiger, *Filippino Lippi's Carafa Chapel in Santa Maria sopra Minerva, Rome, 1488-1493* (Unpublished Ph. D. Diss., Stanford University, 1975). Cortesi depended especially on Aquinas throughout his *Liber sententiarum.* It is interesting that Cortesi chooses this as well as the Sistine Chapel as examples: commissions outstanding in importance for the history of style but which are also specially notable, as well, for their iconographical and visual complexity. Perhaps Cortesi does not fully distinguish between " ingeniousness " of form and content. Carafa had a beautiful palace on the Quirinal which he rented from Francesco Orsini (see P. Leto in *Codice*, p. 248; the chapel is also mentioned in Albertini, *Opusculum*, p. 510). Raffaele Brandolini, a distinguished contemporary orator at the papal court, wrote in a lost dialogue *De Nobilitate*, " In eo licet de vera nobilitate uniuersi disputet: in primis tamen Oliverii Caraphae Card. laudi, generisque claritati studet, cuius etiam Quirinalem Villam elegantissime describit ". (Vat. Lat. 3590, fol. 37 *recto*). See F. Strazzullo, " Il Card. Oliviero Carafa mecenate del Rinascimento ", *Atti dell'Accademia Pontaniana*, N.S. XIV (1964-65), pp. 139-160, and pls. I-II, and most recently F. Petrucci in *Dizionario biografico degli italiani* XIX (1976), pp. 588-596.

112 The following passage is loosely related to and perhaps expanded from Alberti, *Ten Books*, bk. V, ch. III, p. 85, where different modes of reception according to the rank of the visitor are discussed. Indeed a small and a large hall are recommended. Alberti takes the theme from Seneca's *De beneficiis*, in his *Epistulae morales*, R.M. Gunemere, ed. and trans., (Cambridge, 1962), vol. II, pp. 218-241.

113 See S. Bertelli, " Piero Soderini ' vexillifer perpetuus reipublicae Florentinae ' 1502-1512 ", in *Renaissance Studies in Honor of Hans Baron*, A. Mohlo and J.A. Tedeschi, eds., (De Kalb, Ill., 1971), pp. 335-357. Both Piero and his brother Francesco, Bishop of Volterra, were close to Cortesi. Cardinal Soderini visited Cortesi at his villa in September of 1509 (*De Card.*, fol. I 14 *verso*). He lived in a palace next to SS. Apostoli begun in the 1480's (Albertini, *Opusculum*, pp. 525, 546). However, the Palazzo Soderini (Palazzo del Cardinale di Volterra) was next to that of Cortesi's friend Cardinal Adriano Castellesi. See note 85. Cortesi and Piero Soderini exchanged letters (Florence, Biblioteca Nazionale, Naz. II/III/3 fols. 128 *recto* and *verso*, 132 *verso* - 133 *recto*). See also our introduction on the date of *De Card.* Cortesi may have known the Soderini anecdote from Piero or Cardinal Francesco. In *De Card.* (fol. K 8 *recto*), in the chapter " *De Audentia* ", Cortesi describes Piero as a good listener. He was not, of course, a dictator in the modern sense.

114 The Venetian Pope Paul II, Pietro Barbo (1464-1471) who built the Palazzo Venezia, was infamous among humanists for his suppression of the Roman Academy under Pomponio Leto. See R.J. Dunstan, " Pope Paul II and the Humanists ", *The Journal of Religious History*, VII (1973), pp. 287-306.

115 Lodovico " il Moro " Sforza, Duke of Milan (1494-1499) was the son of Francesco Sforza and the the brother of Cardinal Ascanio Sforza. His seizure of the Milanese throne after the deposition of his nephew and his invitation of the French forces into Italy for support against the Neapolitans helped precipitate many ills.

116 The verbs, " cerno " and " specto " are in the subjunctive. Their use in this passage makes their interpretation uncertain. We cannot be sure whether Cortesi is relating anecdotes that might be used as the subjects of pictures or whether he is attempting to describe actual pictures that he imagines in his mind. Were the latter true, these would be abbreviated *ekphrases* and would place Cortesi in the rhetorical tradition that became so fruitful for Vasari's descriptions of works of art. For a summary of this question, see R. Hatfield, " Some Unknown Descriptions of the Medici Palace in 1459 ", *Art Bulletin*, vol. LII, September, 1970, p. 233 n. 3, p. 237, n. 52 as well as Baxandall, *Giotto*, pp. 85 ff.

117 Giovanni de' Medici, the son of Lorenzo il Magnifico, became Card. March 11, 1489, at 14 years of age, with S. Maria in Domnica as titular church, but did not wear cardinal's vestments until March 11, 1492. He was elected Pope as Leo X on March 11, 1513 at 37 years of age. He died on Dec. 1, 1521. His palace after 1503 was the present Palazzo Madama behind the Piazza Navona on the Piazza

Saponara over the Baths of Nero. He had lived in the Palazzo Ottieri (Frommel, *Palastbau*, vol. II, p. 227), which was famous for its collection of antiquities and for its library (Albertini, *Opusculum*, pp. 520, 531). See also notes 112 and 123.

118 See above, notes 60, 113. It is not clear whether a covered or open garden walk, loggia, or terrace is intended here.

119 This differs from Alberti, *Ten Books*, bk. IX, ch. IV, p. 193, who stresses the importance of pleasant and beautiful subjects in the private apartments of the "master of the family and his wife". The reason given is the influence on the conception of children and their beauty. This argument is obviously unsuitable for Cortesi's cardinal. Perhaps it is for the same reason that Cortesi does not follow Alberti in recommending landscape decorations in the private apartments.

120 Francesco Sforza (1401-1466) became Duke of Milan by virtue of his marriage to Bianca Maria Visconti in 1450. His claims were supported by the Medici. Francesco's descendants praised him as the founder of their dynasty and as the paragon of all virtues. Leonardo's plans for the colossal equestrian statue of Francesco would have been the most conspicuous monument to his fame. Laudatory *Lives* of Francesco were written by the poet, Filelfo, and by the historian, Giovanni Simoneta, as well as by by Paolo Giovio. The subject mentioned by Cortesi does not appear in these works but Giovio does praise Francesco's "expedita & incredibil forza di prudenza perfetta & di divin giudicio". (P. Giovio, *Gli elogi: vite brevemente scritte d'huomini illustri di guerra antichi et moderni*, Ludovico Dominici, trans., (Florence, 1554). The annotation to Cortesi's text (fol. 2 *recto*) reads, "Collimare est transuersis oculis sagittam uel iaculum ad signum dirigere: uide Ciceronem li-ii de diuinatione". Nowhere, however, in Cicero's treatise is there any mention of prophecy by marksmanship. We have been unable to trace the source of Cortesi's idea but the annotation at least shows that a contemporary interpreted the text to refer to a means of divination. The concept seems an anticipation of the device of Cardinal Alessandro Farnese: a spear striking the center of a shield that hangs from a tree with the motto from the Iliad (VIII, 282), ΒΑΛΛ' ΟΥΤΩΣ "strike so", first published in 1556. We should like to thank Iris H. Cheney for her help with this problem. For the meaning of the motto as a model of military preparedness and virtuous action, see Partridge, "Divinity and Dynasty at Caprarola", pp. 496-497, who stresses the Aristotelean concept of virtue implied in the motto. Also E. Battisti, "Michelangelo e l'ambiguità iconografica", in J.A. Schmoll gen. Eisenwerth, *et al.*, eds., *Festschrift Luitpold Dussler*, (Munich, 1972), pp. 211-213. Ascanio Sforza may have been the source for Cortesi's image. Later in *De Card.* (fol. V 3 *verso*) Cortesi laments the deaths of Ascanio and Lodovico. It is interesting to note that he makes secular virtue a model for clerical behavior here. Cortesi's suggested painting is related to the tradition of *viri illustres* depicted in Renaissance art and literature. Famous men could, however, also serve as models for the cardinal in the great hall of his palace. Cardinal Orsini had such a cycle, probably painted by Masolino, at Monte Giordano; R. L. Mode, *The Monte Giordano Famous Men Cycle... and the Uomini Famosi Tradition in 15th Century Italian Art* (Ph. D. Diss., University of Michigan, Ann Arbor, 1970).

121 Rodocanachi, *Rome au Temps de Jules II et Léon X*, p. 23, thinks that Cortesi refers specifically to summer bedrooms. We are not certain whether "ratione" refers here to the objects represented or to the means of representation such as perspective. Cortesi's ideas for the subjects to be used in summer apartments derive from his interpretation of Vitruvius, *Ten Books*, bk. VII, ch. V, p. 103. Possibly his affirmation of the value of complicated representations is also an answer to Vitruvius who rejects illusionism in this chapter. For a description of such subjects at the palace of Urbino, see Baldi, *Descrizione*, p. 597. See below, note 123.

122 Vitruvius describes a number of hydraulic machines invented by Ctesibius (*Ten Books*, bk. IX, ch. VIII, p. 295, bk. X, ch. VIII, p. 311) including a water organ and the "Ctesibica machina" proper, which is a pump. Cortesi may, however, also be thinking of the Ctesibian water clock which is the instrument most particularly concerned with precise measurements. See A.G. Drachmann, *The Mechanical Technology of Greek and Roman Antiquity, a Study of the Literary Sources* (Copenhagen-Madison, Wisconsin, 1963). It is not clear whether the machines themselves allow better measurements or whether they are represented in foreshortening. Or, on the other hand, does the complexity of the machines give

the spectator more to look at and think about? We favor the latter reading.

123 Such representations traditionally belong in " studioli ", often decorated with wood intarsia panels. The best known examples are the " studioli " of Federico da Montefeltro from Gubbio and the one still in the palace at Urbino. C.H. Clough, " Federico da Montefeltro ", p. 141, stresses that such " studioli " were understood as reflecting antiquity. Cortesi's prescription for his decorations seems to be based on Vitruvius, *Ten Books*, bk. VII, ch. V. p. 103. Vitruvius mentions both subjects involving " men, buildings, ships and other objects ". The passage can also be read to imply the use of *trompe l'oeil* representations. Cortesi puts these mathematical and mechanical subjects in the " summer rooms " where (see below, note 126) he also advocates something like a Sala del Mappamondo. Does he intend the summer rooms to be used for study? Libraries, such as those at the Vatican and the Palazzo Medici, also displayed " strumenta geometriae et astronomiae et alia quae in liberalibus disciplinis pertinent auro et argento picturis ornata " (Albertini, *Opusculum*, p. 530). See Shearman, " Stanze ", p. 21, pl. 29, for Leonine intarsia on the doors to the Stanza della Segnatura.

124 " Ianensis " is used to mean S. Gimignano in *De Card.* (fol. K 5 *verso*). " Cortesi oppidi " is the author's villa near S. Gimignano which he also calls " castrum Cortesium " in other parts of *De Card.* The villa was still under construction in 1507 and was laid out on grand lines. Cortesi lived there in high humanist style giving fêtes and jousts (*De Card.* fol. Q 12 *recto*). For the site and history of the villa, see P. Paschini, " Una Famiglia di curiali nella Roma del quattrocento: I Cortesi ", *Rivista di storia della chiesa in Italia*, anno IX/1, (1957), pp. 30, 39 and the literature there cited. Cortesi died at the villa in 1510. Its ruins still survive. In *De Card.*, fol. NN 4 *verso*, 5 *recto*, Cortesi states that he had the lake dug on his property in order to give employment to the local inhabitants during a time of famine.

125 The annotation (fol. X 2 *recto*) reads, " Corriuata aqua a rius, riuo, deriuo et corriuo, et hoc quia lacum in Cortesiano effodit: hoc est egerens humum pro aquam corriuatam in scrobibus - novo commento ". Apparently the excavated earth was flushed away by the introduction of a stream. See *De Card.*, fol. 106 *verso* for the dimensions of the artificial lake. See *Pliny's Natural History*, Books *XXXVI-XXXVII*, bk. XXXVI, ch. XXIV, p. 98, where the draining of the Fucine lake is discussed.

126 A " pinax " is mentioned by Vitruvius (*Ten Books*, bk. X, ch. VIII, p. 317) but is clearly the top board of a water organ and not a type of map. However, the word may also mean a painted board or, more broadly, a picture (Lidell and Scott, *Greek English Lexicon*, (Oxford, 1940), p. 1405). Vitruvius does, however, tell of maps of the world (" orbe terrarum chorographiis picta ") in *Ten Books*, bk. VIII, ch. II, p. 147, such as Agrippa had made in the portico of Octavia. Cesariano, *Vitruvius*, fol. CXXIII *verso*, equates " le chorographie depincte " with " mappamundi ". It is interesting that no annotation or gloss is given for " pinax " as though its meaning were perfectly clear to Cortesi's contemporaries. A wall painting of a world map was painted in a triclinium of the Lateran Palace for Pope Zacharias (741-742). See J. Schulz, " Jacopo de' Barberi's View of Venice: Map Making, City Views, and Moralized Geography Before the Year 1500 ", *Art Bulletin* LX, 3, September, 1978, p. 448, *et passim.* Such maps existed in the papal palace at Avignon and in 1495 Burchardus first mentions the map of the world painted for Paul II in the Sala del Mappamondo in the state apartments of the piano nobile of the Palazzo Venezia. This was also designed as a " stantia estiva ". In 1504, Julius II held a banquet there and the room may, possibly, have been intended for this purpose. See I.F. Dengel, " Sulla mappamundi di palazzo Venezia ", in *Archivio della Società Romana di Storia Patria*, vol. LII (1929), pp. 501-508. Later such mappae mundi were painted for the Farnese villa at Caprarola, the Uffizi and, in 1580, at the Vatican (Magnuson, *Quattrocento*, pp. 284-285). Early mappae mundi could actually include elements of natural history like " the habitat of various species of birds, mammals and reptiles " while Cortesi's account of such depictions is reiterated by a letter of 1593 where maps are praised because " servono a molte cose et principalmente a passar l'hore del caldo l'estate et a fuggir l'otio ", See Schulz, " Venice ", pp. 447, n. 66 and 442, n. 46.

127 Note the mercantile associations of " circumvectio ", Cicero, *Letters to Atticus*, D.R. Shackleton-Bailey, ed., (Cambridge, 1965-70). Cortesi does not yet, of course, mean circumnavigation of the globe,

rather he refers to the recent Portuguese expedition to India of Vasco da Gama (1496-97), under Manuel I of Portugal (1495-1521). Cortesi gives these discoveries a Christian interpretation in *De Card.* fol. A 2 *verso*. Manuel's exploratory campaigns elicited strong support from Julius II, who saw them as a means of propagating the faith. Cortesi was not alone among contemporary humanists in echoing the papal view. In December of 1507, for instance, during a three day celebration in Rome to honor Manuel, Egidio da Viterbo delivered an oration before the Pope praising the Portuguese reintroduction of Christianity into India. See J.W. O'Malley, " The Vatican Library and the School of Athens: A Text of Battista Casali, 1508 ", *The Journal of Medieval and Renaissance Studies*, 7 (1977), pp. 271-287, at pp. 275, 285. Raffaele Maffei, *Comm. urb.*, fol. CLXIX *verso* tells that the Cardinal of Portugal (see above, note 13) kept an Indian boy in his palace who, however, remained stubborn in his idolatry.

128 Zographia: a Greek word meaning the art of painting. The verbal form, however, also conveys the idea of painting from life. Cortesi's exact meaning in this passage is unclear. Are the creatures (" animantes ") to be represented, animals, or are all exotic forms of life, such as inhabitants of the Orient, to be shown? Certainly, decorations depicting unusual or newly discovered birds and animals became fashionable decorations for residences. The frieze of birds and animals in the Villa Madama is a fine example of what Cortesi means and the Sala del Pappagallo in the Vatican or the side decorations of the Farnesina Psyche Loggia might also be adduced, as well as Giulio's Camera degli Uccelli in the Palazzo Ducale at Mantua.

129 This is Cortesi's strongest statement in favor of complexity and hermeticism in iconography, both for their own sakes and for their ability to provide intellectual exercise for the viewer as a necessary precondition to the exercise of virtue. This attitude is certainly highly significant but it is worth remembering that Cortesi represented an extremely limited niveau, that of the Curial humanists with their highly cerebral and elitist approach to art and literature and their emphatic allegiance to the doctrine of the imitation of antiquity in its strictest form. See also D. Summers, " Contrapposto: Style and Meaning in Renaissance Art ", *Art Bulletin* LIX, 3, September, 1977, pp. 346-356, for the theoretical basis of Renaissance ideas that the proper audience for painting was composed of " cogniscenti ". Cardinal Giulio de' Medici, on the other hand, took precisely the opposite view in a letter to Bishop Mario Maffei, Raffaele's brother, about the painted decorations planned for the Villa Madama (June, 1520). The Cardinal warns the humanist that he wants recognizable subjects that need not carry inscriptions to be understood. Ovidian subjects will do as long as the meaning is clear. The matter is left up to Bishop Maffei (R. Lefevre, " Un prelato del '500, Mario Maffei, e la costruzione di Villa Madama ", *L'Urbe* XXIII/3 (1969), pp. 1-11. While Cardinal Giulio is more pragmatic and perhaps envisages a broader audience, Cortesi's view is not simply rigidly pedantic or dogmatic. He also wants the meaning of paintings to be understood but believes, on the basis of Aristotle, that their effect will be heightened to the degree that the intellect is engaged. A simple message may not be remembered or acted upon if the spectator's mind is not actively involved in deciphering it. (See above, note 109). Actually the Villa Madama does contain some of the pictorial themes mentioned by Cortesi such as a mappamondo, representations of exotic beasts, and scenes from Philostratus in the loggia. The Palazzo Medici-Madama was also " domus senatoria " and contained decorative themes mentioned by Cortesi. It may well be, as C. L. Frommel has suggested to us, that Mario Maffei constitutes the link between Cortesi's early ideas and their later realization, particularly through Medici patrons.

SELECTED BIBLIOGRAPHY

Alberti, Leon Battista, *Opere volgari*, Anicio Bonucci, ed., Florence, 1845-1849, vol. III.

Alberti, Leon Battista, *Pontifex*, in *Opera inedita et pauca separatim impressa*, Girolamo Mancini, ed., Florence, 1890.

Alberti, Leon Battista, *Ten Books on Architecture*, James Leoni, trans., [1725], Joseph Rykwert., ed., reprint London 1955 ed., London, 1965.

Alberti, Leon Battista, *L'architettura* [*De re aedificatoria*], Giovanni Orlandi, ed. and trans., Paolo Portoghesi, notes, 2 vols., Milan, 1966.

Alberti, Leon Battista, *On Painting and On Sculpture*, Cecil Grayson, ed. and trans., London, 1972.

Albertini, Francesco, *Opusculum de mirabilibus novae et veteris urbis Romae*, in *Codice topografico della città di Roma*, Roberto Valentini and Giuseppe Zacchetti, eds., Rome, 1953, vol. IV, pp. 457-546.

Baldi, Bernardino, *De verborum vitruvianorum significatione sive perpetuus in M. Vitrurium Pollionem commentarius*, Augsburg, 1602.

Baldi, Bernardino, *Descrizione del Palazzo Ducale di Urbino*, in *Versi e prose scelte di Bernardino Baldi*, Florence, 1859, pp. 538-590.

Baxandall, Michael, *Giotto and the Orators*, Oxford, 1971.

Biondo, Flavio, *Roma instaurata*, in *Codice topografico della città di Roma*, Roberto Valentini and Giuseppe Zacchetti, eds., Rome, 1953, vol. IV, pp. 247-323.

Cantimori, Delio, " Questioncine sulle opere progettate da Paolo Cortesi ", in *Studi di bibliografia e di storia in onore di Tammaro de Marinis*, ed., Verona, 1964, vol. 1, pp. 273-280.

Cesariano, Cesare, *Vitruvius, De architettura*, reprint Como, 1521 ed., New York, 1968.

Chambers, D. S., "The Economic Predicament of Renaissance Cardinals", in W. M. Bowsky, ed., *Studies in Medieval and Renaissance History*, III (1966), pp. 289-313.

Chambers, D. S., " The Housing Problems of Cardinal Francesco Gonzaga ", *Journal of the Warburg and Courtauld Institutes*, XXXIX, (1976), pp. 21-58.

Cortesi, Paolo, *De Cardinalatu*, Città Cortesiana, 1510.

Cortesi, Paolo, *De hominibus doctis dialogus*, Maria Teresa Graziosi, ed. and trans., Rome, 1973.

D'Amico, John F., " Humanism and Theology at Papal Rome, 1480-1520 ", Ph. D. diss., University of Rochester, 1977.

Davidson, Bernice F., " The Decoration of the Sala Regia under Pope Paul III ", *Art Bulletin* LVIII (1976), pp. 395-423.

Dickinson, G., *Du Bellay in Rome*, Leiden, 1960.

Dionisotti, Carlo, *Geografia e storia della letteratura italiana*, Turin, 1967.

Dionisotti, Carlo, *Gli umanisti e il volgare fra quattrocento e cinquecento*, Florence, 1968.

Ettlinger, L. D., *The Sistine Chapel Before Michelangelo*, Oxford, 1965.

Filarete (Antonio Averlino), *Trattato di architettura*, A. M. Finoli, ed., Luigi Grassi, notes, 2 vols., Milan, 1972.

Fontana, Vincenzo, and Morachiello, Paolo, *Vitruvio e Raffaello: il ' De architettura ' di Vitruvio nella traduzione inedita di Fabio Calvo Ravennate*, Rome, 1975.

Foster, Philip, " Raphael on the Villa Madama: the Text of a Lost Letter ", *Römisches Jahrbuch für Kunstgeschichte*, vol. XI (1967), pp. 308-312.

Fraser-Jenkins, A. D., " Cosimo de' Medici's Patronage of Architecture and the Theory of Magnificence ", *Journal of the Warburg and Courtauld Institutes*, XXXIII (1970), pp. 162-170.

Freedberg, Sydney J., *Painting in Italy*, 1500-1600, Harmondsworth, Baltimore, 1971.

Frommel, Christoph Luitpold, *Der römische Palastbau der Hochrenaissance*, 3 vols., Tübingen, 1973.

Garin, Eugenio, ed., *Prosatori latini del quattrocento*, Milan, 1958.

Goldthwaite, Richard A., " The Florentine Palace as Domestic Architecture ", *American Historical Review*, vol. LXXVII (1972), pp. 977-1012.

Gombrich, E. H., *Norm and Form*, London, 1966.

Gracci, Anna, " Studi sul Paolo Cortesi da San Gimignano ed il suo ' De Cardinalatu ' ", Tesi di Laurea, University of Florence, 1967.

Grapaldi, Francesco Mario, *De partibus aedium, lexicon utilissimum*, Basel, 1533.

Jacometti, Fabio, " Il primo stampatore senese Simone di Nicolò di Nardo ", *La Diana* vol. 1, no. 3 (1926), pp. 1-13.

Maffei, Raffaele, *Commentariorum urbanorum libri XXXVIII*, Rome, 1506.

Magnuson, Torgil, *Studies in Roman Quattrocento Architecture*, Rome, 1958.

Manetti, Antonio di Tuccio, *The Life of Brunelleschi*, Catherine Enggass, trans., H. Saalman, intr. and notes, University Park, Pa., 1970.

Martini, Francesco di Giorgio, *Trattati di architettura ingegneria e arte militare*, Corrado Maltese, ed., Milan, 1967.

Partner, Peter, *Rome in the Renaissance*, Berkeley, 1977.

Paschini, Pio, " Una famiglia di curiali della Roma del quattrocento: I Cortesi ", *Rivista di storia della chiesa in Italia*, II (1957), pp. 1-48.

Pastor, Ludwig von, *History of the Popes from the Close of the Middle Ages*, F. I. Antrobus and R. F. Kerr, trans., St. Louis, 1898-1923, vols. 6-8.

Pirotta, Nino, " Music and Cultural Tendencies in Fifteenth Century Italy ", *Journal of the American Musicological Society*, XVIIII (1966), pp. 127-161.

Pliny, *The Elder Pliny's Chapters on the History of Art*, K. Jex-Blake and E. Sellers, eds. and trans., reprint 1896 ed., Chicago, 1968.

Pontano, Giovanni, *I trattati delle virtù sociali*, Francesco Tateo, ed. and trans., Rome, 1965.

Portoghesi, Paolo, *Rome of the Renaissance*, P. Sanders, trans., London, 1972.

Priscianese, Francesco, *Del governo della corte d'un signore in Roma*, L. Bartolucci ed., Città di Castello, 1883.

Rodocanachi, Emmanuel, *Rome au temps de Jules II et Léon X*, Paris, 1912.

Shearman, John, " The Vatican Stanze: Function and Decorations ", *Proceedings of the British Academy*, LVII (1971), pp. 3-58.

Shearman, John, *Raphael's Cartoons in the Collection of Her Majesty the Queen and the Tapestries for the Sistine Chapel*, London, 1972.

Schulz, Juergen, " Pinturicchio and the Revival of Antiquity ", *Journal of the Warburg and Courtauld Institutes* XXV (1962), pp. 35-55.

Targioni-Tozzetti, Giovanni, *Relazioni d'alcuni viaggi fatti in diverse parti della Toscana*, Florence, 1775, vol. 8.

Vitruvius, *De architectura*, F. Granger, trans., 2 vols., New York, 1931-34.

Westfall, Carroll William, " Society, Beauty and the Humanist Architect in Alberti's *de re aedificatoria* ", *Studies in the Renaissance* XVI (1969), pp. 61-79.

WILLIAM HOOD

III

THE NARRATIVE MODE IN TITIAN'S *PRESENTATION OF THE VIRGIN**

In memory of Clotilda Brokaw

AS IN EVERYTHING ELSE, there is fashion in charity. Without in any way questioning the motives of those who were concerned for the unfortunate, it can be said that in the 1530s there was what one could call a vogue for a popular spirituality that included helping to better the lot of the sick and poor.[1] In fact, the emergence of a social conscience not unlike our own characterizes much institutional policy in Italy during the period of the Catholic Reform, as witness the proliferation of hospitals and schools, as well as other forms of corporal mercy.

* *The research for this article and major portions of its writing were carried out while I was a guest and, later, Fellow of the American Academy, 1971–74. For those three years I thank the Trustees, Staff, and Fellows of the Academy and the Directors, Bartlett Hayes and Henry Millon. This essay is drawn from my Ph.D. dissertation,* Titian's Narrative Art: Some Religious Paintings for Venetian Patrons, 1518–1545, *written for the New York University Institute of Fine Arts under the supervision of Donald Posner. I should like to acknowledge my gratitude to him, here, for his patience and guidance throughout. I should also like to thank others, most of them members of the Academy community, for their help with my study of the* Presentation: *Sir Ernst Gombrich; Brand Griffin; Charles Hope; Irving Lavin; Marilyn Aronberg Lavin; Eugene O'Brien; Laurie Olin; and Kathleen Weil-Garris. Coincidentally David Rosand, in whose seminar at Columbia University I first became seriously interested in Titian studies, completed his research on the* Presentation *while I was beginning mine. Although the results ("Titian's* Presentation of the Virgin in the Temple *and the Scuola della Carità,"* Art Bulletin, *58 [1976],* pp. *55–84) were published too late for me to use them in my dissertation, I am happy to acknowledge my general indebtedness to him in the footnotes that follow. Our considerations of the picture begin at the same place, a careful visual analysis of the painting and its setting. But from there our viewpoints diverge widely. I encourage readers of this article to consult Rosand's for a radically different interpretation, and to decide for themselves which of our arguments is the most convincing.*

1 For a discussion of Venetian piety and art in the 1530s, see W. Hood and C. Hope, "Titian's Vatican Altarpiece and the Pictures Underneath," *Art Bulletin*, 59 (1977), pp. 534–552, with further references to the bibliography of sixteenth-century spirituality.

In Venice, traditional institutions modified their charitable concerns in the wave of this new consciousness. The Scuole Grandi in particular responded with a renewed interest in founding alms houses and hospitals, and in awarding dowries to impoverished members who could not afford to provide a sure future for their daughters in marriage or the convent. The Scuole Grandi, unlike innumerable smaller pious associations of laymen, were enormously complex organizations that included members from all social classes for mutual benefit. The rich endowed the Scuole for the benefit of the poor, who in turn served their benefactors in various spiritual functions, like participating in funeral masses. Not only were the Scuole Grandi the chief means of transferring wealth from the rich to the poor, but they also became borghese counterparts of aristocratic life. Although membership was open to men of noble birth, they were prohibited by law from holding office.[2]

The citizens who administered the immense wealth of the Scuole Grandi in charity also established these institutions as major patrons of art. By the end of the sixteenth century, all the Scuole Grandi were decorated with a splendor rivaling that of the Palazzo Ducale. Some of Venice's greatest treasures were produced for these Scuole, monuments like the facade of the Scuola di San Marco, built around 1500 by the Lombardi, or Tintoretto's decoration of the Scuola di San Rocco two generations later. Another of the Scuole Grandi was attached to the Augustinian convent and church of Sta. Maria della Carità, on the Grand Canal, now the Accademia. It was this Scuola that in 1534 hired Titian to paint the *Presentation of the Virgin in the Temple* (Fig. 1). It was installed four years later in the albergo, or board room, presently a small gallery of the Accademia. The painting is happily still *in situ*, which allows us the rare opportunity to study a great narrative painting by Titian in its original context. The relationship of the painting to its tradition, to its setting, to its patrons and to contemporary art — all these taken together constitute its narrative mode — is the subject of this essay.[3]

2 The most complete discussion of the Scuole Grandi is to be found in B. Pullan, *Rich and Poor in Renaissance Venice*, Oxford, 1971, pp. 33-197. For an even more thorough-going analysis of the Scuole Grandi as instruments of social reform, see his "Le Scuole Grandi e la loro opera nel quadro della controriforma," *Studi Veneziani*, 14 (1972), pp. 83-110.

3 H. Wethey, *The Paintings of Titian, I. The Religious Paintings*, London, 1969, pp. 123-24, cat. no. 87, with further references; D. Rosand, "Titian's *Presentation*." The documents were published by G. Ludwig ("Archivalische Beiträge zur Geschichte der venezianischen Malerei," *Jahrburch der könglichen preussischen Kunstsammlungen*, Berlin, 26 [1905], Beiheft, pp. 52-53, 143-44, 146). Additional documentary material has been discovered by D. Rosand ("Ti-

The Scuola della Carità had been associated with the Canons Regular of St. Augustine since the thirteenth century. But its inclusion in the life of the convent was grudging, for concessions to build and remodel on the property seem only to have been granted in return for loans of money by the rich Scuola to the poor convent.[4] The Scuola premises are laterally contiguous to the church at the entrance to the cloister. The present first gallery of the Accademia was formerly the Casa Grande, built by the Scuola beginning in 1343 as an annex to the minuscule meeting room granted it in the beginning by the canons.[5] That room, which is immediately over the entrance to the cloister, was enlarged in 1384 and again in the 1440s as the albergo; and its decoration commenced in the middle of the Quattrocento, culminating first in the original commission for the *Presentation* to Pasqualino in 1504, which was never carried out.[6] The albergo owes its skewed shape to the fact that its eastern wall was actually erected in two stages, the first in 1384, when it was allowed to back up to the convent itself, and the second in 1441 when the rebuilding of the church cut into the northeastern corner, resulting in the present L-shaped space (Fig. 2). The north wall, facing the campo below, was never fenestrated, light being admitted to the room through two windows in the south wall overlooking the first cloister.[7] In 1534 the only door was in the west wall, and it jutted above the dado into the area reserved to receive Titian's painting.[8] This is the largest uninterrupted mural space in the room, measuring about 12′ by 23′. The new painting was therefore to have pride of place, although it was by no means the only decoration in the room.

A gilded triptych by Antonio Vivarini and Giovanni d'Alemagna fit into the recess of the east wall; a pale blue and gold wooden ceiling, dating from 1496,

tian's 'Presentation of the Virgin': The Second Door," *Burlington Magazine*, 115 [1973], p. 603); see also his "Titian's *Presentation*," n. 15, 16, 19, 20, 22, 24, 25, 29, 60. Mention should also be made of a rarely noticed study of Titian and narrative, with special emphasis on the *Presentation*: C. Nordenfalk, "Tizians Darstellung des Schauens," *Nationalmusei Årsbok, 1947-48*, Stockholm, 1950, pp. 39-60. I am grateful to Professor Sir Ernst Gombrich for calling this article to my attention.

Titian's *Presentation* commission came to him after a thirty-year hiatus following the death of Pasqualino Veneto, who had been awarded the commission in 1504. See Rosand, "Titian's *Presentation*," p. 60.

4 E. Bassi (*Il Convento della Carità*. Corpus Palladianum, 6. Vicenza, 1971, pp. 13ff.) summarizes the relationship between the Scuola and the canons. See also G. Fogolari, *La Chiesa di Santa Maria della Carità di Venezia*. Venice, 1924.

5 Bassi, *Convento*, p. 13.

6 Bassi, *Convento*, pp. 13-14; see also n. 2 above.

7 See Rosand, "Titian's *Presentation*," p. 66 and n. 60.

8 The south door in the west wall was cut in 1572, and therefore the painting was mutilated in Titian's lifetime. The document (ASV, Scuola Grande di S. Maria della Carità, R. 258, c. 140r) was published by Rosand ("Titian's '*Presentation*'").

covered the space with square coffers, five of which show Christ and the four evangelists in relief (Figs. 3 and 4).[9] The strong south light and the recess of the southeast corner therefore emphasized the left side of Titian's wall. The alcove is three coffers wide, and the relief of Christ is placed in the center one, bridging the two spaces in the room, perhaps in an attempt on the part of the ceiling carver to regulate and unite the space, the four evangelists being placed diagonally in the outer two files.

Just why the Banca, or governing board, decided on the subject for the albergo can only be surmised. However, it is a scene from the Virgin's life that concentrates solely on her, and is therefore an apt choice for the Scuola's title; furthermore, there could have been a no more appropriate episode than the Presentation to hold before the officers of an organization dedicated to works of charity. And as Rosand has pointed out, the theme is also entirely suited for the large-scale, elaborate mural decorations common in Venetian scuole of the period.[10]

The early apocryphal gospels that concern Mary's life relate the legend of her presentation.[11] As the story goes, her aged parents brought the Virgin to the temple in Jerusalem at the age of three to be dedicated to God. Having arrived at the foot of the temple stairs, the little girl left Anna and Joachim and rushed unaided up the fifteen-step grade to be received by the High Priest into the company of maidens who would be educated and serve there until the time of their betrothal.

In itself, the little story seems rather insignificant. Yet it was taken up by the Eastern Church as a feast by the sixth century and its meaning sapped of its mystical sense, the preparation of Mary to become the Mother of God. Although the legend was known in the West for centuries in the context of the apocryphal lives of the Virgin, it was not introduced into the Latin liturgy as a local feast until the end of the fourteenth century. Its observance was extended to the Universal Church only in 1476, but was withdrawn again following the liturgical reforms of the Council of Trent. Consequently its appearance in western European art is much less common than in Byzantine.

9 The picture is dated 1446 and is still in the former albergo. See S. Moschini-Marconi, *Gallerie dell'Accademia di Venezia, I. Opere d'arte dei secoli XIV e XV*, Rome, 1955, No. 36; R. Pallucchini, *I Vivarini*, Venice, N.D., p. 104, cat. no. 62. For the ceiling, see Bassi, *Convento*, p. 21, n. 2. See also Rosand, "Titian's *Presentation*," n. 23, 24.

10 Rosand, "Titian's *Presentation*," p. 61.

11 The earliest accounts are in the *Protevangelium of James* and the *Gospel of the Pseudo-Matthew*. From there the legend moved into the *Gospel of the Nativity of Mary* and the *History of Joseph the Carpenter*, and later into the various medieval *specula* and the *Golden Legend* of Jacobus da Voragine, the chief source for subsequent Lives of the Virgin. For a full treatment of the literature, see Sister Mary Jane Kish-

The fourteenth-century propagandist for the feast was a French layman, Philippe de Mézières, who witnessed its celebration on Cyprus in 1371.[12] He sent a circular letter promoting its observance to several Latin bishops, together with a copy of the Office, and it was celebrated for the first time in the West in the Franciscan church at Avignon on 21 November 1372. Along with the Office Philippe also promoted a *repraesentatio figurata*. A performance on Cyprus had so impressed him that he transcribed it, complete with stage directions and costume descriptions. On his return to Avignon, Philippe stopped over at Venice, where he caused the play to be presented exactly as it had been on Cyprus.[13]

As late as 1529 Philippe's Office, poetically elaborate in the Greek manner, was still being said in Venice; and this is surely the liturgical context in which the officers of the Scuola della Carità thought of the Presentation.[14] By 1530, however, there was already a move to reform the Latin liturgy and to purge it of apocryphal observances. A missal published in Venice that year indicates that the mass for the Presentation is simply to follow the form for the Nativity of Mary, inserting the name of the feast wherever necessary.[15] Cardinal Quiñones, on the command of Pope Clement VII, produced a reformed breviary in 1535. In it, the Office for the Presentation, though not relegated to quite the obscurity assigned the mass in the 1530 missal, is nonetheless considerably reduced in length and elaborateness as compared with Philippe's Office.[16] Titian's painting, then, was executed at just the moment in which the Presentation's importance was being diminished, at least on the official level.

In popular literature, however, the Presentation continued to receive its due place in the many redactions of the *Golden Legend*. Sixteenth-century examples of these

paugh, O.P., *The Feast of the Presentation of the Virgin Mary in the Temple: An Historical and Literary Study*, Washington, D.C., 1941. The most exhaustive study of its representation in art is to be found in J. Lafontaine-Dosogne, *Iconographie de l'enfance de la Vierge...*, II, Brussels, 1965.

12 G. La Pina, "The Byzantine Iconography of the Presentation of the Virgin Mary to the Temple and a Latin Religious Pageant," *Late Classical and Mediaeval Studies in Honor of Albert Mathias Friend, Jr.*, Princeton, 1954, p. 263.

13 K. Young, *The Drama of the Medieval Church*, II, Oxford, 1933, pp. 226-227. Young made the first edition of the play ("Philippe de Mézières', Dramatic Office for the Presentation of the Virgin," *PMLA*, 26 [1911], pp. 181-234). A new edition is presently being prepared by William E. Coleman (Rosand, "Titian's *Presentation*," n. 106).

14 *Breviarum romanum, nuper impressum cum quotationibus in margine... quampluribus figuris decoratum. Additum officium archangeli Gabrielis per s. dominum Leonem approbatum.* Venice, 1529. Office for 21 November.

15 *Missale romanum nouissime ordine quodam impressum...*, Venice, 1530, f. 188.

16 *Breviarum Romanum a Francisco Cardinali Quignino. Editum et recognitum iuxta editionem Venetiis A.D. 1535 impressam*, I, edited by John Wickham Legg, Canterbury, 1888, pp. 170-71.

are Jacopo Sanazzaro's *De Partu Virginis* and Aretino's life of the Virgin, whose description of the episode is very likely based on Titian's painting, if not for narrative detail, at least for effects such as Aretino's stress on the light encompassing the Virgin.[17] But no traditional written source, as we shall see, provides answers to the iconographical anomalies of Titian's *Presentation*.

Titian's composition, in general, conforms to a type for the *Presentation* established in the Quattrocento in the circle of Jacopo Bellini. Representations in the so-called sketchbook show a large open space on the left, and on the right, prominent architectural elements, particularly the temple with its long flight of steps on which the Virgin stands (Fig. 5).[18] Joachim and Anna, together with their relatives, the other maidens at the temple, and onlookers populate the scene. This is the representational tradition maintained by Cima da Conegliano and Carpaccio in their versions of the subject, and it is the same that Titian adopted for his (Figs. 6 and 7).[19] Indeed, it would be surprising, in an artistic climate as conservative as Venice, had he not done so. The *Presentation* belongs to that large group of Venetian paintings adorning the walls of scuole both great and small; and they are almost without exception compositions that reinforce the mural surface, animating the space with vibrantly colored passages and as much elaboration of detail and architecture as the story would bear. Titian was surely enjoined, if that was even necessary, to follow this venerable precedent, just as he was to include portraits of the Scuola officers in a prominent location.[20] There is also reason to believe, as we shall see, that he was also given an iconographic libretto to follow that makes his *Presen-*

[17] Jacopo Sanazzaro, *De Partu Virginis*, Venice, 1527; the earliest edition of Pietro Aretino's *La Vita di Maria Vergine* known to me (Nouamente corretta e ristampata, Venice, 1545) suggests an even earlier one. Rosand ("Titian's *Presentation*," n. 63) maintains that it was first published in 1539.

[18] For the most recent study of the drawings album, with further references, see C. Joost-Gaugier, "Jacopo Bellini's Interest in Perspective and its Iconographical Significance." *Zeitschrift für Kunstgeschichte*, 38 (1975), pp. 1-28. The centralized composition common in Tuscan examples may also be found in the album and in Venice, e.g., Giambono's *Presentation* in San Marco.

[19] L. Coletti, *Cima da Conegliano*, Venice, 1959, p. 79, cat. no 44. Carpaccio's *Presentation* belonged to the cycle for the Scuola degli Albanesi, executed in the first decade largely by the shop. J. Lauts, *Carpaccio. Gemälde und Zeichnungen*. Cologne, 1962, pp. 234-5.

[20] As Wethey reports (*Titian, I*, p. 123) two of the officers have traditionally been identified as Andrea dei Franceschini and Lazzaro Crasso (Ridolfi [1648]-Hadeln, I, p. 153). There is, however, no documentary basis for these claims, and the specific identities of the officials could have little bearing on the main thesis of this article. Rosand has done the most careful work on identifying the sitters; but in the end, it seems to be a vain task (Rosand, "Titian's *Presentation*," p. 76). In the same article (pp. 60-62), he treats the Venetian pictorial tradition of the *Presentation* in great detail.

tation different from all the rest, not only in content, but in important matters of form as well. As an artist, he seems to have been much concerned with the disparate architectural setting for his work: the albergo is low-ceilinged, small and rather dark, and its shape, as we have seen, is highly irregular. Just how Titian managed to unite the programmatic requirements in a single image that at the same time overcame the physical disadvantages of its site is worthy of close observation.

Besides telling the story, the essential function of the design is to overcome the physical and psychological boundaries that separate the real from fictive spaces, and the living viewer from the painted character. This Titian did by every means available to him: design; light; color; and gesture.

The space of Titian's picture is defined by the faces of a cubic architecture parallel to and receding from the picture plane in a regular sequence of voids and solids measurable in the perpendicular on the right by the apparent depth of the dominant element, the temple steps. Closed on the left by a portico and a pyramid, the volume thus created opens in the distance onto a vista of foliated hills, bare mountains, and a sky patterned with broken cloud formations. The perspective further emphasizes this area, since it focuses on the figure of Joachim, turned away from the viewer, on the left.[21]

As in the setting, the figural composition is centered on the vanishing point covered or enclosed by the figure of Joachim on the main axis of the ceiling. To his left stands a group of robed Scuola officers, an acolyte with the Carità emblem on his alb, as well as one or two anonymous figures such as the woman receiving alms from an officer who must surely be, as Jennifer Fletcher pointed out, the Guardian del Matin, charged with distributing money during processions and other public activities of the Scuola.[22] Joachim's gesture, joining the "patrons'" side of the picture to the right, makes a transition from the vertical stasis characteristic of the figures on the left into a horizontal impetus channeled through the figures to the right, where, with some exceptions, they are not portraits but actors in the story. Just as the Scuola officers unite the fictive and real spaces by their glances out of

21 I first became sensitive to the relationship between the painting and its setting in David Rosand's Titian seminar at Columbia University in 1970. It was he who indicated that Joachim is the composition's perspectival focus. See his "Titian's *Presentation*," p. 64, for further comments.

22 J. M. Fletcher, review of B. Pullan, *Rich and Poor in Renaissance Venice*, *Burlington Magazine*, 113 (1971), p. 747. With a step of interpretation I myself would not like to take, Rosand ("Titian's *Presentation*, p. 74) suggests that she is *Caritas*, and therefore a type of personification.

the picture and to each other, forming, with the beholder, a psychologically cohesive group witnessing, if not party to, the Presentation itself, so the actors on the right focus on the event at the temple.[23] There is, in fact, no major linking gesture or glance between the groups of real and imaginary figures, between portraits and types, so that only careful observation of dramatic details like faces and hands reveals the subtle formal continuity. With the exception of joining the left and right groups by Joachim's pose, there is an implosive configuration of the actors which excludes the viewers from the scene viewed. These two main groups are massed within the open space of the piazza, forming a wall of bodies across the transitions from foreground to background and organically reinforcing the strict planarity of space, thereby assuring a uniform surface tension throughout.

Against this mass of agitated figures stands the prominent figure of a young woman in white or pale gold at the foot of the steps, remarkable not only for the quantity of light she reflects but also her reposeful gesture echoing the calm and upright figures of the officers on the left. She in fact prepares the eye for the similar profile stance of the Virgin, small and isolated on the landing, who forms with the young and old woman at the bottom a triad of female figures nearest the dramatic center of the composition. The almost unmoving figures of High Priest and assistant, conical in their vestments, bring the rightward-tending movement of the whole to a stop. The visual rhythms commence, develop and end like a musical phrase within an ordered harmonic sequence, no less interesting for its predictability. The interrelation of figures and their environment is rigorous, and its function is to further the junction of real and painted space. We have seen that the vanishing point coincides with the ceiling's axis and the center of the altarpiece opposite.

23 Such a function for figures in a painting is of course not unique here. Psychological links such as the angel in Leonardo's *Madonna of the Rocks* or Raphael's *Sistine Madonna* are usually generalized, in the sense that no special identity of the viewer with the painted figure is indicated. In this case, however, the viewer would have been a member of the Scuola and would therefore have known the officers whose portraits are used for this narrative purpose; and the focus is consequently much stronger than in a less programmatic situation. A parallel example is Titian's votive picture of the Vendramin family, in which the *pater familias* gazes out of the picture towards, one supposes, other members of the family and invites them to join in adoring the relic of the True Cross. M. Baxandall (*Painting and Experience in Fifteenth-Century Italy. A Primer in the Social History of Pictorial Style*, London and New York, 1972, pp. 72 f.) has treated this theme with regard to perception. For an assessment of Baxandall's interpretation, see J. Ackerman's review in *The Art Quarterly*, 35 (1972), p. 420. For other observations of this device in Venetian painting, see M. Muraro, "Vittore Carpaccio o il teatro in pittura," *Studi sul teatro veneto fra rinascimento ed età barocca*, ed. by M. T. Muraro, *Civiltà veneziana, Studi 24, Florence*, 1971, p. 9.

In like manner, the figure of the Virgin coincides with the wall that separates the narrow from the wide part of the room, and this plane is emphasized by the column of the open loggia that locates her both within the painted space and architecturally within the space of the room. Close examination shows that every figure is placed with a similar concern for the solid, crystalline geometry of the whole composition, resulting in a welding together of compositional elements.

The light has three functions.[24] In the first place, exactly as in Titian's Frari *Assunta,* it furthers the principle of continuity by utilizing the illumination from the windows in the room. This is most obviously seen in the foreground figures on the left. Second, since there are at least three light sources (one from the room and two within the painting through the left portico and in the landscape), the light helps to create an inherent atmospheric space that meliorates, and in a certain sense naturalizes, the rigid geometry of the *disegno.* Third, it reveals color, and plays on certain parts in a superficially arbitrary way to give them emphasis.

As do the architecture and the relief-like plane of figures set close to the front edge on the left, the light in the *Presentation* articulates the various parts of the composition into integral components relative to their special narrative role. The group of officers on the left, with the woman receiving alms, is illuminated by the light from the room itself. This light makes spatially apparent the mediating function assigned the portraits and invites the viewer into the imaginative space. Moreover, this sheet of light illumines all the front plane, a narrow shelf between the flank of the steps and the bottom edge of the picture, where the old egg-seller and the antique torso are placed, outside the space lit internally and occupied by the other actors in the sacred event.

The light for the actors enters through the arched portico on the left, cuts behind the group of officers, and falls first on the backs of Joachim and Anna and then on the rich and simple folds of the attendants' dresses at the bottom of the steps. The risers carry this light in a quicker and more regular rhythm through the right half of the picture where the horizontal movement comes to rest against the simple upright planes of the temple facade. Within this light-formed space,

24 In my opinion, the light is solely an expository device. Exactly as in the theatre, it is arranged to reveal forms according to the dramatic intentions of the director. For Rosand, on the other hand, light in the *Presentation* is the chief carrier of symbolic content ("Titian's *Presentation,*" pp. 62-68). Following M. Meiss ("Light as Form and Symbol in Some Fifteenth-Century Paintings," *Art Bulletin,* 27 [1945], pp. 175ff.), Rosand has elsewhere developed a more comprehensive theory of Titian's using light for symbolic purposes ("Titian's Light as Form and Symbol," *Art Bulletin,* 58 [1975], pp. 58 ff.).

a subspace, likewise created by light, surrounds the figure of the Virgin, and illuminates the step risers just in front of her, the column behind, and the hem of the high priest's white alb. Within this brilliant zone, Titian was thus able to utilize the mandorla image without offending the doctrine of naturalism by the overstated intrusion of an abstract symbol.

Light from the sky reveals the landscape and the background architecture that has a richness commensurate with the distant view, the two forming, with the ceiling, a glittering upper register occupied only by the Virgin, the two priests and ancillary figures that further animate the space. Forms in this area are submitted to the disintegrating effect of shifting light playing over surfaces prepared to catch and accelerate it across a variety of textures and intricate chromatic arrangements. By these means Titian both provided a fulgent setting for the protagonist and allowed the light to disperse the weight of masonry behind the great solids in the more significant frontal planes.

Even with this clear articulation of space by separate light sources, there is no sense in Titian's picture of arbitrary and discontinuous juxtapositions. This unity results in part from the perspectival construction. But the sense of a complementary atmospheric and tonal continuity is achieved by color and the light that in this upper zone subsumes the other two in the unitive general luminosity peculiar to an exterior setting. The contribution of minor passages emerges in this situation. Figures standing in shadow, such as the two behind and flanking the Guardian del Matin and the beggar woman, planes parallel to the light sources, such as the flank of the temple steps, spaces in open shade like the loggia, as well as parts of the sky and much of the landscape, are areas in which local color, unexcited by the incidence of strong directed light, is allowed to compensate with intensity for what is lacking in value.[25]

It is with color even more than with light, though the distinction is surely arbitrary, that Titian further consolidated the parts and emphasized certain of them

[25] For T. Hetzer (*Tizian, Geschichte seiner Farbe*, Frankfurt a/M, 1935, pp. 109 ff.), one of the characteristics of Titian's "Third period" (1530-40) is the painter's exploration of the possibilities of uniting the color and tone of a picture by a single color. In the *Presentation* Hetzer rightly sees that intense primaries are held together by a general tonality tending towards browns and grays, and suggests that the advantages of the medieval gold ground are exploited in this way by Renaissance naturalism. The parallel development in Florentine painting of the 'twenties and 'thirties has suggested to John Shearman (*Andrea del Sarto*, Oxford, 1965, I, pp. 140-3) a most interesting connection of Titian with Sarto. Rosand has written an extensive account of the picture's *fortuna critica*, and takes issue with Hetzer's opinion that the period is, for Titian, one of *détente* ("Titian's *Presentation*," pp. 55-6).

to clarify dramatic relationships. Between the poles of white and black, which are not only poles of light but also of color, the spectrum ranges in secondary and teritiary hues around the three primaries, used here in large and highly saturated passages. In each of the three light zones the painter used a nearer-to-white value than which every other color in that zone is lower. (It is tempting to imagine each of these " whites " as the highest value of a primary hue — blue in the old woman's scarf, yellow in the profile woman's dress and veil, red in the cloud — although subsequent restorations and layers of dirty varnish make this impossible to ascertain.) The relationship between these three parts is the key by which one understands the function of all the color in the painting. In the first place, the brilliance of each white form isolates it and forces that form to one's attention. Second, the whites contravene, in a certain sense, the spatial effects of perspective and light by bringing the fore-, middle- and background into the same plane, just behind the picture surface. These three whites, and along with them the corresponding reds, blues and yellows in the three depths, rise to a common surface and are trapped there, like cells of cloissoné enamel, within the tension of inexorably reticular infrastructures. Third, as with the light, the coordination of three items by color is an expository device by which the artist combined and juxtaposed iconographical content to give special meaning to the story, as will become clear in the discussion of the *Presentation*'s iconography.

Triadic resonances of the same order sound throughout in chords of red, yellow and blue. The figure of Joachim which, it will be remembered, occupies the composition's vanishing point, is painted mostly in a rich yellow, offset in the sleeve and hem of the tunic by a changing pattern of dull crimson and azure. In this way the *disegno* focal point also states the theme of the *colore*. To Joachim's left, beyond the bluish-gray elision provided by Anna, stand the Scuola officer in his blue-black robe and the Guardian Grande in the strong red robes of his office. The primary color scheme is presented most aggressively in this trio of figures and then spreads across the picture, following the light and compositional direction, to the right. It is restated twice in the other two groups of three figures bearing the greatest dramatic weight, while the black-white polarity is concentrated in the figure of the old woman, who otherwise remains outside the system of chromatic sequences.

The sobriety of the first group and the elegance of the second, the women at the base of the steps, converge in the trio of the Virgin, the High Priest and his assistant. Here it is impossible and even meaningless to distinguish between color and light, so deeply did Titian identify the describer with the thing described. The

Virgin stands in her light blue dress with her left arm extended in that Byzantine gesture of greeting, bathed in golden light. The extension of this miraculous radiance is shown with the most commonplace naturalism on the column next to her, on the step risers and in the priests' albs; only by scaling it against the picture's general standard of verisimilitude does one come gradually to understand that this common enclosure in light distinguishes this group from the others and asserts through color the sense of numinous consecration peculiar to these three characters at the heart of the Presentation story. The elaboration of color is more nuanced here than elsewhere, and more extravagant. Far more than in the modest jewelry of the young women, the reflections in the blues and yellows of the High Priest's vestments and in the red mantle of his assistant convey dignity and status to these characters and, as in the female group, replenish with brilliant hues the somberness of the architectural space. Moreover, in these passages the red-yellow-blue theme reaches a final variation that gathers the colors intricately together and brings to a stop all the compositional and dramatic vectors that tended there.

This rather elaborate formal analysis would do little to advance one's understanding of the *Presentation* were it not for the fact that what is revealed is the visual device through which Titian projected the story as he chose, or was required, to relate it. Color, light and composition were designed to achieve two ends: first, to demonstrate the relationships among the characters in the narrative, and the role of the "donors;" second, to narrow the distance between empirical and imaginative experience by the force of an illusionistic system. That the albergo itself, with its light source, exercised a major function in this system is shown by the picture's deep and shallow parts mirroring the space of the room. Such a composition is, to be sure, a feature of Cinquecento Venetian painting in general; but here it is so integral to one's physical experience of the actual space that the invention would almost appear to have been demanded without alternative.[26] Fixed design integers such as the light source through the left portico, adapted from the Quattrocento windows in the room, and the perspectival focus falling on the axis of Vivarini's altarpiece and the ceiling coffer with the relief of Christ underscore the artist's determination to continue the viewer's empirical spatial experience as a setting in which to fulfill the iconographical requirements of the commission.[27]

26 See Rosand, "Titian's *Presentation*," pp. 60-62.

27 The windows were renovated during Titian's campaign on the picture (Rosand, "Titian's *Presentation*," p. 66 and n. 60).

The iconographical requirements are not, as it happens, easy to determine. The problem does not lie, obviously, with the identification of the scene itself, nor with the portraits of Scuola officers, nor with the figures of Joachim, Anna, the Virgin and High Priest.[28] But one must decide what all the other figures are meant to represent; they are either genre types, as in other representations of the theme, or the most prominent figures, at least, must represent specific persons. The antique torso at the right foreground and the farm products surrounding the old rustic at the foot of the steps must likewise be explained either as space-filling window dressing or as bearers of significant symbolic content. Basically, the importance one attaches to these objects and figures reveals one's estimation of Titian as a narrative artist. It is difficult to pass off all these prominent arrangements as mere decoration, as I take the partially visible architectural sculpture to be, especially if one recall the stunning dramatic economy of the great religious paintings that precede the *Presentation*, pictures like the *Assunta* and the *Assassination of St. Peter Martyr.*

Comparison with antecedent versions of the *Presentation* does little to explain these. The setting for the painting was a matter of Venetian convention by the 1530s, dating as far back as the elaborate piazza designed for it by Gentile Bellini and continuing through Carpaccio and Cima da Conegliano.[29] In contrast to Florentine examples such as Ghirlandaio's, where the space is closed up with a dense architecture showing little more than the area just in front of the temple, the pictures of Venetian painters include a grand view of an open piazza behind and to the left of the temple steps, expanded in the case of Cima with an open landscape extending into the distance (Fig. 8). The temple steps are always prominent, as their role in the legend dictates; and the Venetian artists liked to put a répoussoir figure just in front of them, corresponding to the old woman in Titian's picture. The little boy with the unicorn, signifying Mary's virginity, occupies this space in Carpaccio's painting; and a group of four, with four still-life elements, does the same in Cima's.

There can be no doubt, as all scholars have noted, that Titian must have had Cima's model very much in mind as he planned the commission for the Scuola della Carità.[30] Not only in its general layout and similarity of spatial construction

28 The figures of Joachim and Anna, though, have often, and inexplicably, been misidentified. See Rosand, "Titian's *Presentation*," n. 56.

29 See the reference in n. 26 above.

30 See Wethey, *Titian*, *I*, p. 124 for further references. Pasqualino, to whom the commission was originally given, was a pupil of Cima's; and we know that the Scuola kept Pasqualino's design, likely based

does Titian's picture resemble Cima's, but details such as the woman with the child at the far left of the earlier painting and the gesture of embrace in the men at the foot of the steps, as well as some architectural features like the portico façade set at an acute angle to the picture plane occur again, though in greatly modified ways, in Titian's solution. There is not so much resemblance to the Carpaccio version, though the boy and unicorn, together with the tower with its Adam and Eve flanking a clock surrounded by Hebrew characters, suggests an iconographic richness lacking in the Cima, but likely present, as we shall see, in the Titian.

Non-Venetian models possibly known to Titian also reveal the picture's uniqueness as well as its conformity to a general type. Only one, Peruzzi's *Presentation* in Sta. Maria della Pace in Rome, bears a really significant resemblance to Titian's (Fig. 9).[31] Panofsky set great store by the Dürer woodcut of the subject, available to Titian either through a German edition or from Marcantonio's copy (Fig. 10).[32] It is true that Dürer's is the only other example, so far as I know, of a *Presentation* that shows a remnant of classical sculpture; but its appearance together with the money changers does not justify one supposing, without further evidence, that Dürer implied the historical divisions *ante legem*, *sub legem*, and *sub gratias*. Although he was right in the long run, Panofsky too readily took the seated woman in Cima's picture as Synagoga, since she is not distinguished as particularly Jewish by her men companions, as all the male onlookers are similarly turbaned and gowned.[33] Even so, no one has yet explained the identities of the young women, so distinguished in dress and pose, at the foot of the steps in the Carità painting.[34] As it happens, their identity confirms Panofsky's interpretation of Titian's old woman as Synagoga, though for different reasons than his, and also explains the antique fragment near the right edge.

The characters, though not the action itself, of Titian's *Presentation* find their

on Cima's. See Rosand, "Titian's *Presentation*," p. 60; G. Gronau, "Pasqualino da Venezia," *Allgemeines Lexikon der Bildenden Künstler* (*Thieme-Becker*), vol. 26, pp. 273-4.

31 Titian could have known the design only second-hand, of course, through Peruzzi's student, Serlio. See C. L. Frommel, *Baldassare Peruzzi als Maler und Zeichner*, *Römisches Jahrbuch für Kunstgeschichte, XI. Beiheft*, Vienna and Munich, 1967-68, pp. 125 ff., cat. no. 89.

32 E. Panofsky, *Problems in Titian, Mostly Iconographic*, New York, 1969, pp. 38-9.

33 Panofsky, *Problems*, p. 37. Rosand, too, identifies the old woman as Synagoga ("Titian's *Presentation*," pp. 71-2).

34 Rosand ("Titian's *Presentation*," p. 74) seems to follow Leo Steinberg's suggestion that the woman in white is Elizabeth, the mother of John the Baptist, a suggestion I find implausible.

only counterparts in the late Trecento *repraesentatio figurata* recorded by Philippe de Mézières in astonishing detail on Cyprus and performed at Venice before 1372. The script calls for a cast of twenty-two people plus a number of ancillary characters used as a kind of chorus. Costumes, speeches, action and the stage arrangement are all fully described. Although I am aware that a specific connection between Titian's painting and Philippe's play cannot be shown, I should like to offer an interpretation of the painting's iconography based on that script. I know of no other visual or literary source that comes so close to explaining the anomalous, but so prominent, figures in the *Presentation*; and I do feel certain that the artist fully intended to evoke the spirit of a sacred drama, whether it was Philippe's or not.[35]

Philippe's *repraesentatio* requires of course the main characters familiar to us through both verbal and graphic versions of the legend: the Virgin Mary; her parents; young female attendants; the High Priest; and a crowd of relatives. Because the *repraesentatio figurata* was intended to show not only an early scene in the history of Christian salvation but the meaning of salvation as well, there are also characters and episodes that demonstrate what can be regarded as exigetical glosses on the story as it is recorded in a bare and legendary form. For this reason the cast is expanded to include musicians, three archangels, nine other angels representing the orders of the angelic host, as well as personifications of Ecclesia, Synagoga and Lucifer. There were also the bishop (or priest), deacon and subdeacon who took part in the *repraesentatio*, since it was performed in the context of the liturgy.

The action of these characters is just as carefully prescribed as that of the protagonists. There is, for example, a wonderful episode involving Synagoga.[36] After all the characters have processed into the church and taken their places on two raised platforms, there is a sequence of speeches, beginning with the Virgin herself; and then each beneficent character speaks, beginning with Joachim and Anna and finishing with the nine ranks of angels. Synagoga then makes a lament and is expelled from the assembly (that is, forced down the steps into the nave and out of the church) amid loud wailing, tears and, one suspects, the clatter of wood and metal as she drops her attributes, the Tablets of the Law and a standard bearing the Roman motto, SPQR.

35 Philippe's manuscript is reproduced in full by Young, "Philippe de Mézières'," pp. 227-242. Rosand ("Titian's *Presentation*," pp. 72-3) would not, I think, place as much importance on this text as I do.

36 Young, "Philippe de Mézières'," p. 238.

There is a striking similarity between the descriptions of some of Philippe's characters and those prominent figures in Titian's painting. Ecclesia, for example, is described as a beautiful woman about twenty years old who is completely dressed in gold.[37] Synagoga, by contrast, should be dressed in the simple and dark garments "*ad modum antique vetule.*"[38] These two characters from the *repraesentatio* have their counterparts in the young woman at the foot of the steps and the old woman seated among farm products. Titian's Ecclesia, it is true, lacks the crown and cross as well as the dalmatic called for in the script; and it is also true that Titian's old woman carries neither Roman nor Jewish attributes. The artist, however, managed to convey the identities through a code which is more significative than representative. Synagoga's medieval attributes have been replaced by Renaissance "disguised" symbols: the standard inscribed SPQR has become a broken antique torso, and the Tablets of the Law have been replaced by objects used in contemporary Jewish ceremonial.[39] Also, her placement outside the zone reserved, as we have seen, for the actors in the story points not only to her identity but even to that moment in the play after her expulsion from the church. No

37 The first description of Ecclesia (p. 228) says she should be "mulier pulcerrima etatis circiter XX. annorum," whereas later on (p. 230) she is described as "pulcerrimus iuuenes circa XX. annos sine barba, et induetur totem de curro in habitu diaconi," wearing "cappelus pulcerrimis mulieris extensis super humeros" (presumably a wig). In either case, the personification should appear to be female.

38 Young, "Philippe de Mézières'," p. 230.

39 The torso has been discussed by C. Vermuele, *European Art and the Classical Past*, Cambridge, Mass., 1964, p. 88). The sheep or lamb is associated with the Passover meal, the Seder. The custom, dating, apparently, to the ninth century, of symbolically attaching the sins of a person to a fowl (cock or hen), called *Kapparot*, is illustrated time and again in Renaissance *Haggadim*. On the eve of the Day of Atonement, penitential passages from scripture were recited, and then a cock or hen was swung around the head. Although *Kapparot* was officially discouraged, the custom became particularly popular with the Kabbalists, who were concentrated in the sixteenth century in Venice. There is scant mention of eggs in the scriptures; but they are given ceremonial importance in the *Haggadah*. These eggs are chiefly associated with mourning and Passover. Mourners are given eggs to eat on their return from a burial; and eggs dipped in salt are eaten before the Seder. The prevalence of this Passover custom in Renaissance Venice is witnessed by the large number of Seder plates, with indentations for the eggs, which survive from the period. The egg is also an ancient — and self-evident — symbol of parthenogenesis, and is associated in art with the Virgin, for example, in Guido Reni's fresco of her birth at S. Gregorio al Celio in Rome. See H. Schauss, *The Jewish Festivals*, New York, 1938, pp. 149 ff., 164 ff.; "*Eggs*," *Encyclopaedia Judaica*, 6, Jerusalem, 1971, cols. 474-475. For Renaissance ceremonial utensils, consult M. Sandri and P. Alazraki, *Arte e vita ebraica a Venezia, 1516–1797*, Florence, 1971. The complex history of Jewish presence in Venice still awaits serious and unbiased study; Cecil Roth laid some groundwork in two books, *The History of the Jews in Italy* (Philadelphia, 1945) and *Jews in the Renaissance* (New York, 1959), though they are unhappily poorly documented. Brian Pullan, in *Rich and Poor in Renaissance Venice*, has most recently turned to the problem. See also Panofsky, *Problems*, p. 37, n. 26; Rosand, "Titian's *Presentation*," p. 73 for an interpretation of the farm objects and torso parallel to mine.

such iconographic detail allows us to identify Ecclesia with the same accuracy. But Synagoga can hardly occur in this context without her symbolic pendant; and the old woman's gaze at the younger one forms a narrative bond that suggests their pairing. What is more, Ecclesia's profile pose links her to the figure of the Virgin, and therefore to the one who commonly typifies the Church in pre-Reformation ecclesiology, both Eastern and Western.

One can go further with the script, though further identifications become more hypothetical. The little girl leaning on the steps is surely one of those virgins who accompany Mary into the temple, and she has her counterpart in many pictorial representations of the theme. The two young women behind and flanking Ecclesia might also be identified as Raphael and Gabriel. The one on the left would correspond to Raphael because of the child and dog, a reference to Tobias and hence to all Guardian Angel representations.[40] The Archangel Michael is missing from our painting, but so is Lucifer. In the *repraesentatio*, however, his role is completed with the expulsion of Lucifer, while the other two archangels remain as attendants of the Virgin.[41] But the physical absence of these two characters from the scene may have been compensated for by yet another element in the painting, the temple steps with the door underneath. No Venetian could have failed to connect this configuration with the Scala dei Giganti in the courtyard of the Palazzo Ducale (Fig. 11). Although Sansovino's *giganti* had not, of course, been installed there in the 1530s, the architectural arrangement was as we see it today. On the ground floor underneath the landing, a cell was installed to imprison those accused of treason while their sentence was read by the Doge from the top.[42] Since the *Presentation* was the narrative commonly used to signify the Immaculate Conception, it might be supposed that Lucifer is "imprisoned" under the Virgin just as Venice's enemies were held captive under the Doge. Circumstantial support for this hypothesis can be found in the negotiations of the Scuola della Carità with Pordenone, after the completion of Titian's assignment in 1538, when the artist himself suggested that he paint an Assumption on the wall to the right of the *Pre-*

40 On the Renaissance treatment of the Raphael theme, consult E. Gombrich, "Tobias and the Angel," *Symbolic Images. Studies in the Art of the Renaissance*; London, 1972, pp. 26–30. I am grateful to Marilyn Aronberg Lavin, who quieted my misgivings about Titian's having painted female angels by referring me to G. Berefelt, *A Study on the Winged Angel. The Origin of a Motif.* Stockholm Studies in History of Art, 14. Stockholm, 1968, especially pp. 96–111.

41 Young, "Philippe de Mézières'," p. 239.

42 See M. Muraro, "La Scala senza Giganti," *Essays in Honor of Erwin Panofsky*, ed. Millard Meiss, New York, 1961, pp. 351–2.

sentation as a suitable subject both iconographically and formally to serve as a pendant to the just-finished narrative.[43]

Philippe de Mézières' text might explain the identities of those prominent characters in the *Presentation* that have thus far been largely ignored by critics; but unless it can be shown that sacred drama had more to do with Titian's painting than to provide him with a list of actors, we would be left with a simple checklist and the task of explaining how the members of the Scuola della Carità can have been expected to read the picture as we have, unless they were somehow familiar with the script of a play not known to have been performed in Venice after the late Trecento. The most blatant Renaissance content in the composition, the perspective architecture, though, does provide sufficient evidence to allow us to suppose that the *sacra rappresentazione*, as religious drama was called in the sixteenth century, of the Presentation was indeed performed, unrecorded, in Venice in Titian's lifetime. What is more, the connection of the figural identities with the setting is the touchstone of the painting's entire conceit, discussed above, which is a conceptual, rather than visual, illusion.

The *Presentation*, in fact, bears more than a superficial resemblance to Raphael's design for *Paul Preaching at Athens*, known to Titian from the 1520s (Fig. 12).[44] Although the Carità painting belongs to that large class of Venetian compositions decorating the walls of numerous Scuole, and shares their planarity, the device of treating figures in a frieze close to the picture plane, and the filling of the whole with visual richness, its principles of organization and the importance of an aggressive architecture link it also to Raphael's late narrative style, exemplified by the tapestry cartoons. The *Presentation* departs significantly from Raphael's design in three ways, however: the horizon is much lowered, so that the ground in the painting appears parallel to the floor of the albergo; one side opens onto an extensive landscape missing from the Raphael; and the spatial relationships between figures and their setting are not set out with the clarity Raphael sought to achieve. In these three ways, however, Titian's painting compares with another version of the theme, itself derived from the late Raphael, namely Baldassare Peruzzi's painting

43 When approached about filling the albergo's east wall in March 1538, Pordenone suggested that the Assumption was the proper thematic accompaniment to the Presentation, from which one may infer Pordenone's understanding of the Presentation as a type for the Immaculate Conception. The document was published by Ludwig, " Archivalische Beiträge," (1905), p. 147.

44 Three of the men behind the steps in the center of the *Presentation* are closely derived from *Paul at Athens*, but in the reverse sense of the tapestry which, like that of the *Conversion of Saul*, was in Venice by 1528 (Shearman, *Raphael's Cartoons*, pp. 139, 140, 144, n. 62).

in a pendentive in Sta. Maria della Pace in Rome. Titian could not have known Peruzzi's composition first-hand, but happily there is no reason to suppose that he did. During the campaign on the *Presentation* he was free to consult Peruzzi's pupil, Serlio, then in residence in Venice.[45] Peruzzi's and Serlio's activities in theatrical productions are well known, and it is in this connection, I think, that one can understand Titian's process of integrating the idea of a dramatic performance into a visual presentation that would also control the entire physical space with the authority of Central Italian *disegno*.

Ever since Cecil Gould's article outlining Serlio's impact on Venetian painters appeared in 1962 there has been a growing interest in the whole phenomenon of architectural elements in Venetian pictures, as well as the recognition of the role that experiments in theatrical scene design played in Cinquecento art.[46] Unlike Gould, I believe that Titian had a very strong interest, at least for the *Presentation* and the Vienna *Ecce Homo*, in the formal and symbolic possibilities of an architecture which could provide an automatically perceived narrative frame within which the story unfolded.[47] If the suggestion is correct that the medieval dramatic presentation is the key to identifying figures, we are entitled to take the background as not only a perspective loosely organized according to Serlian principles, but as the suggestion, not representation, of an actual stage set constructed to accommodate actors and participants from the audience.[48] Titian's architecture, in fact,

45 See, with further references, C. Gould, "Sebastiano Serlio and Venetian Painting," *Journal of the Warburg and Courtauld Institutes*, 25 (1962), pp. 56–64; E. Forssman, "Über Architekturen in der venezianischen Malerei des Cinquecento," *Wallraf-Richartz Jahrbuch*, 29 (1967), pp. 108–114; D. Howard, "Sebastiano Serlio's Venetian Copyrights," *Burlington Magazine*, 125 (1973), pp. 512–516.

46 Gould ("Sebastiano Serlio," p. 57f.) was the first to notice the specifically theatrical arrangement of Titian's painting and even suggested that Serlio had an actual hand in its rendering. In an excellent analysis of the painting, G. Pochat (*Figur und Landschaft. Eine historische Interpretation der Landschaftsmalerei von der Antike bis zur Renaissance*. Berlin, 1973, pp. 453 ff.) has drawn a similar theatrical analogy. I am grateful to Harold Wethey for calling this study to my attention. Rosand ("Titian in the Frari," *Art Bulletin*, 53 [1971], p. 207) advances a theory in which the architectural settings for Titian's paintings are seen to be a major formative element for their compositions and a basis for connoisseurship. On this point, see A. Harris, "Letter to the Editor," *Art Bulletin*, 54 (1972), pp. 116–18. Recently K. Dorment ("Tomb and Testament: Architectural Significance in Titian's *Pietà*," *Art Quarterly*, 35 [1972], pp. 399–418) has proposed an architectural iconographic program for Titian's *Pietà* in the Accademia, Venice. See also Rosand, "Theater and Structure in the Art of Paolo Veronese," *Art Bulletin* 55 (1973), pp. 217–39, with further references. For Rosand, the architecture, like the light, in the *Presentation* bears specific symbolic meaning: for myself, it is only generally significant, with the exception of the temple steps. See Rosand, "Titian's *Presentation*," pp. 76–9.

47 Titian "had no interest in architectural forms as such." Gould, "Sebastiano Serlio," p. 56. The architecture of the Vienna *Ecce Homo* is discussed in my dissertation (*Titian's Narrative Art*, pp. 150–4).

48 Muraro ("Vittore Carpaccio," pp. 7 ff.) draws

very closely reflects the state of perspective scene design achieved by the 1530s, and by taking it as such we can discover its extremely topical character relative to the Scuola della Carità and the social class from which its officials were drawn.

A sophisticated contemporary viewer could have recognized the architecture of the *Presentation* as "Serlian," since Serlio's drawings were published in 1537.[49] Titian, of course, had access to them previously; and it was surely only an accident that the *Presentation* was installed immediately after its architectural canons were published (Figs. 13 and 14). In fact, the picture belongs less to the specific type of stage sets published by Serlio than to a class of perspective scenes that we can only imagine from descriptions or intuit from surviving drawings and engravings.[50] Venice, surprisingly enough, was not a center of creative dramatic activity in the early Cinquecento.[51] In the years around the time of our picture Ferrara, especially, and the courts of Mantua and Milan seem to have been those centers from which theatrical developments spread to other parts of Italy. The Venetian government manifested an ambivalent and ambiguous attitude towards theatrical presentations from the late fifteenth century through the sixteenth. In the face of

close connections between Carpaccio's St. Ursula cycle and the *sacra rappresentazione* of the same theme; and Zorzi, in the same volume ("Elementi per la visualizzazione della scena veneta prima del Palladio," pp. 21-25) makes the same point. Both authors draw very heavily on the insights of Ludwig and Molmenti who, in their *Vittore Carpaccio. La Vita e le Opere* (Milan, 1906, pp. 112-113), first called attention to the parallels of play and paintings.

49 W. B. Dinsmoor, "The Literary Remains of Sebastiano Serlio," *Art Bulletin*, 24 (1942), pp. 55-91, 115-54; Howard, "Sebastiano Serlio's," pp. 735-6.

50 The bibliography of Italian scene design is immense and overcrowded with a great many studies which are either entirely derivative of Alessandro d'Ancona's fundamental *Origini del teatro italiano* (2 vols., Turin, 1891) or speculative and even imaginary in character. Studies I have found specially useful, besides d'Ancona, are: E. K. Chambers, *The Medieval Stage*, 2 vols., Oxford, 1903; A. Scharff, *Beiträge zur Geschichte des Bühnenbildes von 15. bis zum 17. Jahrhunderts*, Ph.D. Dissertation, Freiburg, 1925; V. Mariani, *Storia della scenografia italiana*, Florence, 1930; K. Young, *The Drama of the Medieval Church*, 2 vols., Oxford, 1933; H. Tintelnot, *Barocktheatre und Barocke Kunst*, Berlin, 1939; G. R. Kernodle, *From Art to Theatre. Form and Convention in the Renaissance*, Chicago, 1944; D. Frey, "Zuschauer und Bühne," *Kunstwissenschaftlichen Grundfragen*, Vienna, 1946, pp. 151-223; R. Krautheimer, "The Tragic and Comic Scene of the Renaissance. The Baltimore and Urbino Panels," *Gazette des Beaux-Arts*, 33 (1948), pp. 327-346 (reprinted with additional comments in his *Studies in Early Christian, Medieval and Renaissance Art*, New York, 1970, pp. 345-359); C. Molinari, "Les rapports entre la scène et les spectateurs dans le théâtre italien du XVIe siecle," *Lieu théâtrale à la Renaissance*, Paris, 1964, pp. 61-71; R. Klein and H. Zerner, "Vitruve et le théâtre de la Renaissance italienne," *Lieu théâtrale*, pp. 49-60; Maria Teresa Muraro, "Le lieu des spectacles (publics ou privés) à Venise au XVe et au XVIe siecles," *Lieu théâtrale*, pp. 85-93; L. Zorzi, "Elementi per la visualizzazione della scena veneta prima del Palladio," *Studi sul teatro veneto fra rinascimento ed età barocca*, edited by Maria Teresa Muraro, *Civiltà veneziana, Studi 24*, Florence, 1971, pp. 25-51; Rosand, "Theatre and Structure," pp. 217-239. A comprehensive review of the theatre in Renaissance Venice is to be found in P. Molmenti, *La Storia di Venezia nella vita privata...* Part 2, Bergamo, 1911, pp. 287-328.

51 Zorzi, "Elementi," p. 21.

these strictures that, considering the frequency of infraction, must have been little more than stern warnings, Sanudo reports a steady succession of theatrical events during the first three decades of the sixteenth century.[52] Venice was not really the place for a continually encouraging climate to nourish the humanist theatre, for there was of course no princely court; and dramatic performances, as distinguished from other kinds of theatrical events like festivals and processions, were primarily an event of Carnival, and sponsored by Compagnie della Calza, social clubs of young aristocrats whose purpose was to provide lavish entertainment for themselves and their friends during the pre-Lenten season, not unlike the Carnival Krewes in present-day New Orleans.[53] With the possible exception of the production of Aretino's *La Talanta*, staged in 1542 by Vasari, the Compagnie della Calza were neither learned enough nor serious enough to promote the kind of theatre that had been flourishing in North Italian courts for the fifty years before 1530.[54]

The perspective set, which was the principal visual motif of the modern theatre, was certainly known in Venice of the 1530s, but it was by no means the only scenographic option there.[55] The few documented associations of Venice and the

52 Sanudo lists the following restrictions placed by the Council of Ten on dramatic performances: "...non si fazi più in questa terra ni a noze ni in nisun loco recitar commedie Tragedie et Egloge sotto pena a quelli in chà de chi di ducati 100. e privation per do anni de offizii et consegni et quelli li fessero et in parte..." (Entry for 30 December 1508); "Fo pubblicata su le scale di San Marco e di Rialto di Ordine di Cai dil Conseio di X. che non si habbi a far comedie in questa terra justa le parte presa dil 1508. nel dito Conseio di X." (Entry for 1 February 1521 [Venetian style]); "Da poi disnar fo Conseio di X con la zonta et posto per il Serimo una parte che non si fazi più Comedie in questa Città nostra aue 2. non sincere 11. di la parte 16. di no et fu preso di no atento che dil 1520..." (Entry for 16 February 1530 [Venetian style]). The large number of dramatic events listed by Sanudo in this period, however, shows that the laws were neither taken very seriously nor enforced. In fact, the day before Sanudo's entry for 1 February 1521, he notes that a comedy was performed at the Papal Legate's house, with senators in attendance. All of Sanudo's entries relative to the theatre were extracted in the nineteenth century and collected in a manuscript now in the Biblioteca Correr, Venice (Cod. Cicogna 1650 [3111]). See also R. Arrigoni, "Notizie ed osservazioni intorno alle origini ed al progresso dei teatri e delle rappresentazioni teatrali in Venezia...," *Miscellanea per nozze Michiel-Morosini*, Venice, 1840, pp. 7 ff.

53 See Bernardo Giustinian, *Historie chronologiche dell'origine degli ordini militari...*, Venice, 1962, I, pp. 114 ff. L. Venturi ("Le compagnie della Calza," Part 2, *Nuovo Archivio Veneto*, 17 [1909], pp. 140 ff.) traced their theatrical activities. On the difference between these aristocratic clubs and the serious religious confraternities of youths, consult R. Trexler's "Ritual in Florence: Adolescence and Salvation in the Renaissance," *The Pursuit of Holiness in Late Medieval and Renaissance Religion*, eds. Charles Trinkaus with Heiko A. Oberman, Leiden, 1974, p. 200 *et passim*.

54 For a reconstruction of Vasari's *apparato* for the performance of Aretino's *La Talanta*, with further references, see J. Schulz, "Vasari at Venice," *Burlington Magazine*, 103 (1961), pp. 500 ff.

55 A manuscript preserved in the Marciana (*Codice Marciano Ital.* XI, 66 [6730]) contains a drawing of the 1530s, accompanying the text of Ruzzante's comedy *Betia*, which shows three simple house fa-

perspective set, Serlio's 1539 stage in Vicenza and Vasari's *apparato* of 1542, are subsequent to the design and completion of the *Presentation.*[56] By that time, however, perspective scenes in Italy had reached a high degree of sophistication after nearly a century of development; and since the most recent signal advances had been made in cities near Venice, one may assume that any group of rich borghesi would have known and understood Titian's architectural setting for their painting.

Giulio Romano had designed a perspective scene for Charles V's visit to Mantua in 1532; and the first permanent perspectival stage construction was set up in Ferrara in 1531 at the d'Este court, actualizing dramatic space commonly rendered by painted backdrops set sometimes on the back walls of cortili, sometimes at the end of a great room in a palace.[57] It is to this latter type that most of the graphic records of perspective scene design belong, painted backdrops such as the Quattrocento Berlin, Baltimore and Urbino panels and Cinquecento examples like a drawing after Bramante in the Ambrosiana and the sketches of Peruzzi (Figs. 15, 16 and 17).[58] It is to the former type, in which the spatial illusion is achieved by constructed houses, temples, shops and so forth, that Titian's *Presentation* setting belongs, in company with the Ferrara set of 1531 and the Serlio one of 1539; and it is this type, in which the actors are free to move within, rather than in front of, the space, which must have appeared to the members of the Scuola della Carità as being the most modern technique of rendering dramatic action. At the very least, they could not have avoided feeling flattered to house a kind of narrative mode which was thoroughly advanced and which was associated with the highest levels of Italian social and intellectual life. Unlike the distant architectural views in contemporary paintings by Paris Bordone and Bonifazio Veronese, which bear little relation to the figure space and which Gould has rightly linked with Serlio's

cades side by side, one labeled " Ostaria " and another " Casa de Bethia," clearly as a record of the very schematic setting for the play. The manuscript was published by M. Cristofari, *Il Codice Marciano Ital. XI, 66 (6730)*, Padua, 1937. See also Zorzi, " Elementi," pp. 31, 42.

56 Klein and Zerner, " Vitruve et le théâtre," pp. 53, 55.

57 Vasari-Milanesi, V, 54 f. D'Ancona (*Origini*, II, 433) offered an interpretation of the documents, which he also published (*Origini*, II, 433, n. 1). Little is known of Ariosto's permanent set in the Este palace, except that it consisted of house and shop fronts, appropriate to comedies performed in front of them. The set burned to the ground the following year, 1532. See F. Gibbons, *Dosso and Battista Dossi, Court Painters at Ferrara*, Princeton, 1968, p. 22.

58 H. Posse, *Die Gemäldegalerie des Kaiser-Friedrich-Museums. I. Die Romanischen Länder*, Berlin, 1909, 76, no. 1615; for the Baltimore and Urbino panels, see Krautheimer, *Studies*, pp. 345-60 and particularly the Postscript (p. 359) for a discussion of bibliography subsequent to the original publication. See also F. Malaguzzi-Valeri, *La Corte di Lodovico il Moro*, II, Milan, 1915, fig. 38.

schemes for the Tragic and Comic Scenes, the setting for the *Presentation* is not so much backdrop as it is ambiance, like the set, insofar as one can tell, for the 1539 stage in Vicenza.[59]

It is well known that the Italian perspective scene evolved in the context of profane drama in the Renaissance. These settings, painted or constructed, were built for both ancient and contemporary drama, for comedies, tragedies and pastorals. By contrast, the setting for sacred drama has a much older history, and the locations of those performances were much more varied. They occurred in churches, in piazze, in private palaces and religious houses; they were mimed, said or sung in verse and prose, in Latin and the vernacular; they were performed as separate plays, as substitutes for the sermon at mass, as *tableaux vivants*; they ranged in importance from part of a great pageant or procession to fully developed dramas divided into acts, with a stage and a stationary audience. What concerns us here is the credibility, in Cinquecento terms, of Titian's setting a sacred drama within the context of a profane scene, a medieval mystery play against an allusion to the Renaissance humanist theatre.[60]

The requirements for profane drama were in many ways simpler than those for the sacred. The perspective scene, in itself, expressed temporal and spatial unity; this unity was both achieved and symbolized by the device of the one-point perspective, in which all the various orthogonals converge within the picture space. The sacred drama, on the other hand, required a multiplicity of time, space and location. Not only was it necessary to be able to show events happening simultaneously in two places, but there was also the need for three clearly defined realms (heaven, earth and hell) and the attendant beings (angels, humans and demons) appropriate to each. Moreover, it was important that certain locations, such as the Temple, Mary's house, Pilate's palace, and so forth, be shown clearly and separately. Renaissance developments in this regard were twofold. On the one hand, the need for elaborate stage machinery for apparitions, miracles, ascents and descents gave rise to a whole craft whose goal was to delight and mystify the audience with the variety and extravagance of effects. This trend, beginning with Brunelleschi, developed through the sixteenth century and was finally incorporated into the profane drama in the seventeenth, with the wonderful stage effects

59 Gould, "Sebastiano Serlio," pp. 58 f.

60 D'Ancona, *Origini*, I, pp. 331-367; Ludwig and Molmenti, *Vittore Carpaccio*, p. 112; Martini, *Storia*, pp. 15-25; Zorzi, "Elementi," pp. 36 ff.; E. Welsford, *The Court Masque* (1927), New York, 1962, pp. 83 f.

for which the baroque theatre is famous. At the same time, the medieval system of *luoghi deputati*, which consisted of a row of schematized buildings across the stage representing the various places of action, beginning on the left with "paradise" and ending on the right with "hell," survived intact well towards the middle of the sixteenth century.[61] It is this arrangement, as intimately connected with sacred drama as the perspective scene is with the profane, that has been shown to be influential on Carpaccio in the working out of his great St. Ursula cycle.[62] Where the perspective scene is a self-contained world to itself, the *luogo deputato* is spreading and conceptually unconfined; where the perspective scene is stable and unified, the *luogo deputato* is animated and spatially fragmented; where the perspective set is psychologically generalized, the *luogo deputato* is intended to excite the eye and arouse the emotions. One is "classical," the other "romantic."

The *sacra rappresentazione* evolved in fifteenth-century Florence as a hybrid of the *repraesentatio figurata* and Renaissance dramatic forms based on antique drama, with the action organized into well-developed plots unfolding in a series of acts on a stage with a stationary audience. Not much is known of these religious "comedies," as they were sometimes called, from the point of view of their production. A great many texts have survived, however, amply to show that the modern *sacre rappresentazioni* were commonly developed as independent plays from medieval texts of *laude*, mysteries and moralities.[63] It was thus not only possible, but even probable, that an old text would be adapted for new uses; and even though there is no record of the *Presentation*'s ever having been performed in Venice after Philippe de Mézières' effort, there is no reason to assume that it was not. By the beginning of the sixteenth century, one might have seen a *sacra rappresentazione* performed in front of nearly any kind of scene — the old *luogo deputato*, a simple painted backdrop in perspective or not, or even before a fully realized perspective set of the type Serlio built in Vicenza. Performances seem to have been rare, at least in Venice, during our period. In a list of some 278 theatrical events, including mummeries, processions and the like, as well as proper dramas, Sanudo lists only two specifically sacred dramas between 1498 and 1533, although it is pos-

61 A manuscript in Valenciennes, dated 1547, looks for all the world as though it could have been illustrated in the thirteenth or fourteenth centuries, so tenacious and satisfactory to the needs of sacred drama was the method of *luoghi deputati*. See Mariani, *Storia*, p. 17; Zorzi, "Elementi," p. 43.

62 Ludwig and Molmenti, *Vittore Carpaccio*, p. 112; Muraro, "Vittore Carpaccio," *passim*; Zorzi, "Elementi," pp. 36 ff.

63 See A. Cioni, *Bibliografia delle Sacre Rappresentazioni*, Florence, 1961.

sible that there may have been some among his anonymous *comedie.*[64] In Florence, on the other hand, the enormous number of editions of *sacre rappresentazioni* points to a more lively interest; and general enthusiam for this kind of theatre has survived in certain places in Italy down to this day.[65] The allusion of Titian's *Presentation*, then, is to a certain theatrical genre: it is to sacred drama, but of a type barely a century old by 1534, constructed along the lines of classically inspired profane drama associated with aristocratic courts in northern Italy, and shown against a setting which was modern, sophisticated and expensive, even as it was appropriate as Scuola decoration. In many ways, one can see the *Presentation* as a parallel to the dramatic performances produced during carnival by the rich sons of Venetian nobles and satisfying, in a vicarious way, the same social energies which the Scuole themselves were designed to mitigate and disperse.

It would be wrong, I think, to claim that Titian, because of this solution for the *Presentation*, was in any special way an artist of the theatre. He did carry out two theatrical commissions for the Compagnia della Calza dei Sempiterni in 1542, the year Vasari equipped the theatre and stage for Aretino's comedy under commission for the same group.[66] In that year, Titian built a *teatro gallegiante* or *teatro del mondo* for the Sempiterni's carnival celebrations. The *teatri del mondo* were circular structures supporting columns carrying an architrave or a domed ceiling. They were often large enough to accomodate two hundred people, and were used to float up and down the Grand Canal and in the Bacino while musicians played for the entertainment of guests on board.[67] A stationary theatre of the same type was built under Titian's directions in the Campo Santo Stefano, which he decorated with paintings, tapestries and *imprese*, as the scene for the elaborate ceremonies surrounding the mass initiating the Sempiterni's Carnival activities.[68]

64 Venice, Biblioteca Correr, Cod. Cicogna 1650 (3111). The proscriptions against replacing the sermon at mass with a sacred drama indicates in a negative way their great popularity in Venice in the sixteenth century.

65 Cioni, *Bibliografia.*

66 Giustinian, *Historie*, p. 114 f. Giustinian's information came to him through Girolamo Duodo, who owned a manuscript containing the constitution and deliberations of the Compagnia dei Sempiterni, founded in 1541. For Titian's *teatro gallegiante* see L. Padoan Urban, "Teatri e 'teatri del Mondo' nella Venezia del Cinquecento," *Arte Veneta*, 20 (1966), p. 142. Zorzi ("Elementi," 40) mistakenly believed that Titian actually painted a backdrop for the festivities in the Campo Santo Stefano, basing his statement on the totally undocumented article by G. Damerini, "Un Teatro per la 'Talanta' del Aretino," *Il Dramma*, 38 (1962), p. 45. Schulz's article ("Vasari at Venice") remains the fundamental study of Vasari's theatrical activity for the Sempiterni.

67 See Padoan Urban ("Teatri") for descriptions of such theatres.

68 Giustinian, *Historie*, p. 114.

Beyond these, however, Titian's efforts in the Venetian theatre, whatever they may have been, are simply not known.

The theatrical allusions of the *Presentation* lead one in three directions away from theatre history proper. To begin with, the architecture alone, whether it be theatrical or not, raises the question of Titian's architectural sensitivity and calls for some investigation of his relationship with Serlio, who is obviously behind this solution. Second, if the *Presentation* is seen not only to reflect in a passive way theatrical developments in the neighborhood of Venice, but to be an essay in the psychological possibilities of narrative painting, one would want to know what the other varieties of theatres were like, and what the general interest in theatre signifies for art as well as for broader social and intellectual issues of the time. Third, since there are so many features of the *Presentation* inconsistent with the practice of perspective scene design, like the landscape, it cannot be said that this painting is intended to give the illusion of an actual performance on an actual stage. The time-space continuum of the picture must, then, point neither to the empirical world nor to the fictive one of the dramatist's imagination, but to a third region which draws on both sets of experiences and attempts to combine them in new ways. This last, or third, mode of experience is what could be called the narrative mode. In the case of the *Presentation* it is a modification of traditional approaches to Scuola decoration. It is entirely consistent with Titian's general approach to a commission, characterized by a fundamental adherence to time-honored Venetian pictorial conventions, that he both satisfied old expectations associated with types of painting and raised new ones.

The most superficial glance at Titian's setting for the *Presentation* reveals this filiation with the long tradition of Venetian Scuola painting in the combination of landscape with large scale architectural portions defining the location and modulating the space. He had had experience, of course, in Padua, with precisely this kind of arrangement; and it would be wrong to maintain that the painting for the Scuola della Carità signifies some radical departure in his thinking. The iconography of a commission is a primary determinant of the kind of setting it will have; and since there are earlier uses of architecture by Titian, and since he was certainly sensitive to the demands and possibilities of architectural space one should not be surprised to find in a subject so closely reliant upon an architectural ambiance the exploitation of all that is possible within that situation.

But however much likeness the *Presentation* bears to a Serlian architectural perspective, and to a stage set, in the end it is not really a Serlian image at all. We have seen how the physical situation in the albergo resonates in the composition of the painting; and the choice of that relationship by Titian precludes any rigorous, symmetrical and evenly balanced system on the order, for example, of Peruzzi's *Presentation* in Rome. Moreover, the importance of landscape in Titian's picture is surely the option of the painter: Serlian perspectives are closed across the back and landscape, where it appears, is never a focus. The high vanishing point of a Serlian perspective allows the viewer to measure the recession in space by the module of paving designs, as in Central Italian painting; but in the *Presentation* Titian lowered the vanishing point so greatly that only a strip of pavement is seen at the very front edge of the composition, and it is in fact impossible to plot either the depth of space or the tempo at which it is created.[69] Finally, the individual elements of the architecture do not seem to come from a Serlian set at all, neither from the Comic nor the Tragic scene. They are instead a pastiche of idealized architectural views available to Titian in prints and drawings, or they are adaptations of actual architectural situations observable by anyone in Venice today, though their ensemble is undoubtedly that of fantasy.

The temple steps, as we have seen, recall the Scala dei Giganti. The strange " market " structure behind, supported on the files of columns, comes on the other hand from a Milanese engraving by Cesariano, most likely based on a scheme by Bramante; and the building behind that, with its Venetian diaper-pattern (visible not only in the Piazzetta but also in the Campo Santa Maria Formosa) looks very much like an illustration from Serlio's Second Book, published in 1537, especially in the nearly identical corbels supporting the balcony (Figs. 18 and 19).[70] The arcade on the left, which operates as one of those links with the albergo itself, is adapted from Peruzzi's *Presentation* and the pyramid belongs in the end to that ubiquitous class of street furniture used by Renaissance artists to mean " old " and " distant " and " exotic ". None of the architectural ele-

69 I am grateful to Irving Lavin, who first encouraged me to think about the theatrical allusions of the *Presentation* by calling my attention to the low vanishing point. Brand Griffin, a Fellow in Architecture at the American Academy in Rome, 1972–74, very generously attempted to make a ground plan of the *Presentation* based on its elevation, and found that distances in the picture's depth are impossible to measure.

70 For Rosand (" Titian's *Presentation*," p. 78) the architectural reference of the whole complex is both to the Palazzo Ducale and to Solomon's Temple, whose *porticum columnarum* he sees echoed in the colonnade. See Malaguzzi-Valeri, *La Corte*, I, p. 309, fig. 362; Krautheimer, *Studies*, p. 354.

ments, with the possible exception of the steps, needs necessarily to refer to anything in actually constructed buildings. The reference instead is to that world of fantasy architecture with which the Cinquecento abounds. It is the architecture of paint, not of stone.

Confronted with numerous programmatic requirements and difficulties of site, Titian searched for a single idea that would solve all his problems. He found this in the visual phenomena, stemming from Central Italy and even the circle of Raphael, associated with the sacred theatre. This provided him not only with an iconographic program but with a conceptual framework as well. The idea of infusing narrative painting with theatrical content had a precedent in Venice, Carpaccio's cycle in the Scuola di Sant'Orsola. Thus, while fulfilling the formal and programmatic requirements for a Venetian Scuola Grande, Titian also found a means of uniting the mundane with the purely imaginary, and in so doing, he invented, or refined, a narrative mode. The result, as I have suggested, can hardly have been anything other than pleasing, and even flattering, to the officials of the Scuola della Carità. Finally, there is some evidence that the *Presentation* even contains a passing reference to the spiritual issues, and personalities, at the forefront of the public interest in 1538.

There exists no evidence that I know of that would allow an interpretation of Titian's *Presentation* in the light of contemporary Venetian piety. It would be a mistake, I think, to look to Scuola decoration for that kind of imagery, topical, immediate, and, one must add, dated. The *Presentation* belongs instead to the realm of public art on the formal level and of iconic representation on the symbolic one. The committee that appointed Titian assigned the subject that had been agreed upon thirty years before, at the time of the initial commission to Pasqualino. There is no reason to suppose that the *Presentation* was to be in any way polemical, although it might be supposed that the narrative medium for the doctrine of the Immaculate Conception might have been chosen by the Scuola della Carità in response to the debates raging between Franciscan supporters of the teaching and its Dominican detractors in the sixteenth century. On the other hand, as I have suggested, the theme of the Presentation is decidedly relevant to the main charitable function of the Banca, the awarding of dowries. In Cinquecento Venice, to be sure, there was, in the popular imagination, an association of the legend with the virtuous, even "immaculate," rearing of young maidens. Evidence of this is given by the foundation in the 1540s, under the title "Presentatione della Madonna" and probably at the instigation of Ignatius Loyola, of the Casa delle Zitelle, whose function it was to " rescue " the daughters of prostitutes and to educate them in useful trade and Christian morality.[71]

Like the Ospedale degli Incurabili, the Casa delle Zitelle was a manifestation of pious works promoted widely in Venice, particularly during the late 'thirties and early 'forties. The foremost preacher of the day was Bernardino Ochino, the Prior General of the Capuchins, a recent Franciscan reform, and a disciple of Juan de Valdés in Naples.[72] Ochino preached the Lenten sermons in Venice from 1538 to 1541, after which he apostatized and fled to Calvin's Geneva. His sermons were attended by hordes of people in 1538, and it was through his efforts there that Venetians responded more enthusiastically than any other Italian population to his call to repentance and conversion of life. The proof of his success may be found in the fact that the basic treatise, the *Beneficio di Gesù Cristo*, of Ochino's movement, nowadays called Evangelism, was not only published in Venice but was also so widely read that its precepts may be found mirrored in the prologues to testaments dating well into the second half of the century, even after the book was condemned in the first Index.[73]

It seems never to have been noticed that the younger assistant standing just to the right of the High Priest in Titian's painting wears a distinctive vestment, a cape of ample proportions and made of scarlet silk (Fig. 20). Unless this vestment is purely the product of Titian's imagination, and there is no reason merely to assume that it is, it must represent some known ecclesiastical garb and therefore suggest an identity for the wearer. In fact, the garment is clearly and unambiguously a *cappa magna*. This is the cape worn on ceremonial occasion by cardinals and certain other dignitaries, when it was allowed to stretch out as a train yards in length. When not worn in processions, it was to be gathered over the left arm, as Titian shows. That the figure in Titian's picture is not a cardinal is indicated by the fact that he does not wear a headdress, but is instead shown tonsured. Therefore, this figure must represent someone else to whom the *cappa magna* was awarded as a singular distinction, and this award could be made only by the pope. As it happens, we know that Ochino was honored in just this way in

71 Pullan, *Rich and Poor*, pp. 385-6.

72 K. Benrath's study (*Bernardino Ochino von Siena*. Braunschweig, 1892) has never been surpassed. See also D. da Portogruaro, *Storia dei Capuccini Veneti*, I, Venice, 1941, pp. 166-203.

73 R. Prelowsky has edited the *Beneficio* and discussed the complex literature on the subject in *Italian Reformation Studies in Honor of Laelius Socinus*, ed. John Tedeschi, Florence, 1965, pp. 23-102. O. Logan (" Grace and Justification. Some Italian Views of the Sixteenth and Early Seventeenth Centuries," *Journal of Ecclesiastical History*, 20 [1959], pp. 67-78) has demonstrated the significance of this movement in Venice through a study of sixteenth-century testaments.

early 1538, when Pope Paul III took upon himself the task of arranging the popular preacher's speaking engagements.[74] Too, the beard would tend to identify this figure as a Capuchin, since they wore full beards. Most telling is the evidence of a woodcut, published a decade after Titian's picture was complete, showing Ochino in profile (Fig. 21).[75] The head in the painting bears a strong resemblance to the somewhat older face in the woodcut not only in the tonsure and beard, but also in the jutting forehead, long, aquiline nose and wide mouth. While none of this evidence is absolutely conclusive, it is tempting to suppose that Titian, having nearly completed the painting, decided towards the end to modify a secondary, but visually prominent, character so that the best-known and most revered preacher of the day, himself a Franciscan and therefore an adherent of the Immaculate Conception doctrine, would be party to the *Presentation.* Such a *pentimento* could only emphasize the directness of experience that the artist had so carefully, and so ingeniously, designed for the albergo of the Scuola della Carità.

[74] *Lexicon Capuccinum. Promptuarium Historico-Bibliographicum Ordinis Fratrum Minorum Capuccinorum* (*1525-1950*), Rome, 1951, col. 1234.

[75] The woodcut portrait was published by Benrath (*Bernardino Ochino*) as the frontispiece to his book. The original appeared with Ochino's *Prediche Nove...* in 1541. The only copy of the *Prediche Nove* to which I have found reference (Benrath, *Bernardino Ochino*, p. 314) stated that it was in the Biblioteca Guicciardini in Florence; but my efforts to locate it were in vain. Fig. 21 is taken from Benrath. It might be argued that both the color scheme and the fact that the figure in Titian's painting looks younger than fifty, Ochino's age in 1538, do not permit this identification. It would, however, be a simple matter to turn an already scarlet mantle into a *cappa magna* and to adjust the features slightly without significantly disturbing the painting which must have been, as I have suggested, very nearly complete.

Fig. 1. Titian, Presentation of the Virgin in the Temple. *Venice, Accademia.*

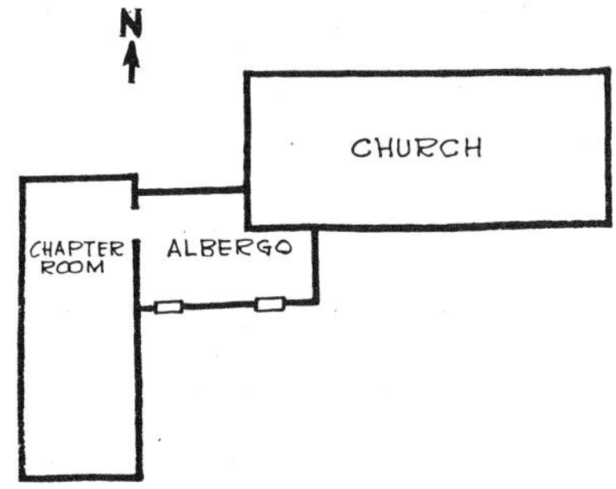

Fig. 2. Schematic plan of the Scuola della Carità. (Forbes Whiteside).

Fig. 3. Antonio Vivarini and Giovanni d'Alemagna, Madonna and Child with Saints. *Venice, Accademia. (Photo: Böhm).*

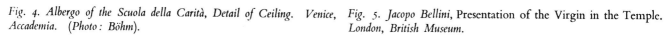

Fig. 4. Albergo of the Scuola della Carità, Detail of Ceiling. Venice, Accademia. (Photo: Böhm).

Fig. 5. Jacopo Bellini, Presentation of the Virgin in the Temple. *London, British Museum.*

Fig. 6. Cima da Conegliano, Presentation of the Virgin in the Temple. *Dresden, Gemäldegalerie.*

Fig. 7. Carpaccio, Presentation of the Virgin in the Temple. *Milan, Brera.*

Fig. 8. Ghirlandaio, Presentation of the Virgin in the Temple. *Florence, Sta. Maria Novella.*

Fig. 9. Peruzzi, Presentation of the Virgin in the Temple. *Rome, Sta. Maria della Pace.*

Fig. 10. Dürer, Presentation of the Virgin in the Temple. *Woodcut.*

Fig. 11. Venice, Palazzo Ducale. Cortile with Scala dei Giganti. (Photo: Böhm).

Fig. 12. Raphael (after), St. Paul Preaching at Athens. *Tapestry. Vatican, Pinacoteca.*

Fig. 13. Serlio, Tragic Scene.

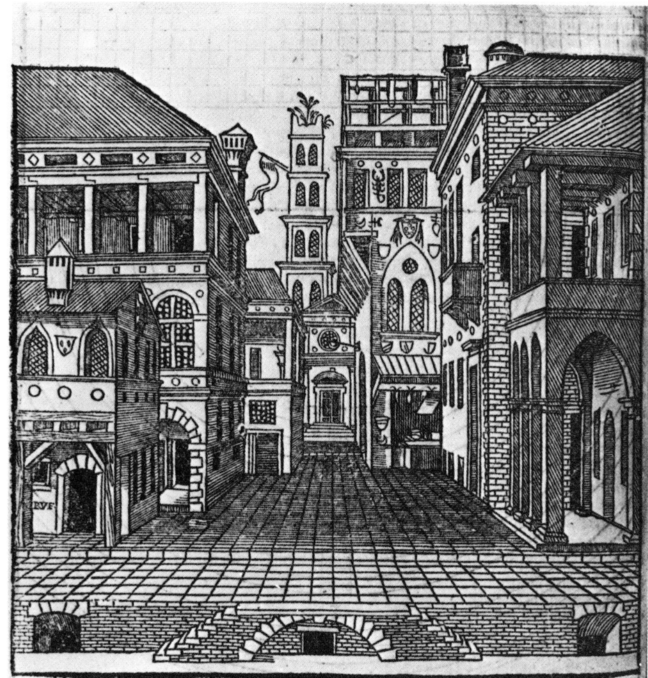

Fig. 14. Serlio, Comic Scene.

Fig. 15. Central Italian School, View of an Ideal City. *Baltimore, Walters Art Gallery.*

Fig. 16. After Bramante, Perspective Drawing. *Milan, Bibliotheca Ambrosiana.*

Fig. 17. Peruzzi, Perspective Scene. *Florence, Uffizi, Gabinetto dei Disegni.*

Fig. 18. Cesariano, Perspective Scene. *Engraving.*

Fig. 19. Serlio, Perspective Scene.

Fig. 20. Titian, Presentation of the Virgin to the Temple. *Detail.*

Fig. 21. Anonymous, Bernardino Ochino. *Woodcut.*

VIRGINIA L. BUSH

IV

BANDINELLI'S *HERCULES AND CACUS* AND FLORENTINE TRADITIONS

THE CHORUS of negative criticism that greeted the unveiling in 1534 of Baccio Bandinelli's *Hercules and Cacus* opposite Michelangelo's *David* in front of the Palazzo Vecchio in Florence (Fig. 30), grew through the centuries into a heated aesthetic and political confrontation.[1] The young David was a favorite Florentine personification of heroic virtue and civic liberty, who had been represented many times in the Quattrocento. The project that eventually resulted in Michelangelo's statue was begun during the early years of the fifteenth century when the freedom of Florence was threatened by the expansion of Milan. It was revived at the beginning of the sixteenth century under the Republican government, which had expelled the Medici but faced enormous pressures from papal and foreign powers and Medicean interests.[2] Hercules was also a popular Florentine hero, who had been Christianized as an embodiment of physical and moral fortitude.[3] The confrontation of

1 A summary of the bibliography on this project is found in G. Vasari, *La vita di Michelangelo*, ed. P. Barocchi, Milan-Naples, 1962, III, 1079ff, to which add D. Heikamp's notes to the *Club del Libro* edition of G. Vasari, *Le Vite*, Milan, 1962, VI, 30ff; J. Pope Hennessy, *Italian High Renaissance and Baroque Sculpture*, 2nd ed., London-New York, 1970, 44-45; 363-364; and M. Weinberger, *Michelangelo the Sculptor*, London-New York, 1967, I, 235ff.

This article was written during a fellowship at the American Academy in Rome and supported in part by a grant from the Rutgers University Research Council. I am grateful to my colleagues at the Academy as well as Kathleen Weil-Garris and Leo Steinberg, for helpful suggestions. The encouragement of Irving Lavin was critical to my research.

2 For the *David* project see C. Seymour, *Michelangelo's David: A Search for Identity*, Pittsburgh, 1967, and Vasari-Barocchi, II, 190ff. For the history of Florence during the era covered by this study see the bibliography in F. Gilbert, *Machiavelli and Guicciardini*, Princeton, 1973.

3 L.D. Ettlinger, "Hercules Florentinus," *Mitteilungen des Kunsthistorischen Institutes in Florenz*, XVI, 1972, 119-142.

the two colossi in the Piazza della Signoria arose from the fact the second statue was originally commissioned by the Florentine Republic from the beloved Michelangelo but was ultimately completed by the unpopular Bandinelli for Medici rulers.

Benvenuto Cellini, whose devotion to Michelangelo was matched only by his competitive hatred for Bandinelli, regarded the *Hercules and Cacus* as a grotesque perversion of its original potential.[4] He claimed that Hercules' skull is too small to contain a brain, that his features resemble a cross between a lion and an ox, that his pose is ungraceful and unclear, that his shoulders look like the pack saddle of an ass, that his musculature resembles a sack of melons, and so on. Bandinelli's abrasive personality, overt ambition, and almost obsequious service to the Medici provided an apt foil for the idolization of Michelangelo from the sixteenth century to the present. In a recent article W.R. Valentiner expressed this same point of view when he asserted that " the character of the two sculptors was such that their works resulted in a divergent expression of idealistic and demonic forces ", the *David* being " the expression of the noblest spirit of fighting youth, a spirit kindled by supernal aspiration, the *Hercules* that of satanic power, slaying mankind with bestial brutality ".[5] Valentiner's anti-Bandinelli bias was so intense that he reversed the subject matter of the statue. After all, Hercules' conquest of the monstrous Cacus, who surrounded his cave with the bones of his human victims, was anything but a defeat for mankind, and since antiquity Hercules' feats had almost always been regarded as a positive force in the world.[6] The personal and artistic clash between Michelangelo and Bandinelli has also been seen as a political allegory, glamorizing the early Medici and the government of the Republic for whom Michelangelo worked as enlightened and democratic while disparaging the later Medici who employed Bandinelli as corrupt and decadent.[7]

Late nineteenth-century critics, devoted to the academic concepts of idealization,

4 *Vita di Benvenuto Cellini*, ed. O. Bacci, Florence, 1901, 353ff.

5. W.R. Valentiner, " Bandinelli, Rival of Michelangelo," *Art Quarterly*, XVIII, 1955, 241-263, is based primarily on Cellini and Vasari (*Le Vite*, ed. G. Milanesi, Florence, 1881, VI, 148ff), as well as Bandinelli's own account of his life and works (A. Colasanti, " Il Memoriale di Baccio Bandinelli," *Repertorium für Kunstwissenschaft*, XXVIII, 1905, 406-443.

6 The most dramatic ancient account of the victory over Cacus is in Virgil's *Aeneid*, VII, 194ff. For further references to and interpretations of the hero see G.K. Galinsky, *The Herakles Theme: The Adaptations of the Hero in Literature from Homer to the Twentieth Century*, Oxford, 1972.

7 J.R. Hale, " Three Centuries of Medicean Rule," *Apollo*, CI, 1975, 409, notes several examples of this tendency. See also C. Tolnay, *Michelangelo*, Princeton, 1948, III, 98-100.

harmony and decorum, often saw in the *Hercules and Cacus* the opposite extremes of ugliness and brutishness. Charles Perkins condemned the statue's "vulgarity, pretentiousness, and bad modelling" and John Addington Symonds referred to it as "the wrestling bout of a porter and a coal-heaver." [8] This negative approach to Bandinelli's statue is still in force. Nearly every mention of the work in recent art historical or topographical literature is accompanied by a reference to or recitation of the statue's alleged failings, no matter how gratuitious those remarks might be. Kenneth Clark says that the statue is "certainly the ugliest Hercules in existence," and Franzsepp Würtemberger calls it a "weak, botched work." [9] Even the normally laconic Touring Club of Italy guide to Florence refers to the statue as "poco felice." [10] While some critical judgments of Bandinelli's statue, such as those by John Pope Hennessy or Creighton Gilbert, are undoubtedly due to real evaluations of the work, I suspect that a greater number result from routine repetitions of earlier prejudices.[11]

My suspicion gains confirmation from the fact that the illustration of the *Hercules and Cacus* used in most modern texts is the one available from Alinari (Fig. 1).[12] This photograph has probably done as much harm to the reputation of Bandinelli's statue as all its verbal critics. With all-too-common insensitivity the photograph was taken from an artificially high and close point of view, level with the center of Hercules' body. The statue was not intended to be seen in this way, nor can it be seen thus under ordinary circumstances. My photograph (Fig. 2), taken from a spectator's normal viewing height and distance, reveals that the Alinari photograph makes Hercules' head look too big for his body, his neck too long, and his arms

8 C.C. Perkins, *Tuscan Sculptors*, London, 1864, II, 149; J.A. Symonds, *The Fine Arts* (1877), in *Renaissance in Italy*, New York, 1961, III, 126.

9 K. Clark, *The Nude*, 1956, 211; F. Würtemberger, *Mannerism*, New York, 1963, 172.

10 Touring Club Italiano, *Firenze e dintorni*, Milan, 1974, 104.

11 Pope Hennessy, *High Renaissance*, 45, and C. Gilbert, *History of Renaissance Art Throughout Europe*, Englewood Cliffs, N.J., 1972, 205-206, stress the statue's structural and geometric character but maintain negative judgments upon it. G. Bazin, *The History of World Sculpture*, Greenwich Conn., 1968, 361, follows Pope Hennessy's analysis, as does C. Avery, *Florentine Renaissance Sculpture*, London, 1970, 189-199, who also permits himself some satisfying tirades against "the fiasco of the Hercules and Cacus."

12 Besides Pope Hennessy, Gilbert, Avery, Würtemberger, and Weinberger, the Alinari photograph (No. 31024A) appears in E.H. Gombrich, "The Leaven of Criticism in Renaissance Art," in *The Heritage of Apelles*, Oxford, 1976, fig. 232; H. Keutner, *Sculpture, Renaissance to Rococo*, London, 1969, fig. ix; P. and L. Murray, *Dictionary of Art and Artists*, London, 1965, pl. 160; *The Thames and Hudson Encyclopaedia of the Arts*, ed. H. Read, London, 1966, I, 61; K. Weil-Garris, *Leonardo and Central Italian Art 1515-1550*, New York, 1974, fig. 51; and L.O. Larsson, *Von allen Seiten gleich schön*, Stockholm, 1974, fig. 140.

and torso too narrow and flat. Other published and commercially available photographs of the work are not much better.[13] Although no photograph can be completely successful in presenting a statue because a camera does not work like human vision, Figure 2 does more closely approach a satisfactory depiction of Bandinelli's work than do previous illustrations.

More important, this review and analysis of the whole project for the statue, which strives to be aesthetically unbiased and politically neutral, demonstrates that even if Bandinelli's *Hercules and Cacus* is ugly, it is not inept. The statue does embody an aesthetic and political confrontation with Michelangelo's *David*, but Bandinelli's handling of artistic and iconological traditions is both more positive and more successful than many critics would admit. Such willingness to judge works of art on their own terms and according to their creators' intentions is, of course, aesthetic relativism. While admitting the possible value of this approach, Ernst Gombrich still condemns the *Hercules and Cacus* because, in aiming to surpass Michelangelo, Bandinelli failed to preserve the Renaissance tradition of accurate and plausible human anatomy, and thus was not playing the game.[14] This claim assumes that Michelangelo's designs were always accurate and plausible, which is far from the the truth, and that Michelangelo's was the only game in town.

Bandinelli did attempt to surpass Michelangelo and often imitated both his works and his life, but in Renaissance Florence there were other games and other traditions. After early training with his goldsmith father,[15] Baccio was apprenticed to

[13] The Brogi photograph (No. 3088) was taken from only slightly lower and further away and includes a wired on figleaf and an unfortunate juxtaposition between Cacus' left shoulder and the statue of Orcagna behind it on the Uffizi Corridor; these two areas of the photograph were purposely blurred in the reproduction in A. Venturi, *Storia dell'arte italiana*, Milan, 1936, X, 2, fig. 170. In the Alinari side view (No. 31024; *ibid.*, fig. 169) the statue is strangely pinched between the wings of the Corridor, which is probably why the background of the image is blacked out in A. Lensi, *Palazzo Vecchio*, Milan-Rome, 1929, 122. Valentiner, "Bandinelli," fig. 4 is an even more peculiar side view, which may be a montage. The Anderson front view (No. 40460), which has a relatively minor distortion from a raised camera level, has not to my knowledge been reproduced in literature. The only photographs I have found taken from a normal viewing position are Bazin, *World Sculpture*, No. 807, a postcard published by Innocenti Editori in Florence (No. 278), and Brogi's view of both colossi (No. 21167; my Fig. 30).

[14] Gombrich, "The Leaven of Criticism," 122-123.

[15] Important studies of Bandinelli's stylistic sources and development include U. Middeldorf, "A Bandinelli Relief," *Burlington Magazine*, LVII, 1930, 65-72, and "A Group of Drawings by Baccio Bandinelli," *Print Collector's Quarterly*, XXIV, 1937, 291-304; D. Heikamp, "Baccio Bandinelli nel Duomo di Firenze," *Paragone*, XV, No. 175, 1964, 32-42, and "In margine alla 'Vita di Baccio Bandinelli' del Vasari, *Paragone*, XVII, No. 191, 1966, 51-62; M.G. Ciardi Dupré, "Per la cronologia dei disegni di Baccio Bandinelli fino al 1540," *Commentarii*, XVII, 1966, 146-170, and "Alcuni aspetti della attività grafica del Bandinelli," *Antichità viva*, V, No. 1, 1966, 22-31; and Weil-Garris, *Leonardo*, 38-41.

Giovanni Francesco Rustici, a close associate of Leonardo da Vinci, whose work remained an inspiration and resource for Bandinelli throughout his career. He also used the example of Raphael's work and the methodology of his shop, although these elements are less evident in the subject under discussion.[16] Beyond these contemporary sources, there was the vast storehouse of antique art, as well as the protean creation of Donatello. All of these alternatives Bandinelli combined into a complex and subtle game, which he may even be said to have won, according to his own political and aesthetic rules.

★★★

In January 1504 a number of officials and artists met in Florence to debate the placement of Michelangelo's nearly completed *David*.[17] The ultimate decision, which is not recorded in the minutes, to place the colossus on the *ringhiera* at the left of the entrance to the Palazzo della Signoria (now Palazzo Vecchio) almost certainly presupposed the initiation of a project to set a comparable statue on the other side of the portal to complete the symmetry [18] and complement the symbolism of the *David*. While single, freestanding statues set in prominent positions were not unknown in Renaissance Italy, they were ordinarily placed as central accents in courtyards or on fountains in gardens. Donatello's *Judith*, which had occupied the site by the portal from 1495 until replaced by the *David*, is a notable exception, but is much smaller than the *David* and created a less emphatic asymmetry. In most of the sites proposed at the *practica* of 1504 — the Cortile or Salone of the Palazzo, or one of the arches of the Loggia dei Lanzi — Michelangelo's statue would have been either centralized within or framed by the surrounding architecture. Cosimo Roselli proposed setting the *David* on the right corner of the steps of the Duomo, and Botticelli immediately added that a *Judith* should be made

16 This and other aspects of Bandinelli's development are discussed by Weil-Garris in "Bandinelli and Michelangelo: A Matter of Temperaments," a lecture first given at the Frick Collection in 1973. Further material will be included in her monograph on the sculptor.

17 C. Neumann, "Die Wahl des Platzes für Michelangelos David in Florenz im Jahr 1504," *Repertorium für Kunstwissenshaft*, XXXVIII, 1916, 1-27; Seymour, *Michelangelo's David*, 57 ff; S. Levine, "The Location of Michelangelo's David," *Art Bulletin*, LVI, 1974, 31-49; N.R. Parks, "The Placement of Michelangelo's *David*," *Art Bulletin*, LVII, 1975, 560-570.

18 M. Marangoni, "A proposito della recollazione del David," *Rivista d'arte*, VII, 1910, 45, notes that the asymmetry was somewhat mitigated by the *ringhiera*, which was removed in 1809. The *David* was moved to the Accademia in 1873 and replaced by a marble copy.

for the other side.[19] Although no such corresponding statue is mentioned in relation to the placement on the steps of the Palazzo, a balanced enframement of that entrance would have seemed equally natural. A pair of statues flanking the portal would have satisfied the Renaissance taste for balanced forms and also would have continued the traditions of paired portal guardians that had existed since early antiquity and had recently been embodied in Paolo Romano's statues of Peter and Paul for the steps of St. Peter's.[20]

David was not as consistently paired with a complementary figure as were Peter and Paul but he did have accepted symbolic counterparts. Perhaps before and certainly after the expulsion of the Medici in 1495 Donatello's bronze *David* had been linked with his *Judith* as images of moral and civic virtue [21] — a combination that probably prompted Botticelli's proposal. Another counterpart of David was Hercules, the biblical hero representing moral fortitude and defense against external enemies and the pagan hero representing physical strength and vigilance against internal enemies.[22] It is easy to see how the virtuous young David's conquest of the giant champion of the Philistine army became identified with the resistance of Florence against larger and more powerful enemies. The identification of Hercules with Florence rests upon the allegorization of the hero that began in late antiquity.[23] For Fulgentius the adversaries of Hercules represented the vices: Antaeus was lust, Cacus evil incarnate, and so on. During the Middle Ages spiritual and intellectual qualities were added to Hercules' strength and morality. In Renaissance Florence Hercules became an *exemplum virtutis*, a model for the active and wise life that benefits mankind. His conquests over tyrants and monsters were seen as the reestablishment of civic order that would bring justice and liberty to the populace. This is the meaning of the image of Hercules on a thirteenth-century seal of the city, the reverse of which was inscribed "The club of Hercules subdues the depravity of Florence." [24] A similar meaning invests other Florentine images of Hercules up to and including Bandinelli's statue in the Piazza della Signoria.

19 Seymour, *Michelangelo's David*, 144-147.

20 A. Riccoboni, *Roma nell'arte*, Rome, 1942, 14; A. Bertolotti "Urkundliche Beiträge zur Biographie des Bildhauers Paolo di Mariano," *Repertorium für Kunstwissenschaft*, IV, 1881, 430 ff. The statues were made during the reign of Paul II (1458-1464); they remained on view there until removed to the Sacristy during the nineteenth century.

21 H.W. Janson, *The Sculpture of Donatello*, Princeton, 1963, 83 and 203, and "La signification politique du David en bronze du Donatello," *Revue de l'art.* No. 39, 1978; 33-38.

22 Tolnay, *Michelangelo*, III, 98.

23 Galinsky, *The Herakles Theme*, 190 ff; Ettlinger, "Hercules Florentinus," 120 ff.

24 *Ibid.*, 120 ff.

There is considerable, albeit circumstantial, evidence that the second colossus for the Piazza was intended to be a Hercules from its inception. It is reasonable to suppose as well that Michelangelo was originally to make the statue, even though he was called to Rome in 1505 to work for Pope Julius II, and even though what seems to be the earliest extant design for the project is by Leonardo da Vinci. Whether or not Leonardo had been considered for the *David* commission as Vasari claims,[25] his drawings do reveal an interest in Michelangelo's completed statue and suggest that he also gave some thought to the composition of the pendant figure. In a drawing of Neptune based on the *David*[26] (Fig. 3) and dated about 1504, Leonardo seems to be criticizing — as Bandinelli did later — Michelangelo's statue as too thin and too static, adding a heavier musculature, more pronounced turns of the head and left arm, and enlivening figures of seahorses at the feet. A similar bulking out and enlivening characterizes Leonardo's drawing of Hercules and the Nemean Lion (Fig. 5), which Pedretti dates about 1504 and regards as "suitable for translation into a statue as a fitting counterpart to Michelangelo's *David*."[27] If the project for the second colossus had already been initiated in 1504, as I believe, Pedretti's suggestion becomes more compelling. The fact that the Hercules is seen from the back and the lion from the front gives it a particularly sculptural feeling. The shift of the left arm back towards the core of the body might also be a sign that Leonardo was thinking in terms of a marble statue.

Documented evidence for the project for the second colossus and its intended authorship by Michelangelo is found by August 21, 1507, when Pietro Soderini, *gonfaloniere* for life of the Florentine Republic, wrote the Marchese of Massa that Michelangelo would soon come to inspect a block of marble found for him at Carrara.[28] Considering the scarcity of enormous blocks of statuary marble — it

25 Vasari's claim (Vasari-Milanesi, VII, 153; Vasari-Barocchi, I, 19) has been discounted because he attributes the deed to Pietro Soderini, who did not become *gonfaloniere a vita* until 1502, and because Leonardo did not return to Florence until after the date of Michelangelo's commission (Seymour, *Michelangelo's David*, 22 ff; K. Clark and C. Pedretti, *The Drawings of Leonardo da Vinci in the Collection of Her Majesty the Queen at Windsor Castle*, London, 1968, No. 12591). However, through his colossal model for the Sforza Monument in Milan, Leonardo was the only living artist known to have worked on the scale of the nine-*braccia* block that became the *David*.

26 E. Solmi, "Il 'David' di Leonardo e il 'David' di Michelangelo," *Rassenga d'arte*, XII, 1912, 128-132; C. Pedretti, "L'Ercole di Leonardo," *L'Arte*, LVII, 1958, 163-172; Clark and Pedretti, *Drawings of Leonardo*, No. 12591.

27 C. Pedretti, *Leonardo*, Berkeley-Los Angeles, 1973, 80. See also his *Disegni di Leonardo da Vinci e della sua scuola alla Biblioteca Reale di Torino*, Florence, 1975, No. 8; A. Bertini, *I Disegni italiani della Biblioteca Reale di Torino*, Rome, 1958, No, 479; and Clark and Pedretti, *Drawings of Leonardo*, No. 19043.

28 C. Frediano, *Ragionamento storico su le diverse*

is fifty years before another block of comparable size is recorded[29] — the initial request for the marble could easily have occurred three or four years earlier, at the time the site for the *David* was selected. On May 10, 1508, Soderini asked the Marchese to continue to reserve the marble, which he says specifically is for a statue for the piazza in Florence, and on December 16 of the same year he insisted that no one but Michelangelo himself take charge of roughing out the block for fear of someone who did not know the artist's idea ruining the marble.[30]

Soderini's words imply that Michelangelo already had a design in mind for his statue by the end of 1508. Tolnay asserts that he was thinking of a *Hercules and Antaeus*, which is reflected in the man carrying his dead son in the *Deluge* on the Sistine Ceiling.[31] A pen sketch in the Casa Buonarroti (Fig. 6) representing a figure with raised arm standing over a crouched victim has also been dated about this time and identified as a *Hercules and Cacus*.[32] As it turned out, Michelangelo was unable to obtain leave from Julius II to pursue the project, and the marble remained in Carrara until 1525,[33] by which time the political situation in Florence had changed greatly, and the significance of the colossus project within that situation had grown more complex.

In 1512 Soderini and the Republican government had been expelled and Florence returned to the control of the Medici. In 1515 Pope Leo X Medici reaffirmed this control by making a triumphal entry into the city, amidst elaborate decorations.[34] Arches ornamented with paintings, tapestries and sculpture, a temporary facade for the Duomo, and several colossal statues stressed the role of the Medici dynasty in Florentine history. Like so much Medici patronage the decor insinuated that the essential identity and interests of the Medici rulers matched

gite fatte a Carrara da Michelangelo Buonarroti, Massa, 1837, 67 ff.

29 The next block of colossal size was found in about 1558 and was ultimately used for Ammanati's Neptune fountain.

30 G. Gaye, *Carteggio inedito d'artisti dei secoli XIV, XV, XVI*, Florence, 1840, II, 97 and 107.

31 Tolnay, *Michelangelo*, III, 101 and 184.

32 H. Thode, *Michelangelo: Kritische Untersuchungen über seine Werke*, Berlin, 1908, II, 297; L. Dussler, *Die Zeichnungen des Michelangelo*, Berlin, 1959, No. 271; P. Barocchi, *Michelangelo e la sua scuola*, Florence, 1962, I, No. 10; and F. Hartt, *The Drawings of Michelangelo*, London 1971, No. 61.

33 Vasari-Milanesi, VI, 148, says that the block was quarried during the reign of Leo X with the marbles for S. Lorenzo, which may be only an assumption, since he was apparently unaware of the negotiations of 1507-1508. Despite Weinberger, *Michelangelo*, I, 243, I doubt that there could have been two different colossal blocks.

34 J. Shearman, "The Florentine Entrata of Leo X, 1515," *Journal of the Warburg and Courtauld Institutes*, XXXVIII, 1975, n. 2, lists 23 descriptions of the entry.

those of the city, by showing the family's links with the land, the history, and the traditions of Florence.[35]

One of the colossi featured in the entry was a *Hercules* made by Bandinelli in stucco covered with bronze paint, which he is said to have boasted would surpass the *David*.[36] The stucco was placed under the leftmost arch of the Loggia dei Lanzi, but it was conceived as a pendant of Michelangelo's statue and a trial-piece for the marble colossus, for which Bandinelli already hoped to obtain the commission. Before the return of the Medici he had made an underlifesize *Hercules* with the dead Cacus lying between his legs, as an exercise in marble carving.[37] Bandinelli's choice of subject matter is highly revealing of the pattern of the nineteen-year-old sculptor's ambition. He seems to have been aware not only that the postponed colossus project was to represent Hercules but also that Michelangelo had carved a *Hercules* on his own initiative when he was seventeen in memory of Lorenzo de'Medici, who had identified himself with the pagan hero.[38] Whether or not one assumes that Bandinelli's early *Hercules and Cacus* was part of this traditional association between the Medici rulers and the hero, his stucco *Hercules* surely was. Like Lorenzo, his father, Leo was linked with Hercules in contemporary literature, and depicted as or associated with the hero in visual representations.[39] A contemporary might not have spelled it out so simply, but the message of Bandinelli's stucco of 1515 was that Leo was Hercules, and since Hercules was Florence, then Leo was Florence.

The design that Bandinelli invented for the stucco cannot be known with certainty because the work is lost, but in the 1560's Vasari included a small image of the figure in his fresco in the Palazzo Vecchio commemorating Leo's entry

35 See n. 41, below; the numerous articles by E. Borsook in the *Mitteilungen des Kunsthistorischen Institutes in Florenz*; and, for additional bibliography, G.G. Bertelà, *Feste e apparati medicei da Cosimo I a Cosimo II*, Florence, 1969.

36 Vasari-Milanesi, VI, 141-142; L. Landucci, *A Florentine Diary from 1450 to 1516*, trans. A. de R. Jervis, London, 1927, 279 ff; G. Cambi, *Istorie*, in *Delizie degli Eruditi Toscani*, Florence, 1785-1786, XXII, 83; E. Schaeffer, "Der Herakles des Baccio Bandinelli," *Monatshefte für Kunstwissenshaft*, III, 1910, 112-114; J. Holderbaum, "The Birth Date and a Destroyed Early Work of Baccio Bandinelli," *Essays in the History of Art Presented to Rudolf Wittkower*, London, 1967, 93-97. The gilding of the statue may indicate a relation to the gilt-bronze *Hercules Boario*, then on the Capitol in Rome (W. Helbig, *Führer durch die offentlichen Sammlungen Klassischer Altertümer in Rom*, Tubingen, 1966, II, No. 1804).

37 Vasari-Milanesi, VI, 137. The work is no longer extant.

38 Ettlinger, "Hercules Florentinus," 119 ff; L. Chatelet-Lange, "Michelangelos Herkules in Fontainbleau," *Pantheon*, XXX, 1972, 455-468.

39 J. Shearman, *Raphael's Cartoons*, London, 1972, 89-90, and "The Florentine Entrata," n. 41.

(Fig. 7), which can be regarded as fairly reliable.[40] In Vasari's painting the stucco *Hercules* stands with his feet spread wide apart and his club held over his left shoulder. If the statue had been set at the right of the entrance to the Palazzo, its shoulders and body would have turned out and away but its head would have looked back towards the *David*. As far as one can tell from the fresco, Bandinelli's stucco had the physiognomy traditional for the mature Hercules: a coarse face with overhanging brow, broad flat nose, and protruding bearded chin. The body had a relatively short torso, long legs, and bulky musculature. Like Leonardo, Bandinelli anticipated pairing the *David* with a figure having a thicker body and less constrained pose. Apparently he planned on the use of a marble block known to be more ample than that of the *David*.

The most interesting aspect of Bandinelli's stucco *Hercules* is not, however, its relation or reaction to the *David*, but rather its use of earlier Florentine representations of Hercules, which reveals a precocious manipulation of traditional images for political symbolism that became more and more common later in the century.[41] Florentine political attitudes during the early sixteenth century were conservative and resisted change. As Felix Gilbert says, "The correct procedure in politics, according to the prevailing mode of thinking, was to seek out the type of political institutions which had existed in the historical — or mythical — past and to model new institutions after the pattern of the old."[42] Bandinelli's procedure in propagandizing the Medici role in Florentine politics was to seek out early visual traditions and to model on them both his stucco *Hercules* and his final marble statue.

The earliest traceable image of Hercules as Florence was the thirteenth-century seal, which is believed to be reproduced in an eighteenth-century woodcut (Fig. 8).[43] Bandinelli's stucco held a club angled over his shoulder, passing behind his head, in almost precisely the same fashion. His other hand rested on his hip, and the arm was covered by drapery from the shoulder down over the hand. In all the

40 Holderbaum, "Bandinelli," 95; Schaeffer, "Der Herakles," 113. Vasari knew Bandinelli well, and although the latter had died before the Quartiere di Leone X was painted, Vasari would have had access to any drawings or models that survived.

41 Ettlinger, "Hercules Florentinus," 139-142; K.W. Forster, "Metaphors of Rule: Political Ideology and History in the Portraits of Cosimo I de' Medici," *Mitteilungen des Kunsthistorischen Institutes in Florenz*, XV, 1971, 72 ff; N. Rubenstein, "Vasari's Painting of *The Foundation of Florence* in the Palazzo Vecchio," *Essays in the History of Architecture Presented to Rudolf Wittkower*, London, 1967, 64-73.

42 Gilbert, *Machiavelli and Guicciardini*, 78-79.

43 Ettlinger, "Hercules Florentinus," 120-121. D.M. Manni, *Osservazioni istoriche sopra i sigilli antichi de' secoli bassi*, Florence, 1739, frontispiece.

thousands of antique representations of Hercules, covering both the shoulder and the hand is extremely unusual, but does appear on two early images of Hercules in Florence: the relief of *Hercules and Cacus* made by Andrea Pisano for the Campanile of the Duomo in the early fourteenth century; and the standing *Hercules* on the decorated jambs of the Porta della Mandorla of the Duomo, carved at the turn of the fifteenth century (Figs. 9 and 10). Aside from this one feature and the position of the club resting on the ground, these two early representations are quite different. It would be interesting to know how they relate to each other or to their sources. But the point here is that Bandinelli evoked them in his stucco *Hercules* because they were old and, therefore, associated with traditional Florentine political institutions.

Although the young Bandinelli's original interest in the project for the second colossus was probably less political than opportunistic, his opportunities were closely tied to politics. His father had already served the Medici rulers, and from 1512 until the death of Leo X in 1521 the bulk of Bandinelli's sculptural work was either for or obtained through Pope Leo or Cardinal Giulio de' Medici.[44] One of the Cardinal's commissions during this period was for two huge stucco figures to flank a garden gate at the Villa Madama, where they still stand, much damaged and partially restored (Fig. 11).[45] The poses of these giants roughly approximate the *David* and the stucco *Hercules*. The giant on the left, like the *David* (Fig. 4), faces forward flatly, supporting his weight on his right leg and bending his left arm towards the shoulder. He is a flabby and lifeless figure and comments unfavorably on his prototype. The giant on the right, on the other hand, has a gyral *contrapposto* that vitalizes the heavy, swollen musculature given to both figures. The right-hand giant, following the stucco *Hercules*, turns his shoulders away from the gate and his head back towards it. A drawing by Marten van Heemskerck[46] (Fig. 12) shows that the right-hand giant held a club over his left shoulder in the same manner as did the stucco *Hercules*, although he extended his other arm forward across his body rather than rested it on his hip. This change was, I believe, Ban-

44 Vasari-Milanesi, VI, 134 ff and 140 ff. These works were a wax model of a *St. Jerome*, the *St. Peter* for the Duomo, the stucco *Hercules*, various parts of the reliefs at the Santa Casa di Loreto, a model of of a *David and Goliath* for the Palazzo Medici, the *Orpheus* for the same Palazzo, the Villa Madama Giants, and a copy of the *Laocoön* (finished after 1523).

45 Vasari-Milanesi, VI, 144; Holderbaum, "Bandinelli," 95 ff; Heikamp, "In margine," 52-53. Heikamp notes the resemblance of the left-hand giant to the *David*.

46 C. Hülsen and H. Egger, *Die römischen Skizzenbücher von Marten van Heemskerck*, Berlin, 1913, I, f. 24*recto*.

dinelli's response to Michelangelo's *Risen Christ,* the first version of which was abandoned because of a flaw in the marble and left behind in Rome in 1516.[47] Figure 14 shows the second version, now in Santa Maria sopra Minerva, which Bandinelli's giant resembles strikingly in reverse (Fig. 13).

It is conceivable that this similarity had an iconographical purpose, since Hercules had long been paralleled with Christ as a mediator between mankind and divinity,[48] and since Christ was closely linked with contemporary Florentine civic iconography. The revolution of 1494 took place on the day of San Salvatore, a few months later Savonarola proclaimed Christ the new king of Florence, and His image was planned as a centerpiece of the new Hall of the Grand Council.[49] The idea gained strength, and after the reestablishment of the Republic in 1527, Christ was formally elected head of the government and His monogram was placed over the portal of the Palazzo Vecchio.[50]

Bandinelli's formal purpose at the Villa Madama was to show how the *David* and a colossus by him would look flanking the portal of the Palazzo. His stucco giants are not symmetrical but have adequate balance to frame the gate and enough interaction to be pendants. Each bears its weight on the right leg, bends the left arm and extends the right; each turns its head inward towards the spectator approaching the gate. Cardinal Giulio appears to have been pleased with Bandinelli's proposal,[51] for later, as Pope Clement VII, he reactivated the much delayed project for the second colossus and gave the commission to Bandinelli.

Even before the block for the second colossus was brought to Florence in July 1525,[52] the project had become the focus of an artistic and political squabble of surprising magnitude. Both Bandinelli and Michelangelo had made designs for for the statue, to which I will return presently. While the block was being taken

47 Tolnay, *Michelangelo,* III, 89 ff and 177 ff.

48 Galinsky, *The Herakles Theme,* 202 ff; M Simon, *Hercule et le Christianisme,* Strassbourg, 1955.

49 J. Wilde, "The Hall of the Great Council of Florence," *Journal of the Warburg and Courtauld Institutes, VII,* 1944, 77-78.

50 L. Passerini, "Del Monogramma di Cristo posto sulla porta del Palazzo della Signoria," in *Del Pretorio di Firenze,* 2nd ed., Florence, 1865, 41-54.

51 Vasari (ed. Milanesi, VI, 142 and 144) says the Villa Madama giants were considered reasonably beautiful, whereas the stucco Hercules cost the sculptor much of his former esteem. Cf. Landucci, *A Florentine Diary,* 285.

52 Gaye, *Carteggio,* II, 464-465; Cambi, *Istorie,* XXII, 274-275; Vasari-Milanesi, VI, 148 ff. Vasari gives the dimensions of the block as 9½ by 5 *braccia* in the life of Bandinelli and the height as nine *braccia* in the life of Michelangelo (VII, 200), but the measurements (8½ by 2½ by 2½ *braccia*) given by Cambi and the document in Gaye are more dependable and conform more closely to the proportions of the finished statue (E. Panofsky, *Studies in Iconology,* New York, 1939, 231).

ashore at Signa because the Arno was too low to continue the trip by boat, it was accidently dropped and sank into the sand of the river bed. A contemporary wit claimed that the marble, having thought that it would be carved by Michelangelo, learned that it would be given to Bandinelli, and tried to commit suicide. But Pope Clement prevented it. An engineer was hired to divert the river and cut away the bank so that the block could be dragged out of the sand with windlasses. The enormous expense of this operation was perhaps justified by the value and rarity of the marble, but also testifies to the Pope's intense interest in the project.

Clement was determined that the statue be finished, and by Bandinelli. Vasari, who was a Medici employee, later blamed the transfer of the commission to Bandinelli on an intrigue at the papal court,[53] but in fact it would have been dangerous to have the colossus completed by Michelangelo, whose political as opposed to professional loyalty to the Medici family was questionable. Bandinelli's was not. Transferring the commission to Bandinelli was a way of neutralizing the Republican associations of the project.[54] Clement continued to employ Michelangelo but was deaf to his requests to regain the commission. In an exchange of letters with the Holy See late in 1525,[55] Michelangelo complained that competition with Bandinelli was destroying his ability to work. Although not usually casual about money and always claiming to be overworked, he offered to carve the statue for Florence as a gift, since he was legally in the exclusive employ of the Pope, or to put off the project for two or three years until he was free, since the Florentines were willing to wait. Clement assured Michelangelo that he gave the commission to Bandinelli only because he did not want Michelangelo over-extended by working on " cose del pubrico " or for other patrons. Clement's real concern was to keep Michelangelo away from the politically sensitive Hercules project. In fact, he proposed an even larger project for a colossus over forty feet high for the Piazza of S. Lorenzo, which would indeed have been public but could not be a symbol of resistance to the Medici, since it would be attached to the family church. The artist's rejection of the proposal in a letter full of bitter humor shows his scorn for this ridiculous attempt to divert him. Clement ended the discussion with a handwritten appeal to Michelangelo to finish the work in hand.

Political considerations continued to effect the history of the project until its

53 Vasari-Milanesi, VI, 148-149.

54 Tolnay, *Michelangelo*, II, 98-99; Weinberger, *Michelangelo*, I, 245.

55 K. Frey, ed., *Sammlung ausgewählter Briefe an Michelagniolo Buonarroti*, Berlin, 1899, 260-271; G. Milanesi, ed., *Le lettere di Michelangelo Buonarroti*, Florence, 1875, 448-453.

completion. When the Florentine Republic was reestablished after the Sack of Rome in 1527, Michelangelo was again given the commission, which called for two figures but left the choice of subject to the artist and the choice of final position to the Signoria.[56] The possibility that the subject be altered and that the statue not be a pendant to the *David* shows that there had been a marked change in attitude towards the project. Michelangelo chose to represent not Hercules, but Samson, his biblical equivalent as a personification of physical strength and moral fortitude. This change was not merely a Christianization of the theme, for Hercules had long been assimilated into contemporary religious thought. Rather, the meaning of Hercules had been poisoned by his link with Medici domination. What had been a positive symbol for the Republic in the first decade of the century had become a focus of resentment against the Medici regime. When the block was returned to Bandinelli after the final victory of the Medici in 1530, some Florentines tried to hinder the sculptor's work. He had to ask Pope Clement to prompt Alessandro de' Medici, who had been installed as Duke of Florence, to provide for the completion and erection of the statue. After the statue was unveiled in 1534 there was an intense reaction against the work and its patrons, expressed as usual in Florence by a flurry of satirical poems. Duke Alessandro imprisoned several persons whose lampoons were too extreme. Bandinelli was rewarded like the political ally that he was: as an extra payment he received the villa confiscated from a personal enemy who had sided with the Republican forces.[57]

I contend that these political events and attitudes had a profound effect on the final *form* of the *Hercules and Cacus*, as well as its history. Before examining the completed statue, however, it is necessary to look at both Bandinelli's and Michelangelo's preliminary designs.

Contemporary sources state that Michelangelo had made designs for a *Hercules and Antaeus* prior to 1525.[58] On two sheets that record those designs [59] the figure

56 Milanesi, *Lettere*, 700; Gaye, *Carteggio*, II, 98-99.

57 Vasari-Milanesi, VI, 155-161. Several verses critical of the *Hercules and Cacus*, and Bandinelli, are published in Perkins, *Tuscan Sculptors*, II, 140, n. 2; 147; 149, n. 5; 151; and *Vita di Benvenuto Cellini*, ed. F. Tassi, Florence, 1829, III, 410, 436-439.

58 Gaye, *Carteggio*, II, 464-465; Cambi, *Istorie*, XXII, 274-275; Milanesi, *Lettere*, 452; Frey, *Briefe*, 260 ff.

59 Thode, *Kritische Untersuchungen*, II, 293-295; Dussler, *Zeichnungen*, Nos. 159 and 196; Hartt, *Drawings of Michelangelo*, Nos. 302 and 496; J. Wilde, *Michelangelo and His Studio*, London, 1953, No. 33; K.T. Parker, *Catalogue of the Collection of Drawings in the Ashmolean Museum*, Oxford, 1956, II, No. 317. Vasari (ed. Milanesi, VI, 168-169) claims that Montorsoli started to execute one of Michelangelo's models for a *Hercules and Antaeus* but that Bandinelli destroyed the marble block. Michelangelo gave a wax model of a *Hercules and Antaeus* to Leone Leoni, but this too is lost.

of Antaeus twists vigorously away from the entwining embrace of Hercules (Figs. 15 and 16). The group is energetic and compact, but it is also top heavy and if executed in marble on a colossal scale, could not have stood without additional support.[60] The *Samson* that Michelangelo designed after 1528 is reflected in a number of small bronzes attributed to Pierino da Vinci.[61] This group is also energetically intertwined and has better internal support because of the Philistine crouched between Samson's legs. A terracotta *bozzetto* in the Casa Buonarroti (Figs. 17 and 19) is generally regarded as a study for the colossus, although no one has proved whether it represents Hercules and Cacus or Samson and a Philistine, or whether it dates before 1525, after 1528, or sometime in-between.[62] I am presently inclined towards the earlier date, because I think that the terracotta, or some similar design, inspired the model that Bandinelli made shortly before the marble was brought to Florence in 1525.

Vasari had seen Bandinelli's model in Duke Cosimo de' Medici's *guardaroba*, and his description agrees in detail with a large wax group in East Berlin:[63] (Figs. 18, 20, 21)

> Hercules... gripped the head of Cacus between two stones with one knee, grasped him with great force with the left arm, and held him crouched under his legs in a tortured attitude; in this Cacus showed his suffering and the strain and weight of Hercules above him, bursting every smallest muscle in his whole body. In the same way Hercules, with his head bent down

60 The Ashmolean sheet suggests that Michelangelo had been considering the statics of the group. In one of the sketches he extended the lower leg of Antaeus to the ground in order to add support. Between the sketches he drew two pairs of lines converging to tiny circles drawn in perspective as if flat on a surface, which I take to be indications of stress or support lines within the figures' legs.

61 Thode, *Kritische Untersuchungen*, II, 297-298; A.E. Brinckmann, "Die Simson-Gruppe des Michelangelo,' *Belvedere*, XI, 1927, 155-159.

62 Thode, *Kritische Untersuchungen*, II, 296; Panofsky, *Studies in Iconology*, 231-233. J. Pope Hennessy and R. Lightbown, *Catalogue of Italian Sculptures in the Victoria and Albert Museum*, London, 1964, II, 423-424, discuss a copy of the *bozzetto*. J. Wilde, "Zwei Modelle Michelangelos für das Julius-Grab," *Jahrbuch der kunsthistorisches Sammlungen in Wein*, n.s., II, 1928, 199-218, and "Due modelli di Michelangelo ricomposti," *Dedalo*, VIII, 1928, 653-671; and Weinberger, *Michelangelo*, I, 245 ff., argue that the terracotta in the the Casa Buonarroti is not a design for the colossus but for a *Victory* for the Tomb of Julius II.

63 A.E. Brinckmann, *Barock-Bozzetti*, Frankfurt am Main, 1923, I, 44-45; F. Schottmüller, *Die italienischen und spanischen Bildwerke der Renaissance und des Barock*, Berlin-Leipzig, 1933, I, 156, No. 2612. The model, broken in several pieces during World War II, is in storage at the Bode Museum. Its high quality and vigorous anatomical detailing lend support to the attribution.

> down towards his crushed enemy, grinding and gnashing his teeth, raised his right arm and gave him another blow with his club, fiercely dashing his head to pieces.[64]

If the model in Berlin is not Bandinelli's original, it must be a near replica in pose and expression. Like Michelangelo's terracotta, Bandinelli's wax model represents two active combatants, the clear victor rising above his fallen adversary. Although Michelangelo's figures are twisted into a compact spiral while Bandinelli's are spread out in a more planar composition, the similarities between the victors' bent legs, turned upper torsos, and raised arms (now missing from the terracotta) suggest a connection between the designs, in which Michelangelo's probably took precedence.[65]

A number of explanations can be advanced for the fact that Bandinelli's design of 1525 was not carried out. Unlike Michelangelo's designs and Bandinelli's own earlier ideas, the Berlin group would have clashed emphatically with the *David*, because of its open pose and violent movement, as well as the large rock base. Valentiner, again distorting the subject matter, argues that the design is in bad taste: " It would have been unbearable, in a sculpture of enormous proportion, to witness the actual moment of murder of the most dastardly kind, trampling a human being into the ground with relentless blows of a heavy club." [66] The design also presents technical problems. The open pose would have been difficult to carry out in marble, and the upper arm would have had to be pieced or braced to support the weight of the club at an angle that puts torsion on the arm.

Vasari says that Bandinelli abandoned the design because it would not fit the block, and presented several others to Pope Clement, who chose the one to be used for the statue.[67] As a Medici employee, Vasari chose not to acknowledge the crucial political factors that influenced the change in design. Even if Bandinelli did miscalculate the measurements of the block, he could have kept more of the ac-

64 Vasari-Milanesi, VI, 149. The translation is from Pope Hennessy, *High Renaissance*, 363.

65 The violence of Bandinelli's conception is anticipated by Rustici's terracotta groups of fighting horsemen that ultimately derive from Leonardo's ideas (Weinberger, *Michelangelo*, I, 244), and the open composition, as well as the pose, of Bandinelli's design, may be reflected in the bronze statuette of a horseman fighting off a lion from the Foulc Collection in the Philadelphia Museum. Weil-Garris has pointed out to me that the pose of the Berlin model also appears in Rosso's *Moses and the Daughters of Jethro*, as well as prints after Rosso and Bandinelli.

66 Valentiner, " Bandinelli," 256.

67 Vasari-Milanesi, VI, 150-151.

tion and impact of the wax model had he, and Pope Clement, chosen to do so. The several models that the sculptor showed the Pope may have included active, conflicting groups, but Vasari specifies that Clement chose the one that showed Hercules standing over Cacus, seizing him by the hair and holding him down like a prisoner.

The model that Clement chose is possibly to be seen in a drawing in the Uffizi, (Fig. 22), which has sometimes been regarded as Bandinelli's final preparatory sketch for the statue.[68] The group is shown from slightly above Hercules' shoulders. The statue cannot be seen from this angle, and it would have been impractical to design from this point of view. However, Bandinelli did keep his models in his studio and had his many students draw from them. The Uffizi drawing is done from the same angle that students are shown viewing and drawing the model for Bandinelli's *Jason* in the 1531 engraving of his Academy.[69] The variations between the Uffizi drawing and the *Hercules and Cacus* are not a sign of tentativeness but rather reveal a previous stage in Bandinelli's thinking. When he made the full-scale clay model from which the statue was faithfully reproduced, he increased the rigidity of his figures and banished all movement. The psychological interaction of glances between victor and vanquished is removed, and the last of the curving lines of the bodies are converted into dominating verticals and horizontals.

The contrast between the Berlin model and the final statue embodies one of the most radical changes of conception that ever took place in the development of a work of art. The wax model is active and savagely violent; the statue is static and hieratic. It was precisely that savagery and conflict that Clement found undesirable. He scarcely wanted to remind the Florentines that the Medici (in the guise

68 Venturi, *Storia*, X, 2, 199, n. 1; R. Galleria degli Uffizi, *Mostra di disegni dei fondatori dell'Accademia delle Arti del Disegno*, Florence, 1963, No. 7; J.B. Shaw, *Drawings by Old Masters at Christ Church Oxford*, Oxford, 1976, No.89. U. Middeldorf pointed out to me that the Uffizi drawing is not preparatory in character and probably derives from a *modello*. The *verso* has several studies of the head and arms of Cacus. The absence of Cacus from the Christ Church drawing does not prove that it precedes the Uffizi drawing, of which it may be a copy; Cacus is also omitted from other derivative drawings, such as Louvre 156 (attributed to Bandinelli) and Uffizi 6992F (Clemente Bandinelli). Uffizi 520F could be a preparatory sketch for the Hercules model, and Louvre 130 and Uffizi 518F probably represent Bandinelli's preparatory work on the pose of Cacus. The head and torso on Uffizi 529F are related to the *Hercules* but with a shift of weight and more open pose of the arms. A number of drawings of the head (Louvre 98, Christ Church 0085*verso*) and legs (Uffizi 521F, 6984F; British Museum 1946-7-13-269) of Hercules also exist, probably as copies from the statue.

69 Museum of Art, Rhode Island School of Design, *Drawings and Prints of the First Maniera, 1515-1535*, Providence, Rhode Island, 1973, No. 117.

of Hercules) could be merciless in surpressing their enemies (in the guise of Cacus).[70] Further, since the *Hercules and Cacus* implied the triumph of the Medici, it was better to show the conflict as resolved rather than ongoing. But the final design of the statue involves more than an avoidance of violence and conflict; it can also be seen as a presentation of a specific political message that Clement wanted advertised.

Contrary to Valentiner's claim, the *Hercules and Cacus* does not represent a bestial murder, but an act of clemency. In the original story Cacus was deservedly executed, but Bandinelli, in keeping with traditional and contemporary ideas, has altered the action and spared Cacus. Hercules was traditionally the personification of force but also of the controlled use of that force. In Ripa's *Iconologia* Hercules appears as the emblem of Heroic Virtue, which has three aspects: the moderation of anger; the tempering of greed; and the contempt for strife, for pleasure and for talking.[71] The lion, whose skin Hercules wears as an attribute, is Ripa's first symbol for *clementia*, because when the lion overpowers a man and throws him to earth, unless wounded by that man, the lion does not tear him to pieces but merely shakes him lightly.[72] The striking feature of Bandinelli's *Hercules and Cacus* is its mildness in contrast with earlier representations of the theme. In the Pisano relief on the Campanile (Fig. 9) Cacus is clearly dead, as he was in Bandinelli's lost marble made in the early 1510's.[73] In the Pollaiuolesque relief in the Palazzo Guicciardini in Florence Hercules is in the process of dispatching his victim,[74] as he is in the Berlin model (Figs. 18, 20 ,21). In the statue of the Piazza della Signoria, however, Hercules

70 The conquest of Cacus is not one of the most commonly described feats of Hercules, although it does appear in Boccaccio's list (*La Geneologia degli dei de gentili*. Venice, 1581, 210 *verso*). Weinberger, *Michelangelo*, I, 244, relates the choice of the Cacus exploit, the only one that took place in Rome, to Clement's conflict with his Roman enemies. Even if this reference is included, the whole history of the project demands that the principal motivation for the subject matter be sought in Florence. If Michelangelo's drawing in the Casa Buonarroti does date *ca.* 1508 and does represent Hercules and Cacus (see n. 32, above), the subject had already been proposed under the Republic. M. Trachtenberg, *The Campanile of Florence Cathedral*, New York, 1971, 86 and 94, interprets the Pisano relief as an image of purifying the earth for civilization, and then (n. 44) asserts that Cacus represents "the lawless nobles who originally had terrorized the land but were finally beaten down by the Florentines." The meaning of the four animal heads around the rocky base of Bandinelli's statue is not clear. The two nearest the portal may refer to the Nemean lion and the Erymanthian Boar, but the dog has neither the two heads of Orthros nor the three of Cerebrus, and no wolf appears in any of the stories.

71 C. Ripa, *Nova Iconologia*, Padua, 1618, 567; Galinsky, *The Herakles Theme*, 198.

72 Ripa, *Iconologia*, 79.

73 See n. 37, above.

74 S. Ortolani, *Il Pollaiuolo*, Milan, 1948, fig. 114. A drawing of Hercules and Cacus after Pollaiuolo is in Turin (*ibid.*, fig. 83).

has moderated his anger. Cacus has been thrown to earth and gazes up at the facade of the Palazzo — the seat of the power represented by Hercules — with an expression that is probably most accurately read as supplication. Hercules, standing proud and secure in his victory, has granted his victim clemency.

The concept of *clementia* was a favorite "political catchword" of the Roman Caesars, ostentatiously displayed if not always exercised.[75] Its ultimate expression was given by divinely elected rulers, who were above human institutions and thus granted mercy freely rather than from fear of punishment.[76] A pope ostensibly elected through the divine inspiration of the College of Cardinals, who had taken the name Clement, can hardly have been uninterested in this tradition, which had been reitered by two of the foremost political thinkers of his day. Nicolò Machiavelli's espousal of the controlled use of force permeates all his writings but is best expressed in the seventeenth chapter of *The Prince* entitled "Concerning Cruelty and Clemency [Pietà], and Whether It Is Better to Be Loved than Feared."[77] Machiavelli says that the prince ought to seek to be considered merciful and not cruel, even though cruelty is often necessary, and that he ought to be feared but not hated. This can be achieved by using force judiciously and not greedily seizing the property and women of his subjects. Francesco Guicciardini also recommends clemency in those cases where it does not endanger a victory. His *ricordo* on clemency (*clementia*) is nearly a verbal equivalent of the visual message of Bandinelli's statue:

> There is nothing that man ought to desire more on this earth and that can be a source of greater pride than to see their enemy prostrate on the ground and at their mercy. This glory is greatly increased by its proper use, that is, by showing mercy and letting it suffice to have conquered.[78]

Pope Clement not only had good reason for advertising his clemency towards

[75] R. Syme, *The Roman Revolution*, Oxford, 1939, 159 ff., 51, and 480.

[76] J.R. Fears, "*Princeps a Diis Electus.*" *The Divine Election of the Emperor as a Political Concept at Rome*, Rome, 1977, 139-140.

[77] N. Machiavelli, *The Prince*, trans. W.K. Marriott, London, 1908, 133 ff. *The Prince* was written in the 1510's and dedicated to Lorenzo di Piero de' Medici. In 1520 Cardinal Giulio commissioned Machiavelli to write his *Florentine History*, which was finished and delivered to Rome about the time that Bandinelli brought his several models.

[78] F. Guicciardini, *Ricordi*, No. 72 (cf. 73), in *Selected Writings*, ed. C. Grayson, trans. M. Grayson, London, 1965. Most of the *Ricordi* were gathered between 1512 and 1525, although the collection was not complete until 1530.

the Florentines; he also had immediate precedent for using a statue by Bandinelli to do so. Karla Langedijk has shown that the *Orpheus* Bandinelli made for the Palazzo Medici in 1516/1517 was Pope Leo's advertisement of his peaceable intentions towards the Florentines and an image of the harmonious manner in which he would rule them.[79]

Bandinelli based his *Orpheus* on the *Apollo Belvedere*, thus linking both the style and the content of his statue with a renowned and venerated antique; he based his *Hercules and Cacus* on a variety of sources but similarly used them to justify and enhance his image. He drew upon antique types and Michelangelesque precedents and incorporated ideas and motifs from Leonardo and Donatello. If read correctly, the *Hercules and Cacus* not only demonstrates Bandinelli's positive aesthetic choices, it also evokes a number of beloved symbols of Florentine civic identity and pride, and thus links its symbolism with theirs.

The statue has not, of course, always been read correctly. Cellini, for one, misinterpreted all the formal features of the statue, although he was probably more aware of Bandinelli's intentions than he chose to admit.[80] The basic configuration of the group was adapted from two antique types: the mature Hercules standing at rest with his club, and the knife sharpener from narratives of the flaying of Marsyas.[81] Cellini's complaint about Hercules' small skull ignores the fact that many ancient statues of Hercules are characterized by similarly modest crania.[82] His condemnation of Hercules' ugly face is irrelevant, because leonine physiognomy was a traditional antique and Renaissance formula for stressing

79 K. Langedijk, "Baccio Bandinelli's Orpheus: A Political Message," *Mitteilungen des Kunsthistorischen Institutes in Florenz*, XX, 1976, 33-52. A similar use of a defensive *impresa* on the *Lacoön* Bandinelli made for Clement VII is mentioned in I. Lavin, "The Sculptor's Last Will and Testament'," *Allen Memorial Art Museum*, Bulletin, XXXV, 1978, n. 25. In Langedijk's opinion Leo rejected Bandinelli's model of David striking off the head of Goliath for political reasons, which would provide a precedent as well for Clement's rejection of the 1525 design. However, that would make Bandinelli's return to a violent image all the more puzzling. For a suggested identification of Bandinelli's *David and Goliath*, see Valentiner, "Bandinelli," 259 and fig. 1. For the purported clemency and actual policy of Leo and Clement, see F. Guicciardini, *The History of Italy*, trans. and ed. S. Alexander, New York, 1969, especially 275, 338 and 361, and C. Roth, *The Last Florentine Republic*, London, 1925, 12 ff.

80 Cellini, *Vita*, ed. Bacci, 353 ff. Although Cellini's *Perseus* has not shown his victim clemency, his impassive, meditative expression, his symbolic victor's stance, and the contrived pose of Medusa's body are all paralleled in the *Hercules and Cacus*.

81 The statue of the *Knife Sharpener* now in the Uffizi was in Rome during Bandinelli's lifetime, and the figure also appears on sarcophagi (Weil-Garris, *Leonardo*, n. 247).

82 M. Reymond, *La sculpture florentine*, Florence, 1900, IV, 120-121.

virility and ferocity in heroic portraits.[83] The turned-down mouth, flattened nose, overhanging brow, and deeply furrowed forehead of Bandinelli's hero resemble the features given to Verrocchio's *Colleoni*, a number of Leonardo's drawings, and Cellini's own later portrait of Duke Cosimo I. The " sack of melons " physique that Bandinelli used complements this physiognomy. The musculature is exaggerated, but not much more so than some of Leonardo's drawings, antique statues such as the *Laocoön*, or Michelangelo's *Allegories* in the Medici Chapel.

Vasari says that when the *Hercules and Cacus* was unveiled in the late spring of 1534 Bandinelli found that it looked too " dolce," and went to work again to strengthen the modelling.[84] Even today bright light tends to wash out the contours of both Bandinelli's and Michelangelo's statues. Before they were weathered and streaked by pollution, the *David* must have seemed even more pale and puny by comparison to the more robust and articulated musculature of Bandinelli's statue. Next to the stolid pyramid of the *Hercules and Cacus* the *David* may also seem attenuated and slightly unstable (Fig. 30). The difference is even more pronounced when observed from the steps entering the Palazzo (Figs. 23 and 24). Cellini criticized the *Hercules and Cacus* for lacking grace and *contrapposto*, but Bandinelli purposely stressed the structural regularity and solidity of his group. Hercules stands with his weight on both legs and both arms almost straight at his sides. Cacus is sharply folded into position, his shoulders paralleling the ground and those of Hercules, and his body giving firm visual and actual support to the masses above. Cellini reported with horror that Bandinelli had criticized the *David* for looking well only from the front,[85] but in fact it is true. In fairness to Michelangelo, one must admit that multiple views in sculpture were not much thought about when he carved the *David* in the first years of the century, and that he did have an usually narrow block which had already been carved in part by earlier hands. Nonetheless, in fairness to Bandinelli, one must give him credit for designing a group that is visually solid and satisfactory from most points of view all around the base.

Besides bemoaning the second colossus' lack of grace, Cellini purports not to understand the pose, since Hercules is not paying attention to what he is doing and it is not clear whether his weight is concentrated on one leg or both. The

83 P. Meller, " Physiognomic Theory in Renaissance Heroic Portraits," *Studies in Western Art: Acts of the Twentieth International Congress of the History of Art*, Princeton, 1963, II, 53-69.

84 Vasari-Milanesi, VI, 160. See also Weil-Garris, *Leonardo*, n. 246.

85 Cellini, *Vita*, ed. Bacci, 386-387.

head is turned to the side, but to avoid implications of ongoing action, and the stance, although not easy to read, is rational and deliberately calculated.

The precedents for the pose of Bandinelli's Hercules are familiar Florentine images, chosen to associate the statue with popular civic ideals. The Quattrocento statue that most closely resembles the overall configuration of Bandinelli's group is the *Abraham and Isaac* (Fig. 25), made by Donatello and Nanni di Bartolo for the Campanile.[86] In both cases the potential victim is held between the legs of the standing figure, who looks off to the side. The form of the turned heads is similar, but the meaning is different, even though both men can be regarded as moral victors. Abraham is presently responding to the miraculous intervention of the angel who pointed out the ram to be substituted for Isaac. Hercules has already spared Cacus and turns away with what might be termed "heroic disdain" to watch for new dangers. The *David* is also a watchful guardian, but Michelangelo was characteristically ambiguous about whether David is shown before or after his victory over Goliath. Bandinelli's representation of a point in time after the victory, and Hercules' internalized detachment from his prisoner, is most akin to Donatello's *Judith* (Fig. 26), who stands in equally hieratic and meditative triumph over Holofernes.[87] Although Judith raises her sword, her gesture is not narrative but symbolic. The fingers of her other hand are casually laced into the hair of the unresisting Holofernes; Bandinelli's Hercules uses no more effort to dominate Cacus. Antique representations of the Labors of Hercules sometimes show him controlling his adversary with a hand in the hair (Fig. 27), but the more immediate precedent for the gesture of Bandinelli's Hercules is Donatello's statue.

The *Judith* was readily available to Bandinelli and had a symbolic content that could be beneficially related to the *Hercules*. In 1495 the *Judith* had been moved from the Palazzo Medici to the position in front of the Palazzo Vecchio taken by the *David* in 1504. After a short stay inside the Palazzo Vecchio, Donatello's statue was installed in the Loggia dei Lanzi, where it remained throughout Bandinelli's lifetime. At the Palazzo Medici the base of the *Judith* bore an inscription that linked her moral victory with civic virtue: "Kingdoms fall through luxury; cities rise through virtues; behold the neck of pride severed by the hand of humility." In the 1460's Piero de' Medici added an inscription rededicating the

86 Janson, *Donatello*, 33 ff. The precedent is cited by Weil-Garris, *Leonardo*, n. 247.

87 Janson, *Donatello*, 198 ff. Heikamp makes the comparison in his notes to the *Club del Libro* edition of Vasari's *Vite*, VI, 10.

statue to "that liberty and fortitude bestowed on the republic by the invincible and constant spirit of the citizens." Janson interprets the rededication as a reference to Piero's victory over the Pitti conspiracy in 1466 and an attempt to turn a personal Medici political triumph into a triumph of the populace at large.[88] Such an implication would have been equally valuable to attach to the *Hercules and Cacus*, to assert that the victory of the Medici rulers was at the same time a victory for the people of Florence. The inscription that replaced these earlier ones in 1495, "The Citizenry Has Erected This Exemplum of Public Wellbeing," appropriated the statue for the Republic and continued to hold up Judith's conquest as a symbol of civic welfare. By linking his *Hercules* with the *Judith*, Bandinelli invested his statue and his patrons with some of her recognized virtue and beneficence.

The stance of the *Hercules*, although different from that of Judith or Abraham, also depends upon and evokes familiar Florentine images of heroic virtue. Both of Hercules' feet are firmly planted on the rocky base. At the same time, the spread legs are straight and tense, the hips are level, and the weight is divided almost equally between the two legs.[89]

Bandinelli's most immediate examples for this type of *anticontrapposto* pose were in the work of Leonardo, who used it frequently in the first decade of the sixteenth century: in the project for *Hercules and the Lion* (Fig. 5), in anatomical studies,[90] and in his fresco of the Battle of Anghiari for the Hall of the Great Council in in the Palazzo Vecchio. Bandinelli would have become closely acquainted with Leonardo's fresco while he was in the Hall in about 1512 drawing from Michelangelo's cartoon for the *Battle of Cascina*. His attention may have been drawn to a figure at the left of Leonardo's design, seen from the rear, standing stalwart amidst the turmoil, and giving cover to two of his Florentine compatriots who are trying to rescue a fallen companion. The figure appears in Gould's and Pedretti's reconstructions of the composition, but is more clearly seen in a drawing in Turin (Fig. 28) that has two studies for the warrior in the upper right.[91] The

88 Janson, *Donatello*, 200.

89 As Weil-Garris, *Leonardo*, 41, points out, this deliberate *antigrazioso* and *anticontrapposto* stance is related to Leonardesque modes. She illustrates a Leonardo drawing of a nude (Clark and Pedretti, *Drawings of Leonardo*, No. 12594) that closely resembles the proportions and musculature of the *Hercules*, as well as the straight arms and spread legs. However, this drawing is more of an anatomical demonstration than a depiction of a real pose, and the figure's feet are both placed directly under his shoulders so that his legs are parallel. In the statue the figure of Cacus obliges Hercules to have his right leg advanced and his left leg extended behind his shoulders.

90 *Ibid.*, No. 19014.

91 C. Gould, "Leonardo's Great Battle-Piece: A

posture of this heroic and humanitarian soldier is remarkably similar to the back view of the *Hercules* (Fig. 29), even to the advanced and retracted position of the legs. The largest study is the closer, although the smaller also holds a weapon in the straight right arm.

In adapting Leonardo's figure Bandinelli again chose a familiar heroic and moral image as a formal precedent for his statue, from a context full of significance for Florentine history, both Republican and pre-Republican. The Hall of the Great Council was built to accommodate the new assembly of Florentine citizens after the reinstitution of the Republic in 1495 and was " the embodiment of Florentine Republicanism."[92] Leonardo and Michelangelo were commissioned to paint murals of Florentine military victories that took place in 1440 and 1364. Pedretti characterizes the image of Leonardo's stalwart soldier as a symbolic and paradigmatic figure: the heroic defender of the liberty and democratic principles of the Florentine Republic.[93] Identification with such a personage would restore to the colossus of Hercules some of the aura of civic virtue that it had lost during the squabbles over the project and the political events of the same years.

It may seem odd to analyze a statue from the back, but Bandinelli did plan his statue from multiple points of view, and for this location. One principal view is obtained by the spectator coming to the Palazzo Vecchio from the Via Calzaioli, the main route from the Duomo and the north part of the city. Other views can be obtained from the steps of the Palazzo, the Uffizi Corridor or the Loggia dei Lanzi, and from the Via della Ninna, a main route from the southeast part of the city. The route from the west or from the south over the Ponte Vecchio enters the Piazza from the Via Vacchereccia, and the spectator gets the view shown in Figure 30, which I consider the most important, because the two colossi can be seen together in their roles as guardians of the portal. From this view one discovers yet another of Bandinelli's references, which is in keeping with the pattern examined already.

The intended echo of the image of *Hercules* from the viewpoint of the spectator approaching the entrance from straight out in the Piazza is Donatello's *St. George*

Conjectural Reconstruction," *Art Bulletin*, XXXVI, 1954, fig. 18; C. Pedretti, *Leonardo da Vinci inedito*, Florence, 1968, fig. 61 and *Disegni di Leonardo*, No. 7; Bertini, *I Disegni Italiani*, No. 227. A connection between the figure and Bandinelli's *Hercules* is suggested by Larsson, *Von allen Seiten*, 49.

92 Gilbert, *Machiavelli and Guicciardini*, 10, See also Wilde, " The Hall of the Great Council."

93 Pedretti, *Disegni di Leonardo*, 17.

(Fig. 31), made about 1416 for the niche of the armorers and swordsmiths' guild at Or San Michele.[94] St. George stands with his left foot and left shoulder advanced, his hips level and his weight evenly distributed over both feet. Bandinelli seems to have reversed the position of Hercules' legs in order to accommodate the figure of Cacus, but otherwise the specific elements of the pose and expression of his *Hercules* are strikingly close to those of the *St. George*. Both figures hold their shoulders level but advance the left one, looking out over it with furrowed brows. Both bend their left arms and relax the hand atop a form that rests between their legs, and both tense their right arms vertically at their sides to grasp a weapon. Although the age, proportions and costume or absence thereof is quite different, watchful concentration emanates from the bodies and faces of both figures.

Commissioned by a guild, the *St. George* was not made as an embodiment of the Florentine government, but does represent a hero who defended a city from a monster, as the relief below depicts. The statue became a great popular favorite in Florence, admired for its " prontezza," " vivacità," and " terribilità," and copied many times.[95] The statue also turns up in literary sources, including a licentious poem by Il Lasca, and a story by Anton Francesco Doni, in which an admirer laments that Bandinelli's *Hercules and Cacus* had such a prominent position by the Palazzo Vecchio, while the *St. George* was in a much less conspicuous location.[96] The story is based on the idea that Donatello's statue was more worthy of the important setting, but at least it does make a connection between the two works.

Two further pieces of evidence help confirm the connection between the statues. One is a small drawing of the *St. George* in the Uffizi that is inscribed and catalogued as Bandinelli (Fig. 32).[97] While the execution is clumsy and contains distortions or misunderstandings of some details of the statue, the brown ink that is clearly visible is traced over faint indications of an original drawing in black chalk. The sheet may be a hasty sketch by Bandinelli gone over later by one of his students, although there is no certainty about the date of either the original sketch or the

94 Janson, *Donatello*, 23 ff. The *St. George* was later moved to the Bargello and replaced by a bronze copy. Larsson, *Von allen Seiten*, 88, compares the stances of the two figures.

95 For example, the St. Michael on Perugino's Adoration altar in the National Gallery, London, and his Lucio Sicinio in the Collegio del Cambio, Perugia.

96 Janson, *Donatello*, 24; A.F. Doni, *I Marmi*, Venice, 1552, III, 10-11.

97 Uffizi 489F. The drawing is inscribed *P. bo. Bandinelli* in black chalk. The *verso* shows a side view of a standing man, wearing a long robe and holding a book.

reworking. The second piece of evidence is more concrete but less direct. In about 1540 Bandinelli was commissioned to carve portrait statues of the Medici rulers for the *Udienza* that was built to replace the dismantled Hall of the Great Council. He turned to the *St. George* again, to serve as the basis for the figure of Alessandro, who had been Duke of Florence when the *Hercules and Cacus* was finally finished.

The hand gestures of Bandinelli's *Alessandro* are taken from Donatello's marble *David* of 1409.[98] The history and symbolism of Donatello's marble *David* are intimately bound up with the government of Florence, and although telling the story of the statue would go far beyond the limits of this study, Bandinelli's use of that historical image gives another example of the pattern of his political propagandizing.

* * *

The political and artistic success of Bandinelli's *Hercules and Cacus* was limited but not entirely lacking. Despite the biased criticism of Bandinelli's immediate contemporaries, the statue did enjoy a certain amount of favorable aesthetic judgment later in the sixteenth century. The large numbers of drawings that copy or adapt the image are one index of its popularity among his followers. One of these followers, Vincenzo de' Rossi, petitioned Duke Cosimo I in 1563 to obtain the full-size clay model.[99] Vasari grudgingly allows the statue approval because it was well studied and because other sculptors had made worse colossi.[100] At least two later statues are based directly on Bandinelli's colossus; Sansovino's *Hercules* in Brescello and his *Mars* at the Palazzo Ducale in Venice.

It is possible that Sansovino's *Hercules* in Brescello was made with an understanding of the political message of Bandinelli's statue. Duke Ercole II d'Este was lavishly praised for his *clementia* in the dedication of Gyraldo's *De Dei Gentium* of 1548.[101] In 1550 the Duke commissioned the statue of his namesake as a

98 Middeldorf, "A Bandinelli Relief," 71, makes the connection with the *St. George*. On the Udienza, see Vasari-Milanesi, VI, 170 ff; Venturi, *Storia*, X, 2, 222-226. On the *David* of 1408 see Janson, *Donatello*, 3 ff.

99 Gaye, *Carteggio*, III, 107-108. For some of the drawings, see n. 68, above.

100 Vasari-Milanesi, VI, 160. Doni, I *Marmi*, III, 10, refers to the *Hercules and Cacus* as "un bellissimo Colosso."

101 L.G. Gyraldo, *De Deis Gentivm*, Basel, 1528, 46B.

symbol of his power in Modena, but later changed its location to Brescello, of which he had recently reacquired control.[102] Since Sansovino's *Hercules* has no figure of Cacus or other victim, it would be presuming too much to interpret the statue as an explicit image of *clementia*, but at least the formal connection with the *Hercules and Cacus* shows that Bandinelli's statue was regarded as an acceptable image of a ruling power.

In Florence Hercules continued to be a common personification of the Medici rulers, as witness Vincenzo de' Rossi's statues in the Palazzo Vecchio and Pietro da Cortona's frescoes in the Palazzo Pitti. Since the later sixteenth and seventeenth-century Medici ruled Florence absolutely, and since Hercules' good reputation had such a long history in the city, it is unlikely that Bandinelli's statue was crucial in the maintenance of that tradition. In the last decades of the sixteenth century, however, when the political conflicts of Republican and Medicean interests had cooled or been thoroughly suppressed, the statue was better understood and even praised. Raffaello Borghini answered complaints about Hercules' lack of ferocity and activity by explaining that the statue does not represent a battle but an embodiment of victory, lauding Bandinelli's artistic judgment in representing the musculature of the figures.[103] In more elegant terms, Francesco Bocchi praised Bandinelli's profound understanding of design and his marvelous skill at depicting the human body, as well as the natural and truthful figure of Cacus and the fierce and heroic image of Hercules.[104]

102 L. Pittoni, *Jacopo Sansovino scultore*, Venice, 1909, 291-297; G. Campori, " Una statua di Iacopo Sansovino," *Atti e memorie delle RR. Deputazioni di Storia Patria per le Provincie Modenesi e Parmensi*, VI 1872, 501-514.

103 R. Borghini, *Il Riposo*, I, 190-191. Borghini also (III, 30) points out that although the statue was once despised, its worth was later recognized (" sebben allora fu biasimata, è stata poi la bontà sua conosciuta ").

104 F. Bocchi, *Le Bellezze della città di Firenze* (1591), ed. J. Shearman, London, 1971, 33-34.

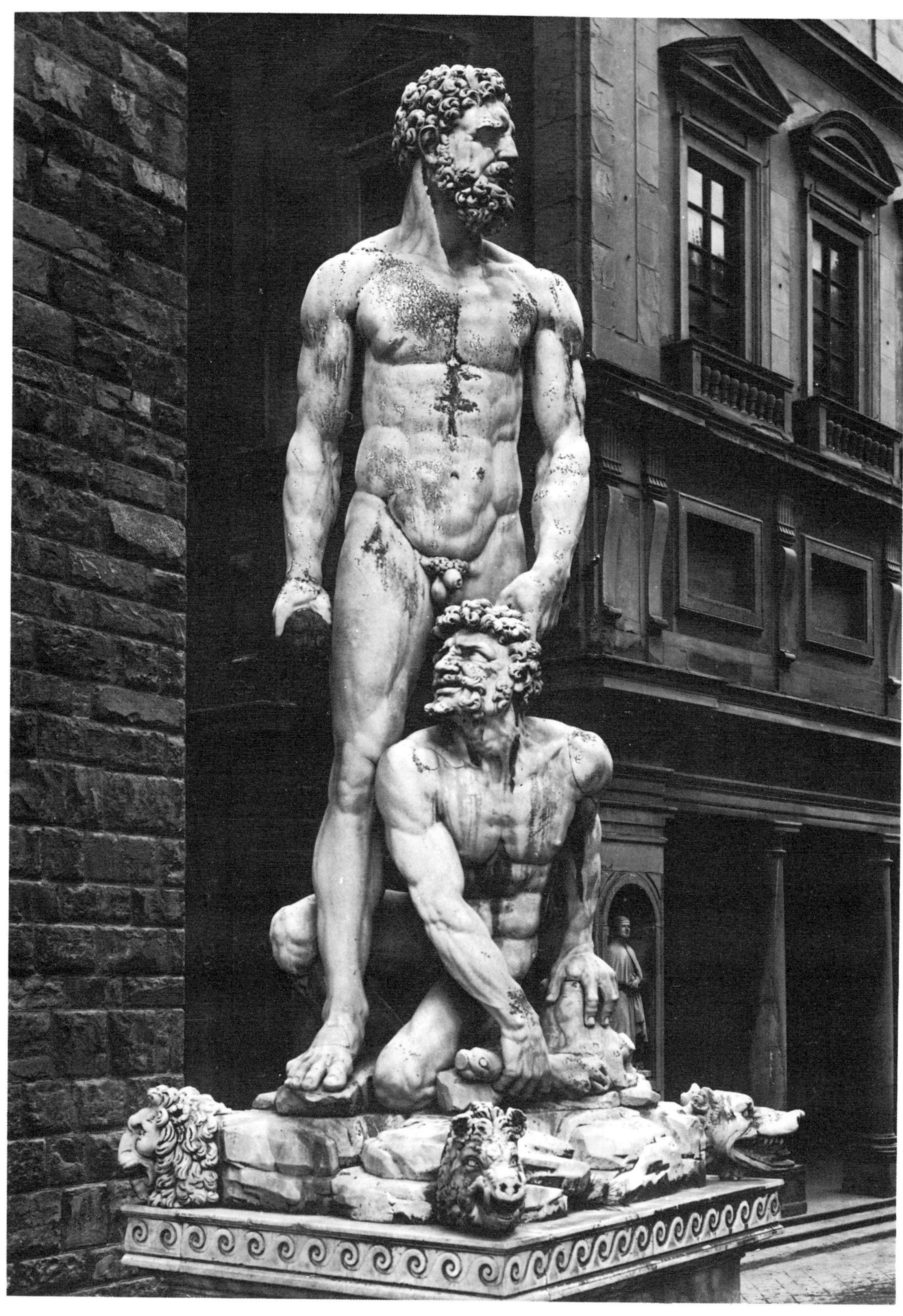

Fig. 1. Bandinelli, Hercules and Cacus, *Piazza della Signoria, Florence (photo Alinari).*

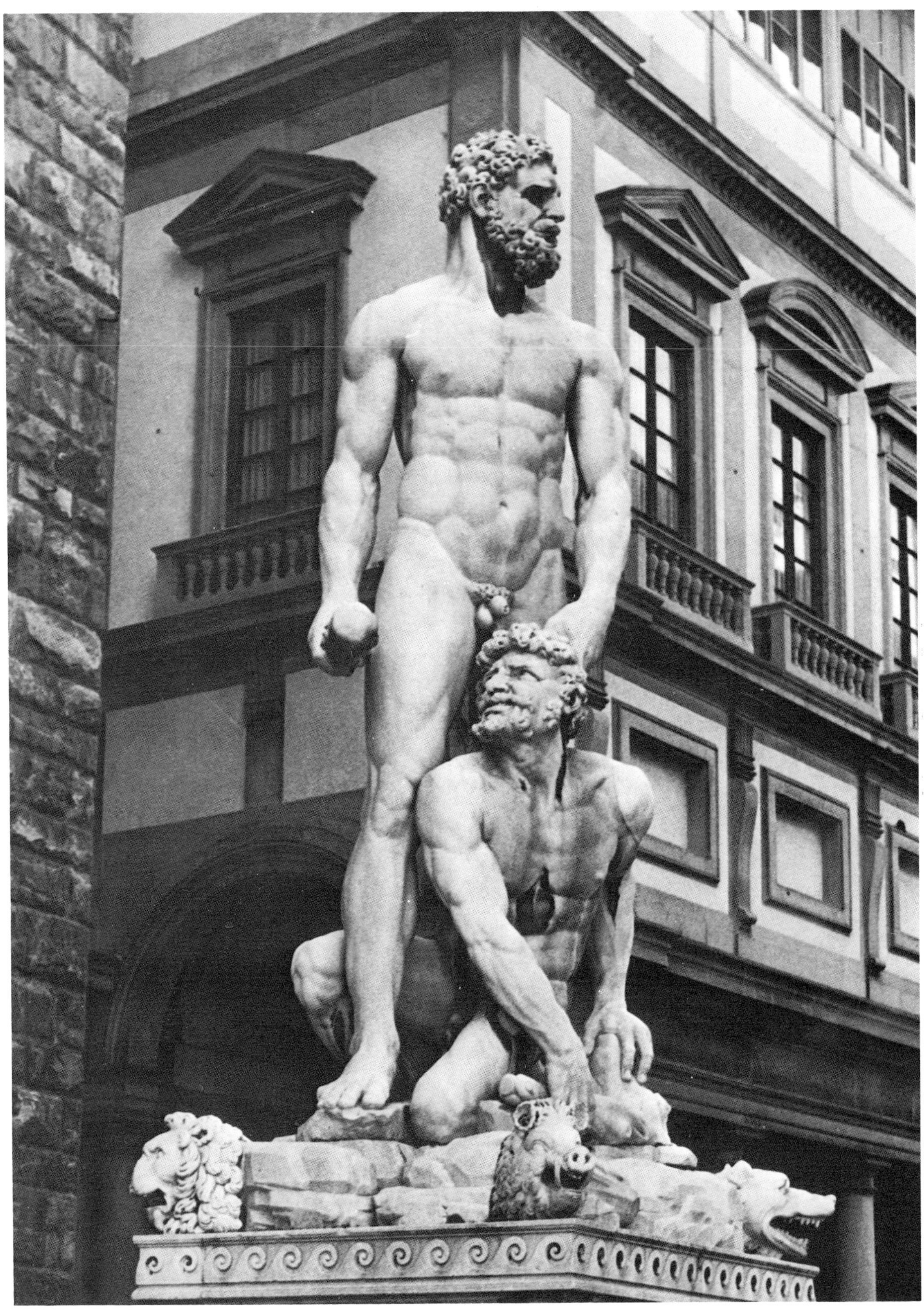

Fig. 2. Bandinelli, Hercules and Cacus, *Piazza della Signoria, Florence (photo Author).*

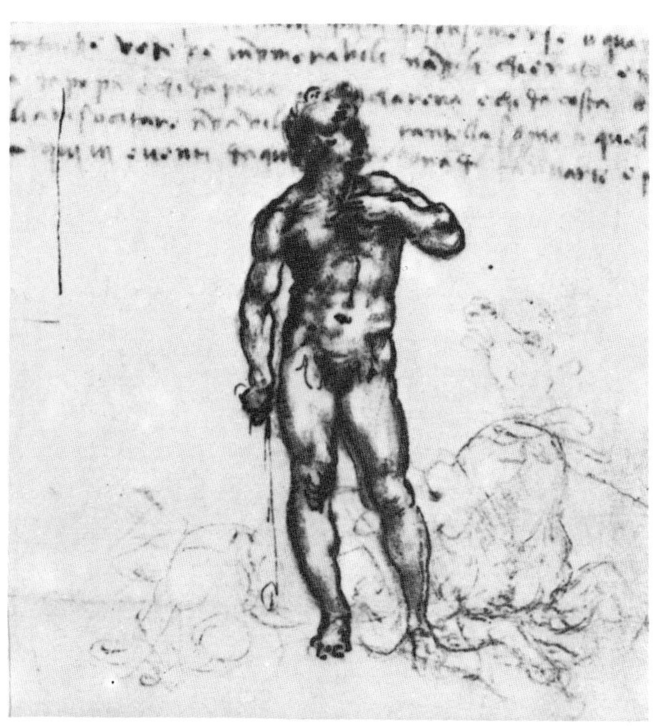

Fig. 3. Leonardo, Neptune (*after Michelangelo's* David), *Royal Library, Windsor, No. 12591 (Copyright reserved).*

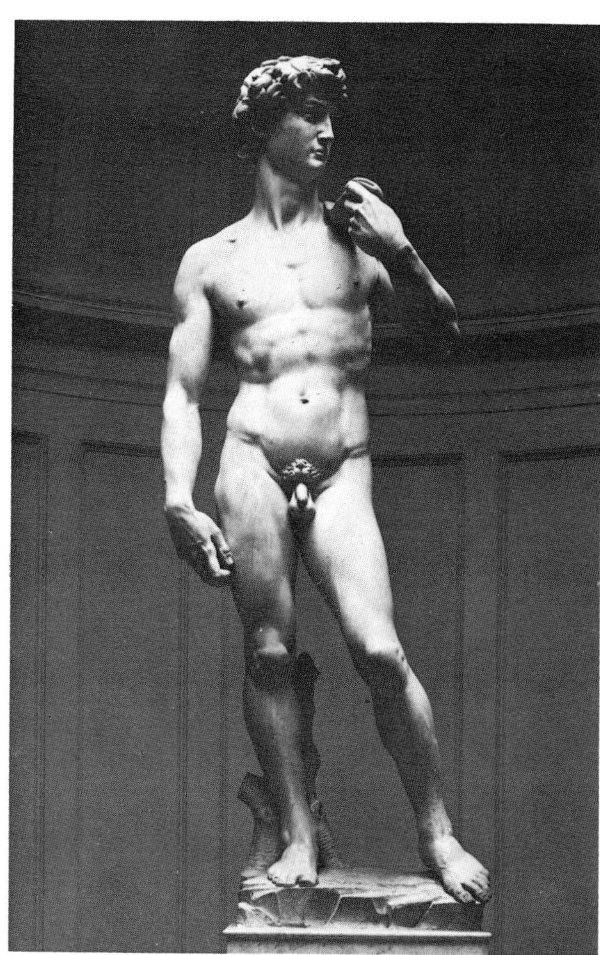

Fig. 4. Michelangelo, David, *Accademia, Florence (photo G.F.S.G., Firenze).*

Fig. 5. Leonardo, Hercules and the Lion, *Biblioteca Reale, Turin, Inv. 15630 (photo Chomon-Perino, Turin).*

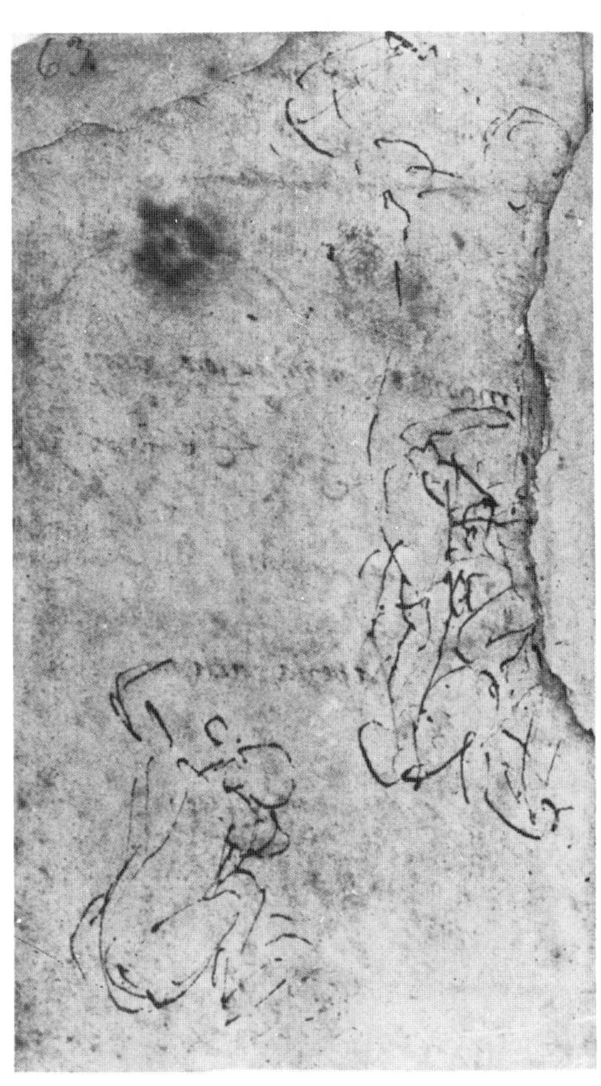

Fig. 6. Michelangelo, Hercules and Cacus (?), *Casa Buonarroti, Florence (photo G.F.S.G., Firenze).*

Fig. 7. Vasari, Entry of Leo X, *Detail, Palazzo Vecchio, Florence (photo Alinari).*

Fig. 8. Hercules Seal, Woodcut from D. M. Manni, Osservazioni istoriche, *Florence, 1739 (photo Author).*

Fig. 9. Andrea Pisano, Hercules and Cacus, *now opera del Duomo, Florence (photo Alinari).*

Fig. 10. Hercules, *Porta della Mandorla, Duomo, Florence (photo Alinari).*

Fig. 11. Bandinelli, Giants, *Villa Madama, Rome (photo Author).*

Fig. 12. Heemskerck, Villa Madama, *Detail,* Skizzenbuch *I, f. 24r, Staatliche Museum Preussicher Kulturbesitz Kupferstichkabinett, Berlin-Dahlem (photo Jörg P. Anders, Berlin).*

Fig. 13. Bandinelli, Giant, *Villa Madama, Rome (photo Author).*

Fig. 14. Michelangelo, Risen Christ, *S. M. sopra Minerva, Rome*

Fig. 15. Michelangelo, Hercules and Antaeus, *British Museum, London (photo by permission of the Trustees).*

Fig. 16. Michelangelo, Hercules and Antaeus, *Ashmolean Museum, Oxford (photo Ashmolean Museum).*

Fig. 17. Michelangelo, Hercules *or* Samson, *Casa Buonarroti, Florence (photo G.F.S.G., Firenze).*

Fig. 18. Bandinelli, Hercules and Cacus, *Bode Museum, East Berlin (photo Staatliche Museen zu Berlin).*

Fig. 19. Michelangelo, Hercules *or* Samson, *Casa Buonarroti, Florence (photo G.F.S.G., Firenze).*

Fig. 20. Bandinelli, Hercules and Cacus, *Bode Museum, East Berlin (photo Staatliche Museen zu Berlin).*

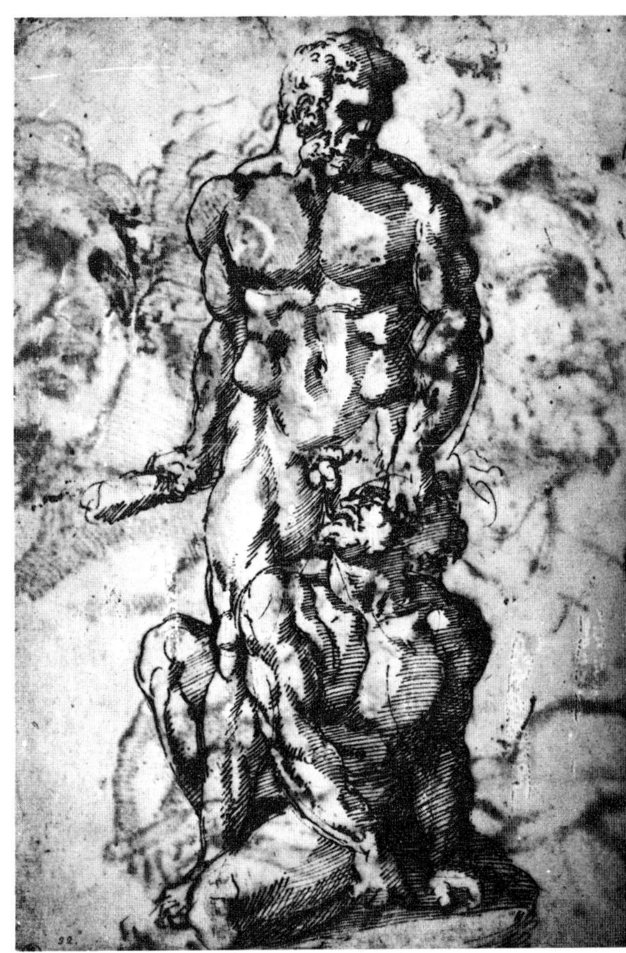

Fig. 22. After (?) *Bandinelli,* Hercules and Cacus, *Uffizi 714E recto (photo G.F.S.G., Firenze).*

Fig. 21. Bandinelli, Hercules and Cacus, *Bode Museum, East Berlin (photo Staatliche Museen zu Berlin).*

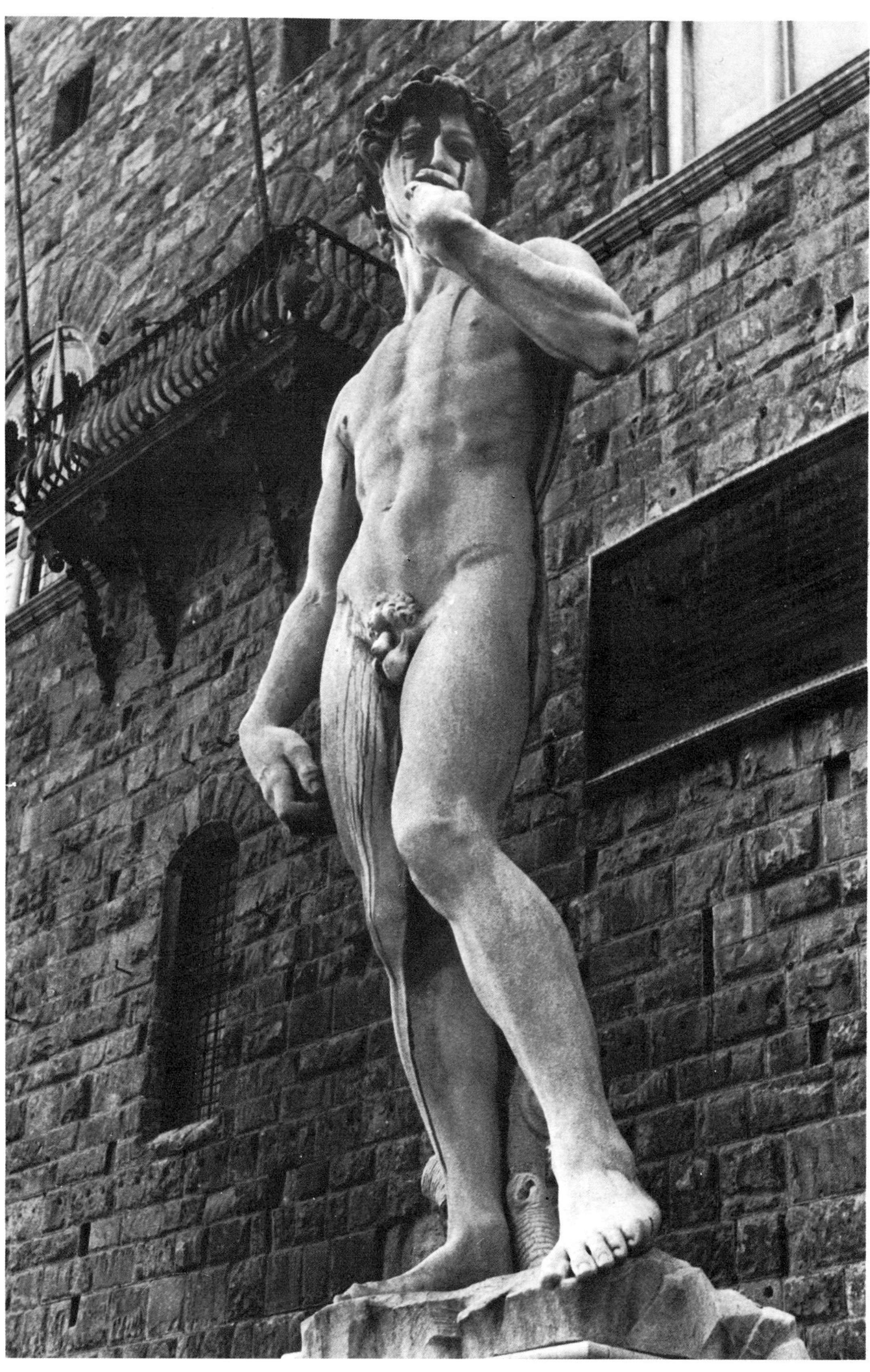

Fig. 23. Michelangelo, David *(copy), Piazza della Signoria, Florence (photo Author).*

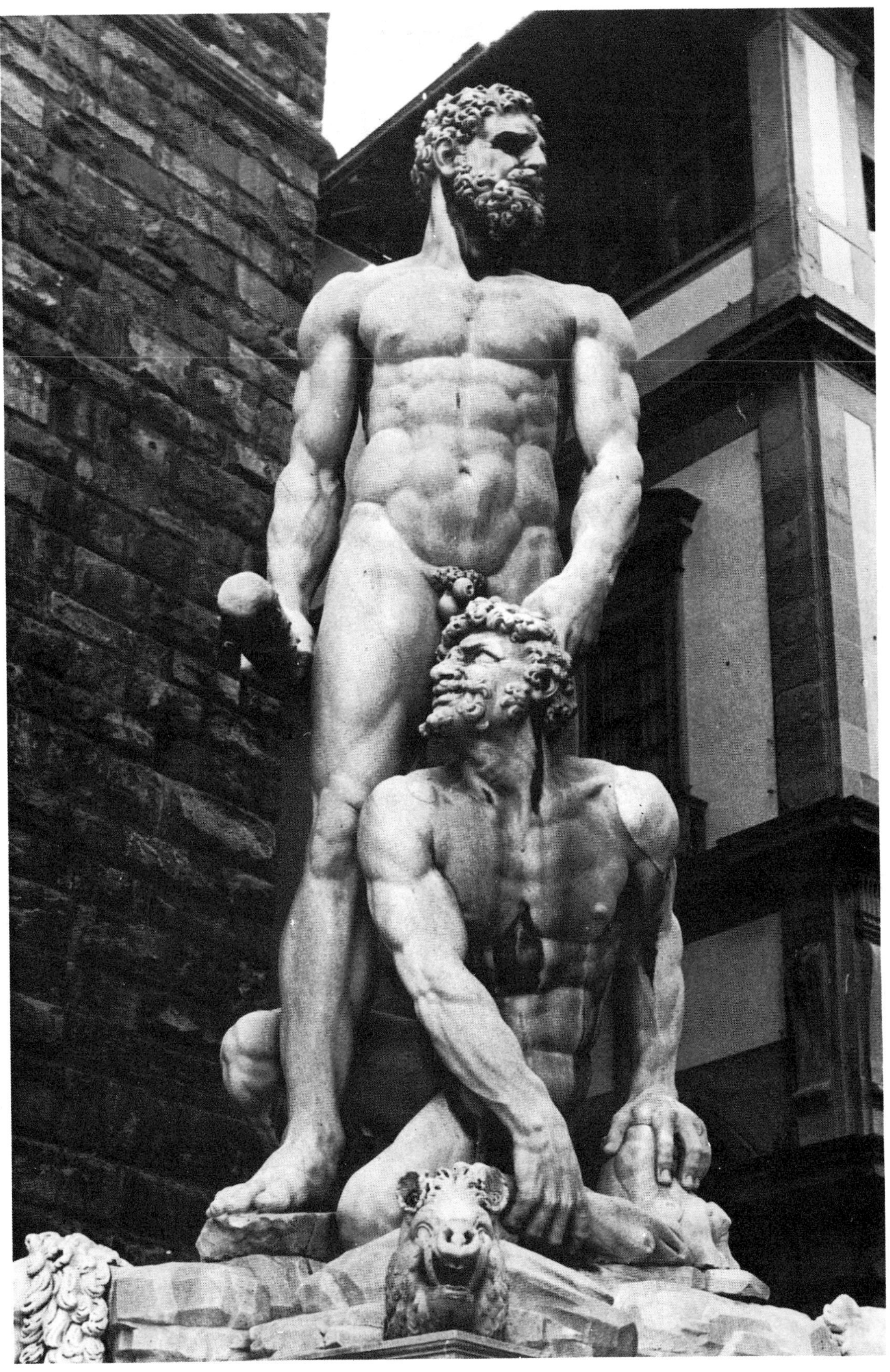

Fig. 24. Bandinelli, Hercules and Cacus, *Piazza della Signoria, Florence (photo Author).*

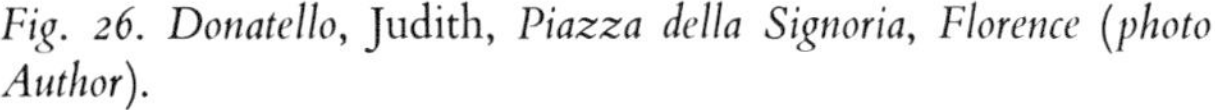

Fig. 25. Donatello and Nanni di Bartolo, Abraham and Isaac, *now Opera del Duomo, Florence (photo Alinari).*

Fig. 26. Donatello, Judith, *Piazza della Signoria, Florence (photo Author).*

Fig. 27. Hercules Sarcophagus, *Detail, Galleria Borghese, Rome* (*photo G.F.N., Roma*).

Fig. 28. Leonardo, Studies for the Battle of Anghiari, *Biblioteca Reale, Turin, Inv. 15567 (photo Chomon-Perino, Turin).*

Fig. 29. Bandinelli, Hercules and Cacus, *Piazza della Signoria, Florence (photo Author).*

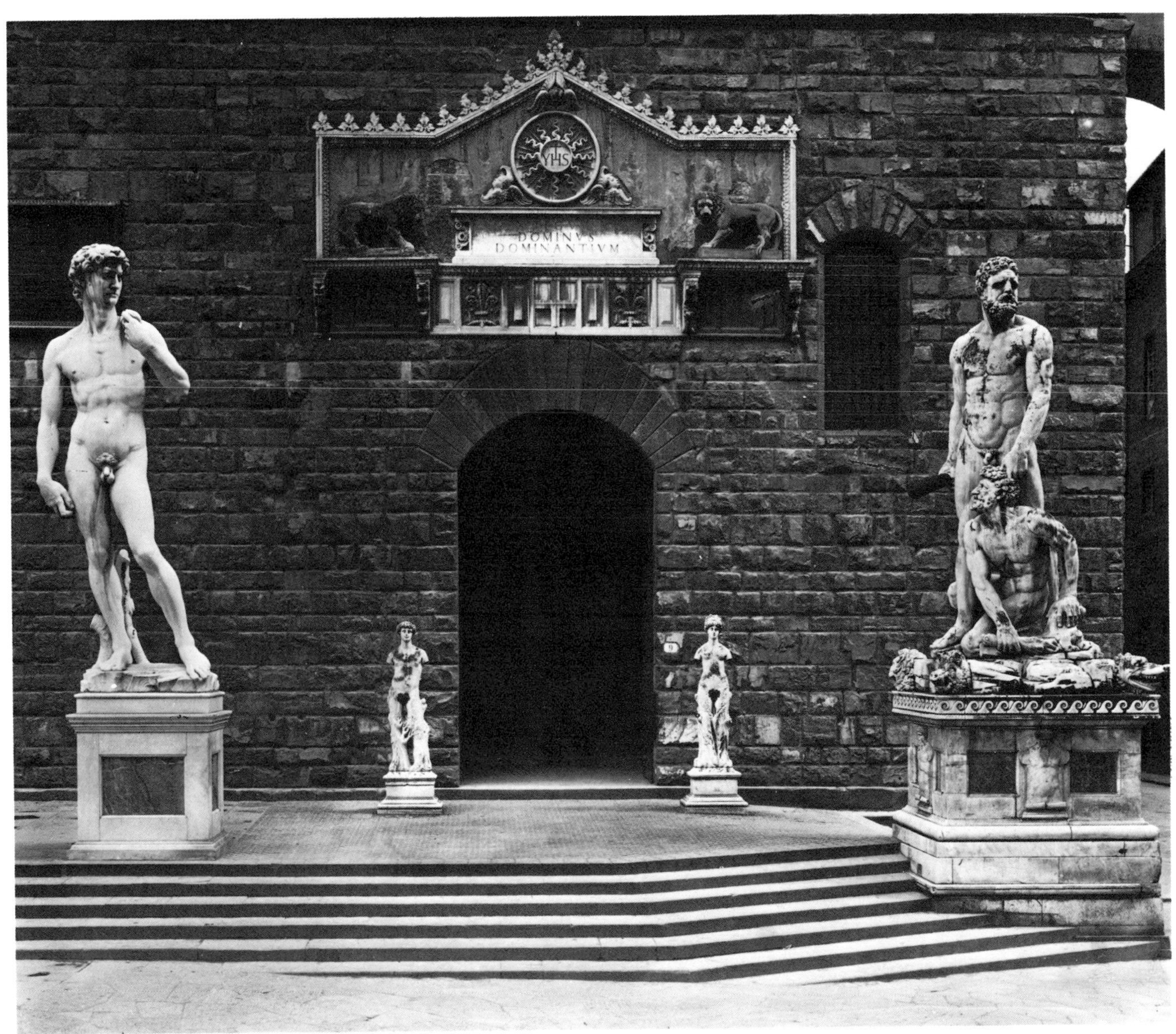

Fig. 30. Michelangelo, David *(copy) and Bandinelli,* Hercules and Cacus, *Piazza della Signoria, Florence (photo Brogi).*

Fig. 31. Donatello, St. George, *Museo Nazionale (Bargello), Florence (photo Anderson).*

Fig. 32. Bandinelli and Follower (?), St. George *(after Donatello), Uffizi 489F verso (photo G.F.S.G., Firenze).*

LEO STEINBERG

V

GUERCINO'S *SAINT PETRONILLA* ★

[A picture] can show what something is at a moment, but it cannot show us how it came to be that way or what will happen to it next.
— W. H. Auden and Elizabeth Mayer, Introduction to Goethe's Italian Journey, *New York,* 1968.

GUERCINO'S colossal altarpiece for St. Peter's (Fig. 1) has been much admired and often discussed — except for its subject, which appears to speak for itself: a young woman has died in the odor of sanctity, is lowered into her grave, and received into heaven. Her name, her identity, her personal or posthumous history — instructive as such information may be, it can hardly improve the sufficiency of the image. Everyone knows that whoever dies on earth is buried in it, and that the elect speed to the welcome of Christ. The painter's realism merely confirms common knowledge and pious faith. As subjects go, Guercino's *St. Petronilla*

★ *Two former students deserve special thanks: John Keating of Hunter College, New York, for arousing my interest in St. Peter's daughter; and Lynn Kaufmann of the University of Pennsylvania, for wise and skillful assistance at every stage of research.*

The St. Petronilla *altarpiece, oil on canvas, measures 7.20 × 4.23 m. It is signed, lower right: GREGO XV PONT MAX / IO: FRANC BARBERIVS CENTENS / FACIEBAT / MDCXXIII. Commissioned for one of the major altars in St. Peter's Basilica in December 1621, the work was probably completed by the spring of 1623. Most of the records of payment are published in Oskar Pollak,* Die Kunsttätigkeit unter Urban VIII, *Vienna, 1931, II, pp. 564 ff. For bibliography, see Denis Mahon,* Studies in Seicento Art and Theory, *London, 1947, p. 84 n.*

seems to leave nothing to question; and no commentator of the past 350 years has thought otherwise.

Yet these same commentators, reviewed together, disagree about what is shown. Is the corpse, in fact, being lowered? Admittedly, the majority read the picture to conform with its conventional title — *Santa Petronilla sepolta e accolta in cielo.* Many, however, have thought they were seeing the body being exhumed, as if all the action, beginning from underground, kept moving up. Thus Goethe on November 3, 1786: "I looked with admiration at a St. Petronilla by Guercino... The body of the dead saint is lifted out of the tomb, and the same person, restored to life, is received in Heaven by a divine youth..." Similarly, the 18th-century inventory of Guercino's drawings at Windsor: "A Capital large Drawing, being the first thought for the Picture of the finding of the Body of Sta. Petronilla..." A century later, Charles Blanc wrote in his *Histoire des Peintres*: "La scène représente, sur le premier plan, l'exhumation du corps de sainte Pétronille; beau cadavre que soutiennent délicatement de rude fossoyeurs..." To this day, an irrepressible minority of scholars (including Semrau, Voss, Künstle, Galassi Paluzzi, and the new Kirschbaum *Lexikon*) persist in reading the picture as a scene of disinterment.[1]

(henceforth cited as Mahon, Studies) *and* idem, Il Guercino. Catalogo critico dei dipinti, *Bologna, 1968, p. 114 (henceforth cited as Mahon,* Dipinti).

In 1730, to preserve it from damp, the painting was moved to the Quirinal Palace. Its place over the altar was taken by a fine mosaic copy (Fig. 7) executed by Pietro Paolo Cristofari (1685-1743). Guercino's original was among the works of art shipped to Paris in 1797. It was returned to Rome in 1815, and, after a brief stay in the Vatican, deposited in the Galleria Capitolina.

Six preparatory drawings for the altarpiece have been published, of which four are reproduced here (Figs. 3, 4, 5, 6); see Mahon, Il Guercino. Catalogo critico dei disegni, *Bologna, 1968 (henceforth cited as Mahon,* Disegni), *nos. 87-91, and p. 97 for reference to the Copenhagen drawing (our Fig. 6).*

Three engravings after the St. Petronilla *are known. The earliest is by Nicolas Dorigny (1657-1746), dedicated to Jules Hardouin Mansart and dated 1700 (Fig. 10). The second — a classicizing attempt to play down Guercino's abrupt tonal contrasts — is by the Swiss Johann Jakob Frey (Lucerne 1681-1752 Rome), dated 1731 (Fig. 11). The third, signed by W. Brown after a drawing by Charles-Edward Perugini (b. ca. 1840), is reproduced in Charles Blanc,* Histoire des Peintres. École Bolonaise, *Paris, 1874, p. 7.*

[1] For the citations in the above paragraph, see: J. W. von Goethe, *Italienische Reise*; Denis Mahon, *Disegni*, p. 94, quoting the 18th-century Windsor inventory (Ms. A, p. 65); Charles Blanc., *op. cit.*, p. 4; Max Semrau, *Die Kunst der Barockzeit und des Rokoko* (*Grundriss der Kunstgeschichte*), Esslingen, 1913, p. 163; Herman Voss in U. Thieme, F. Becker, *Allgemeines Lexikon der bildenden Künstler*, XV, Leipzig, 1922, p. 217; Karl Künstle, *Ikonographie der christlichen Kunst*, Freiburg i. B., 1926, I, p. 493; C. Galassi Paluzzi, *San Pietro in Vaticano*, Rome, 1963, I, p. 107; and L. Schütz in E. Kirschbaum, ed., *Lexikon der christlichen Ikonographie*, VIII, Rome, Freiburg i. B., 1976, p. 157.

To my knowledge, only Louis Réau has observed the confusion over the subject of Guercino's altarpiece — a confusion which he tries, fortunately without success, to settle by fiat. The painting, he writes,

Needless to say, the still image itself offers no certain clues. Nothing in the action of the gravediggers tells whether they are raising the body or letting it down (Fig. 2). Equally neutral is the bier at the left — it may have delivered its burden, or else may be standing by to take the exhumed body away. And though a lament over a recent death seems to be indicated by the presence of weepers, who knows the proximate cause of their tears? At the discovery of a young life cut off in its flower, yet still abloom and incorrupted in a beautiful corpse, weeping would not be ill-timed. And there are further reasons for keeping both possibilities open. The preliminary studies for the altarpiece include one that depicts the opening of a tomb: a slab is being held up as a group of workmen and one curious elder look in (Fig. 3). The alternative, then, the recovery of the body, had been in Guercino's mind while he pondered the subject. It may still have been on his mind when, by means of a pair of hands at the bottom, he implied the cooperation deep down of another gravedigger who would not, during a normal burial, position himself beneath the corpse. And one may add that the averted head of the young man half-seated at right would make better sense if the dead maiden were being raised from her tomb, than if this were the final moment before her disappearance forever.

The body's imminent destination is not the only riddle which this pseudo-narrative leaves unanswered — the picture is filled with evasions and ambiguities. To dispel them is neither within our power nor to be wished. But it does seem desirable to acknowledge their presence, and to consider whether the painter's equivocations spring from weakness or strength; whether they carelessly muddle a simple tale, or satisfy an assignment more complex than had been thought. To do this, we shall have to examine three things: the picture itself, its critical fortunes, and the background of its ostensible content.

To begin at the threshold. Careful hands — huge enough for the little finger to exceed seven inches — rise from the lower edge. They belong to a gravedigger reaching out from inside a sepulcher to support a young woman's corpse seen *in scorto*, head first. Two mates above ground sustain the body by slings: an older man on his knees, bent with reverence; another, half-nude, hard at work. Behind them on our left, huddled at the head of a cushioned bier, stand four troubled

" représente non l'Exhumation de la sainte, mais sa Inhumation " (*Iconographie de l'art chrétien. Iconographie des Saints*, III, 3, Paris, 1959, p. 1065).

One modern scholar entitles the picture, for no apparent reason, " The Martyrdom of St. Petronilla" (Ellis Waterhouse, *Italian Baroque Painting*, London, 1962, fig. 97).

witnesses: women weeping, a puzzled boy, an adolescent with aching heart and flickering candle. At the right, a steep incline is formed by a link of three men, their heads lined up bendwise against the margin: we distinguish a turbaned, black-bearded speaker, a somewhat foppish youth listening, and, between them, a greybeard whose balding brow plays fulcrum to a visionary counter-diagonal — St. Petronilla again, now unforeshortened, kneeling on a supporting cloud before an angel-orbited Christ who, with seignorial grace, welcomes her at the outskirts of heaven.

The celestial orbit is closed on the right by the corner of an Ionic entablature. Of other constructions we see no more than the torus and nethermost drum of an unbuilt column, squat on a dado and plinth; and a platform above the tomb. One detects a remarkably simple counterpoint of human and inanimate forms. Against the latter's steadying horizontals and perpendiculars, the major figures mount three successive diagonals: upward from the emergent gravedigger's hands to the right middle margin; then in a right-angled swerve to top left, where a pair of alerted angels gaze eagerly up- and centerward, promising a third turn (Fig. 6 A). We are given an unbroken concatenation of figures and, midway, unaccountably, a coupling of disparate spatial systems, as if it were commonplace to see heaven and earth overlap.

To cool heads, the seamless conjunction of the two zones has often seemed faintly disturbing. Passeri, writing in the 1670s, regretted that the figures in heaven were shaded with equal emphasis — inappropriate to a "gloria nella quale deve apparire la dolcezza e suavità degli splendori." For Goethe, the picture was beyond price, "whatever objections there may be to this twofold action." Burckhardt, who took the scene for "a momentary event" ("ein momentanes Geschehen"), complained "that the celestial group remains disconnected from the earthly and yet presses too close upon it." Max Semrau was witty: "Guercino feels more at home on earth than in heaven... the terrestrial action is well arranged, lively and interesting, the celestial scene, vapid and conventional." A later critic observes that the division of a painting into two parts occurs in Guercino's altarpieces "with such monotonous regularity that one is inclined to be doubtful of his imagination and ingenuity." [2]

[2] For the quotation from Passeri, see Jacob Hess, ed., *Die Künstlerbiographien von Giovanni Battista Passeri*, Leipzig, Vienna, 1934, p. 351. Goethe's comment follows the remarks quoted on p. 208. Jacob Burckhardt's objection "dass die himmlische Gruppe ausser Verbindung mit der irdischen bleibt und doch zu nahe auf dieselbe drückt" — is made in *Der Cicerone* (1855), ed. Leipzig, 1884, p. 839. The "later critic" is E. J. Richmond, "St. William of Aquitaine by Guercino," *Bulletin of the Rhode Island School of Design*, 20 (July, 1932), p. 37.

Guercino specialists of the last fifty years have focused on the stylistic disparity between the two zones: low naturalism crossed with high classicism, their anomalous co-existence being explained as a double surrender to the influences Guercino encountered in Rome — Caravaggio's influence agitating the bottom, Domenichino's tranquilizing the top. Cesare Gnudi put it explicitly:

> Nel gruppo dei due uomini che calano la Santa martire sorretta dalle mani nodose del terzo invisibile becchino calato nella tomba, vi è qualcosa di nuovo, che non si era prima incontrato nell'arte del Guercino... vi è qualcosa che, più che altrove, risente dello spirito di Michelangelo da Caravaggio. Né viene sostanzialmente intaccata l'unità stilistica dell'opera, se dalla imminenza grandiosa della realtà, dalla immediatezza umana della parte inferiore si passa alla più atteggiata, idealizzata naturalezza della parte alta, e specie della figura della Santa, di impronta già domenichiana.[3]

Implicit in this analysis — that Guercino compromised the unity of the work by swaying in two directions — is the Wölfflinian view of the primacy of style over content. Calvi's assumption (1808), that the creator of the *St. Petronilla* played on a contrast of styles in response to his subject, seems no longer persuasive.[4] The Guercino of modern criticism has become too instinctual, too unsophisticated to be credited with such knowing manipulation. And one suspects this more general inhibition: where competing styles are seen as the driving forces of art-historical evolution, it is difficult to let these same forces be driven like a team, two-in-hand. To recent students of the Seicento, it appears more historical to conceive Guercino as an impressionable provincial, yielding to pressures which he was powerless to resist.

And yet, though the bipartition of the picture is undeniable, though its base portion is heavy-laden with effort and brusque foreshortenings inadmissable in the upper air, Guercino did grasp both decks together, wanting them in one geometric

[3] Cesare Gnudi, introduction to D. Mahon's *Dipinti*, p. xxxvii.

[4] " ...io non so vedere che nobiltà si potesse esigere in un soggetto vulgare, come è quello della sepoltura d'una figlia di un povero Apostolo, anzi parmi che tutto egregiamente corrisponda al soggetto medesimo; il Salvatore poi, e l'Anima della Santa hanno gentilezza e nobiltà quanto a quello stile può convenire » (Jacopo Alessandro Calvi, *Notizie della Vita, e delle Opere del... Guercino da Cento*, Bologna, 1808; reprinted in Giampietro Zanotti, ed., *Felsina Pittrice. Vite de' Pittori Bolognesi del conte Carlo Cesare Malvasia*, Bologna, 1841, II, p. 287. Strangely enough, Mahon recognizes as probably deliberate, a similar, if regrettable, change of style in a later Guercino altarpiece. He is discussing the *Madonna and Child with St. Bruno* (1647) at Bologna: " La differenza fra la metà superiore del quadro e quella inferiore è, sospettiamo, voluta, e certo contrasta direttamente con le abitudini del giovane Guercino quale vediamo esemplificato da un'opera come il *San Guglielmo*. Può darsi che la resa guercinesca di apparizioni celesti in uno stile quasi classico rimanga, per alcuni di noi, difficile da accettare; ma speriamo che a pochi sembri gravoso convenire che è magistrale l'organizzazione armoniosa di forme e colori in tutta la metà inferiore del dipinto." (Mahon, *Dipinti*, p. 183 f.).

configuration. A comparison with a large composition drawing at Windsor demonstrates some of his conscious decisions (Fig. 4).[5] In the drawing the scale of the figures is less, and fairly constant throughout; and the tryst in heaven, with a Christ wholly engaged in giving audience, is confined to one lofty corner. All these features (among many more) Guercino repudiated. In the altarpiece, the otherness of the heavenly vision is not conveyed by remoteness and separation, but by change of style. The *dramatis personae* not only bulk larger within the available field, but diminish progressively from base to summit, the diminution of scale being so gradual and continuous, that the fusion of the two spatial zones becomes but another expression of a continuity already given. And whereas the drawing posits no bond between those on earth and those enskied, the painting makes the antipodes of the field — the face of Christ and the upturned face of the corpse — act as terminals of one axis. Christ's immediate attention may go to the genuflector before him, yet the same person in her mortality twenty-one feet away is not outside his pale. Her supine head, wreathed like a bride's and facing skyward, aligns in a latent vertical with the head of Christ. Stated in geometric terms, the immaterial coordinate that joins the respective faces of Christ and St. Petronilla becomes a hypotenuse that subtends the right angle formed by the bendwise figuration at the right margin. Christ and his saint — face to face — are held apart by expansion, like open compasses. It is the meaning of the event that keeps taut the geometry of the composition.[6]

The literature on the *St. Petronilla* altarpiece is circumscribed by preoccupations with quality, expression and style — chronologically in that order. First came

[5] Composition drawing for the *St. Petronilla* of unusually large size, black chalk, 51.6 × 37.6 cm.; discussed from the stylistic viewpoint in Mahon, *Disegni*, cat. no. 91.

[6] Cf. the observation made by Donald Posner (in "The Guercino Exhibition at Bologna," *Burlington Magazine* 110 [1968], p. 603, n. 6), referring to two Guercino compositions of 1621, the *Taking of Christ* (Fitzwilliam Museum, Cambridge), and the *Incredulity of St. Thomas* (London, National Gallery): "Guercino knew what he was about in these two paintings. They are not the spontaneous products of a '*mostro di natura*,' as Guercino was called by Ludovico Caracci in 1617; they are the creations of a thoughtful mind, inventing different compositional patterns that are expressive of their different subjects." Nevertheless, Posner still calls Guercino "the provincial from Cento," and speaks of "a critical intelligence that Guercino appears not to have had," compensating for the deficiency by "a certitude of intuition and practice [that] often rose above intellectual difficulties." In discussing Guercino's creative process, writers of the past fifty years have been at pains to stress his lack of sophistication. Mahon refers to him as "un giovane niente affatto sofisticato" (*Dipinti*, p. 115); and speaks of "his natural instincts," or his "instinctive ideas for [a] composition" (*Studies*, pp. 107, 101). Gnudi (in Mahon, *Dipinti*, p. xxxii) calls Guercino "alieno dalla speculazione intellettuale."

the disputes over merit, for there were detractors even in the 17th century. The work retained enough of Guercino's habitual manner — his plebeian types, graceless postures, and crepuscular color shot with erratic lights — to affront certain classicists. Hence Passeri's censure: "È dipinto in quel suo stile di tinte, e di costume, che mai s'accomodò ad un certo decoro, e convenienza di nobiltà, ne di forme leggiadre d'attitudini, e di panneggiamenti arteficiosi; ma si posò sempre in quella schiettezza del naturale; ma nella più vile." [7]

How widespread such feelings were is difficult to determine; Passeri himself concedes that impartial cognoscenti approve the work, and the evidence bears him out. "Nel colorito, nell'inventione e nella facilità dell'operare con buon sapere non so chi adesso li passi avanti," writes Mancini; and of the *St. Petronilla*: "non è da dubitare che si sia per acquistar durabil gloria." Lanzi (1795) reports that "alcuni oltramontani lo han chiamato il mago della pittura italiana," and adds in his own voice: "Quanto poi fosse egregio coloritore ne' vestiti sul gusto de' miglior veneti, nel paese, negli accessori, basta vedere la sua S. Petronilla..." Calvi declared that Guercino had surpassed himself in this work: "Maraviglioso fu l'incontro ch'ebbe una tale opera, e tutti anche pittori si sentirono rapiti della robustezza incantatrice del colorito guercinesco, talché si racconta che il Cavalier Giovanni Lanfranco ebbe a dire che quel solo quadro bastava ad atterrire qualunque pittore, nè d'altro si parlava allora per Roma." [8]

Through much of the 19th century, the painting won stintless praise. It was, in Atti's words, "un inarrivabile capolavoro." [9] Goethe admired Guercino for his "great moral beauty and charm"; [10] Stendhal, for his tonality *à la* Shakespeare. "Quand je me trouve devant le tableau de *Sainte Pétronille*," he wrote, "il me semble qu'aucun peintre n'aurait su mieux rendre la couleur d'*Hamlet* ou du *Roi Lear*." But the great novelist fudged the Saint's legend — which, one suspects, he extrapolated somewhat hastily from the two-line legend under the Frey engraving (Fig. 11): "Un jeune homme, habillé comme on l'était du XVIe siècle, revient de voyage, pour épouser Pétronille qu'il aimait. Il arrive pour être témoin de l'enterrement

7 Passeri, *ed. cit.*, p. 351.

8 References to the three authors quoted: Giulio Mancini, *Considerazioni sulla pittura*, ed. A. Marucchi, Rome, 1956, I, pp. 111 and 245. (The *St. Petronilla* altarpiece is mentioned in a marginal comment made after 1621 when the text of the *Considerazioni* had been completed.) Luigi Lanzi, *Storia Pittorica della Italia* (1795-1796), 4th ed., Florence, 1822, V, p. 107; Calvi, *loc. cit.*

9 Gaetano Atti, *Intorno alla vita e alle opere di Gianfrancesco Barbieri detto Il Guercino da Cento*, Rome, 1861, p. 55. Atti's account of the *St. Petronilla*, apart from an occasional phrase such as that cited here, is lifted almost verbatim from Calvi.

10 Goethe, *Italienische Reise*, writing from Cento, October 17, 1786.

de sa maîtresse. On descend dans la fosse le corps de la jeune fille. La tête paraît encore. Brisé par la douleur, le jeune homme, à droite du spectateur, demande des détails à deux personnages dont l'un porte un turban..." A close parallel, then, to the graveyard scene in *Hamlet* and the funeral of Ophelia; matching, not only in subject but in its *tendresse* and the gravity of its shadows, the poetry of the Bard. " Dans ce sens," Stendhal concludes, " la majesté de Guerchin a beaucoup de rapports avec la sienne." [11] It is interesting to see Guercino's subject so idly secularized in Stendhal's imagination.

Most writers on the *St. Petronilla* altarpiece have focused on the stylistic break in Guercino's manner during the 1620s. Scannelli (1657) had commended the painter's general progress towards clarification, and by the end of the 18th century, Luigi Lanzi recognized the *St. Petronilla* as the watershed in Guercino's career, the beginning of his " seconda maniera." It seemed to show a new firmness in modelling and pictorial structure, a use of light no longer as a pervasive solvent but as serving the individuation of forms, and a wholesome refinement in contour and dress. Calvi attributed the change to the salutary stimulus of the Roman scene: " E studiasse di rendere ancor più pregevole, e sorprendente il proprio stile, dacché oltre il giudizioso ritrovamento, e la grandiosità delle parti ottimamente disposte, oltre l'aggiustato disegno, ed il contrasto delle ombre, e de' lumi, espresse con maggior precisione le teste, e l'estremità, le colori con vivo e morbido impasto di vera carne, e diede tanta armonia, e tanta altezza alle tinte, che per la forza, e per lo rilievo pare non potersi andare più oltre; e questa è quella che alcuni chiamano sua seconda maniera." [12]

But the shift to a nobler classical manner, which writers from the 17th century onward had applauded as a change for the better, struck 20th-century critics as a thing to deplore. By 1920, Marangoni was reversing the judgment. The " true Guercino," he protested, was to be found only in the pre-Roman works, the *St. Petronilla* being " un passo addietro " — an essentially academic exercise, an omen of slackening genius and waning sincerity, pointing inexorably to the slippage of Guercino's late works. " Il Guercino ha perduto qui il suo buon gusto misurato. Roma gli ha dato alla testa ed egli ci fa un po' la figura del bourgeois épaté." The altarpiece as a pivot between two phases of style became symptomatic of encroaching

[11] See Jean Seznec, " Stendhal et les peintres bolonais," *Gazette des Beaux-Arts*, sér. 6, 53 (1959), p. 173 f.

[12] For the quotations in the preceding paragraph, see Francesco Scannelli, *Il Microcosmo della Pittura* (1657), ed. G. Giubbini, Milan, 1966, p. 115; Lanzi, *loc. cit.*; Calvi, *loc. cit.*

debility. In Denis Mahon's fundamental analysis of the work, its emergent classicism was diagnosed as a failure of nerve, a submission to prevailing patrician taste. Similarly in Cesare Gnudi's introduction to the catalogue of the Guercino *Mostra*: "La Santa Petronilla resta il testo base... per leggere i primi sintomi e i primi effetti della crisi." [13]

Nowhere do these discussions acknowledge what must have loomed large in the terms of commission, and hence in the painter's mind: the dictates of the subject and the pertinence of the subject to a specific altar within St. Peter's. How set were the mandates and what decisions were open? Which of the characters and situations did the subject prescribe? What determined the choice of St. Petronilla? And why she on such grandiose scale?

The historic identity of Petronilla has given rise to intriguing conjectures. From observations made in the 1860s and '70s by G. B. de Rossi during his excavations in the catacomb of Domitilla, it appears that the original Petronilla was a patrician lady of the Flavian house, probably put to death as a Christian under Domitian. Her tomb — located in a chapel off the catacomb's subterranean basilica — was venerated as early as the 4th century, along with that of the martyred eunuchs (*eunuchi cubicularii*) Nereus and Achilleus. A 4th-century fresco found near her tomb depicts an *orante*, named Veneranda, being conducted to heaven by "Petronella Mart(yr)." [14]

By the 6th century, a legend conflated from diverse sources had been woven around her name. Its main elements derived from the apocryphal *Acts of Peter*, where a daughter of the Apostle is stricken with a wasting paralysis which her

13 Matteo Marangoni, "Il 'vero' Guercino: grandezza e decadenza di un artista," *Dedalo* 1 (1920), pp. 17-40 and 133-142; reprinted in *Arte Barocca* (1927), ed. Florence, 1953, p. 76; Denis Mahon, *Studies*, pp. 83-92. The author's conclusions are briefly restated in Mahon, *Dipinti*, pp. 113-118. For the quotation from Gnudi, see the introduction to the same volume, p. xxxii. Against the above, Donald Posner argues (in his review of the Guercino exhibition, cited above in our n. 6) that the *St. Petronilla* "does not represent a change in stylistic direction; it continues, farther along now, the path Guercino had already begun to travel in Bologna."

14 De Rossi's excavation reports were published in his *La Roma sotterranea cristiana*, I, Rome, 1864, pp. 180, 266 f. and in the *Bollettino di Arch. Crist.*, 1874, pp. 5-35, 122-125; 1875, pp. 5-43; 1878, pp. 125-146; and 1879, pp. 5-20, 139-160. The historical Petronilla is further discussed in the following works: J. P. Kirsch in *The Catholic Encyclopedia*, London, New York, 1911, XI, p. 781, s.v. Petronilla; Emile Mâle, "Les Chapelles de Sainte Pétronille," *Revue des Deux Mondes* 43 (1938), pp. 347 ff. (reprinted in *Rome et ces vieilles Églises*, Paris, 1942, and *The Early Churches of Rome*, Chicago, 1960); C. M. Carpano in *Biblioteca Sanctorum*, Rome, 1968, X, cols. 513-521, s.v. Petronilla. The 4th-century fresco in the catacomb of Domitilla is reproduced in Mâle's *Early Churches...*, fig. 23, and on p. 158 of Schütz's entry in the Kirschbaum *Lexikon*, cited in note 1.

father, despite his healing powers and the pleas of the people, refuses to cure. To prove that he could if he would, Peter bids the girl rise and causes her to walk naturally before them; whereat the people rejoice and praise God. But Peter, to their dismay, commands his daughter — "return to your infirmity, for this is profitable for you and for me." He then relates how, on the day of his daughter's birth, the Lord imparted to him in a vision that she "will do harm to many souls if her body remains healthy." And indeed, when she was ten "she became a temptation to many," including one Ptolomaeus who, having seen her bathe, had her brought to his house to make her his wife. Whereupon, of a sudden, "all one side of her body from her toes to her head was paralyzed and wasted; and we carried her away, praising the Lord who had preserved his servant from uncleanness and shame. And this (Peter concludes) is the cause why the girl continues in this state until this day." To modern readers, one of the less edifying fables in the hagiological corpus: the editors of the *New Testament Apocrypha* describe it as "not especially noteworthy... a miracle-story colored by encratite sympathies... Peter demonstrates in the case of his daughter that outward suffering can be a gift from God if it has the effect of preserving virginity." [15]

The child in this history, which is preserved only in a 2nd-century Coptic papyrus, remains unnamed. But the author of the *Acts of Nereus and Achilleus* (5th-6th century), aware that certain older texts made St. Peter a father, and misled by the assonance of Petronilla and Petrus, identified the Apostle's anonymous daughter with the saint venerated in the cemetery of Domitilla. In these later *Acts* — ultimately incorporated in the *Legenda Aurea* — the tale of the paralytic maiden forms part of a letter addressed to Nereus and Achilleus. The writer, Marcellus, reminds his addressees that they had personally witnessed Peter's refusal to heal his child. The immediate sequel is then retold as in the *Acts of Peter.* At length, having grown perfect in the love of God, Petronilla is relieved of her malady and empowered to restore other sufferers to health by dint of prayer. The rest of the story involves an enamored young Roman count, here called Flaccus, who desires Petronilla in marriage. Being denied, he threatens to have her killed as a Christian if she consent not. Petronilla, her virginity vowed to the Lord, tells the noble youth to send for her after three days; but from that moment forward refuses nourishment until, having taken Holy Communion, she surrenders this life. God himself, to spare her the martyrdom

15 The text of the *Acts of Peter* is published in E. Hennecke, W. Schneemelcher, *New Testament Apocrypha*, Philadelphia, 1965, p. 270 and pp. 276 ff.

which in her heart she had accepted, called her away — leaving the ardent Flaccus to witness her obsequies and to propose marriage to Petronilla's companion Fellicula, from whom, thwarted again, he exacts cruel vengeance.[16] A subsequent source, the *Liber Pontificalis*, assures us that St. Peter, with his own hands, carved the legend on her marble sarcophagus: "Of the golden Petronilla, daughter most sweet."[17]

The turning point in St. Petronilla's posthumous fortunes coincides with one of the critical moments in the history of the West. In the year 753, Pope Stephen II journeyed to Gaul to solicit the help of Pepin the Short against the threat of the Lombards. The Frankish king came to the rescue, campaigned victoriously on Italian soil, and established the pontifical state under Carolingian protection. In return for this timely aid, Pope Stephen promised the Frankish crown a most puissant protectrix, the daughter of the Prince of Apostles, to wit, St. Petronilla; whose remains His Holiness proposed to transfer from their ancient site on the Via Ardeatina to St. Peter's itself. And though the Pope died prematurely, his successor

16 For the *Acts of Nereus and Achilleus*, see R. A. Lipsius, *Die Apokryphen Apostelgeschichten und Apostellegenden*, Braunschweig, 1887, pp. 200-206.

In Jacopo da Voragine's redaction the story is gently cosmeticized. Petronilla is spared the disfiguring paralysis. The infirmity which God visited upon the girl at her father's entreaty — because he judged her too comely of aspect — is only a fever. To show his disciples that he has it in his power to heal Petronilla, Peter orders his daughter to rise and wait upon them at table. Which service performed, the Apostle orders her back to bed, "and again the fever seized her." These last two moments are depicted in a panel by Sano di Pietro, cited on p. 229, below.

See also Boninus Mombritius, *Sanctuarium seu Vitae Sanctorum* (ca. 1479), modern ed. by A. Brunet, Paris, 1910, p. 366 f., for a retelling of the story in the original form of Marcellus' letter to Nereus and Achilleus. Mombritius' version departs from the older sources only in attributing Petronilla's paralysis not to her father alone, but jointly to "the will of Peter and Paul" ("Petronillam bene nostis voluntate Petri et Pauli clinicam factam").

17 For the later history of the sarcophagus, and the corrected reading of its inscription, see below, n. 20. Following, in its entirety, is the passage from the *Liber Pontificalis* relating to St. Petronilla (ed. L. Duchesne, Paris, 1955, I, p. 464): "Hic namque beatissimus pontifex praefati sui senioris germani et praedecessoris pontificis sanctissimi Stephani papae salutifera adimplens praecepta, continuo post eius decessum aggregans sacerdotes et universum clerum atque cunctum populum istius Romanae urbis, operansque in cymiterium ubi prius beata Petronilla sita quiescebat, foris porta Appia, miliario ab urbe Roma plus minus secondo, exinde eius venerabile ac sanctum corpus cum sarcofago marmoreo in quo reconditum inerat abstulit, sculptum litteris eodem sarcofago legente: AVREAE PETRONILLAE FILIAE DVLCISSIMAE. Unde non dubium est quia sculptura illa litterarum propria beati Petri apostoli manu designata esse dinosci ob amore suae dulcissimae natae. Eundemque sanctum corpus cum praefato sarcofago inposito super plaustrum novum in ecclesia beati Petri apostoli cum hymnis et canticis spiritalibus eius beatitudo deportavit et in museleo illo iuxta ecclesiam beati Andreae apostoli, quem praefatus beatissimus Stephanus papa eius germanus, dum adhuc superstes erat, ecclesia in honore ipsius sanctae Christi martyris Petronillae fieri decreverat, ipsum sanctum collocavit corpus. Ubi et ornatum tam in aurum et argentum atque palleis sufficienter tribuit; eandemque ecclesiam restaurans ad honorem sanctae Petronillae picturis miro decore inlustravit."

Paul I (757-767) redeemed his late brother's pledge. St. Petronilla's body was translated to the westerly of the two 4th-century mausolea on the south side of the Old Basilica — known thenceforth as the church or chapel of St. Petronilla, "la chapelle des rois de France." [18]

Emile Mâle's graceful account of these proceedings suggests why the Pope's choice for a special patroness of the treaties concluded between the papacy and the Frankish sovereigns fell upon Petronilla.

> Ce choix de sainte Pétronille semble fort extraordinaire et les vieux chroniqueurs ne nous l'expliquent pas. Mais nous en devinons le raison. En défendant le Pape, en lui donnant un royaume, Pépin le Bref devenait le fils de l'Église, le fils de saint Pierre. Dans une lettre qu'Étienne II lui avait envoyée et que saint Pierre lui-même était censé avoir écrite, il faisait dire à l'apôtre que Pépin et les deux jeunes princes, Charles et Carloman, étaient 'ses fils adoptifs.' Il paraissait donc naturel que sainte Pétronille, fille de saint Pierre, devînt la patronne des rois Francs, qui semblaient maintenant faire partie de sa famille. C'était une soeur qui protégeait ses frères.[19]

The subsequent history of the chapel of St. Petronilla may be passed over briefly. It was honored by Charlemagne and continued for several decades to be lavishly decorated. In 846 it was despoiled by the Sicilian Arabs, and restored thereafter on a more modest scale. We hear of St. Petronilla again at the beginning of the 14th century: during Philippe le Bel's conflict with the papacy, claims were made

[18] See the text from the *Liber Pontificalis* in the foregoing note. Modern accounts of the events described are contained in the sources cited above, n. 14. The exhumation of St. Petronilla appears to be one of the earliest instances of what was to become a major enterprise of the Roman pontiffs. "As the dangers of this lawless period grew, Christians placed their hopes of safety in the intercession of the saints and the power of their relics to avert evil. In 765, Pope Paul I had a large number of catacomb tombs opened and the bodies distributed among the churches of Rome. Shortly afterward began the exodus of these relics, both secretly and with special permits, towards the rest of Europe, chiefly Gaul" (Jean Hubert in *The Carolingian Renaissance*, New York, 1970, p. 54). See also Richard Krautheimer, "The Carolingian Revival of Early Christian Architecture" (1942), *Studies in Early Christian, Medieval, and Renaissance Art*, New York, 1969, p. 215: "Beginning with the middle of the eighth century and continuing through the first half of the ninth, Roman relics were brought in increasing numbers from the catacombs into the city." The author's note 109 lists a number of translations, commencing "in 752 (or 770) with the transfer of St. Sinforosa and her sons to Sant'Angelo in Pescheria"; that of St. Petronilla is not mentioned.

[19] Mâle, *op. cit.*, p. 351. Mâle's notion of the translation of St. Petronilla as a kind of family reunion involves one further step. The saint's sarcophagus was placed in one of two similar 4th-century mausolea. "L'autre mausolée était devenu lui aussi une chapelle et avait été consacré à saint André. Le rapprochement de ces deux noms, saint André et saint Pétronille, nous fait deviner la pensée des papes. Saint André était le frère de saint Pierre et l'on croyait que saint Pétronille était sa fille. Ainsi, un sentiment délicat avait réuni auprès de l'apôtre ceux qui lui avaient été chers pendant sa vie" (p. 352).

that her body had come to France, and a half-dozen towns in the kingdom began venerating her relics. But the Roman claim to her remains was vindicated in 1474, when Petronilla's original marble sarcophagus was rediscovered, bearing a decoration of dolphins at the four corners.[20] This fact, communicated to Louis XI by Pope Sixtus IV, so impressed the French monarch that the dolphin was made the heraldic animal of the Dauphin. When the incumbent Dauphin fell sick and mended, his recovery was ascribed to the sisterly intercession of St. Petronilla. And when this same prince, become Charles VIII, sojourned in Rome during January 1495, he — like his Carolingian predecessor — heard Mass in St. Peter's, then paid homage to *la patronne de la France* in her chapel. It was for this chapel too that a French cardinal in 1498 commissioned the marble *Pietà* from the young Michelangelo.

Not long thereafter, with the building of New St. Peter's begun, the chapel of the Kings of France was pulled down. The remains of St. Petronilla were removed temporarily to the Altar of the Holy Crucifix in Old St. Peter's, where they would rest until 1606.[21]

Meanwhile, certain learned had begun to question Petronilla's family ties. In France itself, St. Francis de Sales pronounced her " not St. Peter's physical but only his spiritual daughter "; and referred to the arguments advanced by Antonio Gallonio and Cesare Baronio.[22] Both authors reason impressively against Petronilla's

20 Duchesne describes the rediscovery of the sarcophagus (*op. cit.*, p. 466, n. 5): " Le sarcophage de sainte Pétronille fut retrouvé en 1474, à l'occasion d'une restauration de son autel, exécutée aux frais du roi Louis XI. Une lettre adressée à ce prince par le pape Sixte IV mentionne cette découverte. Sixte IV dit que c'était une arche de marbre (*arca marmorea*) aux quatre angles supérieurs de laquelle étaient sculptés des dauphins. L'inscription fut relevée alors par plusieurs personnes; nous en avons encore une copie exécutée avec soin par l'archéologue P. Sabino. C'est celle que donne le *Liber Pontificalis*, sauf le nom *Aureae* que est écrit AVR. (*Aureliae*)." Duchesne further reports the later dismemberment of Petronilla's sarcophagus: "Juste un siècle après, en 1574, les reliques de la sainte furent extraites de son sarcophage et renfermées dans une petite urne de marbre. Quant au sarcophage, il fut débité et employé dans le pavé de l'une des chapelles de la basilique." See also J. P. Kirsch in the *Catholic Encyclopedia*, *op. cit.*, p. 781; and C. M. Carpano in the *Biblioteca Sanctorum*, *op. cit.*, col. 516 f. Mâle, *op. cit.*, p. 354 discusses the sequel to the 15th-century rediscovery, involving the visit of Charles VIII to the chapel in 1495.

21 The vicissitudes of St. Petronilla's remains, from the 8th century onward and through the 16th century, are documented by Giacomo Grimaldi in *Descrizione della basilica antica di S. Pietro in Vaticana* (Cod. Barb. lat. 2733), Rome, 1972. See cap. 57, fols. 54v-56r and cap. 61, fol. 59v. Cap. 64, fol. 61v, includes a drawing of the Altar of the Holy Crucifix in Old St. Peter's, bearing the legend: " Exemplum altaris sanctissimi crucifixi unde sacrum corpus sanctae Petronillae virginis in novum templum translatum fuit."

22 St. Francis de Sales, preface to the first edition of his *Introduction to the Devout Life* (1609), trans. J. K. Ryan, New York, 1955, p. 32. The work of Antonio Gallonio (d. 1605) to which St. Francis refers is the *Historia delle sante Vergini Romane*... Rome, 1591. Gallonio's brief account of the Petronilla story introduces the heroine polemically as follows (pp. 98-101): "Petronilla figliuola di San Pietro Apostolo, essendo che figliuole non solamente si chiamano quelle, che secon-

natural filiation with the Apostle. The name, Baronio points out, does not connect her with Peter, since "from Petrus ought to be derived Petrilla, as Priscilla from Priscus and Drusilla from Drusus"; whereas Petronilla derives from Petronius. Furthermore, at the time when Peter could have fathered a daughter, his name was not Peter but Simon. Nor could he have sired her after being renamed, "for both Tertullian and St. Jerome agree that the apostles who were married practiced continence from the time they were called by Christ." Moreover: "The epistle of Marcellus the presbyter, in which mention is made of the aforesaid Petronilla [contained in the *Acts of Nereus and Achilleus*; see p. 216 above], states that she was so beautiful that Flaccus, a nobleman, fell ardently in love with her. Now since a daughter of Peter would have been born before he became an apostle, she would already have attained such an age that she could not have appeared so beautiful as to make men languish for love of her." [23]

But Baronio was a believer first, and the fruits of his reasoning wilted before his faith. "However that may be," he concludes, "these things regarding her are supported by a certain and firm tradition of the fathers, and illustrated by many memorials; Petronilla, the saintly virgin, existed, and has been called by the fathers,

do la carne sono generate, ma quelle ancora, e molto più, che secondo lo spirito." The Saint's legend is followed by a lengthy "Avvertimento al Lettore" (pp. 101-105), wherein Gallonio argues against Petronilla's natural filiation with the Apostle, evolving the arguments upon which Baronio largely relied. E.g., any natural daughter of Peter would have been begotten before his apostolate and, being martyred under Domitian, must then have been at least 53 years old, and more probably 63. "Come è possibile," asks Gallonio, "che Flacco d'una donna di 53. anni potesse così fortemente innamorarsi?" And again: "Anzi pare, che implichi (perservirmi de' termini delle schole) contradittione, l'esser fanciulla, straordinariamente bella, & esser di età di 63. anni."

Gallonio justifies his inclusion of St. Petronilla among Roman Virgins on the grounds that she must have belonged to the well-known house of the Petronii: "Si conferma l'istesso, cioè che Petronilla fosse nobile Romana, e non Hebrea, perchè nella sua historia si racconta, come habbiamo veduto, che Flacco comite la desiderò, & instantemente la domandò per congiungerla seco in matrimonio. Hor come si può credere, ch'vn gentil'huomo Romano nobile, e Palatino, che per essere comite havea luogo appresso l'Imperatore in Palazzo, ricercasse con tanta instanza vna Hebrea figliuola di vn povero pescatore di niuna stima appresso il mondo, e non più presto vna Vergine Romana, nobile, e riccha, conforme allo stato suo?"

Art historians may find it of interest that Gallonio makes a physiological observation which Michelangelo had used forty years earlier to explain the youthful appearance of the Virgin Mother in the St. Peter's *Pietà*: "essendo commune alle Vergini il dimostrare assai minor tempo di quello che elle s'habbino." For the rest, Gallonio argues that Petronilla must have died, not before but well after St. Peter; and that the report of St. Peter's autograph inscription on her sarcophagus is mere fable: "Altro si potrebbe dire, e massime intorno a quell'epitafio, ma mi son risoluto quivi finire." (I have summarized Gallonio at some length since his book appears to be exceedingly rare, no copy of it existing in the United States. For the microfilm of the British Museum copy and other kind acts of assistance, I am deeply indebted to Dana Goodgal of the University of Pennsylvania.)

23 Cesare Baronio, *Annales Ecclesiastici* (1588-1607), ed. Venice, 1738, I, col. 800.

for whatever reason, the daughter of Peter; in her name was constructed an ancient and noble tomb and the anniversary of her birth is commemorated in all the well-known martyrologies." [24]

Thus, despite informed skepticism, St. Petronilla retained her credentials. When New St. Peter's was ready, her remains were translated for a third time, now to their final station. Borne in pomp along with the Basilica's other outstanding relics (the Holy Lance, Veronica's veil, the head of St. Andrew, etc.), they were conveyed to the present altar of St. Petronilla, " in capite ecclesiae " (writes Grimaldi), that is to say, to the western end of the north aisle, or roughly midway between her father's tomb and her father's throne — " the nearest to that of heaven." [25]

It was sixteen years later that Guercino, under the pontificate of his former Bolognese patron Alessandro Ludovisi, now Gregory XV, received the commission

24 St. Petronilla's career in the martyrologies is uneven. The most popular of medieval martyrologies, that of Usuard (9th century), makes no mention of the saint's relationship to St. Peter: " (31 May) Romae, sanctae Petronillae, quae post multa miracula sanitatum, cum eam quidam comes suo vellet coniugio sociare, tridui inducias postulans, ieiuniis atque orationibus vacans, tertio die mox ut Christi sacramentum accepit emisi spiritum " (*Le Martyrologie d'Usuard*, ed. Jacques Dubois, Brussels, 1965, pp. 237 f., and 112). In Mombritius' text of Marcellus' epistle (see note 16) Petronilla's precise relationship to St. Peter is again left undefined. In the Roman Martyrology, compiled for Gregory XIII in 1584 under the editorship of Baronio, the entry is scholarly and carefully referenced — an account rather of the literary tradition than of purported facts. Even Baronio's *dubitationes* are mentioned, and Petronilla's parentage (" of the holy seed of Peter ") is cited only in a verse received from older authors. There is no reference to Count Flaccus, to his offer of marriage, or the manner of St. Petronilla's death — the rediscovery of her body being the one significant datum. The text reads: " Petronillae. a) De eadem Beda, Vsuar. Ado, & Vuandelbert. his versibus: ' Iampridie Petronilla Petri de germine sancto / Fulgida virgo micat Christi trabeata decore.' De eius obitu agitur in actis sanctorũ Nerei & Achillei. De eius corporis invẽtione vide in lib. de Rom. Põt. in Paulo Primo. Cuius aute fidei fit eius historia, consule S. August. lib. contra Adimantũ, c. 17. Nonnullas de ea dubitationes disseruimus in Annal. Eccles. Erat olim Romae nomine S. Petronilla coemiterium nobile, in quo Greg. III. Papa anniuersariam statuit stationẽ, vt constar ex eodẽ lib. de Rõ. Pont. in Greg. III " (*Martyrologium Romanum... Gregorii XIII Pont. Max. iussu editum* [1584], ed. Rome, 1603, p. 345).

Baronio's philological caution was abandoned in the *Martyrologium Romanum* revised under Urban VIII and Clement X. The new standard entry reads: " At Rome, St. Petronilla, Virgin, daughter of the blessed Apostle Peter, who refused to wed Flaccus, a nobleman, and accepting three days' delay for deliberation, spent them in fasting and prayer, and on the third day, after receiving the Sacrament of Christ, gave up the ghost " (*Martyrologium Romanum Gregorii XIII. jussu editum, Urbani VIII et Clementis X*, ed. Rome, 1846, p. 100; englished in *Butler's Lives of the Saints*, ed., 1956).

25 The phrase describing St. Peter's throne as " nearest to that of heaven " occurs in a letter written by Gregory XV (see L. Pastor, *The History of the Popes*, trans. E. Graf, XXVII, London, 1938, p. 244). For minute descriptions of the deconsecration of the Altar of the Holy Crucifix (Jan. 10, 1606), as well as the ceremonial of translation to the present altar in the new Basilica, and the text of the indulgence granted to those attending the ceremony, see Grimaldi, *op. cit.*, fols. 36r, 37r, 38v, 54v, 57v, 59v-61v.

to decorate the altar of St. Petronilla, an altar still appertaining to the French crown. For the thirty-one year-old painter just summoned to Rome, the execution of this gigantic altarpiece, 7.20 meters high, was the most challenging of possible public assignments. And a commission of such importance must have been accompanied by instructions sufficient to assure the painter's grasp of what mattered in the saint's story: her earthly kinship and her status in heaven; the exhumation of her body under a Pope who bestowed her eternally upon France as *auxiliatrix vestra*; [26] and the fact that her sacred remains lay even now in St. Peter's.

That Guercino knew a lot more is indicated by the surviving studies for the altarpiece, above all, by the large composition drawing at Windsor (p. 212, Fig. 4). The drawing represents a circumstantial *istoria* with figures loosely packed on open ground. Far removed from their doings is the reception in heaven — a Christ enthroned to whom a foreshortened angel presents a soft adolescent girl. Down below on the ground lies her corpse, propped up by a bearded worker in a beret. Others prepare the grave; women at lower right cower. And behind all this foreground stir, a young horseman flaunts an insouciant elbow at a rugged male figure at center. The latter — his arms engaged in a demonstrative double gesture — reacts with a fierce glance over his shoulder. While his left index points to the corpse, his other hand fingers a huge upright slab. Obviously, a precise narrative content is being communicated — such punctilious dramatization cannot be arbitrary. The horseman, then, must be the thwarted Flaccus of legend, impenitent at the funeral; from which occasion the loving father of the deceased would not have absented himself. The artist has staged an encounter between St. Peter and Flaccus, incongruous antagonists who are nowhere paired in the sources but whose paths, deduced from the legend, would have crossed here.

Nor was Guercino content merely to characterize. Directing the Apostle's right arm to the stele, he surely recalled that the *Liber Pontificalis* attributes the carving of the inscription on Petronilla's tomb to St. Peter's hand. Accordingly, in the drawing, that hand is already leaving its mark, casting a comet-tail shadow. Visually, that shadow guides Peter's hand. A dart-like accent centering the wide vacant stone, it forecasts and anticipates the action to come. What we are shown — assuming that Guercino was not being thoughtless — is the father's epitaph for his *filia dulcissima* literally foreshadowed on the memorial slab. Thus the Windsor composition

26 Words addressed by Pope Paul I to Pepin the Short, quoted in Duchesne, *op. cit.*, p. 466, n. 5.

confirms what has been observed of the master's drawings in general: " they show us a Guercino who was passionately concerned to tell a story well, to describe an event correctly ... and to make it clear and impressive." [27] In the present instance, the sparse matter of Petronilla's legend is made to yield a dramatic narrative of astonishing density. Guercino's close familiarity with the legend is put beyond doubt, as is his interest in conveying the details of it through direct illustration. All the more reason to wonder at the artist's eventual abandonment of this anecdotal approach. Of the characterizations and interrelations exhibited in the Windsor sheet very little would be retained in the altarpiece.

Whether this change of focus reflects Guercino's own evolution or a new set of instructions is hard to say. Denis Mahon, discussing certain stylistic differences between the Windsor composition and the final painting, has speculated on what might have occurred during a hypothetical meeting of the painter with the Pope's Secretary of State. The Monsignore Agucchi, Mahon suggests, would have tried to divert Guercino from his native manner to one more classicizing and decorous.

> I am inclined to believe that something of Agucchi's mind is to be seen in the " adjustments " which Guercino made in the *Santa Petronilla* ... In any discussions with the artist Agucchi's familiar point of view would have emerged. We can understand the retention, after due refinement, of the figure of Christ; it has that type of *grazia* which Agucchi would have appreciated... As to the lower half we can imagine him perceiving in it, let us say, more *grossolanità* than seemed suitable or necessary, and *un certo disordine Lombardo* about the whole... There are various reasons why Guercino should have paid serious attention to any comments of this kind by Agucchi. It would not be unnatural for the young peasant, a provincial even in Bologna, to be somewhat overwhelmed by Rome and the Papal Court. Moreover Agucchi had had much more familiarity with artists (during a period of twenty years) than the average learned prelate, and one might assume that he would have picked up sufficient of the current jargon to avoid *gaffes* of the cruder sort. Guercino very probably realized that some of the works of art which Agucchi praised were in fact good: why not make some experimental concessions to this method of picture-making so unlike that to which he himself had become accustomed? [28]

Assume that a meeting such as Mahon imagines took place — if not with Agucchi himself (the Secretary's time was chiefly occupied in diplomatic correspondence with papal envoys and heads of state) then with some other representative of official

[27] Posner, *op. cit.*, p. 603.

[28] Mahon, *Studies*, p. 92.

taste. One is still left to wonder whether a painter who had worked successfully for His Holiness in the days of his cardinalate, would have been called to Rome in order to paint in a manner different from that which had caused his success. Nor is it apparent that Guercino heeded Agucchi's hypothetical counsel, since the lower half of his altarpiece shows no abatement of *grossolanità*.[29] If the Windsor composition (or some similar drawing) did serve as a base for discussion between painter and *committente*, Guercino's attention would probably have been drawn to considerations of a different order. He might have been told that the conception was somewhat trifling; that the false fleeting Flaccus was of too small account to merit direct confrontation with the Apostle, whose majesty would be belittled by so mean an encounter; that a St. Petronilla in genuflection before the celestial Christ should not be the slip of a girl shown in the drawing, but a lady of regal port, as befits the patroness of a royal house; and so forth.

All of this is conjecture, of course. We cannot know how much Guercino's revisions owed to official guidance, how much to his own deepening comprehension. Only one conclusion is certain: the Windsor drawing, like other surviving studies, shows what Guercino departed from to find a definitive composition wherein all definition of subject is blurred. In the passage from drawings to altarpiece, he executed a studied withdrawal from the particulars of the story. And the decisions he made with regard to the subject assort so well with his formal modifications, as to suggest a single intelligence advancing on multiple levels towards significant ambiguity.

Consider the posture of Christ: in the three drawings that stage the reception scene, Christ's figure appears enthroned on a cloud. But the pose grows increasingly restive; gusty draperies, windblown hair, and a gracious bend forward bespeak eagerness to embrace the youngest recruit in heaven. In the study at Darmstadt (Fig. 5), the figure still sits, but inclines with impending suddenness, unrestrained by its seat. Finally, in the altarpiece, the pose eludes definition (Fig. 6 A): not sitting down, nor sitting up, but, as it were, sitting forth . To describe this Christ as " assiso in un Trono di nuvole " (Passeri), or as " sedente " (Calvi, Atti), is simple-minded. Like the Christ in the Sistine *Last Judgment*, Guercino's theophany is simultaneously throning, starting up, and approaching.[30]

29 Cf. Mrs. Jameson (*Sacred and Legendary Art* [1848], 3rd ed. Boston, 1857, I, p. 216): " This great picture exhibits, in a surpassing degree, the merits and defects of Guercino; it is effective, dramatic, deeply and forcibly colored, and arrests attention; on the other hand, it is coarse, crowded, vulgar in sentiment, and repugnant to our better taste."

30 Cf. L. Steinberg, " Michelangelo's *Last Judgment*

Another kind of duplicity governs the anatomical disproportions of the glorified Petronilla.[31] Her head is petite; but it is from the amplitude of the silken sleeves that her remaining proportions derive. The body swells in progressive undercover enlargement, trails away to a prodigiously distant foot. The sweep of it is magnificent precisely because the underlying anatomy is untrue. No comparable distortion was risked in the drawings, and copies of the work take care to " correct " it.[32]

The setting, too, gives way to ambiguation, especially in the deployment of the architectural elements. In the drawings they set a scene; in the altarpiece, these same elements promote a suspension of certainties. We may want to dismiss the centered column base or the Ionic pilaster as conventional plugs for leftover intervals. But it is remarkable that we cannot tell whether the column base (rid of the weeds that confer antiquity in Fig. 6) is an antique relic or a building in progress, a vestige or a beginning. Or whether the structure at upper right has any terrestrial foundation. Leveled with the angelic host, it connects neither with the diminutive background landscape, nor with the burial ground. Passeri speaks of " colonne e pilastri dimostrando il di dentro d'un Tempio." In fact, whatever these architectural members suggest in the way of a temple materializes in mystification, and we have no assurance of being indoors.

Or consider the requirement, dictated by the two-phased narration, to keep

as Merciful Heresy," *Art in America* 63 (Nov.-Dec. 1975), p. 50. " Vasari tells us that Christ is seated... 17th-century writers saw him as ' on his feet ' or ' on tiptoe.' Delacroix had him stand. But many keen-eyed observers see him moving to rise — ' ...rising from his throne with the gesture of an angry Hercules ' (Symonds), or as leaping up from it (Panofsky) ...Finally, those who conceive the moment as an Advent, a Coming, perceive a Christ ' advancing with a powerful stride ' (Tolnay). Such differences of opinion proceed less from carelessness in the viewer than from a given ambiguity which the viewer resists."

31 Again, it is Michelangelo who offers the outstanding model of a dual proportionate system — through " undercover enlargement " — within one figure. In the Madonna of the St. Peter's *Pietà*, " augmentation begins at her head, a small head enveloped in many layers of drapery. And this superfluity of cloth, rather than the head itself, scales the next phase. Turbulent draperies mask a continuous escalation..." (L. Steinberg, " The Metaphors of Love and Birth in Michelangelo's *Pietàs*," in *Studies in Erotic Art*, ed. Th. Bowie, New York, 1970, p. 235). Guercino may well have studied Michelangelo's marble group created for the original Chapel of St. Petronilla. And that he could paint a head conspicuously underscaled was observed by at least one later painter. C. N. Cochin, speaking of Guercino's *Angel Appearing to Hagar* (1652), which he saw and admired in Siena in 1750, notes that " la tête de la femme est trop petite " (*Voyage d'Italie*, 1758, I, p. 229; quoted in Mahon, *Dipinti*, p. 201). Note also that the underscaled head of Guercino's glorified Petronilla is significantly enlarged (in relation to the rest of her body or to the Ionic volutes at her back) in the Frey engraving of 1731 (Fig. 11).

32 Cf. the 17th-century drawing (our Fig. 9; Seiferheld Gallery, New York, 1960; present location unknown), and the mosaic copy by Cristofari (Fig. 7A). In the latter, though it is in general remarkably accurate, the trail of the saint's brocaded mantle, by which her left calf is defined, extends only half-way across the width of the pilaster behind it; in Guercino's painting, it reaches three-quarters across.

the air-borne epiphany clear of the earthly zone. In the Windsor drawing (Fig. 4) the problem does not arise; there the meeting in heaven looms like a cloud event out of reach, and a surplus of intervening slack prevents ambiguous transitions. Yet, in the altarpiece the two zones coalesce unintelligibly. The conjunction has been made irrational and unclear, eliciting the sort of complaint one would offer a builder who had failed to separate the *piano nobile* from the street.

Since the figures wear modern dress, the moment depicted cannot be literally assigned to Early Christian antiquity. But Guercino relies on more than sartorial anachronism to un-specify the characters of the story. Who are all these people gathered about the dead Saint? Is St. Peter, for instance, attending his daughter's funeral? In a composition study at Copenhagen for the lower half of the altarpiece (Fig. 6) an elderly man sits weeping in the left foreground: bald-pated, with short square beard, tunic hoist over the knees *all'antica*, he evokes a familiar type — St. Peter penitent at his "task of tears." [33] His prominence in the drawing indicates that the artist at one time considered casting St. Peter in the role of chief mourner. In the altarpiece, however, the clues are unclear, and St. Peter's presence is optional, depending on how the event is interpreted. Those who would read the scene as the Saint's original burial (which, we repeat, her devoted father would not have missed), might ask rhetorically whether a representation of the funeral of St. Peter's daughter in an altarpiece for St. Peter's Basilica is likely to have been negligent about including St. Peter. Accordingly, they will scan the characters for a suitable candidate and recognize the Apostle in the balding greybeard at right. To support their identification they might point to Guercino's *Incredulity of St. Thomas* (London), painted in the preceding year, where an unmistakable St. Peter is the physiognomic double of the greybeard in our altarpiece. And they may rejoice in the latter's felicitous placement, in his telling triangulation with Christ and the dead saint; or in the contact of his noble head with the form of St. Petronilla in glory. But, in fact, the identification has never before been proposed, because the candidacy

[33] The "tears of St. Peter" refer, of course, to the remorse the Apostle felt over his denial of Christ, not to sorrow over the loss of a child. But the image of the weeping St. Peter was sufficiently well-established to be recognizable under alternative circumstances. It had been popularized by the *Lagrime di S. Pietro*, Luigi Tansillo's vastly successful 910-stanza poem, published in its final version in 1585, and followed by numberless paintings. Baronio took the ancient report of St. Peter's chronically bloodshot eyes to mean "that he had wept much" (*op. cit.*, col. 800). The "taske of tears" is quoted from Robert Southwell's "St. Peter's Complaint." For the physical type and dress of the mourner in Guercino's drawing at Copenhagen, cf., for example, Lodovico Carracci's drawing of St. Peter at Windsor (no. 2206, reproduced in H. Bodmer, *Ludovico Carracci*, Burg bei Magdeburg, 1939, fig. 140).

for a St. Peter in the St. Petronilla altarpiece is effectively understated. And with good reason, since the unequivocal presence of the dead maiden's father would restrict the depicted scene to one narrative moment.

Much the same applies to the person of Flaccus, usually recognized in the youthful gallant at right.[34] If this figure stands for the would-be son-in-law of St. Peter (forfeiting much of the dash he had as a cavalier in the Windsor drawing, Fig. 4), Guercino has seen to it that there be no rapport between him and his intended. The space between them is blocked and they look away from each other. Instead of straining, like a lover bereaved, for a last glimpse of his love, our putative Flaccus is caught up in men's talk. Unseasonable inattention! And how bravely Stendhal explained it away: "Crushed by grief, the young man to the right of the spectator asks two men for details..." (see p. 214) — which accords neither with what we see, nor with the story we read.[35]

But does this young man have to be anyone in particular? Passeri gave him no special identity and included him among "alcune altre figure spettatrici." Calvi (followed by Atti) called him "a young squire who seems to be in charge of the place, holding back the crowd of the curious."[36] In other words, emotionally unengaged. And this may be why Denis Mahon adopts the expedient of recognizing Flaccus in the perturbed candle-holder at left[37] — though the latter is surely too young for the role and hardly patrician enough to wrest the title of suitor from the gallant. Calvi rightly calls him "un garzoncello," Atti, "un garzonetto." And so much for the *dramatis personae*. Their identity is diffused in a characteristic equivalent of Guercinesque shadow.[38]

34 "Behind stands Flaccus with a handkerchief in his hand...," asserts Mrs. Jameson (*op. cit.*, p. 216). The figure retained its traditional designation — "un jeune homme élégant, c'est le fiancé de la morte" — even for Charles Blanc (*op. cit.*, p. 4); describing the scene as an "exhumation," Blanc failed to reflect that his Flaccus would have had to haunt the cemetery for 700 years to be on hand for the disinterment.

35 Emile Mâle's curt description of this "oeuvre romantique," as he calls our altarpiece (*op. cit.*, p. 357), follows Stendhal's bad example: "La jeune morte, soutenue par des mains sortant de la nuit du tombeau, montre une dernière fois au comte Flaccus son pâle visage..." Yet it is not to the so-called Flaccus that the saint "shows her face." What, indeed, would he get to see if he looked straight ahead? Nothing but intervening hindquarters.

For a full novelette on the subject of the Flaccus-Petronilla *amour* ("Il parla d'abord de sa passion à ses amis..." etc.), see P. Guérin, *Les Petits Bollandistes. Vie des Saints*, 7th ed., Paris, 1888, VI, p. 322.

36 "Un giovane armigero che sembra guardare il luogo, e tenere addietro la affollata gente curiosa" (Calvi, p. 287, Atti, p. 54).

37 Mahon, *Disegni*, p. 95.

38 A paradigm of Guercino's method is the Copenhagen drawing (Fig. 6), where crucial features, such as heads and faces, receive massive washes of shadow after having been finely delineated in pen and ink (see especially the second figure at upper left). The progress from precision to adumbration in the work-

Returning now to the general subject: what exactly is the moment depicted? Given the persistence of Guercino's equivocations on so many levels, the question is very likely miscast. It presumes the possibility of a definitive answer, whereas the painter's cunning forbids it. The records of payment published by Pollak are no help, since they refer to the altarpiece simply as "il quadro (or l'Ancona) di Santa Petronilla."[39] Some modern writers are similarly noncommittal, whether from indifference or wise caution. Most authors, satisfied that the saint's body is being lowered, describe the scene as a burial. And those who recognize that the movement could go either way, are left to wonder whether the ambiguity was intended or inadvertent — and whether it matters.

The problem of directional ambiguity is endemic to narrative art. It can beset almost any still picture that represents objects moving or being moved.[40] Roger van der Weyden's *Exhumation of St. Hubert*, for instance (London, National Gallery), offers no *visual* certainty that the corpse is not being entombed — except that funeral paraphernalia are wanting. But narrative painters have always known that the problem exists, and have used conventions and artifice to overcome it. They were also aware, at least since the Renaissance, that ambiguous destination could be an expressive resource. In his *De Sculptura* of 1504, Pomponius Gauricus had distinguished between three kinds of motion in the rendering of an action: when the action shows retrospectively what had preceded it (which Pomponius calls *Energeia*); when it shows prospectively what is due (here called *Emphasis*); and *Amphibolia*, or ambiguity, when a movement hovers between possibilities, indeterminate in its trend. As the classic instance of *Amphibolia*, Pomponius cites a painting by Polygnotus which (according to Pliny, *N. H.*, xxxv, 59) caused people

ing out of the altarpiece thus emerges as a mode of thought characteristic of Guercino's approach to form and content alike.

39 See the reference to Pollak under the asterisk at the head of these notes.

40 No uncertainty of destination troubles our reading of moving bodies whose structure is pre-directed — an arrow, a bird, or a fish in motion, or a man or horse on the run. But how would a still picture render a crab or an automobile reversing; or indicate the direction of an object that is not moving under its own power, e.g. a pendulum oscillating? Or consider the following questionnaire: In Giotto's *Presentation* at Padua, is the Child being passed to Simeon or reverting to the Madonna? In Poussin's *Deluge* (Louvre), is the infant in the scene at right being handed up to the safety of higher ground, or down to the safety of the boat? Is Minerva in the Marcantonio-Raphael *Judgment of Paris* stripping down, or hastening to get dressed after missing the prize? In Pontormo's S. Felicita *Annunciation*, is the Madonna turning towards the angel or back to her lectern? In Michelangelo's *Last Judgment* fresco, is the right hand of Christ descending in fulmination, or rising to stay execution? In Picasso's *Minotauromachy* etching, is the man at left climbing the ladder or stepping down? And so forth.

to "argue whether the figure with the shield is ascending or descending." And Pomponius adds proudly that he himself had fashioned just such a figure in bronze.[41] We are thus assured that deliberate suspension of certainty, or ambivalence of direction, was an option available to Italian art from the beginning of the 16th century.

Keeping this option in mind, how confidently may we interpret the action in our altarpiece? Should we see *Energeia* and assume that the body, lifted off from its bier, has just been brought to the brink of its grave? Should we see the body unsteeped from its sepulcher, with continuing upward *Emphasis*? Or should we acknowledge a wilful reservation of clues, which would indicate intentional ambiguity? Since, before the picture was painted, no Frenchman or Roman could think of St. Petronilla's burial without also thinking of her body's subsequent exhumation — this being the symbolic act that had affiliated France with St. Peter — the painter would have had strong incentive to encourage the mutual association of both events, to equivocate between burial and disinterment as between two valid readings. Whereas a candid representation of the original burial alone would have constituted an abridgement of meaning.

It is worth remembering that the cult of St. Petronilla never created an iconographic tradition. Our few scattered images of the saint yield neither canonic scenes nor common attributes. A 12th-century mosaic in the Cappella Palatina, Palermo, shows St. Petronilla veiled, holding a cross. In a 15th-century panel at Saint-Goar, she holds a key; elsewhere a broom — "because she busied herself about the house, whenever her health permitted."[42] In a predella panel by Bartolo di Fredi (d. 1410; Siena, Pinacoteca), she is depicted being cured by St. Peter (similarly on a tapestry in Beauvais Cathedral). Sano di Pietro shows her serving at table and once more, in a subsidiary scene, on her sickbed (Siena, Pinacoteca). An engraving by Marcantonio Raimondi has her holding a palm branch and a little book closed (B. XIV, 183). In Gaudenzio Ferrari's painting of St. Petronilla at Varallo, she wears a white veil and again holds a book — as Mrs. Jameson observed, "she has no distinctive emblem." And when Callot, ca. 1633, etched a Sainte Pétronille under May 31st for his *Images des Saints* (small pithy scenes illustrating the Roman Martyrology), having no type or model to follow, he seated his saint on a mattress outdoors receiving Communion.

41 Pomponius Gauricus, *De Sculptura* (1504), ed. A. Chastel and R. Klein, Geneva, 1969, p. 198 f.

42 "Le *balai*, parce qu'elle s'occupait des soins de ménage, quand sa santé le lui permettait" (P. Guérin, *op. cit.*, p. 322).

Never did it occur to an artist to represent the funeral of Petronilla; nor to a patron to request such an image. Since that occasion held no special significance and played no role in the saint's legend, what cause was there to show her corpse merely going the way of all flesh? Yet someone in 1621 chose the moment of the saint verging upon her grave for a giant altarpiece in St. Peter's. Surely the subject would never have been selected but for the association involved, that is to say, the historic association of St. Petronilla's altar with the French monarchy for whose protection her sacred body had been exhumed.

What part the painter had in inventing the subject we do not know. But whether self-imposed or assigned, Guercino's task was to comprehend the "burial" in a scheme larger than Burckhardt's "momentary event." That is why the persons of St. Peter and Flaccus had to be underplayed — to enable us to discount their presence. Present they are (or may be) insofar as the occasion of St. Petronilla's funeral is represented. Where the picture evokes the saint's exhumation seven centuries later, both characters retreat from the scene. Not that the painting depicts the raising as opposed to the lowering of the body, but that the either-or formula is misapplied. Guercino has made the most of the fact that painted figures are still — that apparent movement accrues to them only by imputation. Under the guise of raw naturalism, the artist contrived a symbolic structure so drained of particularities, that every significant element of the original story and of its aftermath can be found in it.

In one particular, however, Guercino is absolute — in the metric precision whereby he integrated the image of St. Petronilla's corpse with the actual Basilica. Two recent scholars have sensed something of this integration, but in ways contradictory and, I think, unconvincing. Wittkower saw the foreground figures "lowering the body of the saint into the open sepulcher in which the beholder seems to stand." [43] This is unrealistic. The beholder stands, as the celebrant priest does, before the altar (Fig. 7); if he projects himself imaginatively into the painting, he may share the footing of the principal figures, but, in fact, his eye level is given by the landscape horizon, i. e. slightly above the face of the corpse — not in the pit below.

An alternative reading proposes an even closer connection between the depicted world and the real: "Guercino has used the lower frame as the near edge of the grave, so that when the painting was in its original location in St. Peter's, the saint

[43] Rudolph Wittkower, *Art and Architecture in Italy 1600-1750*, Harmondsworth, 1958, p. 54.

seemed to be lowered out of the picture and into the altar-tomb that actually enshrines her remains." [44] But this interpretation, too, is untenable, for the painter has specified with redundance that the corpse not be referred to the altar as its receptacle. Firstly, the altar, being of normal size, is utterly overwhelmed by the gargantuan scale of the foreground figures, St. Petronilla included. Secondly, as regards orientation, the saint's body lies at an angle of 45 degrees to the picture plane — precisely aligned with the obliquity of the grave (Fig. 2), but ill-adapted for bedding inside the altar.[45] Furthermore, the mobility of the body is patently upward or downward, as in a vertical shaft, but not hitherward. Finally, if we tried to imagine the corpse moved "out of the picture and into the altar-tomb," the hidden gravedigger whose hands support the saint's head and shoulder would bar her entry: Guercino inserted him between the saint and the altar, and he cannot be thought away.

The wielder of these enormous hands is understood to stand on the floor of the sepulcher, shielded from our sight by the pictorial threshold and the recessed wall below. We may not know whether he is easing the body's descent or helping to lift it out; but the visible crest of his action is so revealing that, plumbing his altitude down to tiptoes and heels, the inferred depth of the tomb invades our consciousness. Just as higher reaches of heaven are unlocked for us by the glance of the angels in the upper left of the altarpiece, so the hands fringing the threshold produce lower depths. The grave dips as deep as the man's reach is high.

The importance of this conceit is apt to be missed because Guercino's painting no longer occupies its original site. It was removed in 1730, its place over the St. Petronilla altar being taken by an ingenious mosaic replica. Consequently, when we pass the altar in the Basilica, we disregard what we know to be but a copy; and when we contemplate the original in the Galleria Capitolina, we see no cause to remember St. Peter's (Figs. 7 A, 8). This dissociation of picture from

44 Donald Posner in Julius S. Held and D. Posner, *17th and 18th-Century Art. Baroque Painting, Sculpture, and Architecture*, New York, n. d., p. 102. The passage continues: "Thus, for the communicant at the altar, the divine vision was united with the mystery of the Mass through the sacrifice of the saint, and belonged at once to the world of painted illusion and miraculous reality." The conclusion may have seemed too beguiling to admit contradictory data.

45 Posner's argument may be salvageable if we try to divert it to metaphor. Taking the event literally, in terms of the mechanics depicted, the saint's body, whether lowered or raised, lies askew to the plane of the altar. But seen from a distance within the Basilica, her supine attitude, extending from head to arm, could be claiming the altar allusively, or symbolically, as her couch. But this notion, that the dead body is to be understood as lying both oblique and parallel to the altar, would be an extreme case of double functioning; it would credit Guercino with a management of ambiguity beyond anything claimed in this paper.

site breaks a vital link in Guercino's ideological structure. For the device of the cresting fingers unfurled at the base — the incentive they furnish to sound the whole man downward in his full stature — gives us the measure to which the action behind the altar refers. The plummet formed by the gravedigger's body drops ineluctably past the Basilica's floor; not to the real depth of the Vatican grottoes (a dimension outside the compass of the pictorial system), but just low enough to undercut our station, deep enough to bottom beneath the pavement that supports us.

How meaningful we decide to make this implicit sublevel depends somewhat on our prior estimate of Guercino's mentality. Suppose, as we have often been told, that Guercino composed more by instinct than by cogitation; then the hidden gravedigger's stature merely follows from the given scale of the foreground figures, and the fact that its downward projection underruns the Basilica's floor becomes fortuitous. On the other hand, the scale of the foreground figures was never "given" — as we learn from other, equal-sized altarpieces produced for St. Peter's. In these, the magnifying effect of the foreground tends to be neutralized by the use of partial repoussoir figures in collapsed postures; full stature being reserved for diminished figures in middle distance (e. g. Domenichino's *Martyrdom of St. Sebastian*, begun in 1625). But in the *St. Petronilla*, Guercino made the daring decision to thrust the main action up to the picture plane. This gave him a figure scale of spectacular magnitude, appropriate to the largesse of the surrounding architectural space, but gross and monstrous in its dwarfing effect on the very altar which an altarpiece is meant to exalt. What, then, determined the proximity and the cyclopean size of those foreground figures?

There is surely no certain and no single answer; any major decision in so complex a work as the *St. Petronilla* presumably reconciles many motives. But it is tempting to regard the projective scale of the hidden gravedigger as a determinant for the entire proportionate system, so that the immensity of the foreground figures will have followed in consequence. In this inversion of the causal sequence we are assuming that Guercino needed the phantom extension of his undepicted gravedigger to establish a precise measure of depth; and that he needed this measure as the critical means by which to associate the depicted body of St. Petronilla with the actual substance of the Basilica. For Guercino has made the projected stature of the gravedigger testify to the habitation of the saint's body. The scale of those reaching hands at the threshold serves to locate her remains beneath our feet, reminding us that St. Petronilla abides in St. Peter's.

In view of this collocation of place and image, it hardly matters whether the saint's body is being lowered or raised. What matters is the emphatic energy of her hovering at the mouth of a grave — a grave situate underfoot below the Basilica's floor. We are led to realize that the depicted scene invites yet a third reading: the saint's re-interment. Not the recent deposition of St. Petronilla's bones in New St. Peter's, for this is clearly not the event nor the locale represented; the scene was surely not meant to refer to a known public ceremony held sixteen years earlier. But the allusiveness of the presentation could well call to mind her translation in the 8th century when — in token of her new role as protectress of France — St. Petronilla was first re-interred within the precincts of Old St. Peter's. The margin of ambiguity in the picture is wide enough to accommodate, beyond the original burial and the deferred exhumation, a vision of the Apostle's daughter come to rest by the side of her father.

Since the painting was commissioned for the altar that replaced the demolished Chapel of the French Kings, one suspects that Guercino was given some sense of its political import. He may have learned that the French were inclined to lay claim to the possession of their patroness' body; and that impostor relics of Ste. Pétronille were venerated in various French churches, so that the prerogative of St. Peter's required reaffirmation.

There may well have been considerations of greater weight. The national policy of the French during the pontificate of Gregory XV was a source of continual chagrin to His Holiness. He urged without cease that the Tridentine reforms be instituted in France, hoping to wrest control of the ecclesiastical hierarchy from the French crown; but his exertions were vain. As the Thirty Years' War dragged into its fourth and fifth season, he warmly supported the House of Hapsburg; France, though Catholic, remained its implacable foe. The Pope had his heart set on a quick military campaign by the Duke of Savoy against Geneva, and his *nuncio* strove to secure the neutrality of the French, protesting how much their monarchy stood to gain by letting "the Rome of the Calvinists," the font of Huguenot strength, be obliterated; but Paris signalled Savoy that if he stirred against Geneva he would find the French in force barring his passage.[46] With such stubborn resistence to the Pope's plans coming from the French side, it must always have seemed *à propos* to remind the advocates of Gallicanism that the protectrix of the French monarchy lay here in St. Peter's, which — as any viewer of Guercino's painting *in situ* could see — formed a continuum with the Gates of Heaven.

[46] See Pastor, *op. cit.*, pp. 223-227; 236 f.; 206-209.

To encode messages of this sort in a pious hagiological composition required a subtle and keenly conscious pictorial imagination. It was hardly a task for an unsophisticated provincial — no matter how endowed with natural genius. Only a painter of large intellectual resources could have given visual substance to the program underlying the *St. Petronilla* and brought it off. What the work needed was an *intelligent* genius, and this must be why Guercino was called.[47]

[47] The *St. Petronilla* altarpiece may be regarded as an initial test case; for I suspect that Guercino's mental powers have been generally underrated, and that much of the naive late work now passing under his name will be disattributed when our conception of the artist is re-adjusted.

Fig. 1. Guercino, St. Petronilla *Altarpiece. Rome, Galleria Capitolina.*

Fig. 2. Detail of Fig. 1.

Fig. 3. Guercino, Study for the St. Petronilla *Altarpiece. Pen and wash, 25.4 × 32 cm. Windsor Castle, Collection of Her Majesty the Queen.*

Fig. 4. Guercino, Study for the St. Petronilla *Altarpiece. Black chalk,* 51.5 × 37.6 *cm. Windsor Castle, Collection of Her Majesty the Queen.*

Fig. 5. Guercino, Study for the St. Petronilla *Altarpiece. Sanguine, 20.8 × 29.5 cm. Darmstadt, Hessisches Landesmuseum.*

Fig. 6. Guercino, Study for the St. Petronilla *Altarpiece. Pen and wash, 27.1×42.3 cm. Copenhagen, Thorvaldsen Museum.*

Fig. 6 A. Detail of Fig. 1.

Fig. 7. Mosaic copy of the St. Petronilla *Altarpiece by Pietro Paolo Cristofari, 1730. Rome, St. Peter's.*

Fig. 7 A. Mosaic copy of the St. Petronilla *Altarpiece by Pietro Paolo Cristofari, 1730. Rome, St. Peter's.*

Fig. 8. Guercino, St. Petronilla *Altarpiece with scale figure. Rome, Galleria Capitolina.*

Fig. 9. Anonymous 17th-century copy of Guercino's St. Petronilla *Altarpiece. Drawing, formerly in the Seiferheld Gallery, New York City (1950).*

Fig. 10. Nicolas Dorigny after Guercino, St. Petronilla. *Engraving, 1700. London, British Museum.*

Fig. 11. *Johann Jakob Frey after Guercino,* St. Petronilla. *Engraving, 1731. London, British Museum.*

MICHAEL CONFORTI

VI

PLANNING THE LATERAN APOSTLES

WHEN Clement XI assumed the chair of St. Peter in November 1700, the nave of the Lateran Basilica appeared much as Innocent X had left it after his renovation for the Holy Year of 1650. The colored marble niches which Francesco Borromini, the architect of the renovation, had projected from the nave walls failed to receive the statues they were intended to frame. Algardi's stucco models for reliefs in the middle level were never executed in bronze or marble as had been planned. The oval floral surrounds of the upper register still revealed the rough brickwork of the Constantinian basilica and a question had already risen over whether this was intended by the original planners (Figs. 1 and 2). Clement came to power with what appears to have been a four-part program to revive artistic life in Rome. Two of his objectives were the completion of projects begun by earlier pontiffs and the restoration of the early Christian churches of the city. The Lateran Basilica, the mother church of Christendom, whose baroque redecoration had been cut short by a change in Innocent X's objectives, was an obvious candidate for work.[1]

Clement's involvement in the Lateran was more than a result of his artistic program for the city. His own uncle, Annibale Albani, had taken part in the Innocent X renovation, choosing scenes from the Old and New Testaments for the iconog-

[1] Clement XI's four-part program is proposed in my doctoral dissertation (M. Conforti, *The Lateran Apostles*, unpublished dissertation, Harvard University, 1977, pp. 29-36). I have described its objectives as (1) the completion of projects begun by earlier pontiffs; (2) the renovation of early Christian basilicas and restoration of artistic monuments in the city; (3) the construction of buildings to aid the economic and social well-being of the city; (4) the organization of the annual painting, sculpture, and architecture competition, the Concorso Clementino, to preserve Rome's dominant status in the arts.

raphy of the reliefs in the middle register.[2] More importantly, Clement's predecessor, Innocent XII, prompted by the new Lateran archpriest, Cardinal Benedetto Pamphili, had provided 40,000 *scudi* for a new Lateran facade, a sum matched by 20,000 *scudi* from Pamphili himself.[3] This contribution was to inspire numerous Lateran facade projects in the late seventeenth and early eighteenth centuries, but construction did not begin until Alessandro Galilei won Clement XII's Concorso of 1732.[4] Money was indeed available, but Clement XI and Pamphili apparently decided early-on that the interior of the Basilica had to be completed first. In the long years of work on this part of the church the idea of finishing the renovation under Clement XI's patronage somehow dimmed.

While the Lateran decoration was undoubtedly a cornerstone of Clement's artistic program for the city, there is no evidence that the project was seriously considered until early 1702, when the competition for the third class in architecture of the first Concorso Clementino called for the participants to draw a " Rilievo di una nicchia di San Giovanni in Laterano ". Prizes were awarded for this competition on February 25, 1702, and the winning entry, by Pietro Paolo Scaramella, depicted one of Borromini's niches enclosing a figure of a saint placed on a circular pedestal.[5] Plans continued throughout 1702, and later that year a wooden model of one of the niches was begun.[6] In February, 1703, we have the first record of a patron's commitment to the undertaking when Cardinal Francesco Maria de' Medici sent his sculptor Anton Francesco Andreozzi from Florence to discuss the project and the Cardinal's participation in it with Benedetto Pamphili.[7]

Although the Pope took a considerable interest in the Lateran sculptures, many of the major decisions, as well as the day-to-day operations, were carried out by a *Congregazione*, a committee appointed by the Pope, that was headed by Pamphili and included Count Giulio Bussi, Clement's newly appointed Secretary of Me-

2 Alessandro Baldeschi, *Stato della SS. Chiesa Papale Lateranense nell'anno MDCCXXIII*, Rome, 1723, pp. 6–7.

3 Ludwig Freiherr von Pastor, *The History of the Popes*, London, 1940, vol. XXXII, p. 589.

4 For the most recent discussion of the early eighteenth century Lateran facade projects see Hellmut Hager, " On a Project Ascribed to Carlo Fontana for the Facade of S. Giovanni in Laterano," *Burlington Magazine*, CXVII, February, 1975, pp. 105 ff.

5 P. Marconi, et al., *I Disegni di Architettura... dell'Accademia di San Luca*, Rome, 1974, figure 79. The belief that the redecoration commenced in January, 1701, with a 6000 *scudi* gift from Benedetto Pamphili is unfounded (Conforti, *op. cit.*, 1977, pp. 85, 125).

6 Domenico Abbondanza's bill for the model is found in the Archivio Doria Pamphili, Rome, *Benedetto Pamphili, Vol. 39*, no. 1.

7 Andreozzi's letter of introduction from Cardinal de' Medici to Benedetto Pamphili is published in K. Lankheit, *Florentinische Barockplastik*, Munich, 1962, p. 338.

morials Monsignor Curtio Origo, and the Pope's brother, Orazio Albani.[8] Cardinal Pamphili was in charge of the group and he chose most of the secondary figures involved. Origo and Bussi were expected to oversee the daily operations and Orazio Albani acted principally as an emissary to the Pope, reporting to him personally on the progress of the work. The *Congregazione* had enormous responsibility. We are told that they chose the sculptors and examined and approved all the models,[9] but this committee apparatus which was so clearly outlined by Alessandro Baldeschi in his 1723 history of the Lateran should not be considered unusual. There is no reason to believe that most large-scale Papal artistic undertakings were organized in a vastly different way. Although most of the aesthetic decisions had to be approved by the Committee, what is unusual in the Lateran sculpture project is that these decisions were made by two advisory artists who were not sculptors; the painter, Carlo Maratti, and the architect, Carlo Fontana. Each took considerable responsibility in organizing and directing the participating sculptors.

The tradition of appointing an artistic advisor to coordinate and design important Papal commissions was a clearly established one in seventeeth-century Rome. Bernini, as the acknowledged grand master of the city, had orchestrated many of the architectural-sculptural undertakings initiated by the papacy. After his death, and after the lull in artistic activity during Innocent XI's reign (1676-89), the position of artistic advisor, although unofficial, was assumed either by the architect Fontana or the painter Maratti. No sculptor had the experience and the respect of either of these two powerful personalities, thus their positions were never challenged. In the mid-teens of the eighteenth century, after Maratti and Fontana had died, this advisor system was finally broken and sculptors again took a role in the planning stages of official papal works. The tradition was strong around 1700, however, and combined with the need to insure unity in the design of the Lateran sculptures, the call to Maratti for drawings and to Fontana for engineering and complementary aesthetic advice was an obvious one for the time.

Maratti had the more significant role of the two. In early 1703, once the project had been outlined, he began executing the preliminary designs for the figures. These were then given to the sculptors working on the project to produce *bozzetti*.[10]

8 Baldeschi, *op. cit.*, 1723, pp. 9-10.

9 P. H. Hantsch and A. Scherf, *Quellen zur Geschichte des Barocks in Franken unter dem Einfluss des Hauses Schönbrun*, Augsburg, 1931, pp. 92-93.

10 Many of the sculptors were not pleased by this division of responsibilities and in May, 1703, they complained that they did not want to follow the designs Maratti had made for them (E. Scatassa, "I Papi e

A wooden model of one of the niches was finished in early 1703, and it was intended to enclose the larger version of these terra-cottas, testing a proposed figure's relationship to its niche setting.[11] These early *bozzetti* were probably executed as preparation for choosing Maratti's final design.[12] In this way the interests and ideas of the sculptor and the designer could be worked out before the official design for a figure was selected. Afterwards each sculptor had to produce a finished clay model from this final drawing. Once the model was approved by the Committee, it was contractual and no variations on its design could occur at a later stage in the sculptural process.[13]

The sculptors had also agreed to produce a full-scale *creta* version of their proposed sculpture. Producing full-scale models was not uncommon in the late baroque. Marble was expensive and the enormous single blocks planned for each Lateran figure would be particularly costly. To avoid mistakes while carving, a full-scale version would be perfected at a stage when materials could be replaced cheaply. This model would then be used to point the marble in the studio.[14] It would be built, however, within its niche in the Lateran, fulfilling what seems to have been its most important function, the test of scale and proportion of each sculpture within the context of the nave. The question of scale was one of the most serious considerations in the planning stages of the commission. Early in the project, while the sculptors were working on their preliminary *bozzetti*, Carlo Fontana, as an aesthetic advisor to the Committee, was asked for his opinion on the size of the sculptures.

l'arte in un Diario Romano," *Arte e Storia*, 1916, pp. 334-335).

11 These large *modelli* were approximately 3 *palmi* (.67 meters) high (Conforti, *op. cit.*, 1977, pp. 114-138).

12 There are two reasons to make this assumption. To begin with each sculptor had to make many models. One of them, Pietro Balestra, originally employed to execute the *St. Matthew*, made 33 of varying sizes, although he never began one of full-scale (Archivio Capitolare Lateranense, Rome, *Giustificazione delle Statue e Pitture in S. Giovanni Laterano dell'anno 1704 a tt.o l'anno 1714*, no. 222). Also every one of the extant drawings varies to some degree from the final executed marbles. Thus it is likely that the sculptors may have been working towards the production of a final *modello* by fashioning *bozzetti* from various preliminary sketches.

I have discussed the extant drawings, including eleven unpublished Lateran Apostle sketches by Maratti now in the Accademia di San Fernando, Madrid, in Conforti, *op. cit.*, 1977, pp. 218-247.

13 A final presentation terra-cotta model was required of each sculptor. (A. Bertolotti, *Artisti Francesi in Roma nei Secoli XV, XVI, and XVII*, Mantua, 1886, pp. 173-174), and the finality of its design is proven by the existence of a small marble version of the *St. Phillip* by Giuseppe Mazzuoli now in the Germanisches Nationalmuseum, Nürnberg. This marble conforms exactly to the final marble and was executed in early 1705, before the large-scale model of the *Phillip* was even begun (Conforti, *op. cit.*, 1977, pp. 228-229).

14 The construction of framing devices to be used for pointing is described in Archivio Capitolare Lateranense, *op. cit.*, no. 198.

Any project involving sculptures as large as the Apostles would necessitate an architect's advice for engineering and general organization and Fontana and his associates remained with the commission throughout its duration performing many of these tasks.[15] The added request for his opinion on size, however, reflected the difficulty of the project at hand. The niches were unusually large and each had a broken architrave that made the space available for a sculpture much higher than that of a more typical pedimental niche. Having seen such a large open space, some early consultants had assumed that the sculptures themselves had to be nearly as high. Fontana did not agree, and on March 16, 1703, he compiled an argument in a short treatise addressed to Cardinal Corsini, the Papal Treasurer, in which he questioned the correctness of "le statue...gigantee nell'elevazione e latitudine".[16] For him the choice of such large figures stemmed from the misunderstanding of the relationship of architecture to sculpture in enclosures such as these.[17] Too many people were thinking of Borromini's marble enclosures as "nicchie", he said, and instead they should be thought of as "tabernacoli". To him "nicchie" were simple open recesses in the plane of a wall for statuary. The Lateran niches, however, had to have a different designation as they were pedimental structures protruding from a wall.[18] Fontana found his answer to the problem of the size of sculpture enclosed by such architectural surrounds in studying the relationship of the height of sculpture to flanking columns in various pedimental niches around Rome.[19] A figure, he felt, had to be smaller than the column to relate successfully to the niche opening, and keeping it so would also solve the problem of the proportion of each statue within the nave interior.[20] In the drawing he executed to illustrate the points he was making, he placed a design for a *St. Bartholomew*, the sculpture commissioned by his correspondent Cardinal Corsini, within a Lateran niche to show its just relationship to the surround (Fig. 3).

Although Fontana's discussion was conducted in terms of the size of the flanking columns, in his rendering he arranged the figure with greater reference to the rear

15 Carlo Fontana's son and close assistant, Francesco, as well as Filippo Leti, also acted as architectural advisors in the first few years of the project. In the closing years of the commission, Carlo's nephew, Carlo Stefano Fontana, directed most of the operations.

16 Appendix (22) The view of those who felt that the statues should be higher is expressed by Fontana in App. (1-3). Fontana's treatise and its accompanying drawings are discussed most recently in H. Hager and A. Braham, *Carlo Fontana, The Drawings at Windsor Castle*. London, 1977, pp. 86-88.

17 App. (22 ff.).

18 App. (1-16).

19 App. (56 ff.).

20 App. (35-46).

molded panel of Borromini's niche. The saint was to be 16 *palmi* high (about 3.56 meters), and it was to stand on a pedestal about 2 ½ *palmi* (.56 meters) which was to be elliptical to echo the circularity of the pose and keep the figure fully visible from below.[21] Fontana's Apostle design was inserted into another, larger drawing with another figure about the same height, but on a pedestal approximately 5 *palmi* (1.12 meters). The architect hoped the added 2 ½ *palmi* of the new support would prove the disturbing effects of such a large figure and base (Fig. 4).[22]

Fontana's treatise was apparently written in preparation for the construction of a wooden chiaroscuro panel, painted with a Maratti design for a *St. Peter* by the artist's close associate, G. P. Melchiori, and set in one of the Lateran niches for a May 17, 1703, viewing.[23] When the Pope examined the chiaroscuro figure he told the gathering around him that he found it " piccola e secca ".[24] The two-dimensional medium, however, could hardly have given a satisfactory three-dimensional impression of what an actual statue that size would be like. While there is no evidence that a new wooden model was put up, faced with the Pope's complaint, Fontana altered his own plan. In a new treatise of October 20, 1703, this time addressed to Cardinal Pamphili, he kept his argument and wording essentially the same, but changed the size of the figure from sixteen to eighteen *palmi*, placing it on a smaller support (about half a *palmo* high) thereby decreasing the size of the base, increasing that of the figure and keeping the overall height the same (Fig. 5). This enabled the architect to maintain his principle of a sculpture's relationship to its flanking columns while creating the larger figure the Pope felt was necessary.[25]

The essential premise of Fontana's final solution remained unaltered in the statues as executed; the final figures of nineteen *palmi* were not much higher than

21 App. (36–37).

22 App. (47–55).

23 The bill for Melchiori's services is in the Archivio Doria Pamphili, *op. cit.*, no. 6.

24 Scatassa, *op. cit.*, 1916, pp. 334–335.

25 Two copies of Fontana's October 20, 1703 letter to Cardinal Pamphili are preserved in the Royal Library at Windsor, one in vol A/6, another in vol. A/25. The letter in vol. A/6 is accompanied with Fontana's drawing (Fig. 5); the letter in vol. A/25 with the other drawings (Figs. 3 and 4). While the drawing in A/6 is designed to accompany the October text, the drawings in A/25 only fit requirements of the March version, as each of the figures is placed on a pedestal and are approximately 16 *palmi* high [based on the 20¼ *palmi* figure for the columns which Fontana himself gives (App. [13])]. Therefore, while these two drawings are included with the later letters at Windsor, in my discussion I have taken them to represent drawings made to accompany the earlier version. I believe they are a product of his earlier argument.

he suggested.[26] However, the statues' final relationship to the niches, their heavy mass and thicker proportions, appears considerably different from Fontana's own renderings (cf., for example, Figs. 1, 2 and 5). While this is partly due to the extra height and drapery which allowed the sculptors a somewhat broader as well as taller figure, it also results from Fontana's unwillingness to understand the three-dimensionality of the space with which he was dealing. The concavity in the rear of Borromini's niches would never have allowed a figure to be framed by the molding as evenly as Fontana would have had it, whether seen from ground-level or from the idealized perspective he set for himself. He never came to terms with the fact that a statue would fill a considerable volume of space between the rear of the niche and the columns and probably extend outward from the columns, overlapping them. His inability to consider the mass of the sculpture and niche is especially apparent in his choice of precedents of Roman sculpture enclosed within pedimental niches which he used to support his theory and listed at the end of his treatise. While each of these niche figures is indeed smaller than its flanking columns, almost all are seen from afar, usually from the distance of an altar rail fronting a chapel whose main altar is surmounted by such a niche.[27] In only one of the examples, Lorenzetto's *Madonna del Sasso* in the Pantheon, is a viewer able to experience the work from a variety of distances and angles, as one would have to do in the Lateran.[28]

As he formed his ideas essentially from " single-view " examples, Fontana was little bothered by the two-dimensionality of his own design. The extra height and the considerable mass the statues later acquired, changes necessary to successfully fill the great void of Borromini's oval spaces, made his treatise little more than an academic exercise. The real challenge to his principle relating a sculpture to its flanking columns could only come when testing the mass of the figures. This would only be possible when large models were set in the niches and the Committee and experts could sense the appropriateness of a proposed sculpture's dimensions by viewing a full-scale model from various points in the nave.

26 The nineteen *palmi* (4.24 meters) figure is first mentioned by L. Pascoli, *Vite de' Pittori, Scultori, ed Architetti Moderni*, Rome, 1730, I, p. 262. My own measurements of the figure of *St. Matthew* place it at 4.30 meters or 19.2 *palmi*. In terms of Fontana's drawing (Fig. 5), the actual figures as executed would come close to the top of the figure " A " above the head of the saint depicted in that rendering.

27 App. (56-135).

28 App. (97-103).

Fontana's foray into the realm of sculptural planning emphasizes why baroque sculptors produced full-scale models for sculpture within an architectural context. We have already pointed out that the designs of the Lateran Apostles were fixed in early 1704 through the finished, contractual terra-cotta *modelli*. Yet it is known that in June, 1707, the large models were still being broken and refashioned.[29] These alterations were necessitated by the search for the correct relationship of these final *modelli* to an architecture of this scale. Fontana had indeed provided a beginning step, but his theories regarding height could only be proven by different means.

29 Scatassa, *op. cit.*, 1916, pp. 334-335.

APPENDIX

Carlo Fontana's plans for the height of the statues in the Lateran nave are outlined in two letters, one written to Cardinal Lorenzo Corsini on March 16, 1703 (Archivio Segreto Vaticano, Fondo Albani 12, f. 19-21; published by M. Loret, *Archivi d'Italia*, 1935, pp. 75-77) and one written to Benedetto Pamphili on October 20, 1703 (The Royal Library, Windsor, vols. A/6, ff. 4 and 5, and A/25, ff. 32 and 33). The letter to Pamphili is based on the earlier letter to Corsini and here I transcribe the two letters, parenthesizing words which do not appear in the later version and italicizing words appearing in the later version and not in the earlier. If you read the words in parentheses and not the italicized ones, you will be reading the early March version; if you read the italicized words without the parenthesed ones, you will be reading the later October version.

Tal'uni o per dir molti prendono errore nella denominazione di quei luoghi, dove vanno collocate le statue marmoree dentro la Basilica Lateranense, denominandole per Nicchie, e pure il composto degl'ornati di essi fanno vedere essere Tabernacoli, mentre, che ordinariamente le Nicchie non hanno un fasto attorno di sì belle parti, havendo quel grand'Artefice distribute le medesime spaziosamente con eleganza per ricevere nel proprio seno senza angustia la statua per ottenerne un composto correlativo a tutto di quei ornati, che vestono pomposamente quelle nobili Pareti *replicando, che le dette pareti, che circoscrivono le navate non ammettono parimente Statue grandi à causa della poca distanza, che hanno, onde per sfuggire tall' errore L'Artefice sud.o dispose l'ornati, che assegnano la misura della statua medema proportionata al godimento di quelle distanze.*

Il fine (particolare) che havuto l'Artefice nella disposizione ampla di quei Tabernacoli è stato acciò che la statua sia goduta *il suo valore* perfettamente (quasi) in tutto il suo contorno, onde per ottenere un ottimo di perfezzione non dovranno le statue per ivi da farsi gigantee nell'elevazione e latitudine, perchè riuscirebbero molto sconsonanti di proporzione fra la Scultura et Architettura del proprio Tabernacolo, mentre (che) *il grande ingombro restarebbero mai viste, e sconsonanti con* i bassi rilievi, che presentemente risiedono sopra *quali* contribuiscono anche loro norma di proporzione alle statue da farsi, e perciò nel sequente Disegno se ne porta la dimostrazione del fatto, e da farsi con le giuste delineazioni e misure, trovando che la concorrenza vuole, che la statua non ecceda in altezza palmi (16) *18* in circa da situarsi (eminentemente con il suo Piedistallo) *sopra un zoccolo poco elevato dal piano della Base* acciò non venga defraudato quello che richiede il godimento in quegl'ambiti, e distanze; onde però si potrebbe disporre (gli) *li* detti (Piedistalli) *zoccoli* di figura eliptica, overo obliqua per la libertà totale della visualità e per caminare anche (colla) *con la* circolarità della statua, come nella Pianta ed (Altezza) *alzata* s'ammira, certo è che operandosi con queste riflessioni unite con la somma intelligenza di si bravi Artefici, se ne può sperare una perfetta condotta in accrescimento decoroso di quella Basilica, e sommo godimento degl'Astanti; la Proporzione delle colonne laterali del Tabernacolo, (che sono di Palmi 16) danno l'assegna medesima alla statua, che non deve eccedere alla misura del prospetto quì annesso, e per far vedere che il merito di palmi (16) *18 in circa* della statua sia il suo dovere viene corroborato da altre quasi consimili sequenti situate negl'ambiti quasi uniformi, che però se ne sono fatti (tre) *due* Pensieri quì annessi di proporzione (maggiore, e minore) *giusta e* per far costare che la maggioranza (dell'altezza) delle statue sarà, come si crede, nociva *si notifica, che il fuso della colonna s'intende senza Base, e Cappello.*

Tabernacoli overo Altari parte in simil andare di quelli della Basilica Lateranense.

Angeloni delli due Altari nelle Nicchie nella chiesa del Popolo opera del Bernino alti quanto è il fuso della colonna, cioè palmi (16 e mezzo) *14½* circa.

Altare delli Sig.re N.N. dentro la chiesa di S. Domenico e Sisto a Monte Magnanapoli, che si può dir Copia di quelli di S. Gio. opera fatta dal Cav. Bernini; le statue che rappresentano il Redentore e la Madalena sono assai minori d'altezza del fuso della propria colonna (il fuso della colonna s'intende senza Base e capitello) e resta libero della propria statua il convesso del tabernacolo.

Capella di S. Teresa nella Madonna della Vittoria opera del cav. Bernino, la statua di essa Santa con l'angiolo sono di minor proporzione *del fuso* della colonna, che li fà ornato, e resta libero il concavo della Nicchia con quei splendori; viceversa la cappella di rincontro resta deturpata dalla troppa grandezza della statua di S. Giuseppe.

Capella di S. Tomaso di Villanuova nella Chiesa di S. Agostino assai minore di proporzione *del fuso* della colonna che li fà ornato essendo circa un naturale e mezzo d'altezza cioè circa Palmi 12.

La statua di S. Giacomo nella chiesa de' Spagnuoli assai minore *del fuso* della colonna che li fà ornato e alta un naturale, e tre quarti, cioè palmi $(13\frac{1}{2})$ $\mathit{12\frac{1}{2}}$ in circa.

Capella dei Sig.re Ginnetti in S. Andrea della Valle, le loro statue sono di minor misura assai *del fuso* delle colonne, e sono d'altezza circa palmi 11 e mezzo

Cappella de' Sig.ri Strozzi in d.a chiesa opera della scuola di Michel Angiolo, le statue sono assai di minore altezza del fuso delle colonne, e sono alte circa palmi dieci.

La statua di S. Mattia nella chiesa della S.ma Trinità de' Pellegrini è assai minore del fuso della colonna, che li fà ornato, che sarà d'altezza circa palmi 12.

Il Basso rilievo dentro la cappella de' S.ri Alaleoni nella chiesa di S. Pietro in Montorio opera del Cav. Bernini, le figure marmoree sono di proporzioni minori al fuso della colonna che li fà ornato.

Nelli due cappelloni laterali in d.a chiesa una del Card. del Monte, le statue che vi sono, sono assai minori d'altezza del proprio fuso della colonna; la statua della S.ma Vergine situata in un Tabernacolo dentro il Tempio della Rotonda *vicino alla memoria di Rafaele d'Urbino, e si erede sua direzzione*, è assai minore di proporzione del fuso della colonna che li fà ornato e risiede dentro il Telaro nell'intercolumnio *tal regolato milita nel d.o tambernacolo di S. Gio: Laterano*

Giusto appunto il Boromino hà destinato il sito della propria statua de' suoi Tabernacoli in S. Gio. Laterano dentro il proprio telaro, che vi è Le statue del Battesimo dentro il gran cappellone di S. Gio. de' Fiorentini opera del Cav. Boromini in quella grande ampiezza, vi sono le dette statue di altezza circa due naturali, cioè Palmi $15\frac{1}{2}$ e mezzo in circa

Similmente li due Tabernacoli, che fanno Depositi lateralmente al d.o Cappellone quasi consimili agl'altri di S. Gio: le statue, che vi sono non eccedono alla misura del fuso della colonna che fà ornato.

Parimente il Tabernacolo, ò sia ciborio eretto nella Chiesa della Traspontina le Statue tanto dentro, quanto

d'intorno d'esso Tabernacolo sono di misura minore del fuso delle colonne, opera molto imitata dà professori in altre simili.

Si che da tali esempii d'opere così classiche si riconosce, che le statue da farsi di nuovo pare che non divino eccedere circa palmi ($15\frac{1}{2}$) *$18\frac{1}{2}$* in circa *dette statue* da sollevarsi (eminentemente) *al zoccolo* acciò (non) resti (tant'aria) *l'aria* verso il cuppolino di detti Tabernacoli.

Ambiti grandi fuori di proporzione di S. Gio: Laterano

Statua della Cattedra del Vaticano alta palmi 23.

Statue nelli 4 Nicchioni della cuppola Vaticana nei 4 Piloni, alte l'una palmi 20 e mezzo. (Questo sono colossi secondo l'ampiezza del Tempio.)

Statua di S. Leone et Attila nel Vaticano alta palmi 14 e mezzo l'una, e non più.

Statua della Contessa Matilde nel Vaticano alta palmi 12: come anche quella di Leone X quasi consimili.

Regola, e misura della Statua

La Colonna hà d'altezza teste $20\frac{1}{4}$ con base, e Capitello

La statua secondo le misure communi deve essere teste nove della proportione della Colonna, come apunto appare nel disegno, che sarebbe p.mi $18\frac{1}{2}$ in circa, ma p.che hà la residenza alquanto sopra l'Orizonte si potrà farla teste nove, e un quarto p. lo scorcio visuale, che darebbe la sua altezza, come il fuso della Colonna.

Siccome gl'ornati, che compongono cosi leggiadram.te quei Tambernacoli modinati con tal delicatura, che se ne gode un artificiosa armonia di belle parti.

Deve anche il scultore precettivamente scolpire le statue con la medema leggiadria con atti nobili svegliati, e spiritosi non inviluppati di panni alla grossolana, come accade, che p. cuoprire qualche atto, ò parte ignuda faticosa da vedersi con decenza, sogliono alcuni valersi cuoprirli con ingombrati panni, errore molto sfuggito da i grand'huomini antichi, e moderni come s'ammira dall'infiniti, che con molta arte hanno fatto... nel medemo tempo la statua vestita con il contorno dell'ignudo sotto, e questa e una delle maggiori riflessioni, che si deve havere p. accordar la gentilità della statua con l'altre dell'ornati

Contesta dunque con l'esempio di queste, e regole d'architettura, che le dette statue da farsi dovranno essere circa poco più di due naturali *e mezzo* d'altezza *cioè p.mo* $18\frac{1}{2}$ *in circa* da riconoscersi il poco più, o poco meno dai Modelli da farsi sopra la faccia del luogo ben finiti, acciò gl'artefici possino scolpire la statua che faccia la sua comparsa proporzionale nel proprio luogo con quelle regole prospettiche, che sogliono havere la situazione di statue sopra il piano dell'orizzonte e questo e quanto stende la poca abilità del Cav. Carlo Fontana in dare (a V. S. Ill.ma e R.ma) *all'em.za v.ra* tal notizia rimettendomi sempre più al sommo giudizio e sapere di questo linceo de' Virtuosi, che haveranno da operare, e facendole per fine (profonda) *profondissima* riv.a

(Casa li 16, Marzo 1703) *di 20 8bre 1703*

Fig. 1. St. Jude *by Lorenzo Ottoni, S. Giovanni in Laterano, Rome.*

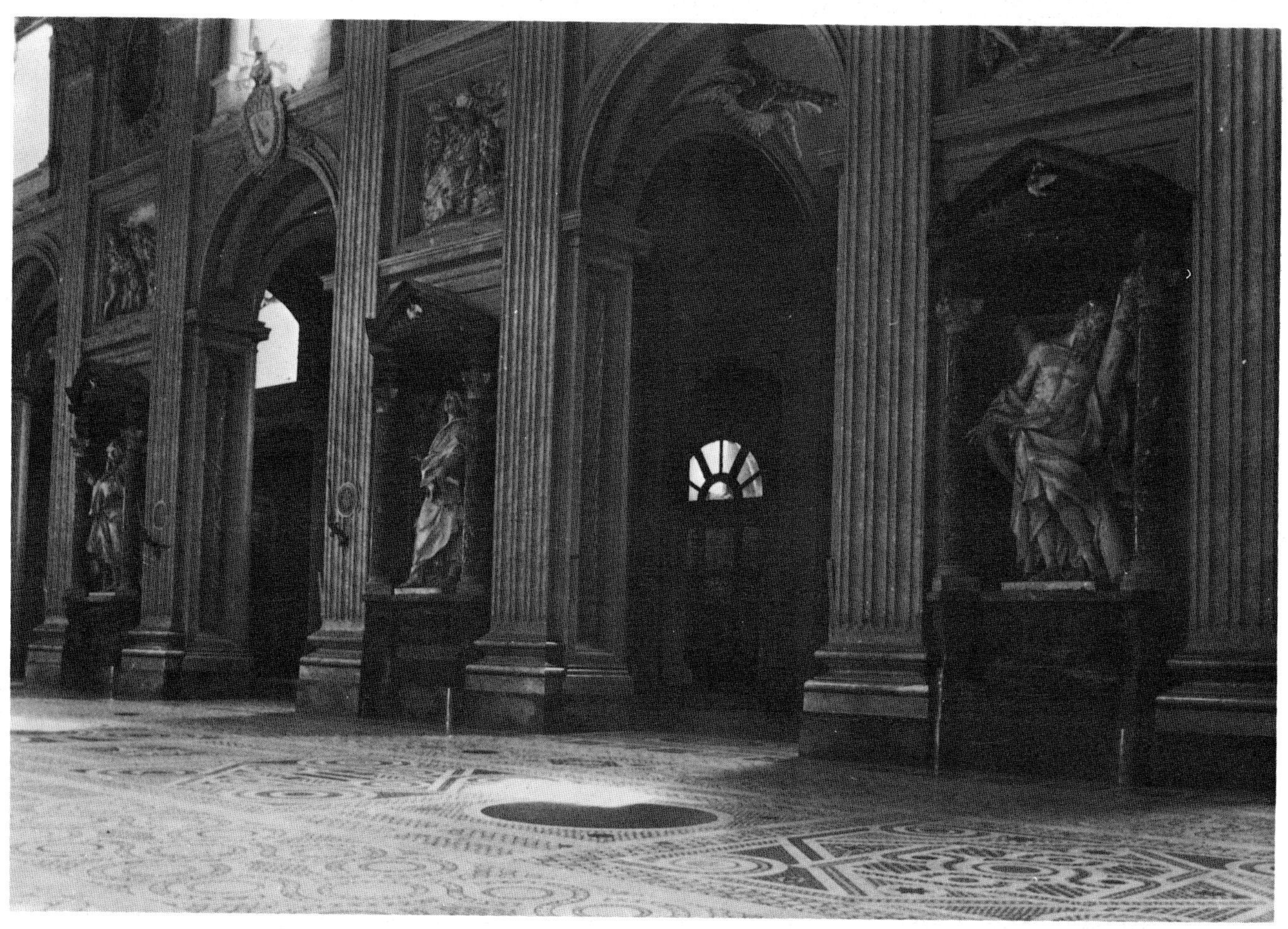

Fig. 2. St. James the Less *by Angelo de' Rossi,* St. John *by Camillo Rusconi,* St. Andrew, *by Camillo Rusconi (l to r) S. Giovanni in Laterano, Rome.*

Fig. 3. St. Bartolomeo *by Carlo Fontana, Royal Library, Windsor* (9919).

Fig. 4. St. Bartolomeo *by Carlo Fontana, Royal Library, Windsor* (9919).

Fig. 5. St. Bartolomeo *by Carlo Fontana, Royal Library, Windsor* (9413).

HENRY A. MILLON

VII

THE ANTAMORO CHAPEL IN S. GIROLAMO DELLA CARITÀ IN ROME: DRAWINGS BY JUVARRA AND AN UNKNOWN DRAFTSMAN

TWO DRAWINGS by Filippo Juvarra for the Antamoro Chapel in San Girolamo della Carità, from an album of Juvarra acquired by the Metropolitan Museum in New York, have recently been discussed and reproduced by Mary L. Myers in her detailed catalogue for an exhibition held at the Museum in 1975 (Figs. 1 and 2).[1] An additional unpublished drawing by Juvarra (not known to Myers) in the Biblioteca Nacional in Madrid (Fig. 3), and a group of three drawings not by Juvarra in the National Museum in Stockholm (Figs. 4, 5, and 6—one reproduced and the other two mentioned by Rudolf Preimesberger),[2] when considered in conjunction with the previously known group of drawings by Juvarra in the Biblioteca Nazionale in Turin (some published by Silvia Battaglia),[3] invite a reassessment of the stages in the design of the project under Juvarra's direction.

1 The album of drawings by Juvarra in the Metropolitan Museum was originally to be published by the late Rudolf Wittkower, as part of one volume in the *Corpus Juvarrianum.* At the suggestion of Margot Wittkower, the project was offered to me as a student of Wittkower's in Piedmontese Baroque architecture. Associate Curator Mary L. Myers has greatly facilitated study of the album and offered many helpful suggestions about drawings on individual sheets in the collection.

A preliminary version of this paper was presented in January 1975 at a symposium chaired by Mary Myers held at the Metropolitan Museum in conjunction with the exhibition *Architectural and Ornamental Drawings* and, in its present state, in October 1978 at the Institute for Advanced Study at Princeton, New Jersey.

The drawings, reproduced in the catalogue of the exhibition, are numbers 36-k and 36-l with entries on 33 and an appendix devoted to the album on 55-56.

2 R. Preimesberger, "Entwürfe Pierre Legros' für Filippo Juvarras Cappella Antamoro," *Römische Historische Mitteilungen*, X [1966/67], fig. 5 (lateral section, or elevation of altar wall) and 203-204 (discussion of the three drawings).

3 S. de Vito Battaglia, "Un'opera romana di Filippo Juvarra," *Bollettino d'Arte*, XXX [1936/37],

The drawing in the Biblioteca Nacional in Madrid (as the two drawings in the Metropolitan album and one of the drawings in the Biblioteca Nazionale in Turin—Fig. 7) contains a rapid perspective sketch in ink of the west half of the chapel as seen from the entrance including the altar and figure of *St. Philip Neri*. The drawing in Madrid is of special interest in that it also includes on the right half of the sheet the only known sketch elevation of the interior face of the entrance wall. The sketches in Turin published by Battaglia, in addition to the perspective mentioned above, include an elevation of both leaves of one of the lateral doors, capitals, a double guilloche band, and two studies for the placement of the Antamoro escutcheon above the entrance to the chapel.[4] Nine additional sketches (five unpublish-

485-498, figs. 5, 6, 7, 10, 11 and 12. Battaglia also reproduces five other drawings by Juvarra of Roman projects other than the Antamoro chapel.

[4] Battaglia undoubtedly knew, but did not mention or reproduce, another drawing of a capital for the Antamoro chapel from the same collection—59.4.1 verso (1), (a) below. In addition, the studies of door leaves found on 59.4.4 (1)—(c) below—and 59.4.5 verso (2)—(e) below—may be for the lateral doors of the chapel. A study for the candelabra found on 59.4.1 (5)—(a) below is unpublished. The doors reproduced by Battaglia (fig. 10) are found on the lower right half of a sheet—59.4.4 verso (3)—that also includes, to the left, an alternative design extending over both leaves which would be complete when both were closed, (d) below. There are, therefore, thirteen sheets containing twenty drawings to be considered. Of these, four show most of the chapel, one a lateral wall, and the remainder, decorative details. Of the details, nine are associated here with the chapel for the first time.

The drawings by Juvarra, arranged by collection, are as follows:

Biblioteca Nazionale, Turin, Raccolta Fea, volume 59.4.

a) folio 1 (5) Study for the candelabra on lateral walls (unpublished)
   1 verso (1) Capital (unpublished)

b) folio 3 (5) Capital (Battaglia, fig. 12)

c) folio 4 (1) Study for lateral doors (unpublished)

d) folio 4 verso (3-right) Study for lateral door (Battaglia, fig. 10)
   4 verso (3-left) Study for lateral door (reproduced in S. Boscarino, *Juvarra architetto*, Rome, 1973, pl. 93—inverted, as it should be)

e) folio 5 verso (2) Three alternatives for a pair of leaves of a door—what may be a crescent in one of the doors suggests connection with the Antamoro chapel (all three unpublished)

f) 108 (2) Escutcheon over door (Battaglia, fig. 7)—right half of a sheet containing a sketch section of a portion of the coliseum (Boscarino [pl. 1])—dated 20 May 1708

g) 116 (2) Double guilloche (Battaglia, fig. 11) which reproduces, however, only the double guilloche that relates to the reveal of the oval surrounding *St. Philip* while omitting the single guilloche, wave scroll, and fret on the same sheet. The latter three unpublished drawings may be studies of unadopted decorative detail.

h) 121 verso (1) Escutcheon over door (Battaglia, fig. 6) alternate to (f) above

i) 127 (1) Perspective of chapel from the entrance *Capella fatta in S. Girolamo del [dal?] S. Avocato/Antemori e da Filippo Juvarra* (Battaglia, fig. 5); also reproduced in L. Rovere, V. Viale, and A. E. Brinckmann, *Filippo Juvarra*, Milan, 1937, pl. 62; Boscarino *op. cit.*, pl. 90).

Metropolitan Museum of Art, New York, Juvarra Album

j) sheet 235 Perspective of chapel from the entrance

ed) of details in Turin (of which seven are likely and two possibly for the chapel) bring to 13 the number of sheets with a total of 20 drawings presumed to be associated with the chapel.

One of the drawings in the Metropolitan—the *primo pensiero* (Fig. 1)—states that the design was *messa in opera* in 1708. The phrase could mean either initiated or completed at that date. Myers, on the basis of Battaglia's citation of the inscription in the pavement of the chapel containing the date 1710 (which states the chapel was initially used to house the remains of the Antamoro family at that date) concludes that Juvarra's note signifies he had finished the design by 1708 when construction was begun and that the chapel was completed in 1710.[5] Preimesberger, on the

Primo pensiero per la Capella di S. Filippo a S. Girolamo/del Sig. Avocato Antemori, messa in opera l'año 1708 (Myers, pl. 36-k)

k) sheet 249 Perspective of chapel from the entrance with plan of altar below *Secondo pensiero/della capella di S. Fi.po in/ S. Girolamo* (Myers, pl. 36-l)

Biblioteca Nacional, Madrid, Drawing Collection

l) sheet 8182 (left) Perspective of chapel from entrance (right) Elevation of interior of entrance wall.

Myers, *op. cit.*, 33, also mentions a plan on page 247 of the Metropolitan album in connection with the chapel. The dimensions of the chapel indicated in plan, 22 × 30 (also shown on sheet 248)—seven *palmi* wider and longer (1.56 m or 5.1 feet)—make it unlikely the two drawings refer to the Antamoro chapel. Space for the chapel was restricted by the sacristy on the left and the cloister behind the altar.

[5] Myers, *op. cit.*, 33. Additional confirmation cited by Battaglia (caption on 490) is supplied perhaps by a date of 20 May 1708 found on the left half of a sheet in Turin—59.4.108 (2), reproduced in Battaglia, fig. 7—which on the right contains a drawing for the Antamoro escutcheon over the entrance (f, n. 4 above). Volume 59.4 which consists of over 500 drawings mostly by Juvarra, many arranged and labelled by him, contains only nineteen dated drawings. The earliest is the title page on folio 1 dated 9 July 1707; the latest 31 June 1714. The detail drawing on folio 108 (2) is, however, on the left half of the sheet which when the album was in its original state may have been pages away from the right half (originally number 38). A date earlier than mid-summer 1707 is, in any case, unlikely for any of the drawings in the volume.

Pierre D'Espezel, on the basis of documents in the archive of S. Girolamo, states that the chapel was complete by 21 September 1706 when the relics of St. Philip were placed in new reliquaries ("Notes historiques sur l'oeuvre et de la vie de Pierre II Le Gros.") *Gazette des Beaux Arts*, Series 6, vol. 12, 1934, 158).

The document cited by D'Espezel from the Archive of S. Girolamo della Carità (*Rubricellone*, f. 1359), is an extract of the actual Antamoro document (itself a copy?) found in Volume 182, 328. The document (see below) is undated. In Vol. 182 the document which precedes (326) the Antamoro declaration is dated 1 May 1706 and that which follows it (dated 20 August 1712 in the *Rubricellone*) is missing.

The three entries in the *Rubricellone* that precede the Antamoro document all bear the date 21 September 1706 (an authentication of relics with two copies). The following entry, a declaration concerning the relics placed in four reliquaries in the Antamoro chapel dedicated to St. Philip, does not have a date in the *Rubricellone*. The succeeding entry, an authentication of the same relics is dated 20 August 1712 (the document missing in Vol. 182).

Not illogically, D'Espezel probably associated the undated Antamoro entry in the *Rubricellone* with the previous dated entry. Without other evidence there is no reason the undated document should be associated with the earlier date. By its collocation within the *Rubricellone* and Vol. 182 the *termini post* and *ante* would be 21 September 1706 and 20 August 1712. If, indeed, the relics were placed in new reliquaries

basis of information from Hellmut Hager, suggests that Juvarra may only have received the commission after the death of Francesco Fontana on 3 July 1708.[6] If this be so, then with all the sketches differing from the executed chapel (Fig. 8), the thirteen sheets must have been prepared in the last half of 1708 prior to the initiation of construction in that year.

The four views by Juvarra of the chapel from the entrance, and the executed building, agree in showing the altarpiece extending upward into the vault area and

in September 1706, the reliquaries must pre-date construction of the chapel. The declaration does not identify the relics:

Le S.te Reliquie che sono state collocate ne'i quattro Reliquiari d'argento, che L'Ill.mo Sig.e Avvocato Antamori à fatti fare per la Sua Cappella di S. Filippo, in questa chiesa di S. Girolamo della Carità, furono ritrovate nella cammera della B.M. del P. Vincenzo Fanucci d' Gubbio dopo la sua morte, e perché vi erano inditij assai forti, che una gran parte d'esse l'havesse havute da' un altro P.re di casa chiamato il P. Giacomo Mochi, morto molti anni p.ma di lui, quale con l'occasione che hebbe di ripulire molte Reliquie di questa chiesa, se' ne' ritenne una particella di tutte, come costa da' un foglio scritto di suo carattere, quale si è ritrovato nell'istesso luogo, dove il P.re Vincenzo teneva queste Sue Reliquie. Onde per questa, et altre Cause L'Ill.mo Sig. Prelato, e Dep.ti della Chiesa volgero, che L'Erede le lasciasse, acciò ritornassero nel suo prestino luogo, come fu fatto. Dal che chiaram.e si vede essere queste SS.e Reliquie appartenenti alla med.a Chiesa, è non ad alcuna persona particolare et in fede (Signed but undated) Archivio, S. Girolamo della Carità, Vol. 182, 328.

It is certain the chapel was completed before 24 November 1710 since on that date the minutes of the deliberations of the Deputati include a request by the Abbot Rovelli that one of the deputies find out who paid for the oil being burned in the lamp *che novamente è stata posta avanti la statua di S. Filippo Nerio, nella Cappella del Sig.e Avoc.to Antamoro*. (On 12 January 1711 the follow-up notes that Antamoro said he would keep the light burning at his expense but also that he had not yet given any money to do so.) Archivio, S. Girolamo, Vol. 243, 186, no. 3, with follow-up on 190, no. 6.

If the chapel is by Juvarra it seems unlikely that it was begun and completed as early as D'Espezel suggests. Juvarra won the Concorso Clementino and received his prize on 5 May 1705. About the middle of 1705 he returned to Messina where he remained until the end of the year. He spent January and most of February 1706 in Naples with Coriolano Orsucci. He is noted in Rome once again in April, August and October 1706, but by the end of December 1706 he was in Lucca where he had prepared new plans for the completion of the Palazzo Pubblico. Juvarra was back in Rome by 3 April 1707 and he remained in or near Rome continuously until 1714 (V. Viale, ed., *Filippo Juvarra architetto e scenografo*, Messina, 1966, 44-46).

[6] *Op. cit.*, 203, n. 18.

As suggested by Hager, Francesco Fontana may have succeeded his father, Carlo Fontana, who from 1669 served as architect to the confraternity (F. Fasola, *L'opera de Hieronimo e Carlo Rainaldi*, Rome, n.d., 278).

Documents in the Archive of S. Girolamo, however, do not record any additional architect between the date Carlo Fontana was elected to replace Paolo Pichetti (21.X.1660 - Vol. 238, 83) until Mattio Sassi was appointed coadjutor with Carlo Fontana (20.VII. 1711 - Vol. 243, 216).

A drawing in the volume in Turin—59.4.100 (1)—demonstrates that Juvarra was close to Francesco Fontana. The sketch of an escutcheon bears an inscription in Juvarra's hand: *Disegno del armi che si fecero del/ funerale del Cav. Francesco Fontana / da F. Juvarra suo amatissimo discepolo* (drawing of the arms that were made at the funeral of Cav. Francesco Fontana by F. Juvarra his very loving follower).

Additionally, sheet 128 in the album by Juvarra in the Metropolitan contains a copy [?] of a letter sent by Francesco Fontana to Juvarra asking him to prepare some plans from two drawings and to color them with watercolor for a presentation later the same day to Cardinal Benedetto Pamphili.

interrupting the entablature. The drawing in the Stockholm Museum of the lateral section (Fig. 5) through the chapel differs in showing the oval contained beneath the entablature. All three drawings in the Stockholm Museum (plan, lateral, and longitudinal section) are not by Juvarra. Hager has suggested they might be by Francesco Fontana, Carlo Fontana's son and also teacher of Juvarra. Although the group displays a number of characteristics in plan and section that are similar to the chapel as constructed, there are major differences that suggest the Stöckholm group be treated first.

The plan (Fig. 4) includes a scale of ten units which allows a measurement to be made of the length and width, wall to wall.[7] Although through transposition it should be possible to calculate the height to the entablature and opening in the dome, the heights in section do not agree. The entablature and dome in the lateral section (Fig. 5) are higher than in the longitudinal section (Fig. 6), and they do not therefore yield useful dimensional comparisons with each other or with the chapel. The plan, however, measures 15.5× 21.2 *palmi*, close to that of the chapel today, c. 15× 23 *palmi*.[8]

The three drawings represent no more than a preliminary project as may be verified by noting in the longitudinal section the lack of connection between the dome

7 Stockholm, National Museum, THC 1961 (plan), 1958 (lateral section), and 1962 (longitudinal section). The ten-unit scale in the plan, when presumed to be Roman *palmi*, yields dimensions similar to those in the chapel as constructed, *i.e.*, 15.5 × 21.2 *palmi* as opposed to scaled dimensions from fig. XIV in Boscarino (3.2 × 5.10 m or 14.34 × 22.85 *palmi*) and as stated by Battaglia, 33 (3.23 × 5.15 m, or 14.47 × × 23.1 *palmi*).

8 For example, while the plan scales close to the present measurement of the chapel (see previous note) the height of the entablature above the pavement in the lateral section scales 4.53 m (if the width of the chapel is assumed to be that shown in the plan) while the same dimension in the longitudinal section scales 2.80 m (again assuming the length of the chapel in section to be the same as in the plan). That dimension in the chapel today measures 3.60 m. The height of the dome above the pavement at the oculus scaled in the lateral section is 5.62 m, while the same dimension in the longitudinal section scales 4.55 m (assuming in both cases the same conditions as previously)—7.28 m today.

In addition to dimensions scaled from the plan drawn and published by Boscarino, the measurements used in this and the following notes were made by Professor Tod Marder who very generously spent a portion of his leave in Rome in the spring of 1978 measuring portions of the chapel.

The main order		360 cm
entablature	54	
capitals	38	
shafts (inc. base)	240	
plinth	28	
Height from pavement to soffit of oval frame		523
Height from pavement to opening in dome		c. 728
Height to head of lateral doors		202
Height of pedestal of statue above altar table		75
Height of altar gradine		25
Height of top of tabernacle		41
Height of altar above steps		99
Height of each step (2) to altar		11

vault and arches at the entrance and altar walls. Also, the central ribs in the longitudinal section do not relate to the pilasters below. The altar wall also lacks any indication of altar or altarpiece.

In plan, the alternate treatment of the corner columns (one in the corner, the other shifted along the wall and both directed at different angles), the uncertain meaning of the treatment of the wall area above and behind the altar (an opening through the wall to admit light or a recess in the wall for an altarpiece?), and the omission of the juncture of the exterior wall of the chapel with the wall of the church to the left of the entrance, all support a reading as a preliminary design.[9]

Similarities found in the drawings in Stockholm to the executed design (Fig. 9) are also present. For example, in the executed design the plan contains: a) corner columns placed diagonally, b) pilasters on the long walls flanking the centrally placed door, c) a doorway with panel above placed in a recess with angled reveals, d) a reverse curve balustrade at the entrance, e) an altar with concave frontal, f) two oval steps up to the altar and, g) steps inset in plan in front of the altar. The sections show when compared with the building (Figs. 8, 10, 11, and 12): a) columns and pilasters on low plinths, b) panels on wall between pilasters and columns, c) *St. Philip* standing on a pedestal with his arms extended and accompanied by two putti set within an oval—a relief or fully-round sculpture, d) double guilloche reveal in oval, e) cherubim above the oval, f) volutes flanking the altar, g) flaming heart on the altar frontal, h) foliate entablature, i) ribs, lined with foliage, terminating in volutes over the columns, j) above the pilasters similar ribs that do not end in volutes, and k) a lantern.

In the Stockholm group in contrast to the chapel as executed, the oval does not rupture the entablature. There are additional significant differences between the two. A few of the differences have been noted above in outlining the preliminary state of the project. The drawings also show: a) nondirectional rather than diagonally placed plinths under the columns, b) Corinthian capitals rather than Composite,

[9] It could be asked whether the drawings in Stockholm might not have been drawn after the chapel was completed by someone who had faulty recollection. That eventuality seems unlikely due to the different proportions and heights in the columns, dome, and lantern, as well as the lack of correspondence between plan and section, and between lateral and longitudinal section. Also indicative of a preliminary state is the lack of connection between the dome vault and the arches at the entrance and apse.

A reconstruction rather than a preliminary design (in which differences can be accounted for due to changes in the idea as it is drawn and studied) would, most likely, at least agree dimensionally as it was laid out in its various parts.

c) an entablature without architrave, d) no coffering between the pairs of ribs in the dome, and e) no relief sculpture in lateral panels in the dome.

The drawings in Stockholm are paradoxical in that, in different aspects, they are both further removed, and yet closer, to the executed project than the *primo pensiero* of Juvarra in the Metropolitan Museum. Before attempting to understand the paradox posed by the drawings in Stockholm, it will be useful to examine the principal drawings by Juvarra for the chapel and the altarpiece to see how the design for the altarpiece changed in its stages from fully-round to relief sculpture or painting, and back to free-standing sculpture.

I *The Drawings for the Chapel*

If we take Juvarra at his word and accept the *primo pensiero* (Fig. 1) as an initial idea, he began with an oval frame the full width of the chapel and extending well up into the vault, enclosing the aureole behind *St. Philip*. The oval is outlined by a moulding covered with a repetitive small transverse oval pattern.[10] A reveal in depth may be indicated at the left edge of the oval. The wall below the oval contains a recessed panel. The corner of the chapel to the left of the oval appears to be curved, perhaps also on the right, but no pilaster or column is shown. There are panels above lateral doors and a continuous entablature above the panels. The wall above the door bay extends as a lunette up into the vault area under an arch. The altar steps appear to extend beyond the lateral doors into the space of the chapel.

The steps of the altar are oval in plan with salient rectangular sections responding to the projecting ends of the altar on either side. In plan the altar is decidedly concave, enlarged at the top by consoles; the flaming heart of St. Philip, and crossed sprays or branches, are displayed in the center of the frontal. The gradine appears to conform to the plan of the altar but bays forward at its center to form the base of the pedestal under the kneeling saint. (The pose of the saint may possibly be taken from the painting by Guido Reni (1615) formerly in the chapel of St. Philip Neri in S. M. in Vallicella.) The pedestal may also contain a tabernacle.

10 Assuming the width of the chapel today (3.20 m) to be that shown in the *primo pensiero*, the width of the oval in the drawing when scaled is roughly 66% wider—2.6 m versus the 1.72 m of the chapel today (scaled from the plan found in Boscarino, *op. cit.*, fig. XIV).

A pair of smooth ribs spring from the thin entablature at either side of the oval and rise to a lobed oculus where they terminate in what may be tight volutes. Trapezoidal coffers with rosettes fill the area between the ribs, the oval, the lateral arches and the oculus. Cherubim peek out of the oculus, hover along the ribs, oval frame, and pedestal, at the left of which one exhibits an appropriate didactic text.

The chapel is shown lighted from the left with shadows in brown wash at the lateral doors, on the altar and steps, beneath the clouds atop the pedestal on the altar, within the oval on the left—outside it on the right—and on the right side of *St. Philip* and all the cherubim. At the oculus, light appears to be entering from above, perhaps from the place toward which *St. Philip* directs his gaze.

The ribs, coffering, oculus, oval, panels above the lateral doors, concave altar, pedestal, free-standing figure of *St. Philip*, and cherubim of the executed chapel (Fig. 8) are present in the initial sketch.

The drawing in Madrid,[11] a small ink sketch (Fig. 3)—kindly pointed out to me by Jennifer Montagu who discovered and identified it—contains a perspective of the chapel from the entrance and an elevation of the interior face to the entrance wall.[12] Both are shown lighted from the left. A number of similarities with the *primo pensiero* suggest it be treated next in the sequence.

The plan of the steps and altar, the pedestal with kneeling saint, the oval aureole, the lunettes above the lateral doors, the ribs and coffering in the vault, and the cherubim—in the oculus, on the oval frame and beneath *St. Philip*—are similar to the *primo pensiero*. The oval is, however, smaller than in the *primo pensiero*, leaving space for a pilaster or column to either side (which may be indicated) while the oculus appears to be wider than the oval below. Above the lateral doors and under the entablature there are indications of a decorative motif or sculptural group not seen in the *primo pensiero*, which is more elaborate than in any of the drawings or in the chapel as executed.

The other sketch on the sheet indicates Juvarra considered making the entrance to the chapel through a doorway the size of the lateral doors rather than the taller

11 Madrid, Biblioteca Nacional, No. 8182. Pen, brown ink. 9.4 × 10.75 cm. Mentioned but not reproduced in R. Enggass, *Early Eighteenth-Century Sculpture in Rome*, University Park/London, 1976, Text, 140.

12 The proportions of the altar wall, width to height (to soffit of oval), remain fairly constant in all four drawings. Approximate ratios are as follows:

Primo pensiero	1:1.53
Madrid drawing	1:1.45
Secondo pensiero	1:1.49
Turin drawing	1:1.50
Chapel today	1:1.64 (from photograph)

arch that is there today. The interior face shows the door crowned by a massive open segmental pediment (probably with Antamoro arms in the center) and above, on a shouldered tablet (with inscription?), a sculptural group that extends upwards across the entablature into a lunette which appears to be glazed. Were it not for Juvarra's statement, the richer, more elaborate scheme for the lateral overdoors and entrance wall in the Madrid drawing might suggest it preceded the *primo pensiero*.

The angled corner columns of the executed project appear in the *secondo pensiero* (Fig. 2), the only view of the chapel by Juvarra which includes a plan. Most notably absent is the oval formerly behind *St. Philip* which has now been replaced by an arched panel extending from altar height through the entablature into the vault ending in a semicircular arch.[13] The Corinthian columns are set on low plinths flanking the altar and have pilasters behind them at either side of the altarpiece. Smooth ribs rise from the columns and disappear into the cloud mass at the oculus. The entablature seems still to be thin. The lunettes over the lateral doors have been eliminated and replaced by panels that descend to the entablature. Urns or busts surmount the cornice over the lateral doors. If the doors are the same height as in the *primo pensiero* and the drawing in Madrid, then the *secondo pensiero* shows an entablature that has been lowered leaving less space for the panels over the doors.[14]

The altar in plan has changed little from the two previous drawings and the steps seem to have the same form in plan. The altar frontal contains a figurative relief displacing the flaming heart which has risen to the center of a cloud-encircled oculus smaller than in the drawing in Madrid. The connection between the saint and the altar is uncertain. The lighting is handled as in the two previous drawings, but the lack of shadow on the altar suggests the figure of the saint may not be fully in the round, but in relief or painted. The pedestal has been eliminated, and *St.*

13 A roughly scaled dimension from the pavement to the soffit of the arch is 4.77 m, lower than the similarly scaled height of the *primo pensiero* (4.90 m) and the Turin drawing (4.8 m), but taller than in the Madrid drawing (4.64 m). The same dimension in the chapel today scales 5.23 m.

14 If the height to the soffit of the head of the lateral doors in each drawing is assumed to be the same and is taken to be one unit, then the top of the entablature in each of the drawings scales to the following ratios (averaging left and right):

Primo pensiero	c. 1:2.16
Madrid drawing	c. 1:2.15
Secondo pensiero	c. 1:1.79
Turin drawing	c. 1:1.68
Chapel today	1:1.78
In the longitudinal section in Stockholm, the ratio of door height to top of entablature	1:1.76

Philip appears to be partly supported by cherubim and partly by a dense cloud mass beneath him that extends to the altar gradine.

The plan sketched below shows space for the columns tucked in quarter-circle niches in the corners but little space for the altarpiece. The columns are not attached to the altar or steps and the altar is attached only to the wall behind. The reveal of the frame of the altarpiece is shown bevelled on the left and with a concave curve on the right. The resultant recessed space is too shallow for a free-standing sculpture, though the shallow oval at the rear of the altar may suggest the base of a relief sculpture, or Juvarra may have considered a painted altarpiece at this stage.[15] In the latter case, the aureole lightly sketched in pencil could be an afterthought, or might indicate its intended depiction on a painted surface.

The drawing closest to the definitive project is the perspective in the Biblioteca Nazionale in Turin (Fig. 7). The oval frame, reduced in size, with what is probably a free-standing figure on a pedestal, reappears. The figure within the frame is larger than in the three previous drawings and approximates the proportions of figure to frame of the executed sculpture. The columns, only lightly sketched, appear to be shorter and the entablature lower than in the *secondo pensiero.*[16] Ribs, vault, oculus, and the shape of the penetration above the oval are firmer. A sculptural relief, in the vault segment above the entablature over the lateral door on the left, makes its first appearance.

The entablature in its final, full depth may be indicated at the left, adjacent to the oval frame. The volutes, that join the lower section of the oval frame to the altar and flank the pedestal for *St. Philip*, are indicated above the altar gradine which has itself been heightened to approximately the executed state. The salient extremities of the altar steps are no longer so pronounced. The lines lightly sketched at the center of the altar gradine may be intended to show the cresting of the cornice of the gradine. As executed, it forms a scrolled pediment over the tabernacle which

15 If the width of the chapel shown in the plan is taken to be 3.2 m as it is today (Boscarino, *op. cit.*, fig. XIV, scaled dimension), then the depth of the reveal for the relief/painting is 16.8 cms (c. 6 5/8 in.) or, if the width of the half-oval is included, 30 cms overall (c. 11 7/8 in.).

16 See note 14. The entablature in the *secondo pensiero* is about 17% lower relative to the head of the lateral door as shown in both the *primo pensiero* and the drawing in Madrid.

If a comparison is made of the size of the figure relative to, say, the height of the altar table (presumed constant) in all four drawings, the resulting ratios are as follows:

Primo pensiero (kneeling)	1:1.62
Madrid drawing (kneeling)	1:2.40
Secondo pensiero (kneeling?)	1:1.92
Turin drawing (pose uncertain)	1:3.00
Chapel today (from photograph)	c. 1:1.77
In the lateral section in the Stockholm group, the ratio of altar height to the standing figure height is:	1:1.69

is set within the gradine. At the bottom of the sheet on the left, the position of the angled column in the left corner at the entrance wall is seen.

The sketch does not, however, show the volutes and plinth at the base of the ribs above the columns, and the altar table spreads more boldly than in execution.

If this sequence for the four drawings be admitted, then Juvarra's idea for the altarpiece began most likely as a fully-round sculpture set in a recessed oval frame. Both the *primo pensiero* and the drawing in Madrid support this reading. In the *secondo pensiero*, the space for the altarpiece became shallow, containing a more traditional arched rectangle suitable for a relief or painting. In the drawing in Turin and in the chapel as built, Juvarra returned to the first idea, to a free-standing sculpture within an oval frame.

On the other hand, the architectural enclosure appears to alternate between largely planal surfaces subordinate to the altar wall and altarpiece (*primo* and *secondo pensiero*) and bold, vigorous articulation (the drawings in Madrid and Turin and the executed project). Or, if the drawing in Madrid is placed earlier than the *primo pensiero*, the sequence would then parallel that of the altarpiece from a more sculptural beginning to a series of more restrained planal studies to return to the bold architecture of the executed project. In either alternative, the changes made by Juvarra as the design evolved cannot be described as linear.

* * *

If we now return to consider the drawings in Stockholm and assume them, as did Preimesberger, to represent a design prepared prior to Juvarra's receiving the commission (a design known to him), we find Juvarra in the *primo pensiero* accepting some elements from them and rejecting others. It is of course possible, should the drawings be by Francesco Fontana, that Juvarra may have discussed the project with him. A sheet in the Juvarra volume in the Metropolitan Museum indicates Juvarra did drawings for Francesco. In the Juvarra volume in Turin Juvarra calls himself Francesco's very loving follower. Juvarra adopted the oval enclosing a free-standing (or relief) sculpture, a ribbed dome, and a concave altar set upon oval steps. Conversely, he interrupted the entablature with the oval frame, rejected the corner column as well as the volutes at the base of the ribs only to return to them both in the final scheme. Juvarra began by obliterating or negating virtually all of his master's design (if it be by Francesco Fontana), and ended by regenerating and integrating many of Fontana's ideas as they became absorbed, digested and transformed in the successive changes of the design.

The sequence of drawings raises additional problems—chief among them, the relation between Legros and Juvarra. If the drawings indicate a development of the altarpiece from sculpture to painting (or possibly relief sculpture) and back to sculpture, then Legros only became involved after the design was settled. If so, the attitude or pose of the saint as shown in the drawing in Stockholm, the *primo pensiero*, and the executed figure seems to derive from the architect and not from Legros.

To be sure, Juvarra and the unknown draftsman of the group in Stockholm had most likely studied the poses of *St. Ignatius* and *S. Luigi Gonzaga* by Legros and were, in any case, representing poses that would have been familiar to any sculptor. Even so, in this case at least, the younger architect apparently had some influence in the selection of the pose, and perhaps, by recommendation, even in the selection of the sculptor.[17]

More information about the collaboration of Juvarra and Legros might help to clarify the purpose of several drawings in the Metropolitan album for some of the statues of the Lateran apostles.[18] Work on these statues was under way in the same years as the chapel.[19] Are these drawings ideas of Juvarra for the apostles, or drawings after designs by others? None of them is precisely like the statues in place, and we know the painter Carlo Maratti supplied drawings for the statues.[20] Did the young Juvarra also seek to influence the sculptural idea of some of the pieces? Two of the apostles were done by Legros—*St. Thomas* and *St. Bartholomew*, but the drawings by Juvarra are not related to the statues executed by Legros.

II *The Chapel and the Altarpiece*

Preimesberger took the Stockholm drawings to be pre-Juvarra and, therefore earlier than the final version in the Biblioteca Nazionale in Turin and discussed the development of the design in Juvarra's hands. Although primarily interested

[17] If this be so, then a reasonable *terminus post quem* for the figure of *St. Philip* would be 1708–09 rather than the "sometime between 1703 and 1710" reported by Enggass *op. cit.*, Text, 140, on the basis of documents published by P. D'Espezel, "Notes historiques sur l'oeuvre et la vie de Pierre II Le Gros," *GBA*, XII [1934].

For a document signalling completion of the statue before 24.XI.1710 see footnote 5.

[18] Drawings that appear to be related to the Apostles in the Lateran are found on sheets 240, 241, and 242 in the album in the Metropolitan Museum.

[19] The sculptural program was worked upon for 15 years. See R. Enggass, *op. cit.*, Text, 39.

[20] Enggass, *op. cit.*, Text, 39.

in Legros sculpture, Preimesberger also discussed Juvarra's architecture, citing parallels and sources for altars flanked by columns, oval altarpieces, sculptural groups, and back-lighting. He left open the question of possible collaboration between Juvarra and Legros as to the pose and gesture of *St. Philip* and the accompanying putti.[21]

Legros was 12 years senior to Juvarra and had an established reputation, having already completed among his many commissions the sculpture for the *S. Luigi Gonzaga* altar (1699) in S. Ignazio: the large silver statue of *St. Ignatius* and the marble group to the right of the altar in the left transept of the Gesù (1699); *St. Francis Xavier* in S. Apollinare (c. 1702); *St. Stanislas Kostka* on his deathbed in S. Andrea al Quirinale (1704); the *Tobit* relief in the Monte di Pietà (1705); and the standing figure of *St. Dominic* in the apse of St. Peter's (1706).[22] He may also have already begun the *Monument to Gregory XV* in S. Ignazio before 1709.[23] Although Juvarra had won first prize in the Concorso Clementino two years earlier,[24] he had built nothing in Rome and only the *coretto* of S. Gregorio in Messina.[25]

On the basis of the Stockholm and the Turin drawings, Preimesberger saw six different elements as potential sources of contribution to the Juvarra design: a) the special relation between altar, flanking columns, and tabernacle; b) the ribbed vault;

21 Preimesberger, *op. cit.* A terracotta *bozzetto* of *St. Philip* by Legros reproduced by Preimesberger (fig. 1) is preserved in the Museum of the Palazzo Venezia in Rome.

22 For reproductions of works by Legros, see R. Enggass, *op. cit.*, Plates, as follows:

S. Ignazio, *S. Luigi Gonzaga*	pl. 100
Gesù, *St. Ignatius*	pl. 96
Gesù, *Religion and Heresy*	pl. 93
S. Apollinare, *St. Francis Xavier*	pl. 110
S. Andrea, *St. Stanislas Kostka*	pl. 114
Monte di Pietà, *Tobit*	pl. 117
St. Peter's, *St. Dominic*	pl. 115
S. Ignazio, *Mon. Gregory XV*	pl. 143

23 Enggass, *op. cit.*, Text, 144 on the basis of new evidence suggests the dates for the tomb and its sculpture to be 1709–c. 1713, but also states that "an entry of 13 September 1709 [by] Valesco reports that work on the tomb is already well under way."

24 Anonymous, "Vita del cavaliere don Filippo Juvarra Abbate di Selve e Primo architetto di S. M. di Sardegna," published by Adamo Rossi in *Giornale di erudizione artistico*, Perugia, 1874; republished recently in V. Viale (ed.), *Filippo Juvarra architetto e scenografo*, Messina, 1966, 22-30; as well as in L. Rovere, V. Viale, and A. E. Brinckmann, *Filippo Juvarra*, Turin, 1937, 22-29. The account of Juvarra's winning the Concorso Clementino is found on 23-24 of both the publications of 1966 and 1937.

25 Anonymous Life, *op. cit.* [1966], 22. There are four sheets with drawings by Juvarra for S. Gregorio in Messina in the Juvarra album in the Metropolitan Museum. Three sheets (nos. 127, 196/197, and 194/199) contain drawings for a *coretto* constructed above the main entrance and one sheet (no. 192) shows four variants for transept altars.

The anonymous life states that after "havendo adornato le finestre e la chiesa di San Gregorio di Messina..." (having embellished the windows and the church of San Gregorio in Messina), one of the nuns, the sister of Monsignor Ruffo, dispatched Juvarra to Rome, to her brother, the Maestro di Camera of Pope Clement XI.

c) the oval altarpiece; d) the use of free-standing sculpture as an altarpiece; e) an oval window behind a tabernacle group; and f) angels and putti supporting an altarpiece. In examining these six elements, he cites completed designs or projects by Carlo Fontana, Andrea Pozzo, GianLorenzo Bernini, and G. A. De Rossi (the Lancelotti chapel in S. Giovanni in Laterano with its ribbed and penetrated vault completed in the 1690's),[26] known to Juvarra which Preimesberger feels may have contributed to the design. He gives considerable weight to Carlo Fontana's work as a source.

Myers, discussing the new drawings in the Metropolitan album,[27] finds that they indicate a greater interest in Bernini than in Fontana. She feels, therefore, too much weight is given by Preimesberger to Fontana's contribution to the design. Additionally, she cites Bernini's transparent glory behind the *Cathedra Petri* in St. Peter's as a possible contributory element, as well as the high altars in S. Tommaso at Castel Gandolfo and S. Andrea al Quirinale, and the chapels in S. Isidoro (Silva—Fig. 13) and S. Lorenzo in Lucina (Fonseca—Fig. 14)—all by Bernini.[28]

The Madrid drawing—perhaps the earliest of them all by my reckoning—makes it clear that Juvarra's first architectural idea contained many elements present in the Fonseca chapel (Fig. 14) and confirms his interest in Bernini. In the Madrid drawing and the Fonseca chapel there are ribbed coffered vaults with oculi, angels and putti. In addition, in the Fonseca chapel, the vaults, modified stilted sail vaults, descend to the mid-point of an oval altarpiece. Juvarra transformed the oval of the Fonseca chapel from an applied frame for a painted altarpiece held aloft by angels and putti into a part of the architecture itself. In his design, the oval penetrated the wall and the putti entered the frame to accompany the free-standing figure. The oval increased in importance and size as it was integrated with the altar below. The transition used by Juvarra from flanking volutes to oval frame recalls also similar volutes of Borromini in the Pamphili Gallery or in S. M. dei Sette Dolori.[29]

26 Reproduced in G. Spagnesi, *Giovanni De Rossi architetto romano*, Rome, 1964: plan, 102; vault, pls. 45 and 46. Spagnesi argues that De Rossi rehabilitated the chapel c. 1650 after it had been damaged in Borromini's reconstruction of the nave of the basilica.

27 Myers, *op. cit.*, 33.

28 The *Cathedra Petri* in St. Peter's, the main altar of the church of S. Tommaso at Castel Gandolfo, and a drawing for the Fonseca chapel in S. Lorenzo in Lucina are reproduced in R. Wittkower, *Gian Lorenzo Bernini, The Sculptor of the Roman Baroque*, 2nd ed., London, 1966, pl. 93, fig. 93, and fig. 91 respectively. For the Fonseca chapel see also our Fig. 14.

For the main altar in S. Andrea al Quirinale see R. Wittkower, *Art and Architecture in Italy, 1600–1750*, 2nd ed., Harmondsworth/Baltimore, 1965, pl. 61 (B).

For the Silva chapel in S. Isidoro see R. Pane, *Bernini architetto*, Venice, 1953, pls. 126 and 127.

29 For example, 1) the volutes flanking the Pam-

The two pairs of columns set on diagonals that intersect at two different centers along the longitudinal axis also recall Borromini's practice. Portoghesi and Boscarino are correct in emphasizing Juvarra's fusion here in his first Roman work of Berninesque and Borrominesque ideas.[30]

Juvarra's eventual selection of free-standing sculpture instead of a painted altarpiece for the chapel perhaps relates to his known interest in the work of Bernini and Andrea Pozzo. The Anonymous Life mentions that Juvarra bought Pozzo's publication.[31] In this period he drew a number of Bernini's works in Rome, Castel Gandolfo and Ariccia. The albums in the Metropolitan Museum and in the Tournon collection in Turin also contain drawings of Pozzo's work in Rome—two drawings after the left transept altar of the Gesù.[32]

Completed in 1698, only a decade before the Antamoro Chapel, the altar of the Gesù contained as an altarpiece a cast silver statue of *St. Ignatius* set in a richly decorated niche. Indeed, the gesture of the arms of *St. Ignatius* on the altar was repeated in the Madrid and Stockholm drawings, although the drawing in Madrid may show the saint kneeling, following more closely the pose depicted in one of the projects for the altar reproduced in Pozzo's *Trattato* (II, 65).

The pose shown in the *secondo pensiero* in the Metropolitan album could relate to yet another of Pozzo's designs, that for the relief by Legros on the altar of *S. Luigi Gonzaga* in the church of S. Ignazio in which the saint is shown with hands crossed on his breast, his head tilted, and his gaze directed to the left.[33] In both the Juvarra sketch and the Legros relief the saint is supported by angels and putti at the sides and below.

phili arms above the window on the interior of the end wall of the Pamphili gallery facing Piazza Navona; 2) the volutes terminating the ends of the segmental pediment (and flanking the spread palm) in the central bay on the *piano nobile* of the facade of the Oratorio dei Filippini; and 3) the arched entablature and split architrave over the entrance to the chapel of S. M. dei Sette Dolori which ends in tight volutes.

30 Four of Borromini's double-ended buildings come to mind: S. Carlo alle Quattro Fontane (reproduced in P. Portoghesi, *Roma Barocca*, Rome, 1966, pl. 113); the chapel of the Propaganda Fide (*Ibid.*, pl. 156); the Oratorio of the Filippini (P. Portoghesi, *The Rome of Borromini: Architecture as Language*, New York, 1968, pl. XXXII and 51); and the church of S. Maria dei Sette Dolori (*Ibid.*, 73 and 74).

For the relation of Juvarra to Bernini and Borromini see: Portoghesi, *Roma Barocca*, Rome, 1966, 418; S. Boscarino, *Juvarra architetto*, Rome, 1973, 148-153.

31 Anonymous Life, *op. cit.*, 22.

32 Sheet 155 in the album in the Metropolitan shows the escutcheon of the Gesuit order placed above the niche which contains the statue of *St. Ignatius* in the left transept. Sheet 111 in the album by Juvarra in the Tournon Collection depicts the plaque above the rectangular relief over the main altar to *St. Ignatius.*

33 Reproduced in Enggass, *op. cit.*, pls. 99 and 100.

Juvarra's contribution in the Antamoro Chapel is, perhaps, the combination or integration of four of these elements: the back-lighted transparent aureole; the partially silhouetted sculpture seen against the aureole; columns set on low plinths that order the chapel and flank the altar; and a choice of a limited-hue range for the marbles that sheathe the chapel.

An aureole lighted from behind had been used above the *Cathedra Petri* but not behind a free-standing figure. At St. Peter's the lighted aureole is a protagonist with its colored light depicting the Holy Spirit descending to the chair and illuminating its occupant. In the Antamoro Chapel the back-lighted aureole is equally the Holy Spirit, probably an intended reference to St. Peter's and the Holy Spirit depicted there, as well as to that moment in St. Philip's life when he, still a layman, was visited by the Holy Spirit who came, we are told, as a visible globe of fire.[34] The glowing light that envelops him each sunny afternoon recreates not only his apotheosis (or a beatific vision) but also the transforming moment of his initial visitation by the Holy Spirit.

Columns flanking an altar (or columns that are viewed in conjunction with an altar) on low plinths resting on the pavement, are unusual. The traditional relationship of columns to altar in 17th century Rome placed flanking columns on pedestals or socles the height of the altar table. Columns on low plinths flanking the altar are usually found only when the main order of columns or pilasters of the church was continued as the main ordering element of the chapel. One example would be the columns in Borromini's S. Carlino; another, S. Marta of Carlo Fontana;[35] or, though placed at a distance, juxtaposed visually with the altar in Bernini's S. Andrea al Quirinale. (The altar in S. Andrea al Quirinale is remarkable in lacking either columns or pilasters flanking the frame of the altarpiece which appears, therefore, unaffixed and suspended by the supporting angels.)

The back-lighted aureole at St. Peter's sits above an altar which is flanked by columns that rise from low plinths. Is it possible Juvarra (and the draftsman of the drawings in Stockholm) wished here also to recall that altar (where the Holy Spirit is shown most vividly) to intensify the notion of the visitation of the Spirit to St. Philip? In any case, the use of altar columns on low plinths did not escape notice and very shortly thereafter Nicola Michetti, another Fontana pupil, used them in

34 Giuseppe De Libero, *S. Girolamo della Carità*, Rome, 1962, 19.

35 Reproduced in H. Hager, "L'intervento di Carlo Fontana per le chiese dei monasteri di Santa Marta e Santa Margherita in Trastevere," *Commentari*, XXV [1974], fig. 5, 229.

the Rospigliosi Chapel in S. Francesco a Ripa begun in 1710. Michetti's model for the chapel shows the traditional arrangement, derived probably from Pozzo's altar of *S. Luigi Gonzaga*. The change to columns on low plinths may be due to Michetti's having seen the Antamoro Chapel underway in 1708 or completed in 1710.[36]

The effect achieved by eliminating the socle under the columns is certainly that of greater association by the viewer with the altar and with the chapel as a whole—an increased intimacy belied, perhaps, by the luxury of the marbles employed. Were it not for the materials one might be tempted to say that the more accessible arrangement was a comment on St. Philip's noted humility and charity, but there is no supporting evidence for such a supposition.

For back-lighting, Juvarra probably knew, and may have considered, Carlo Fontana's projects for the baptistry of St. Peter's.[37] In one of these projects (e.g., Windsor 9916—Fig. 15—first cited in this regard by Preimesberger), a lunette window above the cornice of the secondary order of the baptistry is repeated mirror fashion below forming an oval window against which is silhouetted the upper portion of a tall tabernacle-like cover for the baptismal font.

Tabernacles and other altar terminations placed in a framed opening between chancel and retrochoir and intended to be seen as objects in a defined space with a lighted area behind are numerous from Palladio's time in northern Italy but less frequently seen in Rome. One example known to Juvarra, by G. A. De Rossi (completed by the mid-1690's), is in the church of S. Francesco di Paola (Fig. 16).[38] (Juvarra drew four projects for the altar of the chapel dedicated to S. Giuseppe—the first on the left upon entering).[39]

Pozzo's interest in transparency, enframement, and dramatic focus is evident in his publication and in his realized work, which includes a number of altar tabernacle *baldacchini* which provide a spatial enclosure for a free-standing sculpture as well as provide a modulating element above the altar and between altar and retrochoir.

Bernini's *Baldacchino* in St. Peter's and the *Cathedra* seen through it from the nave

36 Reproduced in E. Lavagnino, G. R. Ansaldi, and L. Salerno, *Altari Barocchi in Roma*, Rome, 1959; S. Francesco a Ripa, Cappella Rospigliosi Pallavicini, model, pl. 66 (201), chapel pl. 67 (203).

37 The albums of drawings by Carlo Fontana in the Royal Collection of Windsor are now published in Allan Braham and Hellmut Hager, *Carlo Fontana*, London, 1977.

38 A plan and section through the nave of S. Francesco di Paola is reproduced in F. Fasolo, *L'Opera di Hieronimo e Carlo Rainaldi*, Rome, n.d., figs. 13 (plan) and 14 (section). The altar may be seen in the section. A photograph of this altar was first reproduced in G. Spagnesi, *Giovanni Antonio de Rossi*, Rome, 1964, fig. on 203.

39 Juvarra's drawings for the altar are in the album in the Metropolitan Museum on sheets 203, 204, 209, and 217.

may have contributed to the development of the chapel by suggesting columns flanking an oval altarpiece. Emphasis on visual juxtapositions and spatial sequences of this kind are frequent in Bernini's work. The main altarpiece in the apse of S. Andrea al Quirinale is framed by a pair of free-standing columns. *St. Teresa* in the Cappella Cornaro in S. M. della Vittoria, the *Beata Ludovica Albertoni* in the Cappella Altieri in S. Francesco a Ripa, and *St. Francis* in the Cappella Raimondi in S. Pietro in Montorio are all conceived to be seen with differing dramatic lighting, through layers of space intended to enhance, through sequential spatial definition, the sacral quality of the image.[40] The view of the Antamoro Chapel from the entrance suggests an intentionally similar measured spatial sequence (Fig. 8).

The adjacent hues selected for the marbles achieve a remarkable unity. Throughout most of the 17th century in Rome, when chapels were sheathed in colored marbles, it was normal to have the major horizontals of architrave and cornice in the entablature of the altar aedicula (and in some cases the entablature of the walls) carved in white marble—probably because of the ease with which it could be carved. In addition, mouldings surrounding panels of more precious and often contrastingly hued colored marble usually were of white marble. In the 17th century capitals and bases of columns were normally either white marble or gilded. Bernini's Cornaro Chapel in S. M. della Vittoria (1647), Cafa's main altar in S. Caterina a Magnanapoli (before 1674), and Carlo Rainaldi's main altar in Gesù and Maria (1690) are examples of the norm.[41]

Towards the end of the century the most luxurious altars and chapels—the Cibo Chapel in S. M. del Popolo by Carlo Fontana (1687), the altars of *S. Luigi Gonzaga* in S. Ignazio and *S. Ignazio* in the Gesù both by Pozzo (1699), and the S. Cecilia Chapel in S. Carlo ai Catinari by Gherardi (1700),—began to use colored marbles for the architrave and cornice (light colored *fior di pesca* or *porta santa* in the chapels by Gherardi and Fontana but a dark rich *verde antico* and a dusky rose (*pavonazetto*?) in the Pozzo chapels.[42] The chapels by Fontana and Gherardi retained white marble

40 Reproduced as follows: S. Andrea al Quirinale (R. Wittkower, *Art and Architecture in Italy 1600–1750*, 2nd ed., Harmondsworth/Baltimore, 1965, pl. 61 [B]); Cornaro chapel, S. M. della Vittoria (*Ibid.*, pl. 50); Altieri chapel, S. Francesco a Ripa (*Ibid.*, pl. 59 [A]); Raimondi chapel, S. Pietro in Montorio (R. Wittkower, *Gian Lorenzo Bernini, The Sculptor of the Italian Baroque*, London, 1955, fig. 55).

41 Reproduced in color in E. Lavagnino, G. R. Ansaldi, and L. Salerno, *Altari Barocchi in Roma*, Rome, 1959; Cappella Cornaro, pl. 26 (83); S. Caterina a Magnanapoli, main altar, pl. 43 (136); Gesù e Maria, main altar, pl. 49 (151).

42 Reproduced in *ibid.*, S. Maria del Popolo, Cappella Cibo, pl. 51 (159); S. Ignazio, altar of *S. Luigi Gonzaga*, pl. 60 (185); SS. Nome di Gesù, altar of *St. Ignatius*, pl. 56 (171); S. Carlo ai Catinari, Cappella di S. Cecilia, pl. 54 (166).

for capitals and bases while in both chapels by Pozzo they are gilded. For Pozzo, white marble was used exclusively for sculpture.

Ten years later than the Antamoro Chapel, when the main altar of S. Agnese in Piazza Navona was begun in 1720, white marble was also used only for sculpture.[43] The entablature follows the color scheme of Pozzo in the church of S. Ignazio. In 1710, immediately after the Antamoro Chapel was completed, in the Rospigliosi chapel Michetti used a Fontanesque *fior di pesca* for the entablature and gilded the capitals and bases of the columns.[44] The evidence indicates a design change concerning altar colors occurred around the turn of the century or just before.

In the Antamoro Chapel in 1708, Juvarra followed closely Pozzo's achievement of the late 1690's but is, I believe, coloristically less assertive than Pozzo, and searches for a more integrated whole.[45] White is used only for marble and stucco sculpture and the column capitals and bases. The warmest colors (yellows and oranges) are in the glass of the aureole and the marble of the altar (which is outlined in *giallo antico*). The walls, entablature, and gilded accents all appear to be of a lower value and in adjacent hue ranges. Only the altar steps, gradine, and over-door panels and mouldings are in a contrasting, but still low-value green hue (which emphasizes the cross axis and lateral doors).

The restraint exercised in the range of hues chosen tends, I believe, to unify the chapel coloristically (even though onyx, jasper, and other precious marbles are used) to a greater degree than in chapels and altars by Pozzo, Gherardi, or Fontana. The restrained hues lend greater emphasis to the oval aureole and *St. Philip*, the focus of the chapel. If Legros was aware of what Juvarra was attempting, theirs must have been a very happy collaboration.

* * *

The sequence of drawings for the Antamoro Chapel and the drawings in Stockholm also suggest reconsideration of our notions of artistic development of an idea. Insofar as the altarpiece is concerned, Juvarra's own labelling of two of the drawings as " first " and " second " ideas when seen in relationship to the finished altar indicate a development that oscillated between free-standing sculpture and a painted surface.

The architecture of the chapel apparently also oscillated between the planal and

43 Reproduced in color in *ibid.*; S. Agnese in Piazza Navona, main altar, pl. 47 (143).

44 Reproduced in color in *ibid.*; S. Francesco a Ripa, Cappella Rospigliosi Pallavicini, pl. 67 (203).

45 Reproduced in color in *ibid.*; S. Girolamo della Carità, Cappella Antamoro, pl. 63 (195).

the highly articulated. The ordering of the chapel began with a planal wall enclosure (*primo pensiero*). The wall surface became richer and more plastic in the Madrid sketch, returned to a more restrained conception in the *secondo pensiero*, and ended in a plastic interior. The initial conception probably did not contain pilasters, and the flanks of the chapel were divided horizontally by a thin, continuous uninflected cornice and lunettes. In its final state, the design is more complex and more integrated vertically and horizontally. Pilasters and columns correspond vertically to counterparts in the vault. The walls relate to sculptural panels, the pilasters to coffering, and the columns to ribs—each successively more salient.

If only the series of perspectives from the entrance are considered, the evolution of the design indicates the development of an increasingly plastic sequence of wall, pilaster, and column (even considering the drawings in Madrid) which culminates in the open oval and fully-round sculpture. Juvarra arrived at a design that shows interest in horizontal hierarchy, continuity, and climax, equal and corresponding to that for vertical continuity and culmination.

The Stockholm drawings further upset notions of neat linear development. If they are taken to represent a preliminary state prior to Juvarra's receiving the commission to design the chapel then, too, an oscillating path would appear to have been followed. The design would originally have had columns related vertically to ribs (with volutes at their lower extremities). Then columns and the volutes at the base of the ribs would have been eliminated in the *primo pensiero* to return only at the end of the developmental sequence. Once the Stockholm drawings are accepted as early (as indeed they appear to be), then non-linear development of the architecture, as well as the altarpiece, appears certain.

It is hardly novel to suggest that in the development of a painting, a sculpture, or even of architecture, the artist may at any point during the process examine a range of alternatives. The drawings by Juvarra for the Antamoro Chapel in the Juvarra album in the Metropolitan demonstrate the extent of his search for a scheme that would provide a singularly forceful and dramatic integration of light, sculpture and architecture. When they are considered in conjunction with the drawings in Stockholm, the *primo* and *secondo pensiero* confirm that, in the absence of other evidence, even with Juvarra's help, the establishment of a sequence for the drawings can be no more than provisional. The drawings in the Metropolitan help to illuminate specific moments during Juvarra's consideration of the design of the chapel, but the sequence of thought processes involved in the development of the concept remain, nevertheless, largely unknown.

Fig. 1. F. Juvarra, Primo Pensiero..., *for the Antamoro Chapel and altar of St. Philip in S. Girolamo della Carità, Rome. Metropolitan Museum of Art, New York.*

Fig. 2. F. Juvarra, Secondo Pensiero..., *for the Antamoro Chapel and altar of St. Philip in S. Girolamo della Carità, Rome. Metropolitan Museum of Art, New York.*

Fig. 3. F. Juvarra, Antamoro Chapel and altar of St. Philip, and elevation of interior entrance wall in S. Girolamo della Carità, Rome. Biblioteca Nacional, Madrid.

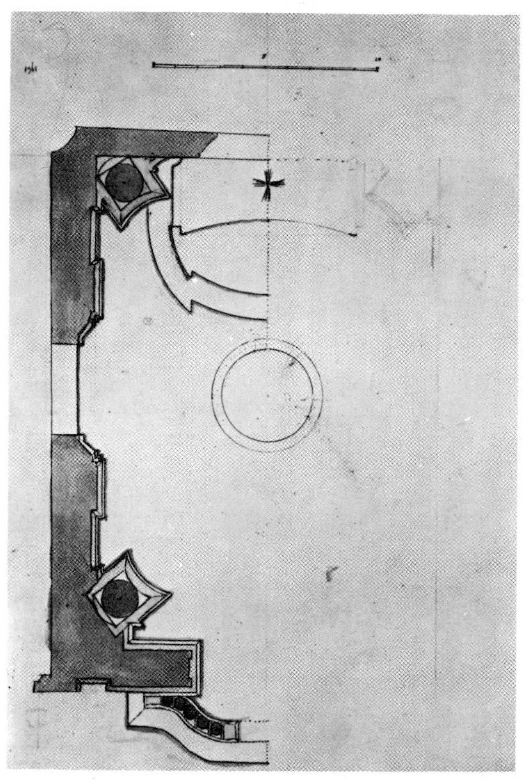

Fig. 4. Unknown Draftsman, Plan, Antamoro Chapel, S. Girolamo della Carità, Rome. Nationalmuseum, Stockholm.

Fig. 5. Unknown Draftsman, Lateral section, Antamoro Chapel and altar of St. Philip, S. Girolamo della Carità, Rome. Nationalmuseum, Stockholm.

Fig. 6. Unknown Draftsman, Longitudinal section, Antamoro Chapel, S. Girolamo della Carità, Rome. Nationalmuseum, Stockholm.

Fig. 7. F. Juvarra, Antamoro Chapel and altar of St. Philip in S. Girolamo della Carità, Rome. Turin, Biblioteca Nazionale.

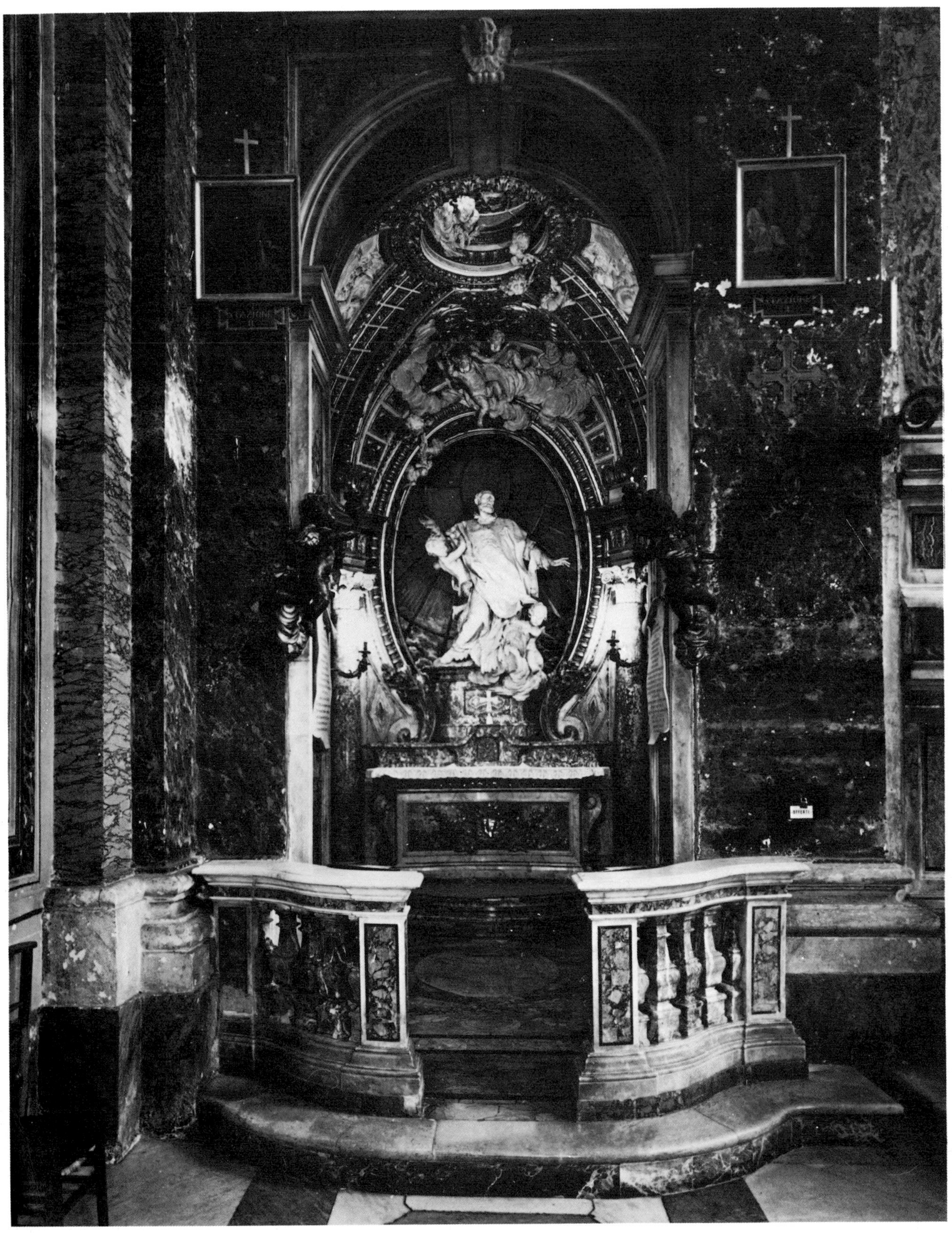

Fig. 8. Antamoro Chapel, S. Girolamo della Carità, Rome, view including entrance. Photo: Birnbaum.

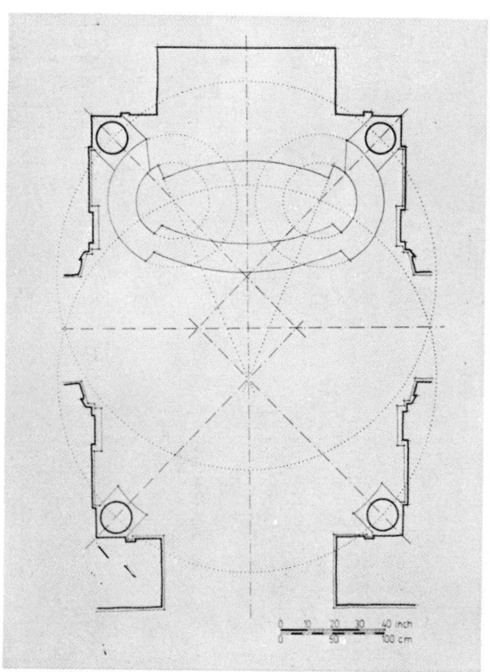

Fig. 9. Plan, Antamoro Chapel, S. Girolamo della Carità, Rome. From Boscarino, Juvarra architetto, *fig. XIV.*

Fig. 10. Antamoro chapel, S. Girolamo della Carità, Rome, view of altar of St. Philip. Photo: Birnbaum.

Fig. 11. Antamoro Chapel, S. Girolamo della Carità, Rome, view of south side of chapel. Photo: Birnbaum.

Fig. 12. Antamoro Chapel, S. Girolamo della Carità, Rome, view of vault. Photo: Gab. Fot. Naz.

Fig. 13. Gianlorenzo Bernini, Silva Chapel, S. Isidoro, view from entrance. Photo: Renzetti.

Fig. 14. Gianlorenzo Bernini, Fonseca Chapel, S. Lorenzo in Lucina, altarpiece and vault. Photo: Renzetti.

Fig. 15. Carlo Fontana, project for the baptistry of St. Peter's, Rome. Royal Library, Windsor, by gracious permission of Her Majesty the Queen.

Fig. 16. G. A. De Rossi, main altar, S. Francesco di Paola, Rome, view from nave. Photo: Renzetti.

JOHN A. PINTO

VIII

NICOLA MICHETTI AND EPHEMERAL DESIGN IN EIGHTEENTH-CENTURY ROME

IN READING diaries and chronicles of daily life in eighteenth-century Rome one is always struck by the extraordinary number of temporary architectural constructions erected to serve a wide variety of functions, both secular and religious. Much of this ephemeral architecture was designed by the most distinguished architects of the period, and while a few did specialize in this kind of work, it was far more common practice for such designs to be provided by men experienced in building more permanent structures. The range of such temporary designs was very great indeed, including triumphal arches, fireworks displays (Figs. 12, 15-20), festive decorations for births and marriages (Figs. 13 and 14), catafalques, illusionistic settings for the display of relics or the sacraments, and, of course, theatre designs [1] (Figs. 1-11). With the exception of the latter category, however, comparatively little has been written on ephemeral design, and almost nothing has been done to examine the relationship between such designs and the permanent structures by the same architects.[2] The main reason for this, of course, is precisely the ephemeral nature of the medium, which can only be studied second- or third- hand by means of original drawings, illustrations or contemporary descriptions. There is no surviving visual documentation for the majority of temporary architectural designs, while in those cases for which there are prints, drawings or an occasional painting, the material is widely scattered and has never been gathered together. Moreover, the

1 Cf. B. Chabrowe, "On the Significance of Temporary Architecture," *Burlington Magazine*, CXVI 1974, 385-391.

2 One notable exception is A. Braham, "Funeral Decorations in Early Eighteenth-Century Rome," *Victoria and Albert Museum Brochure* no. 7, London, 1975.

political and social dimensions of ephemeral architecture designed for festivals and commemorative occasions have never been properly investigated.

Ephemeral design, by its very nature an illusionistic medium intended to represent transitory phenomena, had flourished in the seventeenth century in the work of artists like Bernini and Pietro da Cortona. Carlo Fontana, in his elaborate decorations for the funerals of Leopold I and Joseph I (1705 and 1712 respectively), set a standard for such designs early in the eighteenth century, but by this time Rome was by no means pre-eminent in the field of ephemeral design. In northern Europe as well as to the south in Naples and Sicily, large-scale ephemeral design was frequently employed to divert the populace while captivating their souls and instructing them politically. Two examples of temporary architecture by Fontana's pupils serve to illustrate the international appeal of ephemeral design at this time and the pivotal role of Fontana's studio in its dissemination. In 1690 Fischer von Erlach, who had frequented Fontana's *atelier* in the 1670's, first won public recognition in Vienna by designing two grandiose triumphal arches to commemorate the entry of the imperial family into that city.[3] These arches, lavishly decorated with sculpture, exerted an enormous effect on the populace, which had never seen anything like them before. In 1704, when Filippo Juvarra entered Fontana's studio, he certainly brought with him engravings of a triumphal arch and other temporary decorations he had designed to commemorate the entry of Philip V into Messina two years earlier.[4] Both of Fischer's arches were engraved and the prints surely found their way to Rome where they would have been avidly studied by the younger generation of architects there, among whom was another Fontana student, Nicola Michetti.

Like many of his better known contemporaries, Michetti (active between 1704 and 1758) made numerous designs for temporary architecture, especially for theatre sets and fireworks displays.[5] Michetti's long architectural practice can be conveniently divided into several phases or periods. In the first of these, roughly between 1704 and 1713, he was involved in projects which were out-growths of his train-

[3] Cf. H. Aurenhammer, *J. B. Fischer von Erlach*, Cambridge (Mass.), 1973, figs. 7 and 8.

[4] Cf. S. Boscarino, *Juvarra architetto*, Rome, 1973, figs. 44-48.

[5] The best published account of Michetti's architectural career remains Noak's entry in Thieme-Becker, *Allgemeines Lexikon der Bildenden Künstler* (XXIV, 1930, 532). For further information cf. the author's unpublished doctoral dissertation submitted to Harvard University in 1976: *Nicola Michetti (ca. 1675-1758) and Eighteenth-Century Architecture in Rome and Saint Petersburg*, and " An Early Project by Nicola Michetti for the Trevi Fountain," *Burlington Magazine*, CXIX, 1977, 853-857.

ing in Carlo Fontana's studio, the most important of which were the chapels he designed for two Roman patrons, the Rospigliosi family and Cardinal Giuseppe Sacripante. Also during this time Michetti furnished designs and supervised work on festival decorations for Cardinal Pietro Ottoboni. In a second period, covering the five years between 1713 and his departure to Russia in 1718, he was engaged in two large scale projects: an oval plan church erected in Zagarolo and the preparation of a model of his design for the Sacristy of St. Peter's. Between 1718 and 1723 Michetti was in Russia, where he worked for Peter the Great, primarily in the new imperial capital of Saint Petersburg. The ten years following his return from Russia, and especially between 1729 and 1733, were the most productive of his life. Not only did he build an imposing new facade for the Colonna palace, perhaps his most successful design, but he also was busy providing sets for Cardinal Ottoboni's theatre in the Cancelleria and fireworks displays for the Colonna family. After 1733, and until his death in 1758, Michetti held two salaried positions as architect of both the *Camera Apostolica* and the Theatine Order which demanded most of his attention; in this period he made relatively few designs of importance. Throughout Michetti's career ephemeral design had constituted an important part of his professional activity, from his early work for Cardinal Ottoboni to past the middle of the century. His association with Fontana's studio no doubt first generated Michetti's interest in the design of temporary and illusionistic structures. The most formidable influences on Michetti's ephemeral designs, however, were the treatises of Andrea Pozzo and Ferdinando Galli di Bibiena and the practical experience he gained in observing Juvarra's work for Cardinal Ottoboni's theatre in the Cancelleria between 1709 and 1712.

Cardinal Pietro Ottoboni was the richest and most discerning patron of the arts in Rome during the early eighteenth century. Queen Cristina had died in 1689 and Cardinal Benedetto Pamphili, Ottoboni's other main rival as a patron, left Rome in 1690 to become papal legate in Bologna. Cardinal Ottoboni was especially remarkable because he encouraged all of the arts; his two greatest passions, however, were for music and the theatre, both of which for a brief period around 1710 flourished in his palace as nowhere else in Europe. In 1708 Georg Friedrich Händel, who was then visiting Rome, vied with the Cardinal's favorite musicians, Alessandro Scarlatti and Angelo Corelli, in the Palazzo della Cancelleria.[6] For four years,

[6] Cf. H. J. Marx, "Die Musik am Hofe Pietro Kardinal Ottobonis unter Arcangelo Corelli," *Analecta Musicologica*, V, 1968, 104-117.

from 1709 to 1712, Filippo Juvarra's set designs for Ottoboni's theatre in the Cancelleria, exquisitely uniting art and illusion, established his reputation as the foremost scenographer in Europe.[7] While frequently presenting concerts and plays, the Cardinal was also responsible for embellishing the interior of San Lorenzo in Damaso, which was incorporated in his palace, on the occasion of the Devotion of the Forty Hours, called the *Quarant'ore*. Saint Philip Neri had introduced the celebration of the *Quarant'ore* to Rome in 1548, and since the seventeenth century the public exhibition and veneration of the Eucharist had become the occasion for large-scale sacred representations of an ephemeral nature, a sort of religious theatre employing all the artifice and illusionistic devices of the contemporary stage.[8] Indeed, the splendor of the *Quarant'ore*, which was presented during the Carnival season, was a direct result of the desire to rival the tremendous popularity of secular theatrical spectacles.

Michetti officially entered the household of Cardinal Ottoboni in 1709, the same year as did Juvarra; two years before this, however, he had already been employed by the Cardinal in painting temporary decorations for the *Quarant'ore* in San Lorenzo in Damaso. In the payments for the *Quarant'ore macchine* of 1707 and 1708 Michetti is referred to as a painter, in which capacity — and not as an architect — he seems to have done his first independent work.[9] In 1704 he had been paid more than four-hundred *scudi* for decorating two ceilings in the Vatican Palace with perspective scenes, paintings which unfortunately no longer exist; and in 1718 he would be recommended to the Czar as a perspective painter.[10] The design and execution of illusionistic constructions involved painting as much as it did architecture. Indeed, the greatest ephemeral designs of this kind were almost always the creation of artists gifted in both painting and architecture. Pietro da Cortona's drawing for a *Quarant'ore macchina* of 1633 [11] and Andrea Pozzo's great repre-

[7] Cf. M. Viale Ferrero, *Filippo Juvarra, scenografo e architetto teatrale*, Turin, 1970.

[8] Cf. M. S. Weil, "The Devotion of the Forty Hours and Roman Baroque Illusions," *Journal of the Warburg and Courtauld Institutes*, XXXVII, 1974, 218-248.

[9] Biblioteca Apostolica Vaticana, Archivio Barberini, Computisteria Ottoboni, vol. 1522 (1707), in dates of 1/15, 1/22, 1/29, 2/12, 2/19, 2/25 and 2/26; vol. 1523 (1708), in dates of 1/14, 1/26, 1/28, 2/4, 2/11 and 2/24.

[10] Archivio di Stato di Roma, Camerale I, Registro dei Mandati, Busta 1054, pp. 65, 152 and 271. These payments were called to my attention by Tod Marder. The paintings are also mentioned by G. B. Chattard, *Nuova descrizione del Vaticano o sia del Palazzo Apostolica di San Pietro*, Rome, 1767, III, 176. The rooms described by Chattard, now part of the Museo Etrusco, were remodelled under Pius VI, at which time Michetti's paintings (which were on canvas) were probably removed.

[11] Cf. A. Blunt and H. L. Cooke, *The Roman Drawings of the XVII and XVIII Centuries... at Windsor Castle*, London, 1960, 77.

sentation of the Marriage Feast at Cana, set up in the Gesù in 1685, are but two of the most outstanding such designs by a long line of distinguished painter-architects.[12]

In the documents for 1709, the year in which Michetti became a member of Cardinal Ottoboni's household, and again in 1710, he was no longer called "painter", but clearly had been placed in charge of the team of painters, masons and carpenters building the *Quarant'ore macchina.*[13] This must have constituted a considerable responsibility for the young architect, for the *Quarant'ore* devotions were attended by the most important families and clergy in Rome and reflected directly on the Cardinal's considerable prestige and reputation. While there are no illustrations of Michetti's designs for the *Quarant'ore*, a general ideal of their appearance may be obtained by studying prints of later *macchine* commissioned by Cardinal Ottoboni for the same setting.[14] Fortunately, the Cardinal regularly had pamphlets describing the *Quarant'ore macchina* printed and distributed to the audience. These *relazioni* describe Michetti's designs of 1707-1710 in some detail and comment favorably on his skill as a painter, engineer and mathematician, while at the same time asserting that the subjects were conceived by the Cardinal himself.

The *macchina* for 1707 represented Saints Paul and Barnabas preaching in front of a pagan temple at Lystra, which, as in Raphael's celebrated tapestry cartoon, was shown as a *tholos.*[15] The subject of the next year's *Quarant'ore* devotions was the miraculous levitation of St. Philip Neri as he said Mass in S. Maria in Vallicella.[16] In the following year Michetti depicted the Martyrdom of St. Lawrence as a true *theatrum sacrum*, animated by numerous painted figures shown in violent poses, gesturing rhetorically[17]. The *macchina* for 1710 represented a miracle of St.

12 Cf. A. Pozzo, *Perspectivae pictorum atque architectorum*, Augsburg, 1693-1702, vol. I, tav. 71.

13 Biblioteca Apostolica Vaticana, Archivio Barberini, Computisteria Ottoboni, vol. 1524 (1709), in dates of 1/12, 1/19, 1/26, 2/10 and 2/16; vol. 1525 (1710), in dates of 2/8, 3/8 and 10/31. As many as six masons, seven painters and eleven carpenters were employed at one time working on the 1709 *macchina*, which took more than a month to construct.

14 These include one by A. Mauri for 1728 (Rome, Gab. Naz. d. Stampe no. FC 8782), and two others by G. B. Oliverio for 1734 and 1736 which accompany descriptive pamphlets: *Descrizione del sontuoso sagro apparato fatto erigere nell'Insigne Basilica de' SS. Lorenzo e Damaso per l'esposizione del SS. Sagramento dall'Eminentissimo Cardinale Pietro Ottoboni*, Rome, 1734 and 1736 (Biblioteca Apostolica Vaticana).

15 *Distinta relazione et istorico ragguaglio della sontuosa machina, e di quanto in Essa è figurato fatta inalzare alli tre di Marzo giorno di giovedi grasso dell'anno presente MDCCVII.* (Rome, Archivio Capitolino, *Diario di Valesio*, Credenza XIV, vol. XV, ff. 376-377).

16 *Distinta relazione della sontuosa machina e di quanto in essa è figurato, fatta inalzare alli 16. di febraro giorno di giovedi grasso dell'anno presente MDCCVIII.* (Rome, Archivio Capitolino, *Diario di Valesio*, Credenza XIV, vol. XVI, ff. 16-17).

17 *Distinta relazione della sontuosa machina, e di quanto*

Anthony of Padua, set against the background of a great public square.[18] In this same year Michetti designed another *macchina*, this one depicting the Holy Sepulchre for the Confraternity of the *Santissimo Sagramento* in San Lorenzo in Lucina.[19]

Both the printed *relazioni* and the payments in the Ottoboni papers confirm that the most important feature of these religious spectacles, the *macchina*, was an illusionistic architectural apparatus constructed primarily of wood, plaster and painted canvas which functioned much like an oversize *ciborium* or monstrance in displaying the sacrament. Wax candles and flares in great numbers were employed to illuminate the *macchina*, the systematic use of directed light in varying intensities constituting one of the most overtly theatrical aspects of these designs. A familiar repertoire of pictorial effects — rays of divine light streaming down from heaven, glories of clustered putti buoyed up on clouds, and extravagant architectural structures — all were rendered three dimensionally in compositions resembling *tableaux vivants*. Moreover, these spectacles usually included a musical accompaniment, like the heavenly choir which figures in Michetti's representation of the Holy Sepulchre. *Quarant'ore* designs like Michetti's constituted a powerful instrument of education, persuasion and devotional piety in the hands of the Church and in keeping with the reforms of St. Philip Neri made the liturgy and sacraments more accessible to a large segment of the illiterate population. Along with the *oratorio*, the *Quarant'ore* deserves recognition as an important Baroque artistic expression in multiple media, in many ways the religious counterpart of contemporary theatre. The experience Michetti acquired in the production of religious theatre early in his career undoubtedly served him in good stead when he turned his hand to the design of sets for a secular stage.

In 1710, while Michetti was designing decorations for the *Quarant'ore*, he was receiving a monthly stipend as one of the Cardinal's retainers and living in the Palazzo della Cancelleria.[20] Most important for Michetti's future development,

in essa è figurato. Fatta inalzare alli 7 di febraro giorno di giovedi grasso dell' anno presente MDCCIX. (Rome, Archivio Capitolino, *Diario di Valesio*, Credenza XIV, vol. XVI, ff. 172-173).

18 *Distinta relazione della sontuosa machina, e di quanto in essa è figurato fatta inalzare alli 28 di febraro giorno di giovedi grasso dell' anno presente MDCCX.* (Rome, Biblioteca Corsini, 173-A-7, int. 52).

19 *Breve descrizione della machina del santissimo sepolcro fatto erigere dalli fratelli della Ven. Archiconfraternità del Santissimo Sagramento in S. Lorenzo in Lucina nella loro cappella di S. Gio. Battista nell' anno 1710.* (Rome, Archivio Capitolino, *Diario di Valesio*, Credenza XIV, vol. XVI, ff. 340-341).

20 Between April and July 1710 Carlo Santi Primoli, a carpenter, was paid for repairs in the Cancelleria, and in particular "... nelle stanze dove habita il S. Fran.co Ravenna e il S. Michetti." Biblioteca Apostolica Vaticana, Archivio Barberini, Computisteria Ottoboni, vol. 1482 (1710).

particularly as a set designer, was his connection with Filippo Juvarra, who was also then living in the Cancelleria.[21] Michetti had already demonstrated his abilities as a perspective painter and had certainly mastered the theoretical basis of illusionistic design so exhaustively presented in Padre Pozzo's treatise. Pozzo devoted more space to explaining the mechanics of how the appearance of three-dimensional reality might be illusionistically produced on a two-dimensional surface than he did to the generation of three-dimensional structures from drawings. His exceedingly rational method was essentially pictorial in nature, while Juvarra's scenography was more directly concerned with the architectural arrangement of spaces and the intuitive exploration of their potential to generate new and ever more fantastic forms. In attending performances in the Ottoboni theatre and observing Juvarra's preparations for these productions, Michetti had an unparallelled opportunity to acquire the kind of practical experience which can never be learned from handbooks alone. The extent to which Michetti learned from Juvarra is clearly demonstrated by his own set designs made twenty years later, also for Cardinal Ottoboni.

In 1729, after his sojourn in Saint Petersburg, Michetti once again entered the service of Cardinal Ottoboni, this time as his *ingegniere teatrale*.[22] In this capacity he designed the sets for a lavish theatrical performance entitled *Carlo Magno*, celebrating the birth of the Dauphin in 1729.[23] As one of the representatives of the French King in Rome, Cardinal Ottoboni naturally wanted to commemorate this happy event, all the more so since his rival Cardinal de Polignac, the French minister in Rome, was sponsoring a lavish fireworks display in Piazza Navona for the same purpose. It was to be expected that Cardinal Ottoboni would use his famous theatre to celebrate the Dauphin's birth, and in doing so he selected a play which had been performed once before with sets (including a "Palace of the Sun" in the gothic style) designed by Domenico Vellani.[24] The plot of *Carlo Magno* was already highly political in character, being an imaginative account of Charlemagne's Italian

21 Juvarra first appears on the monthly lists of the Cardinal's retainers in January 1710 as "Cappellano" with a monthly salary of nine scudi. He continues to appear in this capacity until February, 1715. (Biblioteca Apostolica Vaticana, Archivio Barberini, Computisteria Ottoboni, vols. 1482-1487, under "Rollo della Famiglia dell'... Card. Ottoboni").

22 The illustrated libretto of the 1729 performance of *Carlo Magno* (cf. fn. 23 below) credits Michetti as follows: "Inventore delle scene: il Cavalier Nicolò Michetti Romano Ingegniere del Signor Cardinale Ottoboni."

23 *Carlo Magno, Festa teatrale in occasione della nascità del Delfino, offerta alle sacre reali maestà Cristianissime del Re, e Regina di Francia, dal Cardinale Ottoboni, protettore degl' affari della Corona*, Rome, 1729.

24 Described in the *Diario Ordinario di Roma* (no. 1777, p. 4) in date of December 25, 1728.

victories, but the Cardinal brought it up to date by adding an introduction comparing the virtues of Louis XIV to those of the first Holy Roman Emperor and ordering new sets to be designed by Michetti.

Michetti's frontispiece for *Carlo Magno* shows that Cardinal Ottoboni's theatre had changed only slightly in the seventeen years since Juvarra had worked there (Fig. 1). The boxes and orchestra pit appear precisely as they do in a similar frontispiece for *Teodosio il Giovane* (performed in 1711) by Juvarra; the only alterations are the twisted spiral columns framing the stage (which replace pilasters), the proscenium arch (formerly a single segmental arch) and the arms of the King of France, obviously added especially for this performance.[25] The musicians are being conducted by a man at the harpsichord, presumably a portrait of Giovanni Costanzi, who replaced Angelo Corelli after his death in 1713 as the Cardinal's musician and composed the music for *Carlo Magno*. The stage is occupied by a copy of Agostino Cornacchini's equestrian statue of Charlemagne, which had been set up in the portico of St. Peter's only four years earlier in 1725.[26] Michetti also reproduced the highly theatrical background to Cornacchini's statue, an architectural vista glimpsed behind a curtain pulled to one side, which provides a striking example of the scenographic character of all the arts at this time. In employing Cornacchini's statue of Charlemagne in this way Michetti was probably consciously referring to Juvarra's frontispiece for the 1710 performance of *Costantino Pio*, which used Bernini's equestrian statue of Constantine in an identical way.[27]

The set for the first scene of Act I represents Charlemagne enthroned in the temple of Capitoline Jove receiving emissaries of the Roman Senate (Fig. 2). Throughout *Carlo Magno*, the action is set in Imperial Rome, thus providing Michetti with numerous opportunities to create imaginative reconstructions of classical monuments. Nothing, of course, could be further removed from the actual appearance of an ancient temple interior than Michetti's fantastic Baroque hall with its cupola supported by *atlanti* and a fugue of receding balconies. If Renaissance theatre design may be said to have striven for an accurate, realistic representation of Rome in its imperial grandeur, Baroque designers were preoccupied with the scenographic potential of Roman architecture to provide settings of incomparable scale and

25 For Juvarra's frontispiece cf. Viale Ferrero, *Filippo Juvarra*, pl. 17 b.

26 R. Wittkower, "Cornacchini's Reiterstatue Karls des Grossen in St. Peter," *Miscellanea Bibliotecae Hertzianae zu Ehren von L. Bruhns*, Munich, 1961, 464-473.

27 For Juvarra's frontispiece cf. Viale Ferrero, *Filippo Juvarra*, 378, no. 1.

richness. This is certainly true of Juvarra's set designs and continued to characterize one aspect of eighteenth-century artists' appreciation of Roman architecture. However, throughout the eighteenth century, from Juvarra to Piranesi, the exploration of the scenographic potential of Roman architecture ran parallel to the systematic study of ancient remains, which provided the necessary foundation in fact for imaginary and visionary architectural compositions.

The next change of scenery in *Carlo Magno* depicts a garden situated in an oak grove on the Capitoline Hill, in which Charlemagne is walking. The garden contains a fountain of Rome, crowned by a double-headed eagle, one of Cardinal Ottoboni's heraldic devices, and otherwise is somewhat reminiscent of Michetti's design for the gardens at Peterhof.[28] Following the garden scene, the action changes to the Roman Forum, which, rather strangely, resembles an enclosed palace courtyard more than a monumental public space (Fig. 3). This is perhaps due to the fact that Michetti's composition appears to be based on one of Juvarra's engraved set designs, the atrium in *Ciro*, which was performed in 1712.[29] Compared to Juvarra's design, however, Michetti's composition appears static and more confined. At the beginning of the second act the setting changes again to the Porta Carmentale and the countryside outside the walls of Rome. Michetti presents a fantastic reconstruction of the ancient city, including an obelisk and spiral tower which may be glimpsed through the archway and over the ramparts. This scene recalls a number of Renaissance *vedute*, and is also somewhat similar to a drawing made by Juvarra for an unidentified play at the Teatro Capranica, which Michetti may have seen.[30]

Michetti's next set design shows the interior of the Porta Carmentale, which Charlemagne has caused to be closed in preparation for a siege (Fig. 4). This is the only one of Michetti's engraved designs for *Carlo Magno* for which I have been able to find a preparatory drawing (Fig. 5). This sheet is in the collection of the Victoria and Albert Museum and displays Michetti's characteristic draughtsmanship, which employs rapid, nervous strokes of a thin-nibbed pen and rich, layered application of colored washes.[31] Michetti's technique here is quite similar to Juvarra's and much freer than Fontana's, which suggests that he may have closely studied Juvarra's drawings for the theatre. As is the case with almost all of the engravings made after

28 The fountain also intentionally recalls the statue of *Roma Trionfante* set in a niche at the center of the Palazzo Senatorio, where it stands above a fountain basin. The statue was set in place in 1592.

29 Viale Ferrero, *Filippo Juvarra*, pl. 84 b.

30 *Ibid*, pl. 159 a.

31 London, Victoria and Albert Museum, Print Room, no. E. 121-1943.

Juvarra's original designs, the prints accompanying the libretto for *Carlo Magno*, prepared by a number of different artists, lack the spontaneity and range of chiaroscuro contrasts present in Michetti's drawing.[32] Unfortunately, prints and drawings, no matter how brilliant their execution, can only convey a limited idea of the appearance of the actual sets on the evening of the performance, when two-dimensional designs transferred to flats would be animated by directed light and live actors, thereby assuming a third dimension mediating between real and illusionistic space.

The three scenes following the one set within the Porta Carmentale take place in the countryside in the camp of Charlemagne's enemies who are besieging Rome, and are devoid of architectural interest. Following Charlemagne's victory over the rebellious Italians, however, the action returns to Rome, where the Emperor receives the captured Queen Adelinda in a hall in the Capitoline Palace (Fig. 6). This is a characteristic *scena per angolo* showing a relatively small, intimate space.[33] Two features, the flat architraves carried by scrolls flaring out from supporting piers and the window frames incorporating stucco ovals above, anticipate Michetti's design for the interior of the corner pavilion in the Colonna Palace. The following scene is set in a portico on the Capitol, which, perhaps in keeping with ancient literary descriptions of classical porticoes, is decorated by numerous busts and statues (Fig. 7). This in turn is followed closely by the culminating scene of the historical narrative, the triumphal procession of Charlemagne arriving on the Capitol, where the so-called Trophies of Marius are used to adorn his victory (Fig. 8). Architecturally, this is one of the most interesting of Michetti's compositions, in that, while repeating many of the conventions of Juvarra and Bibiena, it manages to create a lively and varied open structure which provides a suitable backdrop for the magnificence of the imperial triumph. It is easy to see how, in designing scenes such as this for the theatre, Michetti had come to terms with the scenographic potential of open structures, which is only a small step away from applying the same principles to the design of actual buildings, like the Palazzo Colonna.

At the conclusion of the historical part of the drama, one of the most characteristic features of the Baroque theatre remained to be presented. This was the miraculous, illusionistic appearance of a great *macchina*, which was intended to overwhelm

[32] The fourteen prints Michetti designed in the libretto for *Carlo Magno* were engraved by five artists: G. Gabbuggiani (frontispiece); F. Vasconi (I, XI, XXXII, XLI, LVI); C. Grandi (VI); G. Massi (XIX, LXII); Paolo Pilaja (XXVI, XXXVI, LXI).

[33] The *scena per angolo*, involving a two-point perspective construction, had been introduced by Francesco Galli di Bibiena in the opening years of the eighteenth century.

the spectators by its sudden apparition and fantastic design. Following the conclusion of Charlemagne's triumph and the happy resolution of the numerous romantic subplots, the curtain closed and then opened again to reveal a chariot carrying Dawn and the three Graces pulled by a pair of doves and miraculously supported by thick clouds (Fig. 9). Slowly, however, the clouds were dissipated by the intense rays of the sun, revealing the *macchina* proper, representing Apollo beneath a circular baldachin in front of his celestial palace, which appears as a projecting exedra (Fig. 10). At the center Apollo stands to greet the three Graces, while to the right a host of heavenly *genii* watch over the chariot of the Sun God. The Palace of Apollo is without question the most imaginative architectural composition among Michetti's set designs for *Carlo Magno*. The sinuous profile of the dome covering the baldachin and the oval perforations at its base are especially remarkable features, as is the extremely classical plan of the ensemble.

Michetti's *macchina* bears a general resemblance to one designed by Juvarra for the tenth scene of the 1714 performance of *Tito e Berenice* in the Ottoboni theatre (Fig. 11).[34] While there can be no doubt that Michetti was familiar with this and other *macchine* designed by Juvarra, his design is much more restrained and classical, deliberately rejecting the dynamic movement of the spiral columns which were one of Juvarra's favorite theatrical devices.[35] This may be the result of the fact that Michetti's design was inspired at least in part by Pietro da Cortona's reconstruction of the temple of Fortuna Primigenia at Palestrina, the crowning feature of which is a classical *tholos* standing in front of a semicircular portico.[36] In the course of his career Michetti designed numerous circular temple-like pavilions, all of which seem to have been quite similar.[37] Three of these were designed for the gardens at Peterhof, each characterized by paired columns, and, in the case of the two for which we have perspective views, domes with onion-like exterior profiles.[38] In contrast to these, the two *tholoi* Michetti designed after his return from Russia look more classical. Both the *macchina* for *Carlo Magno* and a fire-

34 Turin, Cibrario collection. Cf. Viale Ferrero, *Filippo Juvarra*, 373, no. 6.

35 Juvarra designed two other *macchine* of this kind while in Rome. The first was for scene X of *Teodosio il giovane* in 1711 and the second for scene XI of *Ciro* in 1712. Cf. Viale Ferrero, *Filippo Juvarra*, plates 43 and 86 respectively.

36 Cf. R. Wittkower, "Pietro da Cortonas Ergänzungs projekt des Temples in Palestrina," *Festschrift Adolph Goldschmidt zu seinem 70. Geburtstag*, Berlin, 1935, 137-143.

37 It is of course difficult to be precise about the appearance of the circular temples in Michetti's *Quarant'ore* designs of 1707 and 1708, of which we have no visual record.

38 Cf. Michetti's drawings in the collection of the State Hermitage Museum, nos. 4731 a, 4737 and 8465.

works apparatus designed in 1732, which will be discussed shortly, have evenly spaced columns and more orthodox proportions (Fig. 18). This is probably due to the fact that as garden pavilions set on the crest of a hill, Michetti's temples were expected to function at least in part as do the " eyecatchers " which dot so many English landscape gardens, which have lively silhouettes to capture the attention of a distant viewer. Michetti's ephemeral *tholoi*, on the other hand, both house classical deities — Apollo, and in the case of the *Chinea macchina*, the whole population of Olympus — and therefore of necessity had to be more classical in appearance.

Cardinal Ottoboni's celebration of the Dauphin's birth seems to have been greatly enjoyed by the numerous cardinals, ambassadors and prelates who attended the performance.[39] In addition to the exquisite lyrics, music and costumes, one contemporary account singles out the " sontuosità delle macchine " as contributing greatly to the success of the occasion.[40] We have mentioned Michetti's obvious debt to Juvarra's theatrical designs and *macchine*, but the constant repetition and universal appeal of these devices can be traced back much further and is one of the most characteristic expressions of the preoccupation of Baroque artists and audiences with the mechanics of illusionistic representation. Gian Lorenzo Bernini's theatrical compositions, which played on the relationship between audience and spectacle and involved complicated stage machinery to simulate deluges and conflagrations, are well known.

Somewhat less subtle, but for this reason more revealing, is the prologue to Francesco Cavalli's *Il Novello Giasone* performed in 1671 in the Teatro Tordinona in Rome, which had just been completed following designs of Carlo Fontana. The prologue was contrived as an ingenious *tour de force* to draw attention to the elaborate stage machinery of the new theatre and illustrates the extent to which composers, designers and audiences alike were drawn to more and more daring feats of scenographic virtuosity.[41] At the opening of the prologue the Sun appears in his chariot and begins to introduce the drama. No sooner has he begun to speak, however, than his chariot and the entire stage set fall crashing to the ground. In the

39 While performances were held in the Cardinal's theatre on a fairly regular basis in the 1720's, the number of sets and lavish publication of *Carlo Magno* were unusual in the period following Juvarra's departure.

40 *Diario Ordinario di Roma*, no. 1920, p. 7 in date of November 26, 1729.

41 Cf. O. Jander, " The Prologues and Intermezzos of Alessandro Stradella," *Analecta Musicologica*, VII, 1969, 87-111. Bernini's role in encouraging this tendency in Baroque theatre is well known; cf. C. D'Onofrio, editor, *Fontana di Trevi, Commedia inedita*, Rome, 1963.

midst of all this confusion the allegorical figures of Music, Poetry and Painting appear on the stage describing the ruin all about them, for which they blame the architect: "Maladetti i compassi e chi l'adopra!" The architect finally appears, then the following exchange occurs:

Architetto: *Quai stridi, quai lamenti*
Gite spargendo, ò mie compagne, ai venti?

Pittura: *Vedi le prospetive!*

Poesia: *Mira il carro del Sole!*

Musica: *Guarda il Teatro!*
Tutto è del danno commun.
Pietà ti muova!
Di tue false misure ecco la prova!

Architetto: *O come stolte sete*
S'alla apparenza sol belle credete.
Cosi à finger si fa!

(Here, in the matter of an instant, the confusion on the stage is miraculously restored to order.)

Ecco, ogni linea al punto!
All'opera olà!

Tutti: *O leggiadri artifizi!*
Son trionfi dell'arte i precipizi.[42]

The two key lines in this passage are spoken by the architect ("How foolish you are to believe in goodly appearance alone") and the chorus of Music, Poetry and Painting ("Oh charming dissimulations! Art triumphs in approaching the abyss"), which clearly speaks for the audience. In providing designs for the theatre, eighteenth-century architects were continuously striving for new and ever more striking illusionistic effects, and in the process the boundaries between painting and architecture as well as scenography and planning became blurred. For many architects, and this is especially true of Juvarra in his early designs, the theatre was both a laboratory in which new ideas could be tested and an opportunity to project fantastic structures which no patron's resources would ever be sufficient to build.

42 Jander, "The Prologues," 95-96. I am indebted to Professor Jander for calling this passage to my attention.

In 1730, the year after Michetti's sets for *Carlo Magno*, he seems to have provided designs for a second play performed in the Ottoboni theatre in Rome, called *Colombo overo l'India Scoperta.*[43] An unsigned drawing in a private collection has been identified as one of Michetti's set designs for this production of *Colombo*, and the attribution seems a valid one.[44] The fantastic architecture probably is intended to represent the capital of Montezuma in Peru (sic), which was the setting of the 1690 production.[45] Michetti's inventions and the exotic blend of architectural forms in this composition recall the architectural fantasies of Juvarra and the archaeological reconstructions of Fischer von Erlach.

No discussion of Michetti's activity as a scenographer would be complete without recording at least two instances in which he was involved in the design of theatres. In 1714 he was commissioned to build a small theatre not far from the Palazzo di Firenze, which no longer survives, but appears on Gian Battista Nolli's 1748 plan of Rome.[46] Like so many early theatres, the Teatro Pallacorda was constructed within an existing building, in this case a courtyard which had been used to play a variation of hand-ball, from which it took its name.[47] Michetti's theatre, constructed of wood with painted decorations, was ready to be opened for the Carnival of 1715.[48] After fifty years of active life the theatre showed signs of deterioration and was repaired by Giovanni Francesco Fiori. From Fiori's report on the condition of the theatre we learn that it had four levels of boxes supported on columns, and a wooden truss roof.[49] This together with Nolli's rather schematic plan showing a vestibule, a long narrow hall with seating for the audience and space

43 Cf. *Il Settecento a Roma* (Exhibition catalogue), Rome, 1959, no. 1763, and Viale Ferrero, *Filippo Juvarra*, 53 note 36. The libretto for the original performance of this play in 1690 is in the Biblioteca Casanatense (comm. 299/3): *Il Colombo overo l'India scoperta, dramma per musica dedicato all' Illustriss. D. Maria Ottoboni, Da rappresentarsi nel Teatro di Tor di Nona, l'anno MDCXCI*, Rome, 1690.

44 Rome, collezione Ing. A. Sciolla. Museo di Roma, Archivio Fotografico, no. 1763. I have only studied the photograph of this drawing.

45 The drawing, however, does not correspond to any of the specific scenes described in the 1690 libretto. Apparently no libretto was printed for the 1730 performance.

46 F. Ehrle, *Roma, al tempo di Benedetto XIV. La pianta di Roma di Giambattista Nolli del 1748*, Vatican, 1932. The theatre is numbered no. 444 on Nolli's plan.

47 A. Rava, *I teatri di Roma*, Rome, 1953, 116–118.

48 Rava's discussion of the early history of the theatre is based on two documents in the Archivio Capranica (2901 and 3769). This archive, recently transferred to the Archivio Capitolino, was badly damaged before passing to the Comune. Dr. Gian Maria Vian, who is presently engaged in putting it into order, informs me that these volumes cannot be traced. Perhaps they will be identified when a new index to this collection is compiled.

49 Archivio di Stato di Roma, Camerale III, busta 2126, folder 1, document 1, in date of January 7, 1767: "Descrizz.e delli resarcimenti riconosciuti necessarij farsi nelli seguenti Teatri in occasione delle visite fatte alli med.i per le recite del Corre.e Anno... N.o 29 Teatro Pallacorda".

behind the stage for the positioning of flats and machinery, suggests that the Pallacorda was similar to other theatres in Rome at this time. In the same year that Michetti designed the sets for *Carlo Magno* he also appears to have worked on another small theatre which Cardinal Ottoboni was building in his palace in the little town of Fiano Romano.[50] The theatre does not survive and the documents regarding its construction are not clear as to whether Michetti designed the actual theatre or merely the sets for it.[51] It would seem likely, however, that he did design the theatre since at this time he was the Cardinal's *ingegniere teatrale*.

Michetti's reputation for theatre design must have been generally acknowledged in Italy at this time, since in 1729 he was called upon to judge a competition in Naples for a temporary stage which could be folded up and removed with great facility.[52] The model which Michetti preferred was designed by Raimondo del Sangue, Principe di Sanseverino. This suggests the possibility that he may have met the young Neapolitan, whose many bizarre accomplishments included the construction of a *teatro pirotecnico* combining the drama and scenography of the stage with the color, brilliant light effects and spectacle of fireworks.

Throughout the eighteenth century in Italy the theatre was an art form reserved primarily for the enjoyment of the nobility and upper classes of society.[53] Because of the limited size of most Roman theatres and the restricted nature of their audiences the stage was far from being a truly public vehicle of artistic expression. We have seen how, upon certain occasions like the 1729 performance of *Carlo Magno*, the theatre could be used as an instrument of international diplomacy. Architecture was also employed for similar expressive ends, as was the case with the Spanish Steps (perhaps the most monumental piece of urban planning in eighteenth-century Rome), built to assert the French sovereign's claim to be the secular leader of the Christian world.[54] The time and expense involved in building permanent structures as political propaganda, however, tended to discourage the use of architecture in this way except by the most established interest groups.

50 Fiano Romano is thirty kilometers north of Rome.

51 Biblioteca Apostolica Vaticana, Archivio Barberini, Computisteria Ottoboni, vol. 1499 (1729), no. 14, in date of May 17, 1729.

52 " Ma seriamente pensando anch'egli [Raimondo del Sangue], fra breve tempo diè fuora un modello, che fu preferito a tutti gli altri dal famoso Ingegnere di Pietro il Grande Czar di Moscovia Cavalier Michetti, che allora per avventura ritrovavasi in Roma ". G.G. Origlia, *Istoria dello studio di Napoli*, Naples, 1754, II, 325.

53 Cf. H. Tintelnot, " Annotazioni sull' importanza della festa teatrale per la vita artistica e dinastica del barocco," *Retorica e Barocco, Atti del III Congresso Internazionale di Studi Umanistici*, Rome, 1955, 233-241.

54 Cf. W. Lotz, " Die Spanische Treppe; Architektur als Mittle der Diplomatie," *Römisches Jahrbuch für Kunstgeschichte*, XII, 1969, 39-94.

In contrast, temporary architectural structures made of wood, plaster and painted canvas were relatively inexpensive to build, and could be erected to commemorate special occasions like births, marriages, treaties and victories within a fairly short span of time. Moreover, because of the ephemeral materials with which they were composed, such structures readily lent themselves as armatures or backdrops to lavish displays of fireworks, which were frequently employed to dazzle and amuse the crowds that gathered on such occasion. Festivals, and ephemeral architecture designed in conjunction with them, served an important purpose in providing a means of communication between rulers and subjects in eighteenth-century Italy. Not only did they function as vehicles for official propaganda, but they also served to divert the populace from more serious matters. The close interaction between architecture and fireworks in Michetti's ephemeral structures as well as the overtly political messages they convey are characteristic of many eighteenth-century festival designs.

By the end of the seventeenth century the Italians already had a reputation for producing spectacular pyrotechnic compositions using large-scale architectural structures made of ephemeral materials. In contrast, northern European fireworks displays, while technically more sophisticated, rarely attained the degree of monumentality of contemporary Italian designs. For this reason, itinerant Italian fireworks designers were in great demand, some of whom, like the Rugieri of Bologna, even worked for the courts of France and England. Rome was by no means the only center of elaborate fireworks displays in Italy; throughout the eighteenth century Naples was even more active than Rome in this field of ephemeral architecture. The Austrian vice-regents and Bourbon kings employed festivals, and especially fireworks displays, in order to disseminate political propaganda to a largely illiterate populace and to temper popular unrest through the lavish display of royal largess and munificence.[55]

As late as 1700 Naples seems to have relied on foreign masters to provide designs for festival decorations. In 1700 Cristoforo Shor (1655-1701), a Roman who had worked extensively in Spain, designed a fireworks display in honor of the Queen's saint's day, and two years later Ferdinando Bibiena designed and supervised the

55 Cf. F. Mancini, "Feste ed apparati e spettacoli teatrali, *Storia di Napoli*, VI bis, 1970, 1155-1220 and VIII, 649-714.

construction of lavish temporary decorations celebrating the arrival of Philip V, recently acknowledged as king of Spain and Naples.[56] While Naples continued to import foreign talent, it soon became a lively center of festival design, and especially fireworks displays, in its own right. In 1709 Nicola Fiore designed a remarkable *macchina* representing the battle of gods and giants in which Jove, enthroned on top of the orb of the firmament, casts down pyrotechnic thunderbolts upon those presumptious representatives of revolution and chaos seeking to overthrow him, while in the background twin volcanoes erupt torrents of fire (Fig. 12).[57] The political message behind this theme would not have been lost on the Neapolitans, whose city had been captured by the Austrians only two years before in the course of the War of Spanish Succession: any loyalist attempt at rebellion would be futile and violently suppressed.

In Naples, especially after the return of the Bourbons in 1734, ephemeral architecture continued to be employed with great frequency, culminating in the extraordinary designs of Raimondo del Sangue and Vincenzo Re. Raimondo del Sangue, who may have met Michetti in 1729, celebrated the birth of the Infante in 1743 by presenting a *teatro pirotecnico* in which temples, fountains, water-falls and trees were all represented by fireworks of fantastic designs and colors. Indeed, Raimondo appears to have expended a considerable part of his bizarre genius on the invention of pyrotechnic colors, like emerald green, which he perfected in 1739.[58] Unfortunately, only an occasional contemporary description or drawing executed in colored washes survives to breathe life into countless monochrome prints which are the basic source for studying eighteenth-century fireworks designs. Vincenzo Re (active 1737-62), with Pietro Righini the greatest theatrical designer in Naples during the first half of the eighteenth century, was called by Charles I from his native Parma in 1737. In addition to numerous set designs made between 1740 and 1760, Re provided designs for festival decorations, the most memorable of which was a

56 Cf. F. Mancini, *Feste ed apparati civili e religiosi in Napoli*, Naples, 1968, 36-37.

57 In Fiori's design considerable emphasis is placed on the actual fireworks, as distinguished from the supporting architecture. This may be partially due to improved technology and the use of more sophisticated chemical preparations imported by the Austrians. Contemporary handbooks on fireworks go into their chemical compositions in great detail. Cf. for example, A. F. De Freaier, *Traité des feux d'artifice*, The Hague, 1741 (first published in 1707).

58 The prince's biographer described some of the other colors appearing in the 1743 *teatro*, which included "... torchino, il giallo di color di cedro, il giallo a color d'arancio, il bianco inclinante al color di latte, il rosso a color di rubino, il pavonazzo di varie spezie, il verde mare" and "il verde prato". Cf. Origlia, *Istoria*, II, 328-329.

fireworks *macchina* celebrating yet another royal birth in 1747.[59] Re's monumental apparatus is both more formal and exclusively architectural than most Neapolitan *macchine* and appears to be related to contemporary ephemeral design in Rome.

In eighteenth-century Rome the most important festivals involving fireworks were patronized by the ambassadors of Spain, France and the Kingdom of Naples, all of whom sought to influence the policy of the Papacy by public demonstrations of their power and munificence. To this end they competed with one another in employing the best architects and presenting ever more sumptuous and monumental displays. The grandiose *macchine* were almost always erected in the squares in front of their embassies and because they were presented quite frequently came to be closely bound up with the identity and function of these public spaces. The *macchine* of the Spaniards were usually erected in the open space between the Palazzo di Propaganda Fide and Bernini's Fountain of the Barcaccia, those of the French in Piazza Farnese (though occasionally also in Piazza Navona), and those of the Neapolitans in the Piazza SS. Apostoli. On these special occasions temporary stands were usually erected for the aristocracy and frequently fountains providing free wine for the populace as a gesture of largess were also set up. The facades of the buildings fronting on the square were often covered with elaborate decorations, thus transforming the appearance of these large urban spaces. It was also common practice to distribute prints and occasionally even descriptive pamphlets explaining the often all-too-complex significance of the ephemeral decorations to the audience. These, of course, constitute the largest and most valuable group of documents for the study of eighteenth-century Roman fireworks displays.

One of the most interesting *macchine* presented by the Spanish ambassador was designed by Domenico Paradisi in 1721 (Fig. 13). Our knowledge of Paradisi's training and professional activity is extremely sketchy, and judging from this design as well as his work in renovating the interior of Santa Cecilia in Trastevere, is deserving of serious study.[60] He seems to have begun his career as a painter in the 1680's and in this capacity had early contacts with Carlo Fontana; in 1715 along with Michetti he was one of the competitors for the design of the sacristy for St. Peter's. The central portion of Paradisi's composition, which was over a hundred feet tall, was flanked by spiral columns bearing the motto of Spain, recalling designs

59 *Narrazione delle solenni reali feste celebrate in Napoli da Sua Maestà il Re delle Due Sicilie... per la nascità del suo primogenito Filippo Reale Principe delle Due Sicilie*, Naples, 1748 (with fifteen illustrations).

60 Cf. the brief outline of Paradisi's career in H. Hager, *Filippo Juvarra e il concorso di modelli del 1715 bandito da Clemente XI per la nuova sacrestia di S. Pietro*, Rome, 1970, 36.

by Fischer von Erlach. Accompanying Paradisi's printed view of his 1721 *macchina* is a short pamphlet celebrating the marriage of Louis, Prince of Austurias, with the Bourbon princess Luisa Isabella d'Orléans.[61] On top of an octagonal "anfiteatro" are enthroned two allegorical figures representing France and Spain, above which winged *genii* support the crowns of the two monarchies while Hymen joins them with indissoluable bands of gold. At the foot of the throne other allegorical figures personifying the four parts of the earth pay homage, while on the other side (not illustrated) a hydra symbolizing the Protestant heresy and Moslem infidels is cast down by the grand alliance of these two great Christian powers. The marriage celebrated by Paradisi's allegorical figures was a direct expression of Spain's diplomatic policy following the Treaty of the Hague (1720), and sealed her short-lived alliance with France and England. By lavishly publicizing such an important alliance in Rome, Philip V clearly intended to serve notice that in spite of the reverses he had experienced in the course of the War of Spanish Succession, Spain was still a power to be reckoned with.

In 1728 another great fireworks *macchina* was erected in the Piazza di Spagna to celebrate one more in the series of Spanish weddings and alliances, this time with Portugal (Fig. 14). This apparatus, representing the Palace of Hymen, was commissioned by Cardinal Bentivoglio of Aragon and designed by Nicola Salvi, who had yet to establish his reputation by winning the competition for the Trevi Fontain.[62] The resemblance between Salvi's *macchina* resting on an abundant cushion of clouds and similar ephemeral structures designed for the theatre is immediately apparent; Hymen's palace is simply a heavier, more monumental edifice than that of Apollo as designed by Michetti for Cardinal Ottoboni's theatre one year later. Besides the fact that fireworks *macchine* were designed to be blown up, the main characteristic distinguishing them from their theatrical counterparts was their enormous scale. This becomes apparent when it is realized that Salvi's *macchina*, more than a hundred and fifty feet tall, rose considerably higher than the Spanish Steps, the lower portions of which are just visible beneath the clouds to the right of the apparatus. The inscription underneath Vasconi's engraving of Salvi's design identifies the numerous allegorical figures and explains their significance much as Paradisi's pamphlet did

61 D. Paradisi, *Descrizione della macchina de' fuochi di gioja fatti in Piazza di Spagna il xix Dicembre MDCCXXI in occasione di essersi pubblicate le nozze del serenissima Prencipessa Luisa Isabella d'Orleans per ordine dell'Eminentiss., e Reverendiss. Signor Card. Francesco d'Acquaviva, et Aragona incaricato degl' affari di Sua Maestà Cattolica in questa Corte di Roma*, Rome, 1721.

62 Cf. V. Moschini, "La prima opera di Nicola Salvi," *Roma*, VII, 1929, 345-347.

for his *macchina* of seven years before.[63] While the strategy of international diplomacy changed rapidly in the eighteenth century — in 1728 Spain was allied with Portugal *against* France — the means employed for propaganda and the display of power remained essentially the same.

Not to be outdone by Cardinal Ottoboni's theatrical performance of *Carlo Magno* celebrating the birth of the Dauphin in 1729, Cardinal de Polignac, the French ambassador in Rome, put on a lavish fireworks display in the Piazza Navona the following week. The fireworks *macchine* designed by the painter Pier Leone Ghezzi were exceptionally grand in conception, and judging from the lengthy descriptions of contemporary observers and the number of views recording their appearance, were extremely successful.[64] The pyrotechnic decorations were lined up along the main axis of the square in imitation of the *spina* of ancient circuses. As we have seen, imaginative reconstructions of classical monuments were a common feature of contemporary drama, and in seeking to achieve a similar effect on an urban scale, Ghezzi, who was himself an antiquarian of vast erudition, was consciously working within a recognized tradition. Especially interesting is his use of twin spiral columns, a scenographic combination of isolated classical monuments sanctioned by Fischer von Erlach, Paradisi and others, to glorify the French monarchy. On top of one of the columns was a statue of St. Louis IX and on the other a statue of Louis XIV, while painted bas-reliefs on the shafts below illustrated important events in the reigns of these two monarchs. Parallelling Ghezzi's antiquarian interest in the ancient appearance of the Piazza Navona is his profound appreciation of the scenographic potential of the modern square.

By far the most numerous fireworks displays in eighteenth-century Rome were organized by the Contestabile Colonna, the ambassador of the King of Naples. Each year on the feast of Sts. Peter and Paul the King of Naples made the symbolic gesture of giving the Pope a white horse (called *chinea* in Neapolitan dialect) to acknowledge his obeisance to Papal authority.[65] The horse, accompanied by a colorful cavalcade of nobility, was conducted from the Palazzo Colonna to the Vatican Palace, passing the Castel S. Angelo along the way, where it was given

63 Cf. A. Schiavo, *La Fontana di Trevi e le altre opere di Nicola Salvi*, Rome, 1956, 34 for a transcription of these captions.

64 Cf. *Diario Ordinario di Roma*, no. 1924, 10–18 in date of December 3, 1729. G. B. Panini made both an etching and a painting illustrating Ghezzi's design. Cf. F. Arisi, *Gian Paolo Panini*, Piacenza, 1961, II, fig. 128 for a reproduction of the painting which is in the Louvre. Another version is in the Chrysler collection.

65 Accompanying the horse was a yearly donation of seven thousand gold ducats.

an artillery salute. This was the origin of the *Festa della Chinea*, the festival aspect of which was expanded in 1722 by the presentation of fireworks in the Piazza SS. Apostoli on the evenings before and after the cavalcade.[66] For the next sixty years, with few exceptions, two large fireworks *macchine* were presented each year on this occasion, constituting an unbroken sequence of designs of considerable importance to the study of architecture and ephemeral design in this period.[67] Fortunately, in the Casanatense Library in Rome there is a collection of more than a hundred prints illustrating the fireworks displays erected to celebrate the presentation of the *Chinea*.[68] These engravings, which make it possible to study the themes and designs of numerous large-scale architectural compositions, many of them designed by the finest architects practicing in Rome, have long been known but have yet to be studied in a comprehensive way.[69]

A number of contemporary documents, as well as the visual evidence provided by the prints themselves, make it appear likely that Michetti designed six fireworks displays for the *Festa della Chinea* in the period 1731-33. In 1731 Pier Leone Ghezzi described in his diary an accident which occurred in the course of setting off the first of the two fireworks *macchine* for that year (Fig. 15):

> *... giugno, 1731. Fu fatto il fuoco in Casa Colonna e per trascuraggine del focarolo e di Michetti misuratore, e non architetto si brugiò tutto, con tutta l'ossatura, e brugiò la casa contigua, dove vi stava una Gallinara... in cima di detto fuoco vi era un Atlante che sosteneva il mondo, il primo si brugiò l'Atlante, e poi il mondo, e poi cominciò il fuoco da basso, e andiede a fuoco tutto.*[70]

At this time Michetti was the architect of the Colonna family and it is to be expected that his duties would have included the design of the *Chinea macchine*

66 An elaborate temporary structure had been erected in the Piazza SS. Apostoli in 1473 to honor Leonora of Aragon, which suggests that there may have been a tradition of using the square for festival purposes going back to the Renaissance. Cf. T. Magnuson, *Studies in Roman Quattrocento Architecture*, Stockholm, 1958, 314.

67 The series of *Chinea macchine* was broken only in 1734-37 following the Spanish restoration and in 1768, when for some unknown reason the festivities occurred in the morning. In 1745 Piazza Farnese was used for the celebrations, but with this exception the *Chinea macchine* were always erected in front of the Palazzo Colonna.

68 *Raccolta rarissima di tutte le machine de fuochi artifiziali di architettura incendiate in quest'alma città di Roma ne loro respettivi anni e tempi principati dal 1722 a tutto il 1773, e proseguendo felicimente a tutto l'anno... Inventate, disegnate ed incise dai più celebri autori di architettura, di disegno, ed incisure.* (Rome, Biblioteca Casanatense, 20-B-I-17).

69 Sixty of the prints in this collection are reproduced in G. Ferrari, *Bellezze architettoniche per le feste della Chinea in Roma nei secoli XVII e XVIII*, Turin, 1920.

70 C. M. Mancini, "Le 'Memorie del Cav. Leone Ghezzi scritte da sé medesimo da gennaio 1731 a luglio 1734'", *Palatino*, XII, 1968, 484. Just one year

just as had been the case with his predecessor, Gabriele Valvassori. Unfortunately, the architect is not mentioned in the print of the 1731 *macchina*, nor in those of the next two years, but the appearance of these structures, as we shall see, is similar to other designs by Michetti. In addition to this evidence, in the Colonna archives there are a number of payments to masons and other artisans working on the 1733 *macchine* which were approved by Michetti in his capacity of " Architetto dell'Ecc.ma Casa Colonna ", all of which reinforce the impression that he was their designer as well.[71]

The first *macchina* for 1731 consists of an octagonal base carrying an inscription, which is elevated above a basement with a projecting convex center and concave recessions on either side. The curving volutes of a split pediment rise above the center portion of the basement, while statues of Hercules and Minerva flank the central pedestal. Towering above all else is the figure of Atlas supporting the globe, the improper firing of which caused so much damage. The plan of the lower level of this *macchina* repeats that of Michetti's facade of S. Pietro in Zagarolo and the central portion of a palace he designed at Strelna, in Russia. Large circular balls are used as finials, much as they are above the attic level of the pavilions of the Palazzo Colonna, which was under construction at this very time,[72] and on the interior of Michetti's central plan church for St. Petersburg, projected some eight

earlier Michetti had been appointed *misuratore* of the Camera Apostolica, a position which brought him into frequent conflict with Ghezzi. In this diary entry Ghezzi appears to play on Michetti's title, implying that he is not a capable architect, and suited only to evaluate the work of others. Ghezzi's poor opinion of Michetti is confirmed by another reference, a marginal note dated 1733 on a drawing (no. 110) in the Kunstbibliothek der Staatlichen Museen, Berlin, in which he criticizes Michetti's design of the Colonna Palace and execution of the Villa Corsini at Anzio.

71 Archivio Colonna, Giustificazioni del Libro Mastro dell'Anno 1733, part. 6, nos. 254 and 324: " Al di 23 giugno 1733. Misura e stima delli lavori ad uso di muratore fatti a tutta sua robba spese, a fattura da Mro Antonio Giobbi capo mro murat.e per servizio dell'Ill.mo e Ecc.mo Sig.e Principe D. Fabrizio Colonna Gran Contestabile, et Ambasciator straordinario di Sua Maestà Cesarea in occasione che S. Em.za presentò la Chinea la sera della viggilia delli SS. Pietro e Paullo..." The Colonna Archive constitutes a rich and as yet untapped source of documentary material relating to the *Festa della Chinea*. As I was permitted access to the Archive for only one afternoon, however, I am unfortunately unable to make full and systematic use of this information which is essential to further study of the *Chinea* designs.

72 Michetti's design for the facade of the Colonna palace, a long horizontal anchored at both ends by projecting pavilions, is without precedent in Rome and can best be explained by the particular function it served once a year in connection with the *Festa della Chinea*. The prints celebrating this event repeatedly show the low central portion of the facade serving as an unobtrusive backdrop and occasional support for the tall fireworks *macchine*; these were in turn framed by the projecting corner pavilions, which provided a lofty vantage point above the unruly crowd for the ambassador and the Roman aristocracy. The prints representing the *Chinea* displays for 1732 and 1733 provide important visual documentation for the design evolution and execution of Michetti's facade of the Colonna Palace.

years earlier.[73] The *atlanti* and herm figures also recall their counterparts in the first scene of *Carlo Magno*; but more convincing than these details are the over-all proportions and use of the orders, which are characteristic of Michetti's style. The second *macchina* for 1731, which could not be set off due to the destruction of the first, was designed in the form of a triumphal arch (Fig. 16). The arch is surmounted by the imperial eagle supporting a crown and flanked by trophies similar to those which appear in Michetti's set in *Carlo Magno* illustrating Charlemagne's triumphal procession. The basement is articulated by octagonal plaques producing a laminated effect rather like wainscotting which appears in other buildings by Michetti, including the Palazzo Colonna. Although some allowance must be made for the quality of the print, Michetti's design for this triumphal arch is disappointing and far less impressive than that of the first *macchina*.

Both of the *macchine* for 1731 carry inscriptions praising the martial feats of Charles VI in defending the Holy Roman Empire.[74] The Hapsburgs had ruled Naples since 1707, and consequently the political content of the *Chinea* designs was decidedly pro-Austrian until the Hapsburgs were replaced by Charles III Bourbon in 1734. The inscription and battle scenes painted on the base of the first *macchina* show the Austrian army in action in northen Italy denying access to Spanish troops who, in accordance with the treaty of Seville (1729), were seeking to occupy Parma and Piacenza. In 1731, following the death of Antonio Farnese, the Emperor occupied the Duchies of Parma and Piacenza, thereby further increasing the tension between Austria and Spain. Later in the year, however, an agreement was signed in Vienna reconciling Charles VI and Philip V. This ensured only a shaky and short-lived peace which would be broken in 1733 by the War of Polish Succession, in the course of which Austria lost all of her possessions in southern Italy. It is the fragile treaty of Vienna which is celebrated by the triumphal arch of the second *macchina*. Through the convoluted rhetoric of political propaganda, Austrian interests in Italy were identified with the cause of peace at a time when the rest of Europe, including the Papacy, regarded their actions as inflammatory and liable to precipitate a new war.

The two *macchine* designed for next year's *Chinea* in 1732 employ representations of scenes from classical mythology to glorify the emperor.[75] The first

73 Leningrad, State Hermitage Museum, Drawing no. 4728.

74 For a contemporary description of these cf. the *Diario Ordinario di Roma*, no. 2170, pp. 11-12 in date of June 30, 1731.

75 Cf. the description in the *Diario Ordinario*, no. 2329, p. 7 in date of July 5, 1732.

macchina, depicting the Council of the Gods on Olympus, alludes to the continuing efforts of Charles VI to enlarge the Empire and ensure peace throughout the Christian world (Fig. 17). The second *macchina* which was set off following the display of the first shows Ganymede being carried off by Jove in the form of an eagle while two hunters look on (Fig. 18). The Rape of Ganymede is interpreted as having been motivated by the beauty of the young boy's soul, which enabled him to rise to the level of the gods, in which respect the emperor is worthy of being compared to him. The first design representing the Council of the Gods has already been discussed in relation to the concluding scene of *Carlo Magno* depicting the Palace of the Sun and other open circular structures designed by Michetti. As a design for a fireworks display it seems a particularly successful combination of architecture and figures detached from the observers by the illusionistic device of clouds on which the temple seems naturally poised. The composition of the second *macchina* is even more pictorial than the first, primarily because architecture plays no part in it. Instead, Michetti employs the gigantic scale of the mythological figures to great effect; his composition, culminating in the outstretched wings of the eagle, which towers over the surrounding buildings, employs the urban setting as a scenographic backdrop for the depiction of a supernatural event.

The *macchine* for 1733 also employ mythological themes to extol the reign of Charles VI.[76] The first shows Apollo and the Muses gathered on Mount Parnassus, while below, a group of Bacchic revellers dances beneath a grotto cut through the base of the mountain (Fig. 19). According to the explanatory inscription these two scenes serve to illustrate how the emperor's rule has brought peace and prosperity to all of Europe. The second *macchina* depicts Jove and Minerva enthroned in the midst of martial standards as they consult with one another concerning how best to maintain the peace (Fig. 20). In a cave opening into the side of the mountain on which they sit is the forge of Vulcan, where a number of figures are engaged in the manufacture of arms. In contrast to the first, this *macchina* accurately represents the contemporary political situation in Europe, where England, France, Spain and Austria were arming in preparation for the War of Polish Succession, which would begin before the year was out. Both of these *macchine* are raised up on a high arched basement standing isolated at the center of the square and are not attached to the Colonna Palace as was usually the case. Above the

76 Cf. the description in the *Diario Ordinario*, no. 2484, pp. 7-8 in date of July 4, 1733.

level of the architectural basement, however, these *macchine* are essentially large-scale sculptural compositions of figures and rough stone work made of stiff canvas supported by a wooden armature which was covered by a gesso coating and then painted.

Michetti's *macchine* for the *Festa della Chinea* of 1733 were the last ones made for five years. This was due to the change of government in Naples following the War of Polish Succession, as a result of which Austrian rule was replaced by that of the Bourbons. The series of *Chinea* designs picks up again in 1738, but Michetti was no longer involved in their presentation. For a period of six years following 1738 the *macchine* were decidedly non-architectural in character, being instead large pictorial compositions designed by painters in which figures predominate. In 1745 this trend reversed, and from that time onwards, the *Chinea macchine* were essentially architectural compositions in which figures were relegated to a relatively minor role. It would be extremely interesting to know the reasons for these changes in attitude, and whether they were due to changing taste reflected in the choice of French designers, a need for economy, or the introduction of some new technology which made it possible to realize more pictorial effects with fireworks.

Even studied through the less than satisfying medium of monochrome prints, the designs for eighteenth-century ephemeral architecture delight and charm the observer. The scale and volume of the work produced, much of it by first-rate artists, are remarkable, and the designs display an imagination and daring which could never have been incorporated in structures built of more lasting materials. Through prints these designs circulated widely, and once reduced to a two-dimensional format became for all practical purposes indistinguishable from graphic representations of permanent architecture. Due both to the prints' wide circulation and the complex and rapidly changing systems of European alliances, festival architecture employed as political propaganda was more subject to foreign influence than were designs for permanent buildings and took on a truly international character. It is indeed reasonable to speak of an international style of late Baroque architectural design, originally formulated by Carlo Fontana, the full implications of which were realized by his many pupils such as Fischer von Erlach, Juvarra and Michetti. Not only did temporary architecture play an important part in the careers of Fontana's students, particularly Michetti, but it proved a crucial agent in the dissemination of a new, more scenographic approach to architectural design throughout Europe.

Fig. 1. Nicola Michetti, Carlo Magno, *frontispiece. Photograph courtesy of the Biblioteca Apostolica Vaticana.*

Fig. 2. Nicola Michetti, Carlo Magno, *Act I, sc. 1. Photograph courtesy of the BAV.*

Fig. 3. Nicola Michetti, Carlo Magno, *Act I, sc. 11. Photograph courtesy of the BAV.*

Fig. 4. Nicola Michetti, Carlo Magno, *Act. II, sc. 6. Photograph courtesy of the BAV.*

Fig. 5. Nicola Michetti, Carlo Magno, *Act. II, sc. 6, preparatory drawing. London, Victoria and Albert Museum*

Fig. 6. Nicola Michetti, Carlo Magno, *Act. III, sc. 5. Photograph courtesy of the BAV.*

Fig. 7. Nicola Michetti, Carlo Magno, *Act III, sc. 9. Photograph courtesy of the BAV.*

Fig. 8. Nicola Michetti, Carlo Magno, *Act III, sc. 14. Photograph courtesy of the BAV.*

Fig. 9. Nicola Michetti, Carlo Magno, *Act III, sc. 15. Photograph courtesy of the BAV.*

Fig. 10. Nicola Michetti, Carlo Magno, *macchina: "La Reggia di Apollo". Photography courtesy of the BAV.*

Fig. 11. Filippo Juvarra, set design for Tito e Berenice. *Turin, Cibraro collection. After Viale Ferrero, tav. 155.*

Fig. 12. Nicola Fiore, Fireworks Design, 1709. After Mancini, 1970, p. 657.

Fig. 13. *Domenico Paradisi, Fireworks Design, 1721. After Paradisi. Photograph courtesy of the BAV.*

Fig. 14. *Nicola Salvi, Fireworks Design, 1728. Courtesy of the Biblioteca Casanatense, Rome.*

Fig. 15. *Nicola Michetti,* Chinea *Design, 1731* (prima macchina). *After Ferrari, tav. 5.*

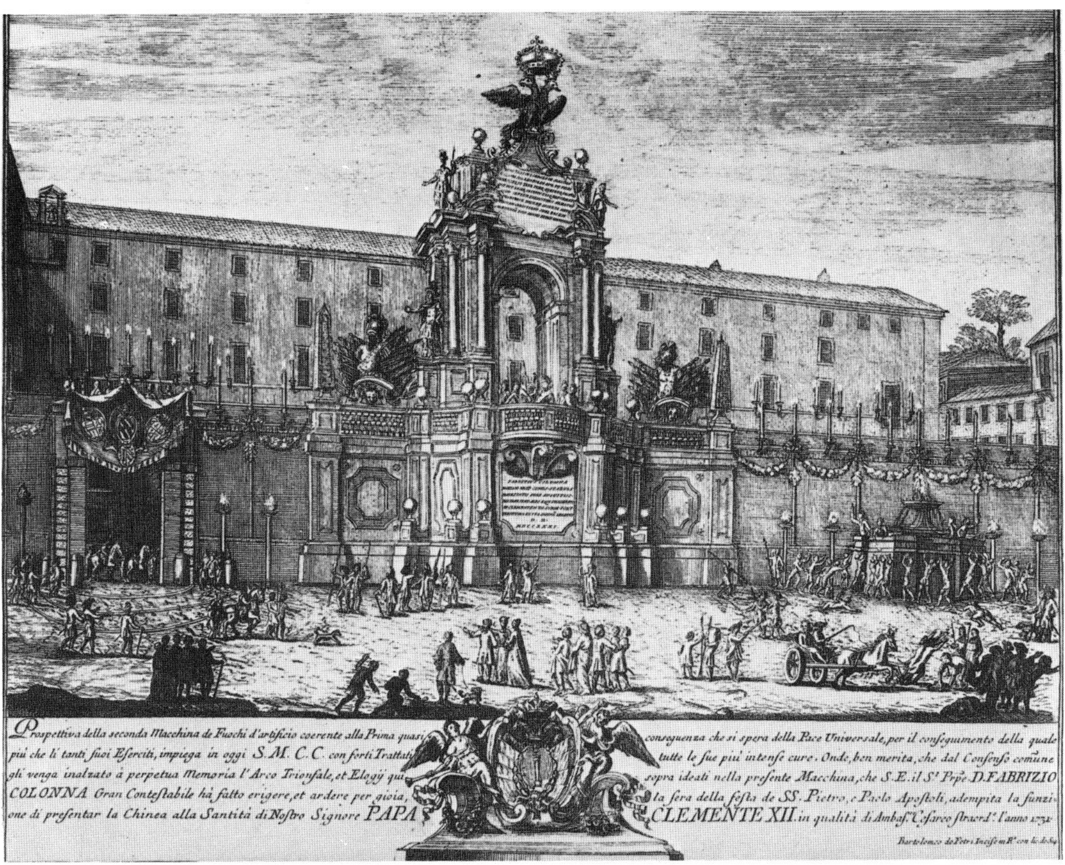

Fig. 16. *Nicola Michetti*, Chinea *Design*, *1731* (seconda macchina). *After Ferrari, tav. 4.*

Fig. 17. *Nicola Michetti*, Chinea *Design*, *1732* (prima macchina). *After* Raccolta rarissima, *fol. 24.*

Fig. 18. Nicola Michetti, Chinea *Design, 1732* (seconda macchina). *After* Raccolta rarissima, *fol. 25.*

Fig. 19. Nicola Michetti, Chinea *Design, 1733* (prima macchina). *After Ferrari, tav. 6.*

Fig. 20. Nicola Michetti, Chinea *Design, 1733* (seconda macchina). *After* Raccolta rarissima, *fol. 27.*

ANTHONY M. CLARK

IX

BATONI'S PROFESSIONAL CAREER AND STYLE *

FROM Batoni's arrival in Rome on May 15, 1727, until his apoplectic attack in mid-September, 1786, there is a career of almost sixty years which is characterized by intense and continuous production. The " omo grande " whom Canova met in 1779 was the most successful painter in Rome — at least when Mengs was not present — from the early 1740's. By 1754 he had gained "nell'Italia la preferenza fra gl'altri Pittore " (Sardini). By 1759 one of his portraits was described as " eins der ersten in der Welt " (Winckelmann); by 1760 " the Italian artists talked of nothing, looked at nothing but the works of Pompeo Batoni " (Benjamin West). Batoni was " the best painter in Italy " (1762, James Bruce of Kinnaird); copied by students along with Caravaggio, Pietro da Cortona, Algardi, Bernini, Domenichino and Raphael (1765, Henry Fuseli); " esteemed the best portrait painter in the world " (1771, Lady Anna Riggs Miller). Although Mengs was " forse più grande e più ricco d'idea del Sig. Batoni è sicuramente più puntuale " (Conte Francesco Carrara), it could be said of Italy in 1783 that "il ne se trouve plus qu'un seul peintre fameux, Pompeo Batoni " (Gustav III of Sweden).

The great number of works upon which Batoni's reputation was based are not yet all recovered and are, mainly, poorly published. Batoni's chronology has never been properly deciphered and his paintings are widely scattered, in Europe, the New World, and from Tashkent to Melbourne, Australia. Despite most courageous efforts in London and Edinburgh by Mr Brinsley Ford, Mr Basil Skinner and the

* *Mostra D. Pompeo Batoni*, cat. ed. I. B. Barsali, Lucca, 1967, 23-50.

Courtauld Institute, some of Batoni's most important British portraits are still unrecognized or unphotographed. To write as I must of Batoni's career is not yet completely easy, and I must begin with an apology for introducing here so many new facts and dates unsupported by reference and appropriate gratitude.

As is well known, Batoni produced a number of church altarpieces, a large *oeuvre* of subjects both profane and religious, and many portraits. The career of Batoni divides naturally into five parts: his training (to 1732), his early works (to 1740), his first flourishing (to 1755), his middle period (to 1780), and a final period. The first period, of special interest today because of the location of the present exhibition, is well recorded by Benaglio and Pascoli, but is also obscure, because of the almost entire lack of artistic evidence. The early works are well known: altarpieces in Rome at S. Gregorio Magno (*ca.* 1732-1734) and at SS. Celso e Giuliano (by Feb., 1738); in Brescia at S. Maria della Pace (erected and unveiled January, 1737) and in Milan (paid 1740); as well as the Colonna ceiling inserts (*ca.* 1737-1740) and the *Trionfo di Venezia* for Marco Foscarini (1737; now in the Raleigh, North Carolina Museum of Art). It is especially notable that at least three of these works are very closely connected with the important patron and cardinal, Angelo Maria Querini. In the flourishing third period, which coincides with the reign of Benedict XIV (who created the artist a *cavaliere*, and for whom Batoni did the 1743 altar in S. Maria Maggiore, the 1743 ceiling of the Quirinale *Caffeaus*, and the controversial altar of 1746-1755 for St. Peter's), Batoni became extremely fashionable in Rome. Now he produced the host of superb history paintings, at first only for the Lucchese and Roman nobility but, by the mid-1740's, eagerly sought in Germany and Great Britain; altarpieces for S. Maria della Pace at Brescia (1744, unveiled 1746); for S. Ponziano e S. Domenico at Lucca (1743 and 1749); for S. Vittore al Corpo at Milan (*ca.* 1745); for an unknown location at Lisbon (1747); for I Filippini at Chiari near Brescia (1750); and for the Chiesa delle Anime del Purgatorio, today a museum, at Messina (1752). His portraits of *milordi* begin by 1744 and were a fashionable necessity by 1755; with the success of the 1753-1754 full-length portraits of the Duke and Duchess of Württemberg (Stuttgart, Württembergerische Landesbibliothek) Batoni became the most noticeable European portraitist. His two copies of his adored Raphael for the Duke of Northumberland (1752-1755) and his copy of a Guido Reni then in Palazzo Colonna also for an Englishman belong to this period, as do the beginnings of the direct purchases of his subject pictures by the German princelings (Schönborn, Pommersfelden, 1747; Harrach, Vienna, Gallery Harrach, 1751; Algarotti's approach for Frederick the Great, 1751).

The long middle period (1755-1780) is dominated by Batoni's difficult but quite friendly rivalry with Mengs. The German's intermittent presence in Rome (absent June, 1761 to March, 1771, and from October, 1773, to March, 1777, dying in June, 1779), his portraits (especially in the 1750's and the favored *Clement XIII* of 1760) and his public commissions (S. Eusebio ceiling by 1760, Villa Albani ceiling of 1761, Camera dei Papiri ceiling of 1772-1773, altar for St. Peter's commissioned in 1772 but never done) meant the serious challenge of an obviously more intellectually able, if not more gifted, painter, and one who had, until 1769, a powerful although controversial aide in J.J. Winckelmann.

If, in this period, Batoni's Roman pre-eminence was at least equalled, the period was nevertheless a deeply successful one and includes the climax of the artist's fame in his portrait of the *Emperor Joseph II with his brother the Grand Duke Leopold* (1769; Vienna, Kunsthistorisches Museum). During Batoni's middle period it was often recorded of the artist (Alessandro Albani, 1753; Mariette, 1764; *Description des Tableaux*, Potsdam, 1771, etc.) that " il s'est ordonné aux portraits," or was delayed because of them. It is true that there is a very large, uninterrupted creation of this, Batoni's most saleable product. However, if paintings of profane and religious subjects have become too expensive for the average wealthy visitor to Rome, Batoni's middle period is the one in which the greatest princes of Europe (who almost universally sat for their portraits to Batoni when in Rome) commissioned such subject pictures in numbers. The list is impressive: *Allegory of Benedict XIV and Duke de Choiseul* for Cardinal Orsini (1757; Minneapolis, The Minneapolis Institute of Arts); *Departure of Hector* for the Duke of Northampton (1758-1761; lost); *Thetis, Achilles and Chiron* for the Duke of Parma (1760-1761; Parma, Galleria Nazionale); *Acis and Galatea* (1761; Stockholm, Private Collection); and *Death of Mark Antony* (1763; Brest, Musée Municipal), both for French noblemen; *Cleopatra and Augustus* (Dijon, Musée) and *Prodigal Son* (Vienna, Kunsthistorisches Museum; both 1773) commissioned with the various Hapsburg portraits by Maria Teresa (1769-1775); the lost pair, *Justizia e Clemenza* and *Valore e Prudenza* (1768; not the Vitetti picture), and another pair, *Scenes of Diana*, for the King of Poland (now lost); the two purchases (the 1746 *Finding of Moses*, Potsdam, Staatliche Schlösser und Gärten Potsdam-Sanssouci; the 1756 *Marriage of Cupid and Psyche*, Berlin, Staatliche Museen, Bodemuseum), and, from 1763, the three commissions of Frederick the Great (*Alexander and the Family of Darius*, done in 1775; Potsdam, Staatliche Schlösser und Gärten; *Coriolanus* and *Venus and Adonis*, both begun 1764, now lost); *Ercole al Bivio*, bought by Count Razoumovsky in 1766 for Catherine the Great (Leningrad, Hermitage), and *Thetis, Achilles and Chiron* and *Continence of Scipio* (both 1771; Hermitage) commissioned for her by Count Chouvaloff in 1768; the 1774 *Bacchus and Ariadne* for Sir W.W. Wynn (Montignoso, Massa, Villa Schiff-Giorgini); the 1776 *Hagar* for Lord Arundel (Rome, Galleria Nazionale); and *Allegory of the Infant Prince of Naples* for Queen Maria Carolina (1780; Caserta, Reggia). To this long list of expensive and highly important works must be added the altars for Madrid (1759), now in the Prado; for the Gesù at Rome (1760, shown 1767); for SS. Trinità at Crema (1761); the second altar for Chiari (commissioned 1763, done 1780); and for S. Antonio Abate at Parma (1778).

Batoni's final period was dominated by the seven very large altarpieces for the Basilica of Estrella in Lisbon (1781-1784; two were done, at least in part, and in 1787 delivered, by Batoni's son Felice), the *Marriage of S. Catherine* now in the Palazzo Quirinale (dated 1779, probably done 1780), the *Holy Family* bought by Russia in 1782 (Leningrad, Hermitage), and the *Venus and Cupid* for Prince Yussupoff (1784). But this period is most memorable for the last portraits done in an *ultima maniera*, simple, direct and more daring than ever before. Of these the most familiar examples are the magnificent full-length of *Thomas Giffard* (1784; Chillington, Private Collection) and the ravishing portraits of *Contessa di San Martino* (1785; Rome, Collection A. Busiri-Vici), and *Marchesa Brignole* (1786; Brussels, Private Collection), although perhaps the most important monuments are the seated full-lengths of the *Grand Duke Paul Petrovic and his Duchess* (1782; Gatchina, USSR) the lost full-length of *Countess Katherine Skawronsky* (1785), and the portrait of the *Balì de Suffren* seated before a view of Malta (1786; Versailles, Musée).

By this brief outline we have noted Batoni's chief works and their patronage and, leaving aside the treatment of his portraits for a moment, it is now possible to turn to the nature of the works and of the career. It seems useful to examine Batoni's training, the influences upon him, and the nature of his talent.

Batoni was the son of, and trained by, a distinguished goldsmith. If the young Pompeo was in constant difficulty with Paolo Batoni (died 1747) and fought him to become a painter and not a goldsmith, I believe Batoni's ornamental finish, which Cicognara called his "laboriosa finitezza olandese," is not just a matter of the spirit and taste of his century but, in Batoni's case, the natural practice of one craft adopted for the advantages of another. Exquisite finish had been an especially Roman characteristic of the late Baroque, one which such French critics as Mariette did, and Cochin did not, like, and which Mengs himself practised in a rather obvious, although more intellectual, way than Batoni. The *finitezza olandese* which accompanied Batoni's exceptional gifts of fresh color, strikingly natural tone, visual intensity and visual elegance, are more than the fashion of a period and often achieve a degree rare in the history of painting, Italian or otherwise. But since the *finitezza* seldom overwhelms Batoni's product — he was rightly said to be " nato pittore " — one cannot, perhaps, give his first teacher large credit.

Batoni's motherless, miserable and disfigured childhood was cured by his discovery of drawing and painting, despite his father's energetic attempts to prevent him from doing either. It is interesting that Batoni always represents the *Arts* as young yet maternal women, and it is poignant to know both that his birth destroyed his own mother and that his native Lucca was later to be a victim of his own artistic success. Long after Batoni's Lucchese patrons (Alessandro Guinigi, Nicolò Mansi, Lodovico Sardini, Michele Barsotti, Francesco Talenti, Francesco Conti, Tommaso Mazzarosa, Francesco Buonvisi) ended his Roman pension because of his sudden and improper marriage (November, 1729), and despite the many commissions from the Lucchese nobility in the early 1740's when Batoni needed them, the artist was finally to refuse not only to favor the Republic in prices and commissions, but even to revisit it. Upon his more important works Batoni did, however, continue to put " Lucensis " in his signature.

Batoni began to draw at seven and by his fifteenth year had copied two Guercino prints and a Salimbeni *Madonna.* He probably was able, in his very last years in Lucca, to use the drawing academies of the two leading painters, G. D. Lombardi and Domenico Brugieri, one of whom later said of a work by Batoni newly arrived from Rome, " desiderarlo più sudico, parendogli così troppo lindo." In his first year in Rome Batoni avoided choosing either Conca or Masucci as his master, but went to Conca's evening drawing academy, and spent a long day copying the famous Raphael and Carracci frescoes and the antique statues of the Belvedere. His first success was in selling drawings of these statues to the British. Francesco Imperiali, the gifted and independent painter who had strong British and German connections, aided both this work (at least by July, 1730) and Batoni's study of painting, and appears to have introduced him to Cav. Girolamo Odam, the artist and intellectual (who was in turn to introduce Batoni to Cardinal Querini), to the draughtsman and antiquary Francesco Bartoli, and to the important cleric and collector, Alessandro Furietti, who commissioned several drawings of antiquities for engravings and, in 1736, the high altar of S. Celso.

Imperiali may be considered Batoni's advisor and, in a literal but limited sense, his teacher. Imperiali's own paintings were more vigorous and yet more classical than those of the official painters of contemporary Rome, the *Maratteschi*, who had twisted Maratti's style towards the young idiom of the rococo. With a rough pastoral nobility and romanticism Imperiali's paintings were also quite different from the work of the two other important independent masters of Rome, Trevisani and Luti. Imperiali's example is closely followed in details of Batoni's S. Gregorio altarpiece, the angel in which is completely in Imperiali's idiom.

And yet Masucci's clarity of vision and form, the porcelain-like finish of Trevisani and the superb tone and effects of light practised by Luti (as well as Luti's intense and characteristic rhetoric) seem more and more in Batoni's mind as the 1730's developed. There is much of Imperiali and of these three other artists in Batoni's early works and, until 1740, nothing of the grandiose rococo style as practised by its most typical Roman exponent, Sebastiano Conca, who gave the color and forms of the late Roman Baroque a rococo Neapolitan dialect. Especially in the middle of the 1730's Batoni seems particularly interested in the classicism of the Renaissance and of the early Baroque: his *Presentation* for Brescia adopts Barocci's *Presentation* and *Visitation* in the Chiesa Nuova (the first monument visited by Batoni on his arrival in Rome), and the high altar of S. Celso is based upon Guercino's *Christ in Glory* in Toulouse reinterpreted by a close study of (and quotations) from Raphael.

There is a noticeable change about 1740 and the paintings of Batoni from the second period in Rome are far less clear and austere: the native poetry is discovered and expressed in ripe and grandiose terms. It is interesting to follow, in Batoni's letters, the development of the artist's handwriting from 1740 to 1745: at first it is intensely *naif*, tormentedly, delightfully and painfully clear; then he practices an unsuccessful but very grand style; finally evolving a robust and open, clear but richly rhythmical manner, which he was always to keep.

The masterpiece of Batoni's first flourishing is the *Fall of Simon Magus* intended for St. Peter's (today in the chiesa di S. Maria degli Angeli), and it is the supreme example of his mature rhetoric. If there is still the lucidity of the 1730 paintings, there is also a language at once grander, more energetic and forceful, and more obviously emotional (and even romantic). The lessons of Trevisani (composition), Masucci (space and form), Conca and Luti (visual emphasis), Imperiali (scale and romanticism) are all assimilated. With very obvious lessons from late Raphael and Annibale Carracci, the *Magus* must have seemed a remarkable summary of Roman pictorial virtues to its early viewers, since what was thought best of the classical tradition from Pergamum, through the Renaissance, the early and very late Baroque, to the new and rather over dramatic position of the *capo scuola*, Batoni himself, are all very much present.

The *Magus* was finished and exhibited in St. Peter's at Easter, 1755, and by the end of that year Winckelmann was in Rome. Batoni's late contemporaries believed the artist had revived the art of painting in Rome, and some of them — and many contemporary scholars — have noticed Batoni's importance in the development of the neoclassical style. Although his paintings of the 1730's are far more neoclassical in a superficial sense than the *Magus*, Batoni is simply not a good candidate for an originator of the neoclassical except for several facts: his obvious admiration for Raphael and the early Baroque; his use of both the new subjects and the more extreme stylistic innovations (to which he added) of the most severe and classicistic Roman artists between 1720 and 1740; and the powerful presence and healthy example he afforded in Rome when the actual neoclassical style was born. If Batoni is not more neoclassical than such an artist as Giacomo Zoboli was in 1724, if Batoni is never more classical than in his works of the 1730's, his own position is nevertheless not really far from that of Mengs or even the J. L. David of *S. Roch* and *Les Serments des Horaces*, two pictures Batoni deeply and publicly admired, and may even have understood. Batoni's position is opposed, however, to that of Winckelmann, for whom Raphael should be studied but not Bernini, an opinion Mengs half-heartedly shared. Mengs, who had " grandissima stima del Batoni," reputedly calling him " a good painter in a bad age " (1760), might not, however, have urged the young Canova towards a " ritornati a S. Pietro; osservati quei vasti sepolchri, le opere del Bernini, dell'Algardi, del Rusconi." Batoni, his contemporaries thought, " ragionava sull'arte assai bene, ma con una certa incolta semplicità, che non dava tuono magistrale ai suoi precetti " (G. G. De' Rossi, 1810). By the style he created, by natural gift, and by the generation to which he belonged, Batoni was an artist of the grand style of the mid-18th century, that unnamed style between the late Baroque (and its brief rococo aftermath) and the actual neoclassicism. Batoni is a perfect example of this style, which Tiepolo practices within the extraordinary dictates of his genius, which Boucher more vulgarly commands, and of which Mengs is the most austere exponent. It is possible once again today to enjoy the intense virtues of Batoni and to reverse the prophecy of Sir Joshua Reynolds, even if critics (who begin to be fair to Batoni but scorch the beauty of Mengs and Greuze with splendid if silly disesteem) still find Batoni *bird-brained*, and can be annoyed with him as Benjamin West was when Batoni, finishing a *Madonna*, put down his brushes and cried: " Viva Batoni! " This simple poet was also the inheritor and continuator of Raphael and Annibale; his contemporaries, whether Roman or British, believed he possessed all the very great intellectual authority — not yet overturned — of the supreme tradition of Roman drawing. One clue to Batoni's intellectual respectability as his contemporaries conceived of it occurs in an unnoticed and surprising place. In Maron's portrait of Winckelmann (1768) the theorist is shown holding Batoni's drawing (lost today but later engraved for the German's *Storia delle Arti del Disegno*) of Cardinal Albani's famous *Antinous*.

The artist's development after 1755 occurs more in superficial than in basic terms. The exhilarating last style (after 1780), so boldly and simply painted, was blamed by some of his contemporaries on Batoni's senility, for which there is absolutely no other evidence. It is, I believe, a happy effect of old age, although it might be argued that there is a conscious adoption of the *maniera inglese*, principally those fresh touches of paint which Angelica Kauffman had made fashionable in Rome and, from Rome, throughout continental Europe.

Other, earlier acceptances of fashion might be mentioned. After 1760, the moment of the emergence of Mengs to Batoni's disadvantage, there are minor revisions of method. Paintings after the late 1750's have a tendency to be not only less grandiose in form and less opulent in effects, but are often positively dry and, even, faintly tired and faintly apologetic. Confidence returns at the end of the 1760's full-force, but it is possible to notice that Batoni's compositions have become more simple and more narrow in depth, and that the pictorial ornaments are more severely chosen, accurate and modest. Lighter colors, although without a brightened tonality, and certain presentational ideas were certainly suggested by the paintings of Mengs and Maron. But, from the 1760's, there is also an elongation of the human figures, an intense, almost tottering spiritualization of the figures which makes one believe that Batoni, in assimilating the new fashions, reacted with the creation of a quite new and personal style. The second altar for Chiari (1780), the paintings at Lisbon, and the late works for Prussia, Austria and Russia are all examples of this and achieve a daring and elegant new kind of monumentality which supersedes both the Roman rococo and the Mengsian classicism. The *Bacchus and Ariadne* for Wynn (1774) and the *Alexander at Darius' Tent* (1775) closely follow earlier treatments of the same subjects by Angelica Kauffman and Charles Lebrun, retain the extreme classicism of both the prototypes, add all of Batoni's charm and artistic skill, and also introduce tight vertical accents which greatly enliven the original compositions and lift them to a more lyrical realm. Many of Batoni's pictorial ideas are feeble; some are frankly silly; some are stolen from very unlikely sources. Yet his pictures themselves are remarkably convincing and are always most impressive artistically. What Batoni showed of the world and its pleasures has become exotic or decorative to modern eyes; yet his art and artifice are potent enough to astound and edify, perhaps more today than when new. However, since modern man usually must deny that there is any place in his predicament for the constant celebration of his pleasures, it is perhaps unacceptable to speak of Batoni as edifying.

Before discussing Batoni's portraits it may be interesting to glance at the artist's relationship with the Accademia di S. Luca, whose oldest and most famous academician Batoni was at his death. Elected in December, 1741, on the recommendation of the *princeps* Sebastiano Conca, Batoni was nominated *princeps* three times himself but never elected: his rivals Mengs, Preciado and Maron were instead. He was extremely inactive and the two most important offices he held (one of the two *Direttori de' Forestieri*, 1752-1771; one of the two *Stimmatori di Pittura*, 1771-1787) Batoni could undertake at home. By my count he visited the monthly meetings of the Accademia only twenty-six times in his forty-five year membership, and of one these times it is recorded: " è sopragiunto dopo il Sig. Pompeo Batoni." While the artist believed himself a faithful member and supporter of the Accademia he was, as Boni wrote, " amante della tranquilità," who delighted in quoting Leonardo that, while " la poesia è l'anima della pittura, la pittura è una poesia muta."

For the student of culture and the art historian Batoni's portraits are apparently the most interesting feature of his work. Because so little is yet known of portraiture in 17th-and 18th-century Rome I believe it necessary to dwell on Batoni's career as a portraitist in some detail.

" L'artista dei forestieri " (as De' Rossi called Batoni) is described in one of his most important aspects by Professor Haskell in the catalogue of the exhibition in Lucca, although it must be remembered that the British *Grand Tourists* were not Batoni's only patrons, if by far the most numerous. It is especially worth remembering that the British patrons were neither willing nor able to force their artistic tastes on Batoni: *Colonel Gordon* (Fyvie Castle, The Fyvie Trustees) is magnificently clothed in his tartans (1766), but is posed before the Colosseum as a conquering Roman emperor, with all the authority of the greatest and oldest school of painting in Europe (as Rome was believed to be). Batoni was fully aware of the latest developments in European portraiture — as the quotation of an Amadée Vanloo engraved in 1765 in Batoni's 1766 portrait of *Sir Sampson Gideon* (Melbourne, National Gallery of Victoria) proves — but, excepting his rivals in Rome and the fashionable Parisians, there was no one to teach Batoni but his own genius and the Roman past. Until the pre-eminence of Reynolds and his sonorous and superficial artistic theories, no one in Britain could have genuinely doubted or seriously undermined Batoni's actual practice, and no one in continental Europe did: for to do so would have been to question the basis of European culture.

British portraiture of the greater part of the 18th century was specifically a provincial version of the Roman practice. It has been said that late 17th and all of 18th century Roman portraiture was itself a provincial version of Parisian practice. If Parisian fashions were undoubtedly important in Rome, and had been for a very long time, Batoni's career itself can belie this opinion. In an earlier stage the influences of the portraits of Maratti, Morandi and Gaulli can be shown in France, as well as French influences upon these Roman artists and their successors. But if Batoni's *Duke of Württemberg* (1753-1754) looks French, it does so because Louis Tocqué thoroughly and successfully adopted it in his *Frederick V of Denmark* (1759-1760). It is more rewarding to trace Batoni's Roman background.

Batoni's earliest portraits date from the 1740's, when the leading Roman portraitists were Trevisani, Antonio David, Masucci, Benefial and Subleyras. Trevisani was the most famous and most old-fashioned of these, and the ingredients of his style, however deeply flavored by the spirit of the early rococo, are rooted in the dignified Roman tradition. This may be said to combine Maratti's glamorous interpretation of Velasquez's *Innocent X* with the the austerities of Raphael's and Domenichino's portraits. Antonio David was a graceful rococo artist who would have been too trivial for Batoni's taste; the cold-eyed and very severe Masucci was David's exact opposite and proved more useful for Batoni's style. Benefial's few portraits possess power and presence, and his 1742 *Louis Charles Montolieu* (formerly, London, Art Market) is as advanced as a Batoni, Mengs or Maron of 1760. Eliminating as much of the Baroque *bravura* as Masucci did, simplifying this *bravura* and making it an internal characteristic of his sitter, Benefial painted Montolieu in the simple strong light of day, emphasizing not the grandly glamorous but the grandly prosaic. Subleyras' earliest portraits are in the careful and dignified Roman manner but soon, apparently under the influence of J.F. Detroy, acquire not only a rich stylishness but a beautiful freshness and directness. In all these artists who were younger than Trevisani there is a radical change of palette and various attempts to achieve freshness and informality, directness and a new kind of nobility.

Batoni's earliest portrait of a British traveller appears to be that of the *First Lord of Milltown* (1744, now in Dublin, National Gallery of Ireland), a more primitive

Batoni than the 1751 portrait of the *Second Lord* in the Lucca exhibition. It is carefully aware of Trevisani's portraits, and is even indebted to that artist's *Self-portrait*, with a conscious preservation of Trevisani's curious rococo echo of Rembrandt. The portrait is exquisitely drawn and conceived, but somewhat timid and without the great decorative flair that graces later Batonis and delays appreciation of the striking resemblances that Batoni is known to have prided himself upon.

18th century portraiture is partially indebted to Trevisani and his French rivals for the presentation of the subject in out-of-door or natural terms which today we still find natural and informal, a development Batoni made fashionable and which, in France, is advanced and withdrawn as a possibility by the elegant constrictions of the rococo style. Batoni's first essays in this new method can be seen in the Fetherstonhaugh portraits at Uppark (1751-1752), which are contemporaneous with the more simple (but not less romantic) early Gainsboroughs. Very few of Batoni's portraits before 1760 place the subject fully out-of-doors and the usual method is for the subject to be in a pseudo-classical interior, separated from a landscape by a balcony. Trevisani and even earlier Roman painters had made such a presentation traditional, and Batoni's difference from his predecessors is his greater force, clarity, freshness and naturalness.

The portrait of the *First Lord Milltown* is more old-fashioned than Batoni's subject pictures of the same date, and this conservatism was appropriate for the cardinals the artist had begun to paint but not for the British tourists. The 1750 portrait of *Lord and Lady Dacre and their daughter* (Horsford Manor, Private Collection) is created along exactly the same principles as one of Batoni's contemporary mythological scenes, and the artist's imagination is now as fully available as his technical and visual ability. Horace Walpole was especially impressed with this lovely picture so full of tenderness and unease (the daughter is a posthumous portrait), and one marvels at the combination of elegant idealism and a naturalism polished but very carefully observed.

Batoni was affable but not flattering, endowing his subjects with elegance and brilliant grace while rendering carefully, and obviously well, their real features. The portrait of the *Second Lord Milltown* (1751; Dublin, National Gallery of Ireland) could not be a more exquisitely elegant artistic performance, nor a more lively likeness of an individual and young Irishman. The emphasis in it upon daring linear patterns within which Batoni, as Boni called it, " scherzava col pennello," is especially characteristic of the early works.

The great portraits of the later 1750's abandon this linear insistence for a more rounded and rich decorative formality of tremendous authority. The power of Batoni's vision and special poetry are nowhere more strongly present than in the *Württemberg* (1753-1754), *Giacinta Orsini* (1757; Paris, Private Collection), *Northampton* (1758, Cambridge, Fitzwillian Museum), *Brudenell* (1758; Kettering, Collection of the Duke of Buccleuch) and *Chevalier Wyndham* (1759; England, Private Collection) portraits, and these will always number among the artist's truly remarkable works. Their range, from the tenderness of the *Lord Brudenell* to the royal and Mozartian grandeur of the *Karl Eugen von Württemberg*, is great and this was obviously the moment of the height and fullness of the artist's powers. The likeness of *Sir Wyndham Knatchbull-Wyndham*, which Winckelmann so strongly praised, is perhaps the most authoritative of those named, but the least attractive because of its somewhat absurd gesture, which the taste of Batoni's day would have easily accepted but ours can't. Most of the pose, and the actual conception of the figure, are the basis of all similar full-length portraits by Mengs, Maron and such diverse later artists as Sir Thomas Lawrence and Gilbert Stuart.

The mistake of Batoni's 1760 standing portrait of *Clement XIII* (Rome, Galleria Nazionale) was exactly the same as Masucci's had been when, in 1740, he painted Benedict XIV in a similar pose and Subleyras' seated portrait had been preferred. It is extremely difficult for a man in the rich vestments of an 18th-century pope to look anything but ridiculous unless painted seated on the throne, and this was how Mengs, who was now preferred to Batoni, showed Clement XIII. Batoni also was both more intimidated by his subject than Mengs and more ornamental, which did not help the pope's fatuous face, which our artist described more intimately than Mengs did. The contemporary criticism of Batoni's portrait, that it overemphasized the richness of the vestments while Mengs was able to be more profound and noble, is superficially true, although Mengs perhaps had only made a more cautious, appealing and elegant portrait.

For the portraits of Northern clients after 1760 Batoni often sets the subject out-of-doors, loosens his style, makes the presentation more informal and lessens his ornamental touches and elegant care. When the customer was of great position or simply of conservative taste, the exquisite care immediately returns, and it is curious to see Batoni serving both the fashionable new informality of the young *lordlings* and the preciosity of the established at one and the same time. Batoni took far greater pains with members of the papal court, with ambassadors to it, and with the more intellectual of the British visitors, such as *James Bruce of Kinnaird* (Edinburgh, Scottish National Portrait Gallery) and *Henry Swinburne* (Newcastle upon Tyne, Laing Gallery and Museum). This is not as true of great British or European titles, and one wonders if the differences amongst their taste or that of their *cicerone* decided whether they should be stately and highly finished or more boldly and informally done. I wonder if the *Duke* (1772) and *Duchess* (1776) *of Gloucester* asked to be painted in an adaptation of the style of Antonio Maron?

While the *Portrait of the infant daughter of the Duke and Duchess of Gloucester throwing a joke upon a lion* (1776) is lost, there exists the delightful treatment of *Louisa Greville* as a small child holding her dog (*ca.* 1767; Chevening House, Private Collection). As if a plain statement by Hogarth had been perfected by Fragonard, this masterpiece of beautiful and simple presentation may be compared with the gaudy and somewhat terrifying portraits by Mengs of the royal children of Spain. The 1774 *Cardinal Malvezzi* (Rome, Collection Malvezzi-Campeggi) and the official likeness of Pius VI, begun in the following year, take full advantage of the contributions of Mengs and Maron, show the usual virtues of Batoni with splendid authority, and introduce new possibilities of particular interest to the arising generation of painters younger than Maron.

In both the original 1769 *Portrait of Joseph II and Leopold* and its full-length version of 1770 (formerly in Vienna, now destroyed) one can see Batoni's late tendency to elongate his figures for the purposes of elegance, and also just how far Batoni was prepared to go in adopting Mengs' hardness and broadness of manner. Boyish charm and feminine grace are suitably present and Batoni still paints and draws in the strong but delicate style adopted three decades before from late Raphael as seen by the later and classical Roman tradition. The grandeur and magnificence of portraits of the late 1750's are greatly moderated and simplified, the Baroque remnants have become little more than the ornamentality of the future Empire Style.

I have written earlier of the extraordinary late portraits painted with a dry virtuosity, speed and suggestiveness which recall Fragonard and Gainsborough, although with clearer drawing and fresher colors. The inspired full-length *Thomas Giffard* of 1784 is among the most beautiful of all Batoni portraits, even if the architectural surroundings and view are a studio assistant's work over Batoni's brief indications. Giffard, whose face in the Batoni resembles that of the Barberini *Faun*, apparently was only normally handsome and had rather brutal features; in Batoni's hands he becomes as beautiful as an angel, yet his young male beauty is totally believable and moving. Mengs painted neither the Hapsburg Princes nor Giffard but, speculating upon what he would have done, one remembers Mengs' portrait of Lord

Brudenell so different from Batoni's, with only the more lugubrious aspects of *British Beef* shown.

Batoni is said to have painted three popes and twenty-two monarchs, although I know actual portraits of only two popes and fifteen or sixteen royal persons, less than half of them ruling princes. Most of the prominent visitors to Rome during his career were painted by him, the British in vast number — with even *Philip Livingston* of New York (1783; New York, Private Collection) — and a scattering of natives of most other European countries as well as Italians both male and female. There is also a missing portrait of the artist's beautiful first wife, a lost self-portrait of 1743, the Munich *Self-portrait* of 1765 (Schleissheim, Neues Schloss, Staatsgalerie) another of 1772 (formerly New York, Germain Seligman; another version, Lucca, Private Collection), and the Uffizi *Self-portrait* interrupted by the last illness. Batoni's face, especially as shown at Munich and at the Uffizi, is work-worn, unpretentious and plain, the typical face of a successful Lucchese dominated by large eyes full of something like human concern.

Batoni painted his many works of portraiture in ever increasing numbers each decade from 1750 to 1780. At least a dozen portraits may be the yearly average in the 1760's and 1770's, and there is no interruption except in 1770 and 1771 when Batoni was almost totally occupied for Maria Teresa, even though an extensive creation of paintings of other types also occurred. After the rarity of portraits in 1780 and 1781, when the artist was mainly occupied by the Lisbon altars, there is a partial return to large-scale production and, although the appetite and talent were prodigious, the results of old age are apparent.

In the 1740's and 1750's a half-length portrait by Batoni cost 30 scudi, a full-length 60 scudi; in 1765 a half-length 50, a full-length 100; and in 1780 a half-length 100 and a full-length 200. There was a further production of copies the large extent of which can be seen in the number of properly signed likenesses of Pius VI. A replica by Batoni of an important sitter was expensive (60 to 200 scudi for a half-length), another by one of his " migliori scolari " would be 100 scudi, and a simple studio copy 10 to 30. It is revealing to compare Batoni's prices with those of the British portraitists. One must remember, however, that to live in Rome was much cheaper than to live in London: a third less at least, although pleasures and luxuries could cost almost the same. I am told that a scudo (two of which made a *zecchino romano*) was worth five shillings and thus, in Batoni's time, four scudi were worth one pound sterling.

The value may be calculated by knowing that the large monthly salary of the general in charge of the Swiss Guards (perhaps somehow comparable to Batoni's position) was 200 scudi, and that in 1760 200 pounds would permit a *milord* to live comfortably in Rome for a year and include the hire of his carriage. A half-length by Reynolds in 1760 cost 24 pounds (soon thereafter 35); in 1777 a full-length by Gainsborough cost 100 and one by Reynolds 200 pounds. To the British customer Batoni's portrait had the added advantage of being cheap.

Batoni's portrait prices also may be compared with the prices of the mythological pictures, which rose from 150 scudi in 1740 to 250 or 300 in 1754 to 700 or 1000 in 1782. The prices of altarpieces varied with the customer and also increased with time: Furietti paid 300 scudi in 1738 for the S. Celso altar; Benedict XIV 250 in 1743 for that in S.M. Maggiore (and 400 scudi for the *Caffeaus* ceiling); the King of Portugal paid 700 scudi in 1747, while the large Lisbon high altar of 1781 cost 3000 scudi.

When its executors, Cardinal Filippo Carandini and the British banker and antiquary James Byres, put into effect Batoni's will of October, 1786, they found that the artist had left about 16,000 scudi " di sole gioie " and 14,000 scudi more in money and property, as well as a studio with important finished paintings, a " vigna in vicolo della Camilluccia " (near Villa Stuart at Monte Mario) and " luoghi de monti " (at Frascati?). His prosperity was fortunate because Batoni also left a widow, four sons (three of them painters and his assistants), two daughters who were nuns, and four unmarried daughters. Another daughter, Apollonia, in 1776 married Pietro Lazzarini and, as the only one of Batoni's many children to marry, her son Sebastiano and her daughter Caterina (who married Giuseppe Soffredini of Nettuno, their son Pietro Antonio being born in 1798) are the sole known sources of descendants of the artist.

In 1819 the last of the Batonis left the large palace at 25 via Bocca di Leone where they had lived since 1759, which had contained the artist's studio, evening drawing class, and exhibition rooms, and which had been graced by those *accademie musicali* of Batoni's gifted daughters that served to attract and distract Batoni's customers. Although the palace had received Pius VI, the Emperor of Austria, the Grand Duke of Russia and so many other distinguished visitors, it bears today no commemorative plaque.

STAMPATO IN ITALIA

NEL MESE DI FEBBRAIO MCMLXXX

SU DISEGNO E PER CURA DELLE EDIZIONI DELL'ELEFANTE

ROMA · PIAZZA DEI CAPRETTARI, 70

Progettazione grafica: Grazia Vascotto